Louis Dyer

Studies of the Gods in Greece at certain sanctuaries recently excavated

Being eight lectures given in 1890 at the Lowell Institute

Louis Dyer

Studies of the Gods in Greece at certain sanctuaries recently excavated
Being eight lectures given in 1890 at the Lowell Institute

ISBN/EAN: 9783743451582

Manufactured in Europe, USA, Canada, Australia, Japa

Cover: Foto ©Lupo / pixelio.de

Manufactured and distributed by brebook publishing software (www.brebook.com)

Louis Dyer

Studies of the Gods in Greece at certain sanctuaries recently excavated

STUDIES OF THE GODS IN GREECE AT CERTAIN SANCTUARIES RECENTLY EXCAVATED

*BEING EIGHT LECTURES GIVEN IN
1890 AT THE LOWELL INSTITUTE*

By LOUIS DYER, B.A. Oxon.

LATE ASSISTANT PROFESSOR IN HARVARD UNIVERSITY

Better stand upon the fragments of antiquity and look about us.
                                    W. S. LANDOR.

London
MACMILLAN AND CO.
AND NEW YORK
1891

All rights reserved

TO
DEMETRIOS BIKELAS

PLANS

                                                                                         PAGE

Plan of the Eleusinian precinct from Proceedings of R. I. B. A.

                                                                    to face page 198

Outline-sketch of the ground-plan of the Hall of Ictinus . . 202

Plan of the temple at Old Paphos from the J. H. S.   *to face page* 310

CONTENTS

I

INTRODUCTION

Latter-day paganism—Greek sanctuaries—Powers of Greek gods—Roman organisation—The kingdom of Earth—The Roman order—Greek individualism—Greek religious thinkers—Anomalies of Greek religion—Apollo at Delphi—Parnassus—Pater, Mannhardt, and Preller—Sanctions of Apollo's power—Apollo's temple at Delphi—Delphian worship—The coming of Apollo . Pages 1-36
APPENDIX I—The deification of Roman emperors . 37-45

II

DEMETER AT ELEUSIS AND CNIDUS

The home goddess of grain—Two Homeric otherworlds—The goddess of enough and to spare—The hallowed fruits of Demeter—The Homeric Hymn to Demeter—The wedlock of Persephone—The *Iliad* and the Odyssean stories—The Eleusinian legend of Demeter—Interlopers in the story—Celeus and Demophoon—Woman's love for woman—Demeter's love for Persephone—Demeter's rules for right living—Demeter of Cnidus 46-74

III

DIONYSUS IN THRACE AND OLD ATTICA

The crazed god of Homer—Contradictions of Dionysus—Probations of Athenian Dionysus—Thracian birth-marks of Dionysus—Asiatic Thracians—Brumalia and Rosalia—Modern May-day festivals—The angel of the darker drink—Elements of wine, fire, water, gold—Dionysus-Silenus the water man—Bassarids, Satyrs, Corybantes, Curetes—The savage Pan or Aegipan—Dionysus Omestes—Dionysus and the Muses—The Icarian legend—Icarius entertains the god—The shepherds slay Icarius—Legends parallel to Icarian story—Winter festivals on Parnassus—Susarion and Thespis at Icaria—First tragedies at Icaria . . . . . Pages 75-117

APPENDIX II—Dionysus Eleuthereus . . . 118-120

IV

DIONYSUS AT ATHENS

Epimenides of Crete—The Pisistratidae and Dionysus—Onomacritus and Orphic myth-making—Epimenides, Pisistratus, and Onomacritus—Reformed Athenian festivals—The people's faith in Dionysus—The greater Dionysia—The *Bacchanals* of Euripides—Messianic vision of Euripides—Analysis of the introduction—Entrance-song of the Bacchanals—Central acts and conclusion—First great act—The probation of Pentheus—Pentheus is deaf to reason—The second great act—The sin of Pentheus—Captive good attending captain ill—The perdition of Pentheus—Cadmus cures Agave's madness 121-163

APPENDIX III—Second birth of Dionysus—his eastern affinities 163-173

V

THE GODS AT ELEUSIS

The coming of Dionysus to Eleusis—The all-welcoming Demeter—Xenophanes and Heraclitus—The holy silence of Eleusis—Dionysus an enhancement of Demeter—The pitiless huntsman Zagreus—

Description of Eleusis—The only church of antiquity—Eleusis fortified in early days—The present condition of Eleusis—The Plutonian precinct—The Hall of Initiation—Halls of Pisistratus, Cimon, Ictinus — Cyclopean traces — Roman restorations — The Hall of Ictinus — The portion of Hades — Greater and Lesser Mysteries—The Greater Mysteries—Yearly procession of the Mystae —The *Frogs* of Aristophanes—The measure led by the Fates—Stations of the yearly pilgrimage . . . . Pages 174-218

VI

AESCULAPIUS AT EPIDAURUS AND ATHENS

The god Aesculapius from the north—Hippocrates and Democedes—The Coan sanctuary—The medicine of Homeric days—The debt of Democedes to Homer—The schooling of Aesculapius—Early history of Greek medicine—Mind and body—Harmony of religion and science—Aesculapius a friend of man—The son of Apollo—The Hieron of Epidaurus—Finding of the infant god—A precinct of Aesculapius—The statue of ivory and gold—The Tholos of Polycletus—The painting of Pausias—Apollonius the intercessor
219-256

APPENDIX IV—Apollonius of Tyana 257-266
APPENDIX V—The status of modern Greek doctors . . 267-269

VII

APHRODITE AT PAPHOS

Aphrodite at Greek sanctuaries — Eastern characteristics — Three regions of Cyprus — Meeting ground of East and West — No Cypriote nationality—Phoenicians in Cyprus—Lack of Greek monuments — Agapenor at Paphos and in Arcadia — Aphrodite always Paphian—From Limassol to Paphos—Cinyras of Paphos—The ubiquity of Cinyras—The temple on the hill—Aphrodite's birth at Paphos—The Greek Aphrodite—The Roman and Assyrian goddess—Aphrodite and Demeter 270-304

CONTENTS

APPENDIX VI—The temple at Old Paphos . . Pages 305-314
APPENDIX VII—Aphrodite of the Greeks, Hittites, and
 Phoenicians 315-323
APPENDIX VIII—The Olympus and the Bocarus in Cyprus
 —Hettore Podocatharo and John
 Meursius 324-354

VIII

APOLLO AT DELOS

Delian nativity of Apollo and Artemis—Delos a wandering island—The consecration of Rhenea—The exile of the Delians—Archilochus the poet of the Aegean—Apollo a King Arthur of the Greeks—Apollo and Cyrene—Self-discipline of Apollo—The Ionians at Delos—Vicissitudes of Delian festivals—From Athens to Delos—The procession of Nicias—The earliest Delian festival—The temple and image of Leto—The Cynthian cave-temple—Latter-day worshippers at Delos—The inheritance of Delos . . 355-390

APPENDIX IX—The Cyclades and Sporades . . . 391-398
APPENDIX X—The worship of Aphrodite and of strange
 gods at Delos 399-403
APPENDIX XI—Photographs referred to for illustrations 404-413

INDICES 414-457

PREFACE

ADEQUATELY to thank all whose help has been lavished upon the preparation of these pages is not possible. Although I can give no catalogue of the names of benefactors, my gratitude is sincere; and this expression of it will, I hope, reach them in Greece, in France, in Italy, in England, and in America. It is but fair, however, to say that constant criticism and suggestion from my wife helped the present work to its shape, and I cannot silence the particular expression of my thanks to Professor Middleton of King's College, Cambridge, and Professor Ker of University College, London, for invaluable aid given most ungrudgingly during the final revision.

Originally prepared as lectures for the Lowell Institute, the eight chapters here given are printed *with corrections and notes, the fruit of a year's deliberation. As lectures they were repeated before various Universities, Colleges, and Societies in various parts of the United States. A lecture on the Cyclades, given before Columbia University, forms the basis of one of the Appendices which, although some of them are unavoidably technical, have seemed necessary to the more or less connected presentation of Greek religious thought here attempted.*

LOUIS DYER

Sunbury Lodge,
Oxford, *April 1891.*

I

INTRODUCTION

I DO not mean to attempt an account of all the Greek gods; eight studies would be insufficient, even if my investigations had already carried me over the whole ground, which is a vast one. I propose in the first place to say what I can of Demeter and Persephone, the two great goddesses of Eleusis in Attica. Here it will be necessary to consider excavations in Asia Minor made some years ago by Sir Charles Newton,[1] as well as the now practically completed diggings of the Greek Archaeological Society at Eleusis.[2] In the second place, the god Dionysus—also worshipped at Eleusis—will be considered, and his early cult in Attica will receive illustration from recent excavations made by the American School of Athens.[3] The

---

[1] *A History of Discoveries at Halicarnassus, Cnidus, Branchidae.* By C. T. N., assisted by R. P. Pullan. London, 1862, folio and 8vo.

[2] See the various publications of the Greek Archaeological Society, particularly the plan, by Dr. Dörpfeld, of the Eleusinian Temple in the *Praktika* of 1885, and *ibid.* Dr. Philios's description, as well as his subsequent reports on inscriptions and discoveries at Eleusis. Dr. Dörpfeld has kindly allowed a reproduction of his plan to appear below in the chapter on "The Gods at Eleusis," p. 202.

[3] See the Seventh Annual Report of the American School at Athens in the *American Journal of Archaeology* for 1889, and cf. the *Nation* of 22d March 1888.

third topic will be Aesculapius and his worship, more particularly at Athens and at Epidaurus, as known through excavations in both places.[1] Fourthly, a consideration of Aphrodite and her worship at Old Paphos will occupy the seventh of my chapters, which will to a large extent be devoted to the problems which have been raised by the recent excavations of the British School at Couclià in Cyprus.[2] My eighth and last chapter will be given to the holy island of Delos, and to Delian Apollo. The French School of Athens, chiefly under the able direction of M. Homolle, has uncovered and discovered of late years all manner of facts about Delos and Delian Apollo;[3] and with these I shall end my studies of five of the greater gods of Greece as worshipped in their recently discovered sanctuaries.

As there are shrines of healing and sanctuaries of especial salvation dedicated to immemorial worship by the medieval world of Christendom, so also in the Hellenic world (much larger, alas! than modern Greece) there were places about which lingered through many centuries a dread and most religious sanctity, a helpful significance. Of such spots in Greece, in Cyprus, in Asia Minor, and of the gods whose presence and whose help was sought in those holy places, I am to speak. I am to speak of several sites lately investigated where the beautiful and ennobling religion, first of Greece, and then—through Greece

[1] Paul Girard, *L'Asclépieion d'Athènes, d'après de récentes découvertes*, Paris, 1881. For discoveries at Epidaurus see in the publications of the Greek Archaeological Society various reports by M. Kabbadias.

[2] See the *Journal of Hellenic Studies* for 1889.

[3] See Professor Jebb's article "Delos" in the first number of the *Journal of Hellenic Studies*; also M. J. Albert Lebègue's *Recherches sur Délos*, Paris, 1876, 8vo, and the publications of the French School at Athens, particularly reports of Delian excavations by M. Homolle in the *Bulletin de Correspondance Hellénique*.

and Rome—of all the ancient world, had its growth; of sanctuaries where that old-time worship of ideals, by some miscalled idolatry, grew pure and yet more pure, broad and broader still, until its inner significance and truth were no longer to be confined within old forms, could be fettered no longer by old bonds; and lo! Christianity was there to gather in a heritage of high-born thoughts from Greece.

In the latter days of paganism there was a two-fold process by which the world was prepared for the dawning of an endless hope, the "dayspring from on high." There was amelioration and purification, as well as a growing superstition and gradual decay. No less distinguished an authority than Professor Jebb[1] has said of latter-day Greek religion:—

"The Greeks were a people peculiarly sensitive to everything that was in the intellectual air of the time, and there was. much in it that helped Christianity . . . there was a tendency to take refuge from polytheism in deism; and in particular there was a spreading belief, half-mystic, in the resurrection of the body,—a belief which drew many votaries to the worship of the Egyptian Serapis, and was in turn strengthened by that cult."

It has unfortunately been habitual, but less so in these latter days of religious tolerance, to accept without question the estimate of paganism made in the heat of conflict by the early fathers of the Christian Church. What those great and good men strove to do has been in the fullest measure accomplished. Christianity has prevailed, and the tanglewood of ancient mythology, the thickets of ancient

[1] *Modern Greece*, two lectures delivered before the Philosophical Institution of Edinburgh by R. C. Jebb.

ritual, have receded from the broadening pathway of our race. But yet the distant view of it remains, its influence is real to-day though more remote. Indeed the purer aspects of Greek ritual and Greek mythology have a counterpart in the most holy Christian places. Surely there is no lack of real Christian piety in feeling, as it were, a reminiscence or a glorified survival of the ancient worship of Dionysus and Demeter at the altar where the bread and wine are given. It was no fanciful parallel which the Christian author of *Christus Patiens* drew [1] between the yearly passion and yearly resurrection of Dionysus in ancient ritual and that passion and resurrection which Christians yearly celebrate to-day.

Consider how much—or shall it rather be said how little?—the ideal equality of all sorts and conditions of men in the presence of God is to-day maintained by Christian ritual and regulation. And consider then what new impulse might perhaps be gained from a careful study of the worship of Aesculapius, of Dionysus, or from a reverential understanding of the Eleusinian mysteries of Demeter. In spring, at the high festival of Dionysus' birthday, one of the marked features in the celebration was a free welcome, extended more than in words, to slaves and day-labourers.[2] First, sacrifices were made with solemnity,

[1] The parallel is drawn by unmistakable implication, since lines from the *Bacchanals* of Euripides are freely applied to the suffering Christ, line 1344 of the *Bacchanals*, e.g., "*Dionysus, we are thy suppliants, we have sinned,*" becomes "*O Redeemer! we are,*" etc. The authorship of *Christ Suffering* was long bestowed on Saint Gregory of Nazianzum, surnamed the Theologian. It is now given to some unknown person belonging to a later day of the Church, when the worship of the Virgin Mary had taken the more definite shape implied by various passages in the poem.

[2] The rural origin of the festival was especially marked by this temporary obliteration of differences in station. See in Hutchinson's *Northumberland*,

and then all alike were invited to come to the banquet of the god, and partake of his freshly opened wine. So also it was with the bread of Demeter. All manner of people were free to come, and be initiated at her Eleusinian sanctuary, excepting only those polluted in some incurable manner, as who should say, those who had committed the sin against the Holy Ghost.

Christianity as we know it, Christianity as we prize it, is not solely and exclusively a gift from Israel. It is time to open our eyes and see the facts new and old that stare us in the face, growing more clear the more investigations and excavations on Greek soil proceed. To the religion of Greece and Rome, to the Eleusinian mysteries, to the worship of Aesculapius and Apollo, to the adoration of Aphrodite is due more of the fulness and comforting power of the Church to-day than many of her leaders have as yet been willing to allow.

The sanctuaries of Demeter at Eleusis and Cnidus, the Icarian demesne of Dionysus, whither he came to meet his earliest Attic worshippers; the Delian shrine of Apollo, and the temples of his son, the healer Aesculapius, at Athens and at Epidaurus,—these and the Paphian precinct of sweetly smiling Aphrodite should be well known to him who seeks understanding of that beautiful religion whose fifth essence and nobler quality has passed into our own. Indeed it is universally true that to understand any religion you must in some sense come under the spell of its sanctuaries, in some way you must visit its holy places.

vol. ii. end, the account of "Mell Supper": "The servants having performed the most valuable part of their labour, are entertained by their masters, *when all distinction is laid aside.* This feast is called the Mell Supper, at which there are dancing, masquing, and disguising, and all other kinds of rural mirth."

This has been most beautifully set forth in the most recent work[1] of a writer whose every utterance on the history of beliefs brings the greatest help. Speaking of the "Creed of Heathen Germany," and of gods very different from those of Greece, but resembling them in that they too had a part in the shaping of Christianity, Mr. Keary most poetically and truly says:—

"If in these days we wish to feel the mystic presence of the great god of the Germans, we must do as our worshipping forefathers did, withdraw from the concourse of men, find out some forest solitude, and wait there. Let it be, if you will, in one of the great stretches of woodland which are to be found in East and West Prussia; or, better still nowadays, go to the vast primeval forests which lie upon the upper slopes of the Scandinavian peninsula, far away from the fjörds and the too frequent steps of tourists. There you will feel, as you should, the strange and awful stillness which from time to time reigns in pine forests such as these. Presently the quiet is broken, first by a sigh, which arises as from the ground itself, and breathes throughout the wood. Anon, from a distance a sound is heard so like the sound of the sea that you might swear (had you never been in such a wood before) that you could hear the waves drawing backwards over a pebbly beach. As it approaches the sound grows into a roar; it is the roar of the tempest, the coming of Wodin."[2]

---

[1] *The Vikings in Western Christendom*, by C. F. Keary, M.A., F.S.A. T. Fisher Unwin, 1891.

[2] To quote this passage without Mr. Keary's justification of it would not be a great harm, since it bears witness in a great measure to its own truth, but what Mr. Keary says seems to me of a very universal importance, and to bear upon the right treatment of Greek as well as of German mythology. Speaking of his own account of Wodin in the forest, he says: "It will be said by some that this description is purely imaginary. I

It is indeed a privilege newly and exclusively granted to the highest moods and broadest minds of to-day, this enlightened tolerance, this "genial catholicity of appreciation," which finds even in paganism a message from the only and the everlasting God. Now at last, thanks to the painstaking work which truly scientific men have done in archaeology, we are receiving something of the legacy bequeathed us by those who lived and loved and prayed of old in Athens and in Rome. Now at last we may feel, with no petty wish to carp or cavil, the sacredness of ancient sanctuaries, and know them for ever consecrated to "the sessions of sweet silent thought," where we summon up not only "remembrance of things past," but also much of the sweet usage and workaday reality in things now present for our spiritual aid.

Let this new privilege console somewhat the praisers of the past, for it makes up for and takes the place of much that modern men have lost. Let malcontents consider in this new-dawned light of tolerance the early worship of both Greece and Rome, and then they may forget to remember how their lots and their lives are cast into a world so filled with quantity, so choked and crammed to bursting with millions whether of men or money, that quality seems lost, or even to be, when rarely found,

make a distinction between what is imaginative and what is imaginary. If you choose not to go into the study of mythology or of beliefs of any kind until you have first stripped yourself of your imagination, you will travel indeed lightly burdened, and you will arrive at strange results. Because, as belief of all kinds is born of the imagination, and *Aberglaube* is, as Goethe says, the poetry of life, you will have taken the precaution of going into the dark unprovided with a lantern. To avoid doing this you are not obliged, however, to give free rein to your fancy. Nor have we done so here."
I have taken the liveliest interest in seeing how near to my own point of view Mr. Keary arrived, and how the idea of studying the Pagan religion in its sanctuaries had presented itself to him in another part of the field.

neglected and misprized. Let us then exhort the pessimists of this, the golden hour of the broadest and most real Christianity — that truest consecration of democracy — to look not backward but upward, and discern in the broad humanity and strength, and above all in the toleration [1] of latter-day religion, a gleam from Olympus of the Greeks. Their religion, so far as it was true, still lives and shines in the light of to-day. In the high types of excellence and beauty which Greek religion created, and Roman practice made more all-embracing and enduring, there is manifested a mercy whose overruling providence leads us towards the best.

Indeed the quality of Greek divinities is that of mercy. Demeter's love is faithful, although the heavens seem to fall, and though earth withholds all comfort for a time; her chastened joy (when at last it comes) is divinely pure and gracious in the fulness of its perfect peace. Apollo, that most truly Greek of all divinities, is a gloriously dazzling exemplar of purity and light. He, the sun-god, is mirrored like the sun from a thousand angles of refraction. Understand this god, and straightway his image, shaped this way or that by accident, or even distorted by some chance, will be always

[1] It is a fact well known that regular offerings were made on behalf of Augustus at the Temple in Jerusalem. This was but one of many small practices which grew out of the *Theocrasia* or commingling of gods, a result of that all-embracing toleration which led Greeks and Romans alike to treat as their own the gods of other nations. See the opening plea in the *Octavius* of Quintus Minucius Felix, p. 6 B-E. It was a pious duty for travellers in remote parts of the empire to sacrifice to the local gods wherever they went. When the absolute antagonism between paganism and Christianity brought persecution to pass, there was still a lack of thoroughgoing intolerance as compared with that of the Inquisition. A comparison of the numbers put to death by Roman and Spanish intolerance respectively establishes this fact. See Friedlaender, *Darstellungen aus der Sittengeschichte Rom's in der Zeit von August bis zum Ausgang der Antonine*, iii. p. 586.

returning to your wandering eye from every corner and surface of Greek story and Greek song. Achilles had the swiftness and the pure white heat that make Apollo known,[1] and that nobly moulded youth, who bursts, divine in righteous anger, on our view upon the western pediment of the temple of great Zeus,[2] is a very incarnation of the power of Apollo. Whether he be Apollo, or, as some think, Pirithous,[3] the act of quenching lust and foiling brutal crime is most pure [4] Apollo's own.

Dionysus, the dread, the deep, the darkly irresistible, a god of mystery and of intensity, the all-possessor of men, and even of beasts and things upborne by onrush and inrush of his power—Dionysus lives on to-day in the fairy-land of poetry, mirrored by the motley throng of Orpheus tales and songs of wine and stories of overpowering inspirations. All and each of the greater Greek gods still live their charmed life, and even to-day each one in some sense is the centre of a scheme of things, a universe all his own.

There was, in fact, little or no thought in early Greece of how one god's power might be made compatible with that attributed to and exercised by another. Each Greek state was, according to Greek theory, absolutely independent of all and every other. Therefore it was not unnatural for Greeks to think of each one of their great divinities as in some sense partaking of an absolute independence. Each great god had been worshipped, no doubt, at some time,

---

[1] For some admirable remarks on this parallelism, which scarcely needs to be pointed out, see Keary's *Outlines of Primitive Belief*, p. 192: "Each is the ideal youth, the representative, one might fairly say, of 'young Greece,' that which was to become in after years Hellas."
[2] See Appendix XI. i. 141 and 143.
[3] Pausanias, V. x. 8.
[4] For Apollo as the god of purity see the last chapter below on Apollo at Delos.

somewhere in broad and various Hellas, as the supreme arbiter of destiny, the wielder of all power, and the hearer of all prayer. Thus we have glimpses of an earliest time [1] when Greek religion was, if the word be insisted upon, monotheistic. At each centre of political life it would seem that men worshipped a god whose omnipotence was bounded by the boundaries of that particular state. The difference in relative importance noticeable between the gods connects itself with the history of the chief place of this and that god's worship. A certain early importance in matters religious belonged to Dodona for instance, and the national character borne in later days by the festival of Olympian Zeus was partly the cause and not wholly the effect of the kingship attributed by universal consent to Zeus among the great gods on Olympus as well as at Olympia.

Judge Greek religion not by all its moods, but by all its highest and most characteristic ones. Avoid as you would the very spirit of untruth a judgment of Greek political and religious ideas, founded on notions of politics and religion that only came into being in modern times, and then you will say that Greek religion was a polytheism where each of many great gods was potentially the one and only god for every Greek, but actually and more particularly in one place and for one people of Greece. The Greek religion of polytheism was more monotheistic than monotheism itself, for the Greeks were not content with one only God Almighty and Supreme, they had and they worshipped many such.[2]

---

[1] Of this earliest day we can have only glimpses, and it must be to a large extent ideal, as retrospects of the kind always are. In reality many disturbing causes came in, such as the relics of an utterly barbarous phase of religion and a certain compatibility between local all-importance and ideal subordination in a rough scheme of the religious world, such as a peasant's mind could form.

[2] Lehrs (*Populäre Aufsätze*, p. 130) expresses substantially the same

The truth which this paradox contains is shown by the course of Greek political history—a stream which ran curiously and closely parallel to that of Greek religion. The whole range and expanse of ancient Greek life were requisite before the Greeks could win from struggles and adversity the lesson of political subordination and national unity. While this life-giving knowledge was most vivacious within it, the mind of Greece was merged with its territory in the body politic of Rome, and Rome was livened for her task by Grecian wit.[1] Indeed, humanity has possessed the power of potent organisation and broader growth only since the day when Hellas died as a separate political power, conscious at last, though late, that captious independence overstrained had brought destruction in its train. Rome —imperial Rome—showed forth most plain the moral of Hellenic failure, and Roman success made way for the conception of something higher even than political organisation of the broadest kind. After and because of the heathen empire came the Holy Empire which crowned all others, the empire of the universal Church.

At Marathon and Plataea, Greece defeated the patriarchal order of politics and religion. There was a moment of universal history when the clan was succeeded by the commonwealth, when the spirit of humankind required new room for growth, more room than the oriental polity of

idea by drawing a distinction which eludes translation. "The Greek," he says, "could perfectly well apprehend (*begreifen*) one sole God, but his mental requirements and endowments were utterly averse to any real comprehension (*ergreifen*). He always fell short of a realising sense, and accordingly never lived up to, never acted out the idea."

[1] "The Roman conquest of Greece was a welcome event to the mass of the European Greeks. The popular sentiment at the time was expressed by a parody of the saying attributed to Themistocles in exile to the effect that his ruin had made his fortune." Jebb's *Modern Greece*, p. 3.

Persia could afford it. To the old Persian order succeeded the new era of Greece and Rome.

Sir Alfred Lyall, in his *Asiatic Studies*, most acutely says that Greece invented "political . citizenship, and rules of conduct under State sanction. Between the clans and the commonwealths the difference is not so much between lawlessness and free institutions as between the primitive man, whose social and political customs are as much a part of his species as the inherited habit of an animal, and the highly civilised man who consciously chooses his own laws and form of government according to expediency and logic." The props of tribe and caste were dispensed with, that the wider and freer political organisation of our day might come into being. For the evolution of so vast a system the ground had first of all to be cleared. This took place before the battle of Marathon, on the very restricted scale which Greece allowed, but not to the same extent everywhere in Greece. The Spartan institutions of Lycurgus (so far as we can know them) are a curious crystallisation of primitive, social, and political habits, hardly in advance of what to-day excites wonder and defies a casual comprehension in India and Central Asia. Athens, the typically free, the truly modern Greek state, had her triumph at Marathon, Salamis, and Plataea. For a time this new way of living required a very restricted sphere of action, these new states had to be small. Independence rather than interdependence was the watchword of this dawning period. The time was not yet come for federations or confederations, and hence the Athenian Confederacy failed. Years and years of political experience had to be gathered in by Athenians and by Romans before a solidly constituted state of this new type became possible on a large scale.

To those who cannot see how different in kind from anything known before was the small Greek *Polis*, it must seem that the Greek world was far more hopelessly split up after the Peloponnesian war than it had been in the days of Homeric song. In politics the new principle made coalition impossible, and in religion it left to local divinities their old-time omnipotence. The loose and unsettled organisation of the government in heaven by Zeus was still what Homer had made it.

But this was only for a time. When at last the world from which we spring, and of whose life we are, had been qualified for wider things, and had outgrown Greek individualism, then Greece had grown into Rome, and had allied itself with that spirit of subordination and self-discipline by which alone the Romans conquered all mankind. Imperial Rome at its best has seemed a realisation of Plato's dream, a state where philosophers were kings and kings were philosophers. This was truly the kingdom of Heaven upon earth, and a comparison forced itself upon religious minds between the perfect union and solidarity of all functionaries of the empire and that loose government of the spiritual world on Olympus which tradition ascribed to Zeus. According to these latter-day notions the power of Zeus over his fellow-gods and subjects was contemptibly small and precarious. A desire asserted itself gradually that the kingdom of earth should arrive in the heavens.[1] The

[1] This desire showed itself very vigorously even in the lifetime of Augustus, having already found expression under Julius Caesar in a very extreme form. Professor Merriam (see the next note) has gathered most interesting proofs. See also Giacomo Lumbroso, *L'Egitto al tempo dei Greci e dei Romani*. Both of these writers correct the errors of Mommsen, who maintains that the Caesareum at Alexandria was dedicated to Caesar *Appulsor*. This epithet is a mistranslation; the real equivalent of ἐπιβατήριος is the deity to whom the ἐπιβατήρια—*sacrifices* at embarkation

Roman emperors were deified, *inter alia*, as the representatives of a more logically ordered scheme of things than that presented by the poetical figures that ruled Olympus. Nowhere was this new hierarchy of the heavens more sedulously cultivated than by the Greek members of the Roman Empire. Zeal for this new worship has earned for Greece much slander from unreflecting persons. Servility and base flattery are attributed to men who really were following in the footsteps of their forefathers, and seeking an organised religion which their poetical traditions could not give, though it did suggest the lack of it. Indeed Zeus or

and disembarkation—were made, who rules and protects all sailors. For this aspect of Imperial divinity see Virgil, *Georgics*, i. 29-31, and Propertius, iii. 11, 71. Apollo and Zeus were the two other divinities, beside Poseidon, with whom Augustus was identified. Professor Merriam's array of inscriptions is particularly interesting. Philo Judaeus, *Legatio ad Caium*, describes Augustus as "the source of worshipful majesty to his successors, the defender from evil ('Αλεξίκακος). The entire habitable world decreed honours to him co-equal with those of the Olympian gods." Caesar (ἐπιβατήριος) at Alexandria (*navigantium praeses*) was, as the same Philo describes him, "the saving hope of all who weigh anchor or enter within its (the harbour's) shelter." The seriousness of Alexandrine sailors in this conception of the divinity ot Augustus (the Caesareum of Alexandria was not, as Mommsen says, for the worship of Julius but for that of Augustus Caesar) is picturesquely shown in chapter xcviii. of Suetonius' *Life*. Catilius placed at Egyptian Philae a dedication "to Caesar ruler of the sea, a mighty Zeus swaying limitless regions, son of Zeus (Caesar) the Deliverer . . . star of all Hellas that rose as a mighty Zeus the Saviour." At the temple of Isis at Tenbyris in the year 1 A.D., Octavius, of the emperor's own gens, styles Augustus Zeus Eleutherios. At Herod's Caesarea-by-the-sea Augustus was worshipped under the aspect of the well-known statue of Zeus at Olympia. The Athenian temple of Olympian Zeus was finally dedicated to the *genius Augusti*. Of Augustus worshipped under the guise of Apollo Dr. Merriam gives many instances; his Egyptian style is, "autocrator Caesar, son of the Sun, King of Upper and Lower Egypt." Moreover, upon two Demotic stelae (in the British Museum) from Memphis are interesting records of two brothers who were priests. One of them died, and his brother was appointed in his place by Augustus "in the first year of the god, the son of the god, the great foreign god Caesar autocrator"; and, furthermore, he was made "Prophet of Caesar." Inscriptions exist dated during Augustus's lifetime (qualifying him—in spite of his prohibition—as a god) from Apamea (*C. I. G.* 3525), Lesbos, Delos.

Jupiter could not very long remain the emperor of Olympus when once the deifications of Roman emperors had accustomed men to think of the ordered rule of heaven as a counterpart in some way of the ordered and most plainly organised rule on earth.[1]

This impulse to sanctify the secular arm of government marked the reigns of many Roman princes, and made all good emperors, and some even whose vices earned the scorn of those near by, the idols of the provinces. Hence arose that consecration of a universal headship covering all affairs, both spiritual and temporal, which has survived in the Roman Church and in the Russian part of what to-day still bears the title of the Greek Church. This glorification of imperial attributes at Rome helped to undermine men's faith in the established Greco-Roman religion. Each of the careless gods on Greek Olympus trenched too palpably upon the prerogatives of various of his fellows. There was no loophole of escape for the ingenuity even of Roman jurisprudence. Zeus had too many affinities with Dionysus, who resembled Apollo in his powers and Aesculapius in his story. Apollo the healer was more than Aesculapius' father, he often seemed to be all there was of the godhead of Aesculapius. Was Apollo the god and Aesculapius but a man? But then what became of the miracles and divine pretensions of the latter? How came both Dionysus and Aesculapius to birth by the

[1] Appendix I. below deals with the deification of the emperors (see Horace, *Od.* i. 2, and elsewhere), and on the general subject read Gaston Boissier, " La religion romaine d'Auguste aux Antonins," and also consult A. E. Egger, " Examen critique des historiens anciens de la vie et du règne d'Auguste." An interesting account of *The Caesareum and the worship of Augustus at Alexandria* by Professor A. C. Merriam will be found in the "Transactions of the Am. Philological Association for 1883." The conclusions in this paper are the more interesting because arrived at without any knowledge of Boissier's views. They confirm the view taken in this lecture and its Appendix.

same miraculous and premature intervention of fire? These perplexities and others remained unanswered even by the clumsy hocus-pocus of venal priests, or the more disinterested but equally unconvincing lucubrations of Orphic brotherhoods. Hence arose a want unsatisfied and universal; from the natural evolution of political and religious life in antiquity arose a cry to which then came the answer of Christianity: *Illimitable hope has new made heaven and earth, and order has supplanted shapeless and unseemly riot in the spiritual realms through which we have true life.* Universal Christianity was called into being to meet the new and Roman order of things where organisation was everything. Then the turbulence of Greek individualism had to keep the peace or cease to be.

The religion of Greece as such was guiltless of system and wholly devoid of method. It may be compared to a wayward prayer poetically prayed, according to the whimsies of many daring flights of devotional ecstasy,[1] and not to a scheme of the ordered universe so reasoned out and so systematised that it could be written down in creeds or expressed in articles. But now arises the question, How could worship or prayer of any kind be possible unless there was some definite understanding of the powers and provinces of various gods? This is really the same question of which we tried to dispose a moment since. We are forced to ask it in this day of clear-cut creeds because of all the history of religious ideas between us and early Greece. This question, however, no really Greek-minded person could

---

[1] "We can reason out the growth of a belief; for looked at over a wide area and followed through a sufficient period of time, every belief has a kind of reason and a kind of reality. But to each individual in his brief span of life it is like the wind; he cannot tell whence it cometh or whither it goeth."—Keary, *The Vikings*, p. 59.

have understood, let alone answering it. Indeed the possibility of maintaining the old ritual and of worshipping the old divinities depended somewhat upon the impossibility of asking this question. From this it is evident that in considering the past, and more especially in dealing with a bygone religion, we must perform the feat of leaving out our own peculiar selves, and all the ready-made ideas with which our minds have been upholstered. This involves a scrupulous self-examination, and brings before us again the old first law of Delphian Apollo—*know thyself*. Think yourself away, if it were possible, from all this workaday world of business, with its majority whose thinking is more or less at second hand—borrowed from tradition or echoed from great leaders' lips—think that you have neither heard nor dreamed of a large state solidly organised as we know states to-day. Think of a condition of mind where the management of a large railway would be deemed impossible; where the notion of policing a town of half a million had not dawned, and the thought had not entered in of combining large states into one political aggregate otherwise than by the lash of an overpowering master,—of the Great King, as the Greeks in their most independent days named under their breath the ruler of Persia.

Incapable as the Greeks were even of the Persian counterfeit of political organisation, they never raised nice questions in theology about the prerogatives of their gods. Apollo, Dionysus, Zeus, Demeter, and many others were coexistent and all-powerful, yet there was room for the new divinities that came from Egypt and the East. The abstract question of subordination among the gods did not dawn even upon the greatest and most far-reaching minds of Greece. Many and subtle are Plato's arguments about the gods. Difficulties springing from the various and often discreditable tales told about them crowd upon his truly pious mind; but he is never distracted by the desire to fix exact limits of power for each. Plato, Pindar, and Euripides, Greek minds which were especially pre-occupied by religious problems, devoted their efforts in this direction to disentangling the wisdom and omnipotent strength of God from the follies and frailties of man, as well as from the more than human infirmities attributed to ancient gods in old-time stories. To vindicate the poetic purity and truth of Apollo, to show forth the uncalculating and tragical intensity of Dionysus, was their chosen task,—a far more important one at that time than the elaborating of a heavenly hierarchy or the formulation of a creed. All divinities, says Plato, are false if they are not spotless and free from imputations of falsehood; in his perfect commonwealth the poets shall be forbidden to sing of gods who can be bribed like unjust men. With similar intent Pindar piously remoulds the story of the house of Tantalus, since it is unlawful to attribute evil to the gods; while almost every page of Euripides bears the impress of a conflict in men's minds between the noblest ideal conception of godhead and the popular stories and superstitions concerning the gods.

The Greek poets and philosophers are among our intellectual progenitors, and therefore the religion of to-day has requirements which include all that the noblest Greek could dream of—requirements which the aspirations of Israel alone could not satisfy. Our complex life had need not only of a supreme god of power, universal and irresistible, of a jealous god beside whom there was no other god, but also of a god of love and grace and purity. To these ideal qualities present in the diviner godhead of the Gospels the evolution of Greek mythology brought much that satisfies our hearts. This I say because the purity inculcated in the religion of the Jews and enforced by penalties, as recited in various episodes of the Old Testament, rarely imposes itself by the inner charm of native worth and loveliness. It comes upon us frequently as the will of a resistless and often unrelenting God, a religious point of view transcended by Plato, Pindar, and Euripides. Both these presentations were doubtless needed, but the importance of this latter must not blind us to the power for good inherent in the former. And here we may remember the quaint and solemn words of Henry More in the *Mysterie of Godliness*: "Christianity is so excellent in itself that we need not phansy any Religions worse then they are, the better to set off its eminency. Besides the more tolerable sense we can make of the affairs of the ancient Pagans, the easier Province we shall have to maintain against prophane and Atheistical men, to whom if you would grant that Providence had utterly neglected for so many ages together all the nations of the world except that little handfull of the Jews, they would, whether you would or no, from thence infer that there was no Providence over them neither, and consequently no God."

All these considerations certainly arouse a feeling of thankfulness that the great religious leaders of Greek thought should before all things have occupied themselves with the goodness of their various ideal divinities. Had their preoccupation been to show that one god was more powerful than another, rather than the total superiority of gods to humankind, then the charm of goodness "hearted in high hearts" would never have ended by attaching to the best man's conception of the best god in Olympus. It is, in fact, difficult to see how the spontaneous charm of Demeter's love, the glorifying efficacy of her sorrows, could have been set before the human mind, could have been dramatised otherwise than in a community of gods no one of whom had an absolute and omnipresent supremacy. It is fortunate perhaps for us that the Greeks were poetical and dramatic rather than logical and literal-minded in their theology,—if theology we choose to call it,—for in the charmed realm of their great gods where as equals they suffered and struggled, hoped and helped, loved and were loved, the ideal character of the perfect god—a man divine, a human god—was gradually brought to be.[1]

[1] It was not omnipotence so much as solitude, lack of good fellowship, of susceptibility to comforts and delights, that Pagans found fault with in the Christian ideal. "Whence comes, who is, and where lives their precious god?" asks Caecilius, and then he gives his own answer by qualifying the god as " Unicus, solitarius, destitutus,"—*without a fellow, solitary, wholly forsaken.* For the full passage see the *Octavius* of Minucius Felix, p. 13. Possibly the mere fact that the Christians boasted of the oneness of their god enhanced the Pagan appreciation of mere multiplicity; and yet there is a genuine ring in the saying attributed to one of the imperial defenders of Paganism that a universe emptied of numerous divinities was uninhabitable.

Lehrs has given the best account of the matter as it affected fundamentally Greek notions of religion. "The very circles long accustomed to a view of myths which either abandoned or explained them away, the very people who (like the influential Stoics) had definitely made up their minds against all gods in human shape, entertained side by side with the metaphysical conception of one highest god a present belief in many gods. Nor was this belief a mere matter of formal dogma; it lived and glowed with a power that influenced men's lives." Again Lehrs says in the same essay, entitled, *Gott, Götter und Dämonen*, "When your Greek contemplated nature and the feebleness and dependence of man, there arose before him not one god ... but there was a spontaneous outburst of the fulness of life divine. He saw a world of gods." The gifted author at the close of this interesting passage finds an adequate though untranslatable phrase for the lives and loves of the gods on Olympus, "Dieses vielgestaltige Götterineinanderleben."—*Populäre Aufsätze*, p. 130.

In searching out the development of an ideal character, divine and human, through the tangles of poetic fiction that served at once to hide and to protect it till its growth was strong, we must be ready for surprises. We must forget that Zeus was ruler in Olympus, and be often prepared to treat him like the least among his attendant divinities. His looks and even his attributes are given sometimes to Aesculapius, one of the latest of partakers in Olympian immortality. Apollo and Dionysus will often seem almost convertible, and the worship of Demeter merges into that of Rhea on the one hand, and on the other into that of Cybele, while all three goddesses are continually exercising powers, giving ear to prayers, and receiving offerings which might be equally well associated with the name of Aphrodite.

In fact, the most profitable state of mind for one who would learn about Greek religion treats each god and goddess in turn as if he or she alone existed, and at the same time always bears in vivid mind the history and attributes of all and several of the other gods.[1]

There was noticeable in the last days of Paganism a breaking down of barriers, an effacement of the individual status of each god. This process began much earlier, however, in the case of some gods than in that of others. Indeed one of the greatest Greek divinities, Dionysus, seems

[1] In dealing with this difficulty one thing chiefly needful, according to Lehrs, is to accustom our minds to the notion of an extended sphere of action for each and all of the several gods. "Every god had his own peculiar and appropriate range of usefulness and activity, and yet every god was besought for every manner of help, in any place where he was close at hand, where he was propitious, where he was especially worshipped."— *Populäre Aufsätze*, p. 138. Indeed a very close parallel to this overlapping of the spheres of power assigned to the various gods may be found in cases of appeal made to patron saints in the Greek and in the Roman Church.

never to have been to-day what yesterday had shown him, and on every morrow he was changed again. He began as the great god of Thrace, a prophet-ruler of the dead. Introduced in more southerly climes, he became in one place a god of clemency, and in another the avenging deity. So far as the religious consciousness of Hellas was ever wholly awakened, just so far was there an attempt to frame the universal Dionysus out of elements drawn from all this revelling rout of fairy-tales. In one direction the differences fell away that divided Dionysus from his father Zeus; on another side—and this is a vital point for understanding the history not only of Greek but especially of Attic religion—a close affinity showed itself between Dionysus[1] and Apollo, more especially Delphian Apollo.

Delphi was the seat of a joint worship of Dionysus and Apollo. Apollo absented himself from his shrine on Parnassus as well as from his holy island of Delos during the bitterer winter months. At Delphi Dionysus naturally ruled supreme while Apollo was thus absent, since he was there before Apollo came at all. I shall now speak of Delphi, not only because of this interesting coupling of two great gods, this dwelling together in unity at Delphi of two divine and blessed brethren, but also because there is a certain present appropriateness in the theme. How could I more suitably close an introduction to lectures that are to deal with excavations already achieved than by talking of a far-famed site where all is yet to be done, and showing what

---

[1] Dionysus finally reached a point which may be described as a confluence of epithets derived from all the various forms of his own story, and also from the closely allied worship and myths of Osiris as well as from other sources farther away. See the Plutarchian tract on Isis and Osiris; and for the mass of epithets see *Orphic Hymns*, No. 51, which gives forty-five epithets, and No. 30, where there are twenty-eight.

vital questions may be answered by successful diggings there?

The clearness and the almost intellectual sparkle of the fountain of Castalia[1] can be neither overpraised nor overprized. To slake the thirst at this bright stream, and look from Delphian heights downward and see the far-off glimmer of a distant sea descried from aloft and afar across the Crissaean plain,—memorable for the sacred wars fought that none might pollute it by tillage of any kind,—is an experience never to be forgotten. Then turn away and see the sun-illumined glories of those high-heaved bulwarks on Parnassus' side, the rocks once called Phaedriades. High above the ledge, where ancient Delphi rose, are reared these sheer walls of living light; and one of the mysterious places which some connect with the Apolline oracle is a seemingly unmeasurable rift in these Phaedriades that may be entered by adventurous climbers from the gathering-place of the Castalian spring.

Here, truly, is a place where pilgrims would resort, and at Delphi the traveller in Greece may even now fitly bring to a climax all those feelings of wonder and exultation awakened by the sight of Greece, the common and inalienable fatherland of generous souls. If two friends were shortly to be parted, and each to see the other's living face no more, I could wish for them no more solemn place for their last days of fellowship than Delphi,—Delphi as it is to-day.

Here they could read together that most solemn, sweet, and pious play[2] where Euripides shows forth the spirit of

[1] Appendix XI. ii. 76.
[2] Such, I maintain, is the character of the play which has recently been described by a distinguished authority as an "attack upon Delphi." My reasons for dissenting from this unusual view of the *Ion* have been fully presented in the *Nation*, No. 1329 (18th December 1890).

truth and noble-hearted kindliness that inspired the Delphian worship of Apollo. Above the actors in the play of *Ion* towers Parnassus; the brighter, purer air of its twin peaks exhales from every line of this tragedy, which may after all be deemed no tragedy, since it comes to a happy issue, that involves neither murder nor sudden death. Both of these twin Parnassus peaks belonged to Apollo and Dionysus, as Dante remembered in his invocation of Apollo at the beginning of his *Paradise*; but, so far as Apollo alone stood for the highest reach of the poetic spirit, the highest summit was peculiarly his. Hence Dante says:

> Most kind Apollo, for my final task
> Make thou of me such vessel of thy grace
> As with thy laurel-crown thou canst reward.
> One peak thus far of high Parnassus' twain
> I found enough; but now must have them both,[1]
> Or enter not the contest that impends.
> Now enter thou my breast, inspire me thou!

---

[1] This is a far truer and more effective picture than that of Cervantes in the "Journey to Parnassus," where Helicon with its Hippocrene, its Pegasus, and its Aganippe is made a part of Parnassus. Dante only remembered (as Scartazzini says) the beautiful lines of Lucan (*Phars.* v. 71-74) describing the Parnassus:

" Hesperio tantum, quantum semotus Eoo
Cardine, Parnassus gemino petit aethera colle,
Mons Phoebo, Bromioque sacer: cui numine mixto
Delphica Thebanae referunt trieterica Bacchae."

It is interesting to see that Dante was not, as Cervantes was, appealed to by the array of misguided learning which he might easily have derived from the commentary of Servius on Virgil, much resorted to in his day. See Servius on *Georg.* iii. 43; *Ecl.* vi. 29, x. 11. In his commentary on the *Aeneid*, Servius carries this confusion farther by saying on *Aeneid* vii. 641: *Parnassus, mons Thessaliae, dividitur in Cithaeronem, Liberi, et Heliconem, Apollinis, cuius sunt Musae*; and again on the same line repeated, *Aeneid* x. 163: *Parnassus mons est Thessaliae iuxta Boeotiam, qui in duo finditur iuga, Cithaeronem Liberi, et Heliconem Apollinis et Musarum.* The origin of this confusion between the two peaks of Parnassus and the neighbouring pair of Boeotian peaks is probably to be found

In Dante's mind Apollo stood aloof from all other exemplars of the pure poetic spirit, from all other inspirers of majestic song. The Muses and Dionysus were enough for him while he but sang of torments and of earth, but for the upward winging of his song through the heavens, Apollo's inspiration was required. It came to him as a crowning consummation and a grace ineffable from God to uplift his soul and transfigure his body until he could have a perfect vision of heaven, the wonderland of man's nativity, the fatherland of every righteous soul.

This true insight into the unperishable function, the indestructible potency of Apollo, was possessed not by Dante alone, but by many poets ancient and modern. It has been indeed a true instinct, an unfaltering flight of

in the vague recollection of certain details in a quotation from Hermesianax of Cyprus made in the Plutarchian work *De Fluviis* (II. 'Ισμηνός). Parnassus generically includes all peaks between Mounts Oeta and Corax on the one hand, and Cirrha and Anticirrha on the other; specifically the name Parnassus applies to the two highest peaks in this range which are named Tithorea (Herod. viii. 32, Strabo, p. 417, and Pausan. X. xxxii. 6) and Lycorea (Pausan. *ibid.* and Strabo, p. 418). For the Greek poets these peaks were inseparable, and were associated with rites more frequently connected with Dionysus than with Apollo (Aeschylus, *Eum.* 22 ff.; Soph. *Ant.* 1126 ff. and 1144 f.; Eurip. *I. T.* 1244, *Phoen.* 205 ff., 226 ff., *Ion*, 713, and *Hypsipyle*, fr. 752). Apollo was not however excluded, but his presence was involved in that of Dionysus. Pausanias, speaking of the peaks of Parnassus (X. xxxii. 7), says: τὰ δὲ νεφῶν τέ ἐστιν ἀνωτέρω τὰ ἄκρα, καὶ αἱ Θυιάδες ἐπὶ τούτοις τῷ Διονύσῳ καὶ τῷ Ἀπόλλωνι μαίνονται. Virgil and Ovid say nothing new about the two peaks. Ovid agrees with Pindar in making Parnassus the Mount Ararat of Deucalion's deluge. Lucan does not exclude either god from either peak; but, nevertheless, Benvenuto da Imola has rightly interpreted Dante's meaning here by saying: "Unum iugum Parnassi deputatum Baccho suffecit sibi hucusque, nunc vero et illud et aliud consecratum Apollini est sibi necessarium. Per Bacchum autem figuratur scientia naturalis quae haberi potest per acquisitionem humanam, sicut physica et ethica." Apollo represents *metaphysica* or *sacra scientia*; Bacchus stands for eloquence, "quae hucusque suffecit sibi"; but Apollo is *sapientia*. Then he maintains that Apollo and Bacchus represent the same god under different names, quoting Macrobius, and "Orpheus sacer poeta." Dante himself here adopts Orphic views. See Appendix XI. ii. 86-89, and iii. 9.

poetic inspiration, which has preserved Apollo more than any other of the gods in Greece. Let us then see at last that Apollo rather than Zeus was governor of Olympus, that the only real discipline—if such a word be applicable at all—submitted to even momentarily by all the gods in Greece emanated from Delphi and the far-sighted, wide-minded oracle of Apollo at that holy place.

Zeus was a king among gods, who reigned but governed not.[1] His Premier was the Delphian god. This way of stating the facts is new, but still the very nature of Greek mythology and religion warrants us in adopting it. The god of purest highest poetry alone was competent rightly to order a religion which was pure poesy. Instinctively the poets Homer and Hesiod shaped Greek religion, and Herodotus speaks of them as its originators, the first theologians. It is against the poets and their poetical theology that Plato makes his protest. All this, together with the necessity laid upon us, even to this present hour, of going to school, to the great Greek poets, when we seek to inform ourselves about the Greek gods and their sanctuaries, will prepare us for one of the many exquisitely true utterances exquisitely made by Mr. Walter Pater, to whose various

---

[1] A certain latter-day enhancement of the supreme power of Zeus is one of the interesting differences that distinguish Greco-Roman from early Greek religion. This was but the natural result of the political preponderance of Rome and the *Theocrasy* or commingling of heterogeneous gods taken in conjunction with the new place made for imperial ideas in the religious service of the empire. No doubt philosophy and the clearly thought-out belief in one supreme power, to which so many leaders of later Pagan thought gave utterance, also played its part. To Jupiter or Zeus, as the titular representatives among the traditional gods of this supreme maker and orderer of the universe, universal prayers were made. It must, however, be remembered just here that we are prone to read into the religion of the ancients something of our own clear-cut notion about an indisputably supreme author of all being.

essays[1] I earnestly refer for much that enlightened me in the preparation of these lectures. To him, and also to the well-known book of Preller, and to essays by William Mannhardt,[2] that deserve to be better known than they are, I desire to make especial acknowledgment.

In his first essay on the Myth of Demeter and Persephone, Mr. Pater draws to his close with words for which I claim a wider application than he gives to them. After truly saying that "there is a certain cynicism in that over-positive temper, which is so jealous of our catching any resemblance in the earlier world to the thoughts that really occupy our minds, and which, in its estimate of the actual fragments of antiquity, is content to find no seal of human intelligence upon them," he speaks of the theory of comparative mythology and of the specific and most helpful doctrine or theory of animism.[3] "Only," he adds, in the

[1] Two essays on "The Myth of Demeter and Proserpina" in the *Fortnightly* for January and February 1876, and in December of the same year, "A Study of Dionysus." This last is completed by an essay on "The Bacchanals of Euripides," published in *Macmillan's Magazine* for May 1889.

[2] *Mythologische Forschungen*, posthumously published by H. Patzig in 1874.

[3] Since the preparation and delivery of these studies as lectures this whole subject has been elaborated in Mr. Frazer's *Golden Bough*, which is a treasure-house of information in regard to primitive religious customs. Especial attention is there given to customs and stories which embody this doctrine of animism. As a matter of course the elements of especial interest in Greek myths as such reach immeasurably above and beyond any traces of primitive religion or fetichism discernible in their beginning. Still, since the absence of a right account means almost inevitably a wrong account of these beginnings, Mr. Frazer's book is relevant to the study of Greek mythology and religion. His readers are, however, in serious danger of thinking otherwise because the centre of gravity in his *Golden Bough* falls beyond its base. The picturesque but comparatively unimportant rite of the Arician Grove is no proper nucleus for the important material which Mr. Frazer has gathered into his book.

Much light is thrown upon various questions discussed below in another and most welcome publication, *The Monuments and Mythology of Ancient Athens*, by Miss Harrison and Mrs. Verrall. I can only regret that I had not the great advantage of using both these books in preparing my lectures.

application of these theories, "the critic must not forget that after all it is with poetry he has to do. The abstract poet of that first period of mythology, creating in this wholly impersonal, intensely spiritual way, — the abstract spirit of poetry itself, rises before the mind, and in speaking of this poetical age the critic must take heed before all things not to offend the poets."

The poets, then, and Apollo, or the personified spirit of poetry, form our court of final appeal which sits upon the loftier peak of Parnassus, and judges all matters of vital concern to the gods in Greece and to Greek religion. With this proviso it may be said that Apollo's was the only authority which really swayed Olympus. When, however, a more extended power over all the other gods is attributed to Apollo, the fact becomes so nearly a fact of poetry, that the statement of it in prose almost deprives it of its truth. Let there be, then, an appeal to some poet. Hear an echo, a translation from the sweetest strains divine of poet Aristophanes:—

"Come to me, partner mine," sings the hoopoe to the nightingale, "cease from slumbers, unloose the flights of sacred songs, that through thy lips divine dost wail, for mine and thine, for Itys of many tears trilling and shrilling in the liquid melodies of thy tawny throat. Pure ascends through the greenwood thicket their echoing refrain even unto Zeus's throne, where golden-haired Phoebus, giving attentive ear and making responsive music to thy mournful lays, upon his lyre of ivory wrought, marshalls the dances of the gods. Lo! from deathless lips proceed the while concordant with thy strains most heavenly acclamations from the blessed gods." Here was no place for father Zeus to interfere; like all the other gods, he too obeyed Apollo, and followed after Phoebus, leader of the dance. Delphian Apollo was mightier in song and in prophetic wisdom than even Zeus himself. The poet's poet-god wielded the sceptre of poetry and gave his law to all the gods in Greece.[1]

After all is said and done such rule and right to guide as attached to Apollo among other gods belonged to him by divine right of righteousness, and has the final sanction of a sense of tolerance and fair dealing conspicuous in the justice of Apollo's acts and the generosity of what he abstained from doing. His rule was based upon a truly poetical sense of right and wrong. Had he not been generous and broadly tolerant of powers and pretensions which prosaic minds and gods of prose would certainly have resented and opposed, he never could have prevailed at Delphi. It was this supremely poetical quality in the Delphian god, his possession, so to speak, of imagination, which enabled him serenely to contemplate and wisely to further the welldoing of other divinities and of various worships often seemingly the rivals of his own. The best instance of this Delphian tolerance of Apollo is in the union of Apollo and Dionysus at Delphi itself, and in the cordial and useful support given by Apollo's Delphian oracle to the propagation and elaboration of Dionysus worship elsewhere, particularly in Attica. Like Apollo, Dionysus was a poet-god and a giver of oracles, an inspirer of the souls, and a possessor of the bodies of men. And yet

---

[1] This is a very different primacy from that primacy of fear attributed to Apollo in the Homeric Hymn. The difference may serve as a measure of the advance in nobility of religious thought made by the Greeks under the leadership of great and deeply religious thinkers like Euripides, Plato, and Pindar. And yet something of the later strain of Apollo is heard in the prayer of Glaucus, *Iliad*, xvi. 514 ff. : "Hear, O Lord, who art somewhere in Lycia's rich land or in Troy ; for thou canst hear in every place when a man is in grief such as now is the grief that is on me."

Dionysus and Apollo went hand in hand through all the length of Hellas.

Another way of stating the case would be to say, as has recently been done, and most truly, that one great reason for the prosperity and renown of the oracle and temple at Delphi was the cleverness shown by Apollo's priests in combining and maintaining with equal hand the various cults of various divinities that centred there. But this way of counting those who may in some sense have been wire-pullers as wire-pullers only, of counting their manœuvres for everything, and the reality of the cause for which their work was done for nothing, leads nowhere. It is profitless, because falsehood always lurks in the reasoning of those who, from the heights of imagined superiority, look down upon the great religion of a great epoch in the world's history, deeming it a sheer delusion through and through. Thank Heaven! we can let the eighteenth century have all for its own that canting talk about the "trickery of priests." No vital religious fact was ever materially affected by the trickery of priests, and it is no accident therefore, but a deeply significant fact in the course of Greek mythology and the history of Greek religion, that Apollo and Dionysus, the sublime and the intense, dwelt together in unity before the eyes of those who came and worshipped at the mountain shrine of Delphi.

"*Apollo, ivy-god and prophet bacchanal,*"[1] cries Aeschylus, sublimest of the singers at Dionysus' Attic theatre, giving to Apollo the characteristic insignia of Dionysus. "*Lord Bacchus, lover of the laurel tree,*"[2] says Euripides, lending

[1] Fr. 394, cf. Macrobius, *Saturn.* 18, 6.
[2] Macrobius, *ibid.*: Euripides in Licymnio, Apollinem Liberumque unum eundemque deum esse significans, scribit "δέσποτα φιλόδαφνε Βάκχε, Παιὰν Ἄπολλον εὔλυρε."

Apollo's sacred laurel bough to Dionysus for the nonce. Traditions kept alive in far-away places show the brotherhood of these two gods of poetry. In one place record was preserved of it by a worship of Apollo under the special epithet of "one sent by Dionysus."[1] In popular pictures, such as decorated vases, the ivy often crowns not Dionysus but the slenderer Apollo. The Muses, represented as Apollo's attendants upon the front pediment of his great Delphian temple, are frequently given in popular pictures to be the companions of Dionysus, who also borrows very often his brother Apollo's lyre. To close these instances with the strongest proof of the good fellowship and mutual tolerance between them as conceived by their worshippers, consider the western pediment or gable of the great temple of Apollo just before mentioned. To correspond to Apollo and the Muses of the other, this pediment presented Dionysus and his Thyades, his maenad band of bacchanalian women. The temple being that of Apollo, Dionysus still could be made most prominent, since, like Apollo, he was an inspirer of song.

Many other reasons, but especially the date of this Delphian temple, built in the middle of the sixth century B.C. by Spintharus of Corinth, indicate how early this bond of brotherhood between Apollo and Dionysus received conspicuous sanction from the Delphian priests and in Greece at large. Within the temple, just in the Holy of Holies, where the golden statue of Apollo stood, was a tomb of Chthonian Dionysus, not far from the rounded stone that marked the absolute centre or "navel" of the earth. This last was flanked by two golden eagles,[2] for it was well known that Zeus sent forth

[1] Διονυσόδοτος, Pausanias, I. xxxi. 4.   [2] Appendix XI. i. 126.

two of his own imperial birds—one from the north, the other from the south,—and the fact of their meeting just in this spot, and perching on either side of this particular stone, witnesses that Delphi is at the centre of the world. This original meeting was commemorated by the two golden eagles set up upon the spot and sanctified to Apollo. Another feature of this shrine that goes to prove that it was no ordinary sanctuary of Apollo, but rather a meeting ground for many worshippers of many divinities, was an altar to Poseidon, the shaker of the earth, which was anciently erected and always maintained.

Such points as these, and others to be gained from Pausanias' description of the great Delphian temple, show how much may be learned from excavations on this site. To make excavations at Delphi will be a glorious task for any to whom it may be allotted, and would indeed be a fitting continuation of the work which our countrymen, inspired and directed in those days by Dr. Merriam, a scholar of whose great attainments and sound judgment America is proud, have already done among the Attic mountains at Icaria. But the friends of the American School of Classical Studies at Athens have not forgotten that it is the youngest but one of the four schools there established.[1] Therefore they will not sorrow but rejoice if the first established of all schools at Athens, the French School, with its well established traditions and a liberal grant from the Government, carries out work so well begun

[1] Rumour has it that the Italians are about to add theirs to the four established already. Those who are familiar with the organisation of excavations in Italy and know the Italian system of local reports will understand the gain to Greek archaeology which an Italian School at Athens must bring.

at Delphi by M. Homolle and M. Foucart.[1] What could not be done with a sufficient grant of money by a School that accomplished with next to no money at all the excavations and investigations at Delos which have made us all M. Homolle's debtors?[2]

A disentangling of the relations between Apollo and the other Delphian gods, some of whom seem to have preceded him and to have been eclipsed by his arrival, will perhaps be possible in the future. But this can only be when much work upon the site shall have yielded many new inscriptions. With only such knowledge as is now available, contained, be it said, in an admirable paper recently published by Professor Middleton in the *Journal of Hellenic Studies*,[3] it seems possible to say little with positiveness. It is not, however, rash to declare even now that the terms upon which Apollo's worship finally obtained supremacy at Delphi are likely to have enlarged the final range of his influence. The compromises involved in his first coming no doubt begot in him a wide and tolerant strain.

With the earlier history of worship at Delphi is bound up the growth and increase of the great power that made for order in Olympus and began to bring into the religious ideas of Greece a spirit of reasonableness if not of logic. Just as the highest ideal of poetry, the work of a poet's poet like Dante, presents the universe as an ordered whole, so the highest and really most supreme divinity in that poetry of poetry, Greek religion, will be Apollo on Parnassus, the poet's god of poetry, seeking to organise, to make reason-

---

[1] Foucart, *Ruines et Histoire de Delphes*, 1865.
[2] See chap. viii.
[3] See the *Journal* for 1888, vol. ix. p. 282.

able, and justify the worship and the ways of all the gods in Greece, and to present the world of Olympus as an ordered whole.

This was accomplished chiefly by oracular responses. A constant interchange of influence is perceptible in the relations between Delphi and Athens. When the hitherto-despised Dionysus-worship was brought into honour at Athens and no longer hidden in the country demes, the influence of the Delphian oracle of Apollo was one of the determining forces that wrought the change. It is certain that the Delphian oracle sanctioned and promoted just at this time an additional worship of Dionysus not known of old to the country demes of Attica. Under this new aspect from abroad, Dionysus was known as the god of Eleutherae, a town on the frontier towards Boeotia. His worship was characterised by moderation, and Pegasus, his high priest of Eleutherae, is associated with the practice of tempering the strength of wine with water. Accordingly the Dionysus of Eleutherae was not the awful Dionysus of the nether world, not the "angel of the darker drink," but Dionysus the Saviour, who came to show men, tired and dazed by his orgies, how they might make themselves clear-eyed once more and have untroubled hearts as they betook themselves again to their wonted avocations.

By such a mitigation of the more outrageous features in the rude and early Attic worship of Dionysus did Apollo repay that god who had made place for him when he came to Delphi. Of that coming Euripides gives a beautiful picture in his *Taurian Iphigenia*: "Sweet was the babe of Leto born, Phoebus, a god with golden hair. Borne by Leto, on he came unto Parnassus, whose peak leaps in the bacchanalian dance that honours Dionysus. There of mottled hue and glance wine-flashing lurked a dragon, shaded by laurel leafage; sheathed as in brass, Earth's monstrous portent guarded the seat of nether-world prophecy. Him didst thou slay, a mere babe though thou wert, Phoebus, and didst enter in to possess it the seat of oracles most divine, and now thou art throned on thy tripod all-golden, even thy throne unacquainted with falsehood, rendering there unto mortals thy prophecies that ascend from beneath the divine Holy of Holies close to the streams of Castaly, in thy house at the midpoint of earth." The dragon slain, here alluded to, is the Pythian monster. Him and all the oracles rendered by earth at Delphi Apollo caused to disappear by the irresistible power of his coming. All that was antagonistic to Apollo Euripides here looks upon as evil. Perhaps he thought of it as embodying all the unpitying relentlessness of the earlier and inhuman phase of Greek religion, against which his own poems are a dramatised protest. The good that existed in local rites was not affrighted by Apollo's coming. The dawning sun-god, lately born of Leto on that miracle of the Grecian seas, the holy isle of Delos, could banish none of the powers of light; only darkness fled before his rising.

This coming of Apollo to Delphi, this dawning of the light in which we see revealed the highest and the best that worship could inspire in Greeks, and wherein we learn to know the loftiest characters and characteristics among the gods in Greece, may fitly be associated with another song of Euripides, sung by Ion at the open door of his father Apollo's Delphian temple:

"Lo from his gleaming chariot drawn by coursers four the sun now flashes light far down to earth; the stars in flight are swiftly plunged into holy night by the fires of day. Parnassus' peaks untrodden, bathed in its radiance, receive for men below this wheel of day. Meanwhile the smoke of parchéd frankincense and myrrh wings its way upward to Phoebus' roof. Yea, and a woman on the thrice hallowed tripod is sitting, the Delphian one, singing forth such sounds for Greece even as Apollo's voice proclaims."

This tripod at Delphi was the symbol of Apollo's primacy on earth; at Athens and in Attica the same tripod was awarded as the victor's prize in the tragic and the dithyrambic [1] contest. The winner always consecrated it to Dionysus. Thus may the tripod, so constantly present on the Delphian coins and in all manner of Greek religious pictures, stand for one of the most vital facts in the Greek world: the unison of Apollo and Dionysus in concordant rule upon the double peak of Delphian Parnassus.

[1] It was certainly awarded for tragic victory at Icaria, and as certainly for dithyrambs at Athens, where it was probably also given for tragedy.

APPENDIX I

THE DEIFICATION OF ROMAN EMPERORS

ROMAN imperialism has not usually been judged upon its merits. Perhaps this would have been otherwise if Julius Caesar, the first and in many ways the greatest of the emperors, had lived longer. But his heir Augustus was a man of other mould. His whole effort was to persuade Rome and the Romans that their worn-out commonwealth and all its antiquated simplicity of religion was still surviving. He wished to be supreme without seeming so, to govern but not to reign. This masquerading scheme had a marvellous success, and here is one reason why the new religious sanction of Roman imperialism, the deification of the emperors, has not as yet been very generally understood as it deserves to be. The senate, before Julius Caesar died, ordered the institution of worship in his honour; and, if the report of Dio and Zonaras were considered more than a misconception of Cicero's mocking allusion, they styled him Jupiter Julius.[1] However that may be,

---

[1] See Dio Cassius (44, 6), for the completest account : καὶ τέλος Δία τε αὐτὸν ἄντικρυς Ἰούλιον προσηγόρευσαν, καὶ ναὸν αὐτῷ τῇ τ' ἐπιεικείᾳ αὐτοῦ τεμενισθῆναι ἔγνωσαν, ἱερέα σφίσι τὸν Ἀντώνιον, ὥσπερ τινὰ διάλιον, προχειρισάμενοι ; Zonaras (x. ch. 12, p. 492 A-C) brings in as a climax to his long list of honours voted and given to Caesar while he yet lived Δία τε αὐτὸν Ἰούλιον προσηγόρευσαν. Cf. Cicero (*Phil.* ii. 43, 110)— Est ergo flamen ut Jovi, ut Marti, ut Quirino, sic Divo Julio M. Antonius ? Cf. *Phil.* xiii. 19, 41—Cujus, homo ingratissime, flaminium cur reliquisti ? See Suetonius, *Caesar*, 76. Since Leunclavius' and Fabricius' notes on

Mark Antony was nominated to be his flamen or master of sacrifice. But then came Augustus deprecating, so far as he was personally concerned, the establishment of temples for the new imperial worship, all but forbidding it in Rome and barely permitting it elsewhere. He deprecated so conspicuous a religious innovation in the full glare of publicity at Rome, but apparently did all in his power to extend a similar worship in dark corners of Rome itself[1] and in various parts of the Roman empire. So successful was this policy of artfully dissimulating the new and artificially reviving the old cults that many of the important sources for understanding the deification of the emperors are outside of the known literature of imperial days. Obscure and fragmentary inscriptions have to be appealed to. Many of the great men of imperial administration, including some of the emperors themselves, found it difficult always to take the new religion seriously; it is therefore not surprising that men of another day and generation should pass it by unheeding.

And yet, if a close connection between religion and morality can be taken for granted, a new religion was required to give sanction to the new morality of imperial days, and this religion finds expression in the Augustan poets. In a

the passage in Dio above cited, the fashion has been to ignore it. Scholars have dispensed themselves of the trouble required to sift the testimony of Dio, rejecting it summarily as coming too long after the facts. But see Dr. R. Wilmans, *De Dionis Cassii fontibus*, etc., Berlin, 1836, pp. 24 and 25. Speaking of the *acta publica*, Dr. Wilmans says: "Ex hoc igitur fonte multae apud Dionem derivandae sunt narratiunculae." Dio took his point about Jupiter Julius from the *acta publica* no doubt. On such a point Cicero could not afford to be explicit, therefore he was ironical. See also Hugo Grohs, *Der Wert des Geschichtswerkes des Cassius Dio*, etc., Züllichan, 1884. Livy neglected daily events that happened in Rome. Dio's merit lies in his account of these, "für die *Interna* sah er noch (besides what Livy notes) die Geschichte Sueton's und die *acta publica* an." It is evident that his account of honours voted to Caesar is an additional proof that he took pains about daily events at Rome.

[1] The genius of Augustus was associated with the Lares Compitales. See Marquardt (*Staatsverwaltung*, iii. p. 199), who refers to Ovid (*F.* v. 145) and Horace (*Od.* iv. 5, 34), and for a similar worship of the Genii of later emperors to inscriptions.

lecture before the Royal Institution on Roman Imperialism, Professor Seeley contrasts the Republican and the Imperial ideals of conduct as follows: "Men ceased to be adventurous, patriotic, just, magnanimous; but, on the other hand, they became chaste, tender-hearted, loyal, religious, and capable of infinite endurance in a good cause." They cultivated the virtues of the pious Aeneas. Even though the details of these contrasted catalogues of virtue may not be to everybody's mind, the fact of a changed standard must be admitted; and consequently the religious alterations, the distinctively imperial innovations in worship, should be scrupulously investigated and carefully pondered.

From Virgil, and also from Horace, Ovid, and others, we may learn of the new ideals of this wider and broader day which transformed even traditional religion in the Roman dominions. The hearts of the subjects of imperial Rome, the hopes of the Roman proletariat, were centred not so much in the old-time Roman religion as in the new-come reign of peace. The emperors could not, if they would, escape the homage of their subjects. It was the part of wisdom not to stifle but to guide this spontaneous zeal, this uplifting of grateful hearts toward the ideal of a beneficent and omnipotent imperial fatherhood. Those ancient Caesars could as little escape such a worship as can the modern Caesars of Russia. Therefore it was well to bind up with the new worship the religious, social, and political life of various orders and classes, particularly that of the lower and most numerous class, which was more or less unprovided for by traditionally existing religious usage and ceremonial. Certainly a beginning of social and religious life was absolutely needed for those whom Republican Rome had left in outer darkness. Without the part assigned in imperial services to freedmen and small tradesmen the empire would never have been in so advantageous a position for reaping the benefits of Christianity as it really was when the critical moment arrived.

Let us view this imperial service in its relation (1) to

the earlier religion of Greece and Rome; (2) to the new political and religious needs of the hour; and (3) to the political, social, and religious needs of a new class of people, *i.e.* of a class of people who had hitherto been almost completely ignored.

It is certain that the notion of deifying the emperor or any human being must have been rooted in previous habits of mind. No flattery, however base, could on the spur of the moment have invented just this form of homage with any chance of securing its adoption. The fact is that it was not the work of clever men. They had to set their hands to it in obedience to a popular impulse which they were too clever to withstand. No one supposes that the Senate would have done homage to Jupiter Julius of their own accord. The burst of popular admiration and gratitude which in Greece required that divine honours should be paid to Flamininus,[1] was analogous to the enthusiasm felt by the Roman populace for their benefactor Caesar. Precedents therefore must be sought in the religion of the people. The time-honoured worship of the genius of the Roman people or of Rome had always appealed especially to the people, and this was naturally and promptly associated with and finally passed into a worship of the emperor. Was not he their good genius? the people asked. Even Augustus allowed himself to be worshipped by circumlocution as "the clemency of Augustus," and throughout the empire, if not in Rome itself, were erected, with his officially reluctant sanction, altars and shrines for Rome and Augustus like the one on the Athenian Acropolis.

This Athenian homage may serve to recall the history of deification in Greece, which can be read plainly and had run a long course before the days of the Caesars at Rome.

In the middle of the Peloponnesian war a gallant Spartan

[1] See his life by Plutarch (chap. xvi.), where mention of a survival of this worship down to Plutarch's time is made. It is interesting to note that this deification of Flamininus was by the Greeks of Chalcidice, near neighbours of the Amphipolitans who long before paid divine honours to Brasidas.

soldier, Brasidas, died in Thrace while defending Amphipolis from the attacks of Athens. The enthusiastic Amphipolitans put Brasidas in the place of their Athenian founder Hagnon, ordering an altar to be dedicated to him, and bestowing upon him the other quasi-divine honours usually given by Greek colonists to the founder. What a hold was gained by this manner of testifying to the great qualities of a contemporary is shown by the deification of Lysander, which took place at the end of this same war. The novelty here consists in the fact that Lysander received sacrifices and all the rest of it while he was yet living. Brasidas, on the other hand, had died before Amphipolis worshipped him. Thus long before the Ptolemies and the days of Roman imperialism the Greeks in Asia had capped the climax of apotheosis for Lysander. So far Rome did not easily go. It was, in fact, so little habitual at any time to deify a living emperor that the bare proposal was treated as involving his "promotion into the next world." There was a moderating common-sense at Rome which kept this custom—half Greek and wholly Oriental—within certain bounds, and associated it with the reasonable and popular worship of the genius of Rome.

Such were the Greek and Roman possibilities of which imperial apotheosis was the enhancement and the realisation. Now a word may be said of the new religious needs to which this apotheosis gave a measure of satisfaction. These new needs were felt alike by the higher and lower orders in the empire, though by the latter most keenly and consistently. Quintilian, Tacitus, and Pliny may fairly represent the higher orders. They stood aloof from the popular religious point of view, and, like many who took refuge in Stoicism or Epicureanism, rejected much if not most of the mythology in which the popular mind still found a religious satisfaction. It is curious, in spite of all this, to note the way in which Tacitus reports a miracle performed by Vespasian. He really seems to be willing, for a moment at least, to recognise a supernatural power in the emperor.¹ Quintilian, without having a systematised philosophy of his own, talks of a god who is the "father and contriver of the world," one who "administers" the universe.² Plainly the emperor ruling the Roman world is the prototype in this case. Quintilian does not think of the emperor as god, but he thinks of god as the emperor.³ Pliny, the sceptical naturalist, was especially proud of being superior to popular religion. Few things awake his enthusiasm, and his usually limping prose takes sudden wings only for a moment when he soars toward his god made manifest, the shining sun, "mind of the universe."⁴ But Pliny himself has not wholly escaped the religious contagion of his time. His thoughts constantly hover around the person of the emperor; his illustrations and explanations are always bringing the emperor in. He calls Nero the "foe of mankind," and mentions, as it were with bated breath, that he came into the world feet foremost.⁵ Again, after rejecting various superstitions, he exclaims— "The help that man lends to man is god; this is the way of glory eternal. This is the way taken by Roman worthies of old, and this way with heavenly step now goes that 'maximus aevi rector' (*greatest latter-day guide*), Vespasian Augustus, and by his side his children walk." And then he adds—"Of all ways for paying due thanks to men of great desert, to enrol them as gods is the most time-honoured."⁶

If the new and incalculable power of the Roman emperors had such a dazzling influence over minds trained

---

[1] Igitur Vespasianus cuncta fortunae suae patere ratus nec quicquam ultra incredibile, laeto ipse vultu, erecta quae adstabat multitudine, iussa exsequitur. Statim conversa ad usum manus, ac caeco reluxit dies. Utrumque, qui interfuere, nunc quoque memorant, postquam nullum mendacio pretium (*Hist*. iv. 81). Cf. *Ann*. iv. 20, where, in the account of Lepidus and Tiberius, Tacitus represents the favour of an emperor as a sort of gift of grace, not to be won but allotted by fate.

[2] *Inst. Or.* ii. 16, 12. Cf. *ibid*. xii. 2, 21.

[3] Cf. one of Dante's phrases for the deity, "Il consiglio che il mondo governa" (*Par*. xxi. 71).   [4] *Nat. Hist*. II. vi. 12.

[5] *Ibid*. VII. viii. 45.   [6] *Ibid*. II. vii. 18 and 19.

by habits of philosophic thought, what must have been the popular state of mind? Certain bursts of enthusiasm which are chronicled, numerous dedications inscribed on stone, may help us to some conception of this. The successful career of demagogic and unscrupulous informers gives further light. No doubt Eprius Marcellus, one of the ablest and most unscrupulous of these informers, depended for his backing upon the populace, or he would never have taken the tone which he did in the Senate. Eprius and others like him were backed by popular indignation in their fierce attacks upon those who refused to take the prescribed oath, "In acta divi Augusti et divi Iulii."[1] His motto was also the people's—*Pray for good emperors, but take any you can get*; and this represented the people's state of mind.

Among the people who were thus blindly loyal to the imperial master, were large numbers whose first franchise connected itself with this new order of things. It is curious to note—as far as the scanty means of information allow—what a seemingly incongruous compound of Asiatic piety and European bureaucracy gathered around the institution of this new imperial rite.

In Italy, Sicily, Gaul, Spain, on the Danube, and in Africa a new class of men sprang into notice. They were freedmen and small tradesmen, and formed an especial class or caste, calling themselves Augustales. They had to do with local celebrations analogous to the Augustalia at Rome. Furthermore there were provincial meetings of notables.

---

[1] Eprius Marcellus was identified with the new cult since he was one of the Sodales Augustales (see Henzen's Inscription 5425, quoted in Nipperdey's note on Tacitus, *Ann.* xii. 4). The customary oath, "In acta divi Augusti et divi Iulii" may be insisted upon as a purely secular act, since it was required as a preliminary to the performance of secular functions (*Ann.* iv. 42; xiii. 11). Still the use of the word *divus* certainly involves a religious attitude toward those to whom it applies. Moreover Tiberius plainly regarded this *sollemne iusiurandum* as promoting him to a condition beyond mortal mishaps, if Tacitus speaks truly (*Ann.* i. 72)—Neque in acta sua iurari, quamquam censente senatu, permisit, cuncta mortalium incerta, quantoque plus adeptus foret, tanto se magis in lubrico dictitans.

Convened for the purposes of the new worship, these assemblies soon became centres of provincial life, and played in later Roman days no unimportant political part, although Christianity deprived them of all connection with religion.

Such conventions of notables existed in the East as well as in the West; but not so the new order of Augustales.[1] In Greece and Asia Minor, and in general wherever the empire of Alexander had planted the seeds of specifically Greek political organisation, there was noticeable here and there a sort of church organisation. The old hieratic term νεωκόρος (familiar at Eleusis, for example), quite removed at last from its original meaning of temple-sweeper, got itself applied rather to whole communities than to individual men,[2] and is found upon many coins of Asiatic cities where periodical festivals in honour of deified emperors were held. There was competition for this privilege of holding high imperial festivals,—for the νεωκορία.[3] Ephesus stood pre-eminent in having had it granted four times.[4] In conjunction probably with these, and certainly with other features of the imperial worship, there came into existence a board of ten High Priests for the province of Asia. To take one Eastern province as an example of many, they were called Ἀσιάρχαι,[5] and were necessarily men of substance and position. They were elected by representatives from various cities who assembled yearly at Ephesus. Of these ten Ἀσιάρχαι one apparently ranked[6] above all the others, and

[1] Although no evidence of the fact is forthcoming, the Augustales probably existed in the free municipia established in the East. But these as well as the colonies may be neglected in speaking broadly, since they were not of the East as such.

[2] See, in Pauly, Krause's articles "Certamina" and "Neocoroi"; also his more detailed monograph on the νεωκορία.

[3] See Tacitus, *Ann.* iv. 55, where it is plain that something like the νεωκορία is involved.

[4] Coins of Caracalla's and of Elagabalus' reign bear the inscription—Ἐφεσίων μόνων ἀπασῶν τετράκις νεωκόρων.

[5] For other provinces there were other titles—Βιθυνιάρχης, Ποντάρχης, Καππαδοκάρχης, etc.

[6] See Marquardt, *Röm. Staatsverwalt.* i. p. 513.

bore either the unqualified title of Ἀσιάρχης, or of ἀρχιερεὺς τῆς Ἀσίας. He performed functions analogous to those of a bishop. Thus it came to pass that the chief rallying point of Paganism in its last battle with Christianity was one of its very latest phases—the worship of Rome and Augustus elaborated in two ways, one for the West and one for the East.

II

DEMETER AT ELEUSIS AND CNIDUS

THE worship of Demeter does not agree with war, since she never used her golden sword [1] to slay. Remembering, when wronged even, that she was the giver of good things, she found comfort to her griefs in blessing all mankind. Such a goddess had no place in Homer's *Iliad*; the whole of its heroism is alien to her. Other peaceful gods might go to war, limping Hephaestus might join the force that favoured Greece, while Aphrodite smiling fought for Troy; but neither side claimed Demeter. So far from seeking her aid were the haughty heroes of Homeric song, that her good gifts were sometimes even misprized. Ajax defied all who were mortal and ate of the fruits of Demeter, all whom a spear-thrust could pierce or a rock could crush and maim.[2] The golden grain in abundance, for which a farmer will always be thankful, often seemed to those valiant men of war an unwelcome mark of mortality and weakness, a blot upon the brightness of undying fame. When the Achaean host is under a cloud of dust and its burnished helmets and bristling spears are tarnished, then the poet bethinks him of Demeter the yellow-haired, where she so often stands

[1] *Hymn to Demeter*, l. 4.   [2] *Iliad*, xxi. 76; xiii. 322.

among the winnowers on a farm, parting the wheat from the chaff that spreads over the brightness of day like the dust that chokes the Achaeans.[1] Plainly it is rather in moments of trial and humiliation that the kindly goddess of earth's fruits is remembered in the *Iliad*. Demeter had in fact been left at home when the host set sail for Troy. She remained among the farms and flowery fields of Thessalian Pyrasus where was her sanctuary, and its name of Pyrasus[2] came from the abundance of wheat which was her gift.

In the *Odyssey*, on the other hand, farmers and farming are looked upon with more interest; and naturally, since the intense theme of the Trojan war is there exchanged for a less thrilling but more charming narrative of adventure. In the *Iliad*, when nothing is said to the contrary, we may be sure of fighting; in the *Odyssey*, no matter what else is going on, there is continual feasting. The whole of the last half of the *Odyssey* has its scene laid at home among the farmsteads or in the hall of Odysseus. Unhappily the domain of Odysseus was no Pyrasus, no *wheatland*, and therefore though we become familiar with the domestic economy of Eumaeus, whose faithfulness to his lord Odysseus tempts the translator to be absolutely literal and to call him the "divine swineherd,"[3] this brings no mention of Demeter the home goddess of grain, the Kornmutter or Mother of Corn. Something of her history may be gathered from Homer, though he chiefly knows that Zeus was her husband, and that he slew her beloved Iasion, whom she met upon a thrice-ploughed fallow field of Crete.[4]

Homer either did not imagine that Persephone was

[1] *Iliad*, v. 500. [2] *Ibid*. ii. 695.
[3] Mr. Gladstone has recently and truly said that in point of goodness Eumaeus excels every one of the Homeric gods.
[4] *Odyssey*, v. 125.

daughter to Demeter, or did not think that the relation, so ineffably beautiful according to the story which finally prevailed, had any very great significance. He speaks of Persephone simply as the daughter of Zeus,[1] whereas the idea that finally prevailed made Persephone nothing if not her mother's daughter,[2] and sometimes indeed left a doubt whether Zeus or Poseidon were her father. It mattered little to her later worshippers who her father was, since she became all her mother's,—the eternal type of a daughter dearly loved and lost, sought for in grief and found at last. But to Homer Persephone was nothing of all this ; she was the queen of the dead ;[3] dread Persephone. Terror was in her name, and in spite of the lovelier phases through which she passed, a word of slaughter can still be heard when she is named. For Homer she was always to be feared,[4] a divinity only then to be called glorious when by so naming her you might forestall some dreadful harm. She could send forth, from where she ruled among the dead, that awful Gorgon's head that turned to stone all those whose eyes it met; her anger was therefore to be feared and in every way to be appeased. This gloomy picture of Persephone is drawn in the *Odyssey*, where she dwells and queens it in a dusky realm that may be above or below ground; the only thing which is certain about it is its situation with reference to the rest of the world. It is a land far off in the darkness of the west, beyond the twilight of

---

[1] *Iliad*, xiv. 326 ; *Odyssey*, xi. 217.
[2] Eur. *Phoen.* 687.
[3] Arcadian legends give Persephone the name Δέσποινα (Paus. VIII. xxxvii.) and her mother is Demeter Erinys. At Eleusis under this aspect Persephone was named Daeira. See Preller's *Greek Mythology*.
[4] Persephone is called ἐπαινή four times in the *Iliad* and four times in the *Odyssey*, where she is also (euphemistically) four times called ἀγαυή, and once ἁγνή.

Cimmeria. It is an outer or utter world, not necessarily an under world.

In the *Iliad*, on the other hand, we hear of Hades or Aidoneus, the husband of dread Persephone. So awful were the abodes where these two dwelt and ruled supreme that the poet speaks of the disclosure of Hades' dominions to the light of day as a thing too awful almost to mention. Unlike the far off country of the dead visited by Odysseus, the otherworld of the *Iliad* is under men's feet. The fighting of the gods before Troy, Poseidon shaking the earth, and Zeus filling the air with his thunders, nearly broke through into the undiscovered country of the dead. Aidoneus upon his nether throne was filled with fear and trembled.

It cannot be too often repeated that the Demeter known to the Homeric poems had no affinity with Persephone in either of her two realms. According to a flickering tradition we hear that Persephone was deemed by some to be not Demeter's daughter but a child borne by the dreadful river goddess Styx.[1] Perhaps if Persephone's mother had been named by Homer, he would have said she was the Styx. Anything rather than mother to the queen of death was Homer's Demeter. She is a goddess of peace and plenty. For another presence like hers we may look to a place far nearer home than Greece, to English Northumberland. Hutchinson says in his history,[2] "In some places I have seen an image aparelled in great finery, a sheaf of corn placed under her arm and a scycle in her hand,

[1] Apollodorus, *Bibl.* i. 3, 5.
[2] *A View of Northumberland, with an Excursion to the Abbey of Mailross in Scotland*, by W. Hutchinson, Anno 1776, published at Newcastle in 1778, vol. ii. p. 17 of the Appendix in the account of *Mell Supper*.

carried out of the village on the morning of the conclusive reaping day, with music and much clamour of the reapers into the field, where it stands fixed on a pole all day, and when the reaping is done is brought home in like manner. This they call the Harvest Queen, and it represents the Roman Ceres." Hutchinson might have added that it corresponded to what we know from Homer of Demeter, who resembles nothing so much in those earliest stories as this Harvest Queen of England or the Corn Lady whose divinity is honoured in Scotland by hanging up a small package of grain when the reapers have finished.[1]

After the Homeric poems came the works of Hesiod, but it is uncertain whether all the traditions preserved by Hesiod and not recorded by Homer are of an origin later than Homer. In fact they both give us glimpses of customs and habits of mind as old as time. It is convenient, however, and not seriously misleading, to think of the cheerful yellow-haired Homeric Demeter as of one coming to woman's estate through the deeper experiences with which Hesiod's poems invest her. Here she becomes acquainted with grief through her dear daughter Persephone. Hesiod knows far more of the goddess's kindred than Homer. Rhea is Demeter's mother and Cronos is her father; Zeus is her husband, to whom she bore white-armed Persephone. Hesiod also has heard, while Homer has not, of the carrying off of Persephone by Aidoneus.[2] To him Zeus granted his daughter's hand, and by him Persephone is seized and carried off in a chariot. Still, Hesiod is not always very far in his notion of Demeter from the simple

---

[1] Parallels from various country customs are multiplied by Mannhardt, and also by Frazer in the *Golden Bough*. [2] *Theog.* 912.

THE GODDESS OF ENOUGH AND TO SPARE

and uncomplicated idea of Homer. Demeter the goddess, crowned with those very fruits which she alone can give, is famine's foe. "Work, Perseus, make famine your foe and fair-crowned Demeter your friend."[1] This is Hesiod's advice to his kinsman.

The Greeks in Sicily worshipped Demeter from the earliest days, and well they might, since the island of their homes was so especially favoured by her that it came to deserve the name of the granary of Rome. One Sicilian sanctuary was dedicated to Hadephagia,[2]—a strange name indeed until by translation you discover that this object of Sicilian reverence was simply the Genius of a square meal, the goddess of Enough-and-to-spare, a divinity much prayed to even now by cow-boys and many other people who have long wildernesses to cross, and often fast perforce for many hours together. At this same Sicilian shrine Demeter herself was worshipped under the surname of Sito, that is, of Mother Rye. This Sicilian service paid to Demeter Sito and to Hadephagia is but the logical outcome of the utilitarian view of Demeter as famine's foe presented by Hesiod in his *Works and Days*, that oldest of farmers' almanacs.

But beyond the simple aspect of Demeter as the giver of food there lurked in the earliest adoration of her something most solemn and secret. How early Herodotus[3] considered this worship to have come into Greece may be judged by his story that the daughters of Egyptian Danaus showed unto the women in Pelasgian days what were the rites to be celebrated in honour of Demeter. Herodotus is speaking more especially of the special festival in her honour called the Thesmophoria, where she was worshipped as giving sanction to certain Thesmoi or laws upon which

[1] *Works and Days*, 298.   [2] Athenaeus, x. 9.   [3] ii. 171.

the family and other social facts were based. This somewhat vague statement of Herodotus is at least sufficiently definite to show that he regarded Demeter's worship as among the most ancient forms of divine service. Before Homer or Hesiod sang, Demeter was; and the sentiment of awe which consecrated her goddess and mistress of what men held most sacred and most dear had existed in Greece from the very first. Before the poets came, a whole ritual must have grown up, the significance of which Demeter's peasant worshippers could not expound. These were men whose only argument was the observance of times and ceremonies, and who knew no higher logic than the telling of a tale about this god or that.[1] Hesiod, who first chronicles in full their stories of Demeter's parentage, and who first though briefly mentions the grief that came when her daughter was stolen away from earth, must surely somewhere indicate a deep and solemn view of the fair-haired Demeter's power upon the lives of men. Of this deeper view there are traces, though it may be necessary, if we would clearly understand, to read between his lines.

In place of Homer's phrase, "the fruits of Demeter,"[2] Hesiod prefers to speak of "the holy fruits of Demeter."[3] This adjective *holy* contains a first and half articulated expression of the mystery and awe which overpowered the pious adorers at Eleusis when it found its full utterance in ritual. Another hint is given by Hesiod that throws light upon this homely farm-religion of the early days in Greece.

---

[1] "There is a certain illogical logic about all mythologies. Where philosophy leaps at once to abstract terms and speaks of an omniscient, omnipotent, omnipresent deity—mythology, aiming at the same notions, proceeds, agreeably to its nature, by positive imagery in place of negative *abs*-tractions."
—C. F. Keary, *The Vikings*, p. 61.

[2] *Iliad*, xiii. 322.   [3] *Works and Days*, 466.

I mean where he says, in words not always rightly understood, that a field new ploughed and newly sown has power to charm a babe and still his cries. That is, if the babe be only laid upon it, no doubt. This receives illustration from various customs not yet extinct in Europe, which bring the new sowing of seed and the tending and growth of young babes into one and the same scheme. Hesiod, just after dwelling upon the above point in regard to stilling young children, proceeds, "Now make prayer to Zeus and to holy Demeter, that they may make perfect and heavy of growth the hallowed fruits of Demeter."[1] Plainly the inscrutable power which gives and withholds abundance in harvests can somehow hinder or help the health and growth of a babe. Every language and every country works out in some way the old story and utters with a new voice the time-worn truth that the growth of babes and children is one with the growth of trees and flowers and grass.[2] All fruitfulness, every species of multiplication in the land, is linked to that of every other kind by some mystical bond which makes one of them all, and binds the growth of men and of things into a single and continuous scheme. This belief, now argued out by science and subjected to scrutiny in all its parts and all its meanings, was represented among the peoples of all times in a thousand quaint customs of the countryside, many of which survive among the innocent and unlearned to-day. Akin to all these customs, but

[1] The whole passage runs as follows :—

νειὸν δὲ σπείρειν ἔτι κουφίζουσαν ἄρουραν·
νειὸς ἀλεξιάρη παίδων εὐκηλήτειρα·
Εὔχεσθαι δὲ Διὶ χθονίῳ, Δημήτερί θ' ἁγνῇ,
ἐκτελέα βρίθειν Δημήτερος ἱερὸν ἀκτήν.
Works and Days, 463–466.

[2] See Mannhardt's posthumously printed essay " Korn und Kind."

fuller of the perfect truth of poetry which is beauty, and beauty, and once again beauty, was the service of fair-crowned Demeter in Greece by chosen spirits of Greece, and when Rome came, in Rome.

Plainly the godhead of Demeter and her kinship with the queen and king of darkness were bound up somehow with the deeper and more mysterious suggestions made ever and anon by Hesiod. Homer knew nothing of all this, and accordingly Homer knows little or nothing of the real godhead of Demeter. The first complete account of the myth of Demeter is contained in a poem of later date than the *Iliad*, the *Odyssey*, or the writings of Hesiod. This is the Homeric Hymn to Demeter,[1] called Homeric not because it was written by Homer but as the work of some poet versed in Homeric lore, and its probable date is about 600 B.C.—five hundred hexameter lines written at least 2500 years ago, which remained absolutely unknown from the fourteenth to the end of the eighteenth century of our era. Mr. Sidney Colvin[2] has most aptly described this beautiful poem, and gives the following account of its substance and style:—
" There is nothing liturgical about it; it is rather in the nature of a ballad, recited, it may be, by a patriotic minstrel of Eleusis to the groups of strangers who thronged to the city, or in competition with other such ballads at one of those poetical tournaments which formed part, we know, of many of the Greek religious festivals. I say a minstrel of Eleusis, because of his special tone of pride in the town and locality, and because he ignores Athens, while his Ionian dialect would be quite proper to an Attic rhapsodist. It is their

[1] About one hundred years ago Ruhnken received it for publication from a learned friend who stumbled upon it in an old monkish library at Moscow.
[2] *Cornhill Magazine*, vol. xxxiii. June 1876, "A Greek Hymn."

ballad character, and the community they have of style and diction with the *Iliad* and *Odyssey*, which have earned the title of Homeric for a certain number of Greek hymns or narrative poems in praise of particular divinities which have come down to us. This is the most beautiful of them all."

This beautiful Hymn contains, according to the view set forth below, at least three ballads or stories, and the inconsistencies and roughnesses in its composition spring from a too conscientious effort to make the three into one. At the time when this Hymn was composed, or perhaps we should say compiled, many interesting facts and fancies about Demeter and her worship were at the author's command. The most conspicuous of these are two stories telling how Aidoneus carried off Proserpina, and of Proserpina's final restoration to Demeter. One of these may be called the *Iliad* story, since it is based upon the *Iliad* conception of the world of death as an underworld. The other may be called the *Odyssean* version, since according to it Persephone was spirited away into the land beyond Cimmerian darkness, whither Odysseus went to talk with dead Tiresias. Over and above these two accounts of Persephone's disappearance and reappearance, that had woven themselves into consistency upon the lips of men, there were other tales inextricably connected, now in one way and now in another, with the two just named, which gave to the bereavement of Demeter and the robbery of Persephone a local habitation and a name. These stories may be conceived of as having been as numerous as were the temples of Demeter, but certainly the one that men most heeded was the one which localised the whole myth at Eleusis in Attica. Eleusis is about twelve miles from Athens, but the fertile and extensive Thriasian and Rarian plains, the first one towards Athens, and the second one towards Megara, surround it and make it a natural home for the goddess of grain. It is evident that many generations of simple people on the farms of the Thriasian and the Rarian plains in Attica had been absorbed in the due worship of the goddess Demeter. Gradually, in this direction and in that, connected accounts of the goddess and of the Eleusinian rites in her honour grew up and found credence. The most pleasing and popular of these were woven into one narrative, which forms the beautiful and yet most bewildering Hymn in question.

The perseverance of Dr. Wegener has triumphed over the author of this Hymn to Demeter. What the poet joined together Wegener has triumphantly put asunder. Too anxious, like many compilers of religious articles and creeds, that no one concerned should find cause of offence in his work, the author, in spite of the poetic exquisiteness of his touch, left such inconsistencies and patent incongruities that each tradition can with more or less certainty be disentangled from the others; and this is what Dr. Wegener has done.[1]

The *Iliad* story of the carrying off of Proserpina is briefly as follows :—Zeus conspired with Gaia, the earth, to get Persephone, his child by Demeter, for his brother Aidoneus to wife. Earth snared the smiling maid by a most fatal blossom called the narcissus. Persephone reached forth to pluck the wondrous flower, and lo! the ground opened, and Aidoneus dragged the shrieking girl down to his underworld home. Hecate meanwhile was sitting in her cave thinking delicate thoughts. She and she alone could see the robber on his downward way, and she it was who made haste with the news to Demeter. The

[1] *Philologus*, xxxv. (1876) pp. 227-254.

bereaved mother stands at Zeus's throne and asks for restitution. Zeus urges that Aidoneus is a worthy husband for Persephone. Then Demeter shuns Olympus, and resorts to the fields and towns of men. She retires into her temple (at Eleusis), where she passes a whole year. The world is stricken in all the produce and increase of earth. Zeus, forced by the cutting off of all fruits, sends Iris first, and then the other gods. All others fail, and Rhea, Demeter's mother, last of all goes to her and she makes peace. Zeus grants a compromise. Two-thirds of the year Persephone is to stay with her mother and see the glad light of day, but for one-third of each twelve months, during the sad season of winter and darkness, the daughter and mother are to be parted, Persephone is to be with her husband Aidoneus. Appeased at last, the mother welcomes back her child, and earth once more covers itself with the holy fruits of Demeter.

The second version, told in the same breath by the Homeric author of Demeter's Hymn, is the *Odyssean* version, and it must be admitted that the landscape of Eleusis does not suit the demands of this form of the story so well as it does the *Iliad* tale just given, but on the other hand this account of the story brings in the pomegranate seed—a mystical emblem often seen in the hands of Demeter and Persephone at Eleusis and elsewhere. There is much to tempt an unwary person here; certainly the rash would incline to pronounce this *Odyssean* tale the older of the two. However this question of age be decided, there is no doubt as to a strong affinity with the *Odyssey*, not only in the *Odyssean* aspect of the tale which has yet to be given, but in the whole of the poem. Mr. Colvin has descried and inimitably described the likeness as follows: "It (the

Hymn) moves with much of the same easy grandeur as the *Odyssey*, it has the same romantic charm, and delights us with similar pictures of heroic manners, of chiefs trusted by their people, of beautiful unabashed virgins, of noble hospitality to strangers. Like the *Odyssey*, it tells us of gods going to and fro among mortals, unrecognised till they choose; of disguises and feigning answers and sudden revelations."

And now,—to turn from the *Odyssean* touch in the whole poem to what has been talked of as the *Odyssean* version of the carrying off of Proserpina,—that runs as follows :—On a flowery mead close by Oceanus, Persephone is gathering flowers with the daughters of Oceanus. But a sudden fear arrives—Hades dashes across the flowery field with his chariot and spirits the maiden away. Zeus knows nothing of the deed, but is busy in a far off temple accepting sacrifice from men. The robber king of death meanwhile drives ever onward toward the darkling West. Persephone cries ever and anon, but most of all when at the very last of the weary journey she sees that she must lose the sight of day. Hades comforts her by telling her of the honours she shall have as queen among the dead; and furthermore, that fate may never take her from him quite, he secretly thrusts a pomegranate seed into her mouth. Demeter hears her daughter scream, and rends her garments, and wraps her shoulders in the garb of mourning. Thus, seeking and asking, for nine days long does she pass over land and sea. None of Persephone's playmates, not one of all the gods and men, can tell her who the robber is, or where her daughter tarries. So therefore she goes to the all-seeing sun, and he shows to her the utmost regard and kindness. Filled with pity, he tells her who the robber is, and whither

Persephone has been carried. Then Demeter in wrath betakes her to her Eleusinian temple. Zeus meanwhile hears her wrongs, and sends his messenger Hermes with instant reprimand, and with command that Hades make restitution. Hades, the Zeus of the netherworld, made no retort in anger, but smiled serenely and bade Persephone do as the word of Hermes commanded. He was sure, through the fatal seed of the pomegranate which she had taken, that Persephone would not forsake him utterly. Hermes accordingly leads her back to her mother, who is glad of her return, but grieves to find what an unbreakable spell from Hades is on her.

These two legends are curiously but not at all indistinguishably interwoven through the whole of the first and the last portions of the Homeric Hymn to Demeter. If in no other material detail, they coincide in taking for granted the existence of a temple of Demeter. This temple is not necessarily at Eleusis. Both of these versions would suit any other centre for the worship of Demeter just as well or ill as they suit Eleusis, for it is possible to substitute another name, and thus, so to speak, the venue of the myth can be changed with the alteration of one word. The second or *Odyssean* story lays the scene of the robbery in a far off land, which is certainly neither Eleusis nor any other centre of Greek life, and as for the place whither the stricken Demeter retires, it is simply spoken of as her temple, and no local details are given, but only the name Eleusis. The *Iliad* tale, on the contrary, might be supposed to consecrate Eleusis, not only as the place where Demeter's temple was, but as the actual theatre of the robbery of Proserpina. But Cnidus (whither the story wandered by sea from Thessaly no later perhaps than it went to Eleusis) would answer just as well. The same may be said of any other place where Demeter was worshipped, and where there was a rock-formation suggestive of the rending and yawning of the earth, and a smiling and fertile plain near by for the flower gathering of Persephone. Accordingly neither of these stories of the carrying off of Proserpina necessarily localises the myth and worship of the two goddesses, mother and daughter, at Eleusis. But towards the hundredth line of the Homeric Hymn a strange thing suddenly happens. Just as the earth opened when Persephone reached out her hand to gather the fatal narcissus, so when the reader seeks to follow onward the narrative thread of Persephone's robbery, woven together out of two strands, he finds that it becomes tangled suddenly from one line to the next, and, before he knows it, he is dragged down to where sorrowing Demeter sits on the Laughless Stone by the Eleusinian well called Maidenswell. The way of Persephone's story comes to a sudden chasm, and a legend of different quality, though not less beautiful, is disclosed.

This is the purely and most sweetly Attic tale of Demeter's stay at Eleusis. Here we have united together certain local traditions that grew up at and near Eleusis in the early days when Athens and Eleusis were on so nearly equal a footing as independent states, each exercising a local leadership, that they with ten others could eventually become the twelve members of the Attic confederation—if it were sure that this word suited the politics of those earliest days. This interjected Eleusinian tale of Demeter's stay at Eleusis gives the needed consecration—the only one respected in those early days—to the temple and observances of Demeter at Eleusis. By this tradition is founded the Eleusinian claim to be the greatest centre for Demeter-worship in

Greece. This story, however, is not told in one way only any more than that of Persephone's taking away. Here again the scrutiny of minute perseverance discovers various inconsistencies and a double version. As the points of difference seem less vital here, they shall for the most part be given in one narrative, while a few matters can be kept till the end for consideration.

The Eleusinian legend of how Demeter came to dwell at Eleusis is then substantially as follows :—Near a well close to the Acropolis of Eleusis the sorrowing goddess Demeter rested from exhaustion, for she had been long in search of her lost Persephone. What was the name of the well, Parthenos (Maidenswell) or Callichoros (Dancewell)? However that may be decided, the goddess rested there on the Laughless Stone, the *Agelastos Petra*. Was Demeter disguised as an old woman, or was she there in the undisguised majesty of her divine beauty? The stories varied; but in this they agree, that the four daughters of the king of Eleusis, Celeus son of Eleusin by name, came thither with pitchers of bronze that they might draw water from the well. They question the goddess, who tells them a tale neither plain nor unvarnished. She has been enslaved by men who kidnapped her in Crete.[1] When her captor landed at Thori-

---

[1] The use of Crete in this feigned narrative is by some supposed to amount to a recognition of Crete as an early cradle of the worship of Demeter. It should, however, be remembered that Crete was the most obvious of places to mention in any invented tale of seafarers and seafaring. This is proved by its constant occurrence in feigned adventures in the *Odyssey* (xiii. 256 and ff.; xix. 171 and ff.), and by the way in which it often creeps into the Homeric MSS., either instead of places of less frequent resort or in addition to them (cf. *Odyssey*, i. 93, where two verses about Crete are added; *ibid.* 285, where Zenodotus substituted Crete for Sparta ; the same thing occurs in *Odyssey*, ii. 214 and 359. See La Roche's critical edition, Teubner, 1867. Something of the kind is reported at *Odyssey*, iv. 702). The real proof of a widespread and very early belief in Crete as one of the starting-points of the Demeter myth is in Hesiod's localising in

cus in Attica she made her escape under cover of night. Now she wishes to be taken into service. The girls go to their mother, Metanira, and return with a message that she will be welcomed as their brother Demophoon's nurse. According to one story Demeter, in the undisguised splendour of her divinity, dazzled Metanira, the babe's mother, who arose as if to give the place of honour to the entering guest, whose more than human skill was required to deliver the infant Demophoon from the evil spells cast over his life by a wicked nurse. The other way of telling the tale makes Demeter none the less a good fairy, only her gentle offices are given in the disguise of a grief-stricken woman overburdened with years and misfortunes. Thus disguised she takes the boy—the child of Metanira and Celeus latest born —and gives him the care without which he could never have been brought to man's estate. Of whatever nature the goddess's service was, all tales agree in saying that the child grew apace, without the ordinary food of mortal babes, fondly cherished upon her immortal bosom and lulled to rest. At this point a curious turn is taken by the myth, which relates that Demeter sought to make the boy Demophoon immortal, and to that end, when all the house was asleep, set him in the flames. One night she was watched either by one of the sisters or by the mother Metanira. Catching sight of Demophoon in the flames, his indiscreet and misguided

Crete (*Theogony*, 969 and ff.) the commerce between Demeter and Iasion, reported but not localised in the fifth Odyssey, vv. 125 and ff. This is confirmed by a reference to Bacchylides (Bergk, fr. 64), where the rape of Proserpina is localised in Crete. Common report, however, had it with equal certainty that Proserpina was carried off from the fertile fields of Sicily. I think it therefore unjustifiable to appeal to the early poets as giving an undisputed pre-eminence in Demeter-worship to Cretan traditions. Ariadne—a sort of Persephone—came from Crete, it will be remembered, and she has little or no direct connection with Demeter. See Appendix X.

kinswoman screamed aloud, whereupon the goddess, having laid hold upon him, was moved to sudden anger and let him fall. The family is awakened, and the women minister to the affrighted child. Then Demeter takes her departure, but not, as the previous episode would seem to suggest, in anger. No; she waits to give full commands concerning the building of her temple at Eleusis, and she enters into all the rites, the orgies, as they were called, which were to be celebrated in her service there. These commands, according to one story, were laid by the goddess upon Metanira and her daughters, who did not call upon Celeus and his sons,—among whom was Triptolemus,—until morning dawned. The intervening hours through all the night were spent by the women in propitiating the goddess. The alternative version is that Demeter on the eve of departure spoke to the women of her worship and its orgies, and then summoned King Celeus and his sons Triptolemus, Diocles, Eumolpus and Polyxenus, and gave to them all needful commands for the building of her temple and the institution of her service.

As points of divergence arose, they have been indicated in the above summary of the Eleusinian story of Demeter. Two main versions there plainly were, but even after making allowance for such a variation, there remain difficulties to be cleared up. First of all the whole story of Demeter's seeking to make Demophoon immortal by immersing him in fire seems incongruous and incomprehensible. This fact, taken together with the identity not only in substance of the account of the fire-baptism of Demophoon by Demeter, and one preserved elsewhere[1] of the fire-baptism

[1] Apollodorus, *Bibliotheca*, iii. 13, 6. Compare the account of Demophoon's fire-baptism given also by Apollodorus, i. 5, 4. The story suits

of Achilles attempted by his mother Thetis and foiled by his father Peleus, removes one difficulty. The whole fire episode was probably imposed upon this story; it has no place there, at least not in the form in which it has been transmitted. And this smooths the way for clearing the second difficulty. It is plain that there is a surplus of proper names here. The king of Eleusis, in whose house Demeter tarried, is not in all accounts of the myth called Celeus. Panyasis[1] names the Eleusinian king Eleusis or Eleusin,[2] whereas in this Homeric Hymn the king is Celeus, and his *father's* name is Eleusin. Moreover the youthful hero worshipped at Eleusis, and especially in the Rarian plain near by, as Demeter's favoured child, whom she had instructed in the arts of farm labour, is Triptolemus, not Demophoon. This circumstance would lead us to expect Triptolemus to take Demophoon's place in the story of Eleusis given in the Homeric Hymn, and such is the case in what are considered later, but may represent earlier versions of it.[3] Now if from the Homeric Hymn be subtracted the fire-baptism of Demophoon, there is nothing left for Demophoon in all the story.

It looks as if Demophoon and his father Celeus were interlopers in this Eleusinian tale, and it is not impossible that their presence here may be a chapter of early

Achilles, and does not suit Demophoon. Thetis wished to make him immortal by burning out the mortal part which he had from his father. We are not told how the thrusting of Demophoon "like a torch into fire" was supposed to make him—of mortal father and mortal mother—superior to mortality. Furthermore Achilles never tasted mother's milk, and hence his first name was Ligyon. A point is made of Demophoon's not taking the breast, but nothing remarkable comes of it. The whole Achillean fire-legend loses reality in the alien story of Eleusis.

[1] Apollodorus, *Bibliotheca*, i. 5, 2 (where Pherecydes is quoted as saying Eleusis was a son of Oceanus and Ge. In these tales Eleusis figures as Cecrops and Cychreus do at Athens and Salamis); Hyginus, *Fab.* 147.
[2] Cf. Pausanias, I. xxxviii. 7, end.
[3] Hyginus, *Fab.* 147, who was followed by Ovid.

religious history in disguise. Supposing the religious importance of Phliasian Celeae[1] to have been overshadowed and all but clean forgot in very early days, we should then have a survival of it if the local hero of Celeae was Celeus. Accordingly the supposition would be that, before Eleusis and its legends completely won the day, there was an interregnum, a period when neither Eleusis nor Celeae nor Andania[2] had appropriated exclusively the story of Demeter's sorrows upon earth. What variety of names and episodes there may have been in all these rival tales cannot be known. But the uncertainty of many of the important proper names in the Attic story as it has reached us is most significant. For Metanira some give Cothonea;[3] the name Demophoon crowds Triptolemus—Demeter's real favourite—into the position of an elder brother; and Celeus is invited into the Eleusinian story of Demeter, taking the place of Eleusin, who becomes his father. Celeus could easily (in a compromise-version) fill the unimportant place of the child's father Eleusin in the narrative, but it was not so easy to supplant Triptolemus, a local demi-god whose worship was almost on a par with that of Demeter herself. This is the reason why Demophoon appears in this story only to disappear, and indeed there is very little beyond the record of a Demophoon, son of Theseus, to show where Demophoon came from.[4] Of him we have but the name, though it is certain that in some early story he played a leading part, for the name reappears in Euripides'

[1] Pausanias, II. xiv.   [2] *Ibid.* IV. iii. 10.
[3] Pausanias (I. xxxviii. 3) says that Pamphos "κατὰ ταὐτὰ καὶ Ὅμηρος" calls the daughters of Celeus, Diogenia, Pammerope, and Saisara. These names are unknown in our Homeric poems.
[4] Hyginus tells of the nine journeys to the shore near Amphipolis in Thrace of Phyllis, betrayed by Demophoon, *Fab.* 59. Cf. Ovid, *Her.* ii.

Heraclidae, where a Demophoon figures as king of Athens, and indeed elsewhere frequently but with no defined associations. The original Demophoon, unlike Celeus, could hardly have belonged to Celeae.

The composer of the Homeric Hymn to Demeter escaped some embarrassment by leaving out entirely the great Eleusinian myth of Triptolemus. The record of this, which has been preserved, is chiefly in the shape of pictures and a few fragmentary lines of poetry from a lost play of Sophocles. Plainly Triptolemus, the hero-prince of Eleusis, was adopted by Demeter; he was her son in whom she was well pleased, and through whom she granted to men all manner of good things above and beyond what it was his especial province and privilege to give, the boon of plenteous grain, and the knowledge needed for its planting and due preservation.[1] Temples were built and altars established for the grateful worship of Triptolemus, the especial favourite not of Demeter only but also of Persephone. Especially sacred to him was the plain where first he showed men how to plant and plough, the Rarian plain, which was set apart as holy ground for ever, and from which was derived the grain for making the cakes offered up in the Eleusinian temples. Its produce came as a part of the revenue of the Eleusinian temple of Demeter, and one of the peculiar duties of the priests in charge at Eleusis was to keep this plain of Triptolemus free from all pollution.

Thus by examining closely the Homeric Hymn more

[1] Whether, as I have perhaps too positively suggested above, Triptolemus should play Demophoon's vacated part in the Demeter myth is another question. On this whole point M. Lenormant's article " Cérès," in Daremberg and Saglio's *Dictionnaire des antiquités grecques et romaines*, may be profitably consulted.

even than a phase of the religious activity of the early Attic mind has come to light. Stories grouped themselves about Demeter at Eleusis which first revealed the greatness of the goddess herself, next the bond between her and her child Persephone. With this was involved the worship of Aidoneus—more or less identified with the local hero Eubouleus—and Persephone, rulers in the undiscovered country of the dead. Quite unexpectedly at the end of the story, where the immemorial observances in Eleusinian worship are receiving sanction and institution from Demeter, it is borne in upon the attentive reader that Demophoon and Triptolemus do not belong to the same group of local traditions, and thus a glimpse at the local history of early Eleusis and of some neighbouring shrine, say its Peloponnesian neighbour Celeae, is given. Furthermore Triptolemus, and perhaps, in his own forgotten story at home, Demophoon also, represent the beneficent influence of Demeter the mother of corn and the goddess of beautiful abundance. This beneficence of hers, this overflowing generosity in her nature, provides for more than creature comforts,—it makes for what is highest and best in home existence and civilised life.

One noticeable touch of poetic truth in the story of Demeter at Eleusis is the way in which woman's love and care and need for woman are portrayed. When Demeter is sitting all forlorn the daughters of Celeus come upon her, cheerful and careless maidens sent forth to fetch water. The spectacle of self-forgetful sorrow which the goddess presents seems to transform them; they ask her why she tarries in so lonely a place, quite aloof from the town. She ought to be in some home, they urge, for there in the shadowing halls dwell women of her age and older too.

They will be kind in word and in deed. Such is the tender promise of consolation which the maidens give,—and the promise is fulfilled; Demeter is as much loved as she herself is loving in the house of Eleusinian Celeus, her home on earth. Through the whole story men are kept in the background. Iambe, the wayward daughter of the house, cheers Demeter with her gibes, and Metanira refreshes her not with wine, but water perfumed with herbs and made more strong and sweeter for the tired taste with barley. Demeter is thus made whole by her own bounteous gift of grain. Silent and eloquently sad was Demeter, as she moved with the gentle maidens towards their home. Not a sound was heard as they went, nothing save her footfall and the dulled rustle of her heavy raiment, dark with the colour of mourning. Ministered to at last by these kindly womenfolk she smiled, she laughed, and her spirit was glad within her.

This pathetic picture lends a divine sanction, as it were, to the need which woman in trial has for kindly women, and throws light upon one whole side of the worship of Demeter. For Demeter, as the upholder of the ties of marriage, was called Thesmophoros, and a festival in her honour called the Thesmophoria was celebrated by women and women only. To this worship some of the very noblest aspects of the Eleusinian service would seem to be allied. In his little-known picture of the *Women at the Thesmophoria*, Aristophanes has made abundantly merry at the expense of Demeter's Thesmophorian woman's festival, but for all that it remains more than ever sacred.

How is it possible to translate into modern words the pious aspirations of the old-time farmers who worshipped Demeter at Eleusis? How can the divinity of Demeter be made comprehensible or even plausible to us? Perhaps not at all, but yet there is a charm in the goddess's simple story of trial and triumph through sorrow that seems to claim the hearts of men, no matter how alien to Greece their birth and breeding may chance to be. The central, the efficacious and communicable grace of Demeter's story is the love she bears Persephone. This is a home tie, and through this Demeter becomes the home goddess. It sometimes seems that the whole range of ideas dwelt upon in Demeter's service by Greeks is covered by that beautiful and nobly, broadly English word *harvest-home*. Under the mastery of the home impulse, of love for her own, the great goddess's whole beneficent nature gradually unfolded itself. If you should say that Aphrodite [1] loved to be loved, I might by way of contrast maintain that Demeter asked only and chiefly to love, to lavish her care and minute pains upon some one who needed protection.

The daughter thus beloved of Demeter was a wondrous creature, in no way resembling that dread Persephone of Homeric song. A child of Demeter and not of the awful Styx, her face bears the look of a flower freshly opened. The gentle and shyly smiling curves of her lips show the lines sometimes seen in blossoms, delicately closed because the day is done. The maiden's only care is for flowers, and the unmeasured love of her mother is her shield against all harms, until the fatal hour when Hades comes and robs her of the pleasant light of day, snatching her away from joy in flowery things. There is an almost adequate representation of Persephone the flower maiden, the dear and delicate child in whom dwelt the graces, the perfumes and

---

[1] For a further presentation of the relation between these two divinities see chapter vii. below, on Aphrodite at Paphos, near the end.

the colours, all that earth shows forth in all the lilies of all her fields. This representation is a statue of whitest Parian marble, so small that were it less perfect it would be what Mr. Pater so prettily calls it, the merest toy. This wondrous figure was found by Sir Charles Newton within the sanctuary of Demeter and Persephone—one of their most ancient sanctuaries, that of Cnidus on the Triopian promontory in south-west Asia Minor. The first and untried loveliness of a maiden unacquainted as yet with grief and untested by the world has passed into this most delicate Praxitelean work.

No greater contrast can be imagined than that between this statue of Persephone and another found near it, and like it to be seen now in the British Museum. This second statue is possibly that of an aged and careworn priestess of Demeter. But at the same time in it we have before us the embodiment of Demeter herself, as she was in act of going sad and despairing to the house of Celeus. Upon this speaking marble the unwitting artist, under the unconscious inspiration of the sad sweet story, has set the impress of sorrow, and with it a touch of that remembrance of happier things, which is "sorrow's crown of sorrow." Here truly is the goddess Demeter,[1] in outward semblance like her priestess, a stricken woman well advanced in years,

---

[1] See M. Lenormant in his article "Cérès" above referred to :—" On parle d'une Déméter Γραῖα (Hesych. *s.v.*) ou 'vieille femme'; ce surnom fait allusion à la forme que la déesse avait prise en arrivant à Eleusis et pendant son séjour dans la maison de Celeos. Il semblerait en résulter que l'on a quelquefois adoré, et par suite représenté Déméter sous ce déguisement emprunté. M. Newton (*Discov. at Halic.*, etc., p. 399), M. R. Foerster (*Raub der Kora*, p. 248), et M. Heuzey (*Monum. de l'Assoc. des études Grecques*, p. 10), ont même cru reconnaître la Déméter *Graia* dans une statue de vieille femme en pied, d'un travail fort remarquable et d'un accent très élevé, qui provient des ruines du sanctuaire des grandes déesses à Cnide (Newton, *op. cit.* planche lvi.)"

but noble in her mien. The folds of her apparel, the eager forward leaning of her head, tell of vain seeking and unavailing grief. Here stands the *mater dolorosa* mourning for her child. But somehow hers is not a passive woe, for her there is still room for hope. There is therefore a strenuousness in Demeter's sorrow unlike the total self-surrender to grief of many sweet portrayals of the fainting Mother Mary at the Cross.

For Demeter there was still hope, and while she waited all her sorrow and the fruitlessness of her search only served to bring into active life and motion her impulse to do good. Many a home has been blessed and cheered by some such selfless presence as was sorrowing Demeter's at Eleusis. Deprived of the home love, and of the light of her sweet daughter, Demeter became the good fairy and the friend of the Eleusinian home of Celeus, the faithful and all-wise nurse and instructress of the son of the house, and through them the devoted friend and helper of all the homes of men on earth.[1] For Triptolemus, with the knowledge of agriculture, gave the laws of Demeter to men. These, the goddess's rules for right living, were no doubt preserved, with momentary glimpses at one of the most elevating of the many beautiful myths of early Attica, by Sophocles in his lost play called *Triptolemus*. We almost see the kindly goddess appearing on the scene and giving her beneficent injunctions to young Triptolemus, for a learned expounder of the eleventh Olympian Ode of Pindar quotes from the play, which lay open before him, these solemn words, "Set my commandments on the tablets of

---

[1] Ovid brings out the human side of the story by an artifice used in Euripides' *Electra*. He discrowns Celeus, and brings Demeter to a poor man's home.

thy heart." But we really know nothing except that these words occurred in the play. The sacred words may have been given by Demeter to Triptolemus, or quoted from her by Triptolemus to some favoured man. It would be best of all to know what the commandments were. Perhaps some notion of their import is contained in the Pythagorean rules of life which Porphyry[1] puts into the mouth of Triptolemus.

"Thou shalt honour thy father and thy mother, thou shalt make glad the gods with offerings, and do no wanton harm to beasts." Upon some such commandments as these Demeter based her laws, and the penalty for disobeying them was a withdrawal of her favour and a denial of all her good gifts. Our own Jewish fifth commandment is not very different from Demeter's, which required men to honour their parents in order that the earth might yield her increase. Before Demeter gave her gifts, wretched men, so say the poets, were forced to live upon acorns. The Demeter who preserved the homes and hearths of men from want, and sanctified the bonds of family life, was a noble type of divine womanhood, above and beyond all other types that Greek men worshipped, and the noblest of the three great Cnidian statues found by Sir Charles Newton is undoubtedly a representation of this Demeter. Mother of peace and giver of plenty, there she sits, the Lady Bountiful and Beautiful of Greece. Her gaze is now at last more nearly serene, but in it there is sadness as a memory of past sorrows.[2] The goddess has made her

---

[1] *De Abstin.* iv. 22.

[2] As I see this statue, the sadness of its look is not overpowering. Hence I venture to differ from those who see in it Demeter *Achaia*, the mother of lamentations, so to say. If I understand Mr. Pater aright, I see it as he does.

peace with evil and the power of death, and takes joy in such sweet communion with her child as the fates allowed. It would be too much to say that this Demeter smiles, but cheerfulness lurks half suppressed about her mouth, just as in her attitude there is relief and great repose in spite of something that seems almost to be constraint. A curious mingling of opposites there is both in her posture and her face. A cheerful look that tells of mystery and wherein lurks the memory of woe, a contradiction, as it were, between her eyes that are not glad, and the lower lines of mouth and chin that are not sorrowful. A posture of evident rest and yet an impression of bashfulness and almost of hesitancy. These contrasting expressions existing side by side, hard to seize and harder still to describe, together with the manner of holding the head, and the .uneasy grace with which the limbs are disposed, are seen alike in the Demeter and the Persephone of Cnidus which are attributed to the Praxitelean School. There both mother and daughter are marked by these same family traits, a shyness which goes with all natures delicately noble and free from self-seeking, that shyness which men learn by wandering much alone, and musing oft when only the trees and the streams, only the green earth and her fruitful fields, are there to sympathise and understand.

On many vases and in some bas-reliefs it is hardly possible to distinguish Demeter from Persephone. This is as it should be according to the worship rendered them at Eleusis. Excepting in her days of thoughtless youth, before her trial came, Demeter's Persephone is Demeter's self twice told. During the third of every year, the wintry season when Persephone was the unwilling bride of Hades and abode with him in sadness, Demeter was forlorn. Joy came back to her with spring when Persephone was freed again to stay with her. Their sorrows and their joys, their life, their love, their happiness, are always one. If under Demeter's name be symbolised power to grow and bear full fruit inherent in each living thing, then Persephone may be called the outward blossoming into leaf and flower and fruit. But who shall surely say which of these two processes or powers is Demeter and which Persephone? Where does the domain of either begin or end? Demeter and Persephone each represent the power to grow and the process of growth. Of these two elements commingled is their soul, which is one though it dwells in two bodies. Both are two aspects of one and the same fact in nature, and each is the incarnation in her joy of the yearly burst of springtide life on earth, and of the glad abundance of the riper year, while in the sorrows suffered alike by each is shown the yearly march of living things towards death. Each of these goddesses, linking her happiness to sorrow and rising out of grief to gladness, bears the testimony of her being to the indissoluble link that joins life to death and death to life; while the unfathomable love that joins them both, and makes them live one life when they are sundered just as when they are together,—this mirrors for us that unity which pervades the world and makes all growth and all life a blossoming from the unknown depths of ever-fruitful love—tokens of the "never-dying flowers of joy eternal,"[1] given for a space and for a space withdrawn.

[1] Perpetui fiori dell' eterna letizia. Dante, *Par.* xix. 22.

III

DIONYSUS IN THRACE AND OLD ATTICA

THE goddess Persephone, like many tragic heroines of more mortal mould, whose mischances moved Athenian hearts in the theatre of Dionysus, loved light and life. The queen of the netherworld tarried in her realm of darkness, longing always for the upper earth and its bright ray. Nevertheless she was the wife of Hades, and stayed in his underworld for one third of every year. This bestowal of the loveliest life divine, even for a brief season, on the fellowship of the dead—or, if you will, this transfiguration of Homer's death-dealing goddess of the dead into a creature so lovely and so loving that she charms alike and comforts the realms of life and death—indicates a progress. The wondrous flower-change suffered by Demeter's daughter images a widened and deepened view of the life beyond.

This progress began even in those minds from which the Homeric poems sprang, but here was only its beginning. Homer's Elysium was but a shadowy and merely painless place of abode when compared with the islands of the blest of the latter-day Greeks. Such satisfactions as Homer granted in that neutral-tinted place to a favoured few were not a well-earned meed of righteousness, nor were the punishments of Tantalus or Sisyphus conceived of by Homer as more than shadows of their life on earth; they were dim semblances of what those men of unworth suffered ere they died.

The new Persephone, flower-changed from Persephone the dread, went down and lighted up the silent home where hitherto the spirits of men, of just alike and unjust, had led a shadowy life where joy laughed not but only smiled, where sorrow brought no pain. Men's ideas underwent a corresponding change, and we can read between the lines of the new legend of Eleusis[1] that a great revolution came to pass in the belief concerning immortality. Hand in hand with this there was, partly its cause and partly its result, an alteration in men's ideals of duty and perfection in the present life.

The clearest and most musically devout expression of these new feelings and thoughts is found in Pindar, a poet of Boeotian Thebes, who flourished in the first half of the fifth century B.C. It is not surprising that a Theban should have spoken as one having authority about the life hereafter, since the transformation of religious belief in question was especially associated with Thebes through Dionysus. The more definite and substantial expectation of future rewards and punishments, to which the Greeks finally accustomed their meditations, was connected everywhere with the worship of Dionysus, a late-born god, whose Theban mother died at Thebes in Boeotia, that he might come to being. In Attica this changed point of view which Dionysus everywhere brought with him was associ-

---

[1] An interesting connection by way of derivation has been suggested between the words Eleusis and Elysium.

ated not alone with him, but with a holy alliance sealed at Eleusis in secrecy and mystery between Demeter and Persephone, with Hades hovering near, on the one hand, and on the other this new godhead of Dionysus freshly come[1] to Greece from the north and east.

From Thrace in the north, and from Phrygia, where his first worshippers called him by many names, but chiefly Sabazius, Dionysus brought much that was barbarous. And the barbarous and non-Hellenic quality of the new god made him a sad puzzle to the Homeric public. In the only extended and discriminating Homeric account of Dionysus,[2] his behaviour is represented as the reverse of courageous, and he is surnamed "mainomenos," "beside himself," or "crazed." The Greeks before Troy knew as little of Dionysus as of Demeter, and the ideal heroic quality was inconsistent with the worship of either divinity. The most that Homer's heroes did was to admit that Bacchus was a god, and to own a wholesome fear of scorning him.

Lycurgus, the fierce Thracian, so runs the short and simple story of Homer, warred against the new divinity. He pursued the crazed young god, and drove him to fling himself into the ocean. In the depths of the sea Thetis showed him kindness, and kept him safe from the dread hatchet of Lycurgus, whose ferocity was finally punished by total blindness. In the eyes of a typically vigorous hero,

---

[1] Herodot. ii. 52 ; see also iv. 79.
[2] *Iliad*, vi. 135 ; it is not uncommon to regard this, and that other Homeric place where Dionysus appears, as *untergeschoben* or supposititious. Until some knowledge is positively gained of the circumstances under which they made their way into the text, the whole question may be neglected. Whoever formulated these accounts had behind him or them a really established conception of the god, and this is what concerns the present inquiry.

Ajax, let us say, Dionysus was disgraced by his incompetence for war if not by his flight, and no punishment miraculously overtaking the enemy could make him other than a crazed and cowering being.[1] Therefore it is not wonderful that this late-born god was not a favourite in the days of Homeric chivalry, so far as he was then known.

The truth is that Dionysus was, from the outset, a god of contradictions. He represented death as well as life. He was a god of fiery manifestations, though born in the lowland plain of mountain-watered Nysa, and though he is constantly worshipped as the representative of abundant vegetation. He was attended by the seasons, by the nymphs of flowing waters and of growing trees,[2] by the Muses and by old Silenus—the type of all things that flow upon the earth—by the Satyrs, always half beasts and half men. A prophet divine, Dionysus was sometimes overcome by his own gift of wine. The leader and inspirer of holy choral song, the god whose worship awakened and

[1] Whatever may be said of the Homeric conception of courage and cowardice, it cannot be successfully denied that a certain grotesqueness as of cowardice attached to some aspects of Dionysus as popularly conceived. The jokes at his expense in the *Frogs* of Aristophanes are always harping on this string, and they certainly did not shock but pleased the people assembled to do him honour.

[2] Of course at the time when these personifications of the various movements and growths in nature sprang into being, there was nowhere any consciousness of the relation they bore to what we should distinguish from them as "the real things" or "the things themselves"; they were the real things for those in whose imaginations they first sprang into being, and their confusing multiplicity and elusive nature reproduce the confusion which lies upon the shifting face of woodlands, streams, and meadows. After generations had dreamed and talked of these baffling wildwood creatures, at a time when there was a conscious analysis of popular stories, and a systematic attempt to revive ancient belief, we find the poet Callimachus giving the true account of what nymphs were. In the *Hymn to Delos*, vv. 82 and ff., he exclaims: "O Muses, tell me truly, goddesses mine, did oak-trees then come to be when the nymphs were born? Nymphs are glad when showers bring increase to the oaks, nymphs are sad when the oak-trees have lost their leaves."

sustained the loftiest strains of sacred tragedy, was himself amid the brawls of leering drunkards, and his unreproving presence sanctioned all the worst excesses bred of unmixed wine. His Maenads and his Bassarids, when they wandered off to honour him by penance in the wilderness, were often seized by frenzy fits, that made his name a signal for most murderous deeds of harm, and yet he was a saviour god who suffered death and insult every year to redeem mankind. Such was the conflict of elements in this new divinity. With wandering tribes Dionysus came from Thrace; and Daulis on Mount Parnassus with Boeotian Thebes received him in the earliest days.

The gradual adoption of this strange worship throughout Greece may be called a first Macedonian conquest or supremacy, which had its day in the world of the spirit, long before that of Philip the crafty and his son Alexander, the "great Emathian conqueror" of Milton's song. Indeed Emathia, the cradle of Philip's power, was that district north of Mount Olympus, where upon the spurs of Mount Bermius were those fabled rose-gardens of Midas that early harboured the myth of Dionysus. These prehistoric associations gave to Philip's intrigues and Alexander's masterful ambitions a sort of home sanction from the god of their home, and hence perhaps came the great conqueror's fondness for appearing with the attributes of Dionysus.[1] Dionysus was the first Thracian conqueror of the spirit of Hellas, and the later Greeks so conceived him when they created the type called the Indian Dionysus, who is the arch-conqueror,—a deification, as it were, of the Eastern exploits of Alexander.

[1] Compare the masquerade of Antony as Dionysus at Ephesus. Plut. *Antony*, 24.

The undeniable touch of his original Thracian ferocity which Dionysus has, even in his most highly developed and sweetly civilised aspects, is startling at first, and never easy either to understand or to combine with his other aspects. Nevertheless a contemplation of the god throughout his whole career, and especially as he was worshipped at Athens, will outweigh whatever disgust might be felt at the lower phases of his ritual, and leads us to wonder at the high purposes and great truths which finally associated themselves with him.

Now it is important to define terms and explain the meaning here attached to the word Thracians. Those Thracians from whom Greece learned to worship Dionysus were, of course, not the Thracians personally known to Herodotus. Before his day the earlier Thracians had migrated southward from Thrace, and had established themselves, first of all in Phocian Daulis, and then in various parts of Boeotia. The mountains of Attica near Marathon appear to have been visited by these early invaders from Thrace, and a record of this survives in the legends of the mountain-deme Icaria. Cadmus, the maternal grandparent of Dionysus in the Theban story, is said to have sojourned in Thrace on his way from Phoenicia to Greece. The fabled visit of Dionysus to Icaria and King Icarius is perhaps best explained by connecting it with the migration headed by Butes. Thracians are known to have wandered over the islands of the Aegean under his leadership, and not far from their track was Marathon, whence they might easily penetrate into Attic Icaria. With the name of Butes associates itself the so-called Thracian sea supremacy, a time in prehistoric days when Thracians are said to have controlled the Archipelago. The seat of their power was

Naxos. The early presence of Thracians on Naxos accounts for the plentiful growth of stories connecting Dionysus with that island, called in the end especially his own, and described as having the shape of his vine-leaf. Naxos, we hear, was the place where Dionysus was born and bred. This tale and that of the god's visit to Icarius have plainly no close affinity to the Theban story. In Crete also there was during the two hundred years traditionally allotted to the Thracian sea supremacy abundant chance for the creation of a vigorous legend of Dionysus.[1]

Now the local tales of Dionysus in vogue upon Naxos, the other Cyclades and Crete,[2] would be sure to play no inconsiderable part at Athens, which was in especially close communion with the islands of the Aegean. From the Archipelago, therefore, as well as from Boeotian Thebes and the favouring oracle of Apollo at Delphi, can be traced influences that combined at Athens with the aboriginal and old Attic tale of Icarius and Icaria. A late comer in Athens, the Thracian god was the gainer through long waiting; for an unconscious selection performed by his Athenian votaries neglected the wildest and basest features of his story, taking from Icaria, Thebes and Naxos only the higher traits. Thus Dionysus at Athens became the godhead and the centre of the widest and best worship known to the best spirits in the best days of the best community of Hellas.

His ritual underwent a triple probation before Athens fully adopted him and he so shone before men that he became the tutelary god and great inspirer of Aeschylus, Sophocles, Euripides, and Aristophanes. There was first

---

[1] For a different view of these Thracians, see the second note on chapter vi. below.   [2] See an account of them by Hoeck in his *Creta*.

the Icarian or old Attic probation, then the probation in Naxos and Crete, and thirdly, the probation in Thebes and Boeotia. All these were preceded by the god's first estate in Thrace, and succeeded by his public adoption and glorification in Athens. We ought, therefore, to consider five stages of Dionysus: 1st, Dionysus in Thrace; 2d, Dionysus in old Attica, *i.e.* Icaria; 3d, Dionysus in the Archipelago at Naxos and Crete; 4th, Dionysus at Thebes; and 5th, Dionysus in Athens. But it will be neither convenient nor possible to consider these five stages with equal fulness.

After an account of Dionysus in Thrace, the consideration of certain debatable points belonging to Dionysus everywhere will lead to such treatment of him in Thebes and in the Archipelago as is required for understanding him first in old Attica or Icaria, and finally in Athens. In Athens he reached his final stage of perfection, and a consideration of his worship there will form the climax and be our abundant reward for the present rather perplexing study of the details of earlier phases. And yet the most painstaking scrutiny, the minutest examination of such evidence as may be had, will never disentangle completely, never make perfectly plain, just what elements constituted the Dionysus first worshipped in early Greece. His character was composite from the moment Greeks worshipped him; for in Boeotia,[1] as in Attica[2] and on Naxos,[3] some part of him was native to the soil, and he was nowhere wholly Thracian. There are dimly visible traces of the merging of an early Greek worship of trees into the more soul-stirring rites of the Thracian newcomer. The confusing

---

[1] Dionysus, surnamed ἐνδενδρος, was a Boeotian god.—Hesychius.
[2] Pausanias, I. xxxi. 4.   [3] Athenaeus, iii. p. 78.

thing about him is that in Thrace as well as in Greece he appears as in part a tree-god, attaching to himself the attributes of a primitive and barbarous Jack-in-the-Green. But it is convenient to make abstraction for the moment of his vegetable antecedents in Thrace. We may safely consider that their chief effect upon him in his new Hellenic dwelling-places was to give him instincts which were the remote ties of a half-forgotten kinship allying him with indigenous tree-spirits and tree-worships. The probably milder and less clearly marked observances which he found in Greece were soon merged into, and were obliterated by, his intenser and more brilliant strain.[1] This belonged to him by Thracian birthright, and here we have his birth-mark, the one constant element in early Dionysus worship,—he was and is and always will be a god of Thracian quality. The great modern historian of Rome has thus indicated what this Thracian quality was.[2] "Maidens dashing at midnight down the mountainside with brandished torches, the boom of deafening instruments, the rush of streaming wine and streaming blood, a religious holiday-making that lashed all the senses to a furious pitch of frenzy and hurled men headlong on to madness,— Dionysus, in all the glory and the terror of his name, was a Thracian god." That portion of the god's character which came from Thrace in early times may therefore claim examination first.

In such an examination it must be taken for granted that the latter-day Thracians (and so far as religion is concerned, the Macedonians) reproduce the leading qualities of the

[1] I have not been able to look at Rapp's *Beziehungen des Dionysoskultes zu Thracien*, but he is reported as taking this view.
[2] Mommsen in his 5th vol. ch. vi. p. 189.

earlier tribes, who finally left Thrace (whether of Asia Minor or of Europe is not certain) and wandered westward and southward with their native god to Greece. Making this proviso, we may say that the Thracians were of stubborn spirit, uncompromising like the rocky lands which they have always defended as their home. A wild race of mountain robbers, skilled in some things beyond the measure of barbarians, they would not be brought under the yoke. "The Satrae," says Herodotus, "have never been the subjects of any," and Thucydides, himself of semi-Thracian parentage, tells of mountain-dwelling Thracians, men whom nothing could force into military service. In later days they were ferocious in rejection of Christianity, and then, when Christianised at last, they proved most faithful defenders of the Church. To their reckless defiance of all invaders these Thracians joined certain views about religion, death, and life hereafter, which bear directly upon the early type of Dionysus. There was a great contempt for this present life, a vivid faith in a better, and to them a more real and important life hereafter. The saying that the body is the grave of the soul was originally Thracian, and the Thracians used to gather in bitter mourning around each new-born child. They wept for sorrows sure to come. But if a tribesman died they rejoiced and spoke of his happy deliverance. A dying chieftain left many wives, and after his death high court was held to know which wife he loved most dearly. The chosen widow was rewarded by death upon her husband's tomb, and all the others envied her good fortune.[1]

Without some personal god to lead the tribes of the dead, such an intense realisation of life hereafter would

---

[1] Herodot. v. 4, 5.

hardly have thriven. Indeed the real beginning of it all was an intensely real person whose dwelling-place and whose power interested the tribes in Thrace more than even their native hills, whose favour they prized more highly than liberty itself. Such a person possessed their pious souls, and was the god of Thracians everywhere. Herodotus was astonished at the intensity of their devotion, and remarks especially that they believed that there was no other god save only their own god. This enthusiastic intensity and almost Mohammedan intolerance imposed the Thracian worship even upon communities otherwise far in advance of them. Here then is an Asiatic touch[1] in the beginnings of Dionysus; indeed his Thracian origin was partly Asiatic.[2] Thracians in Thrace, Thracians in Asia Minor where were settled their Phrygian cousins,[3]—all these tribes worshipped Dionysus under a name of their own choosing, and celebrated in his honour most strange and violent festivals,

[1] For admirable suggestions about the eastern aspects of Dionysus worship, see the quotation from Sir George Birdwood, K.C.I.E. (who suggests that the name Dionysus is of Phoenician origin), given in Appendix III., p. 164.

[2] Aristophanes, *Birds*, 874, with scholiast's note, and *Wasps*, 9.

[3] Servius on *Aeneid*, iii. 15 *ad fin.*; and especially Herodot. i. 28; iii. 90; vii. 75. See also Strabo *passim*. He is constantly harping on the affinity between Thracians and Mysians, Bithynians, and the like. But Mommsen himself could not be more in despair about confusions and uncertainties regarding the peoples of Thrace and the interior of Asia Minor. See xii. p. 564, where he gives for this state of things the same reason given recently by Mommsen: διορίσαι δὲ χαλεπόν. αἴτιον δὲ τὸ τοὺς ἐπήλυδας βαρβάρους καὶ στρατιώτας ὄντας μὴ βεβαίως κατέχειν τὴν κρατηθεῖσαν, ἀλλὰ πλανήτας εἶναι τὸ πλέον ἐκβάλλοντας καὶ ἐκβαλλομένους. ἅπαντα δὲ τὰ ἔθνη ταῦτα Θρᾴκιά τις εἰκάζοι ἂν διὰ τὸ τὴν περαίαν νέμεσθαι τούτους καὶ διὰ τὸ μὴ πολὺ ἐξαλλάττειν ἀλλήλων ἑκατέρους. We know as little (perhaps less) of this region of the Balkan peninsula and of Asia Minor as Strabo did, simply because the confusing cause has continued to work. Here has been and is still a confused maelstrom of tribal and national antagonisms in constant motion, occasional waves of more or less temporary invasion have always broken in upon any permanent and clearly defined shaping of political life in the ancient realm of the Thracian tribes.

both by night and by day. The barbarian violence of these led, no doubt, to the epithet of the "crazed god" for Dionysus, who had not been very long or very far away from Thrace in Homer's day. So close a love bound worshippers to this god that they sent solemn messages to him, informing him of their needs, once in every five years. A messenger once appointed by lot, the faithful first gave their messages, then three tribesmen stood forth holding with points stretched firmly heavenwards three upright spears. Others then laid hold upon the favoured emissary's hands and feet, and tossed him upward. He was greatly blamed and another messenger was chosen if he did not light upon the spearpoints and die; if he died all was well.[1]

It is wonderful to see how indestructible was this worship in Thrace of the leader of Elysian joys, of the marshaller of the blessed dead, the real king of the real world, call him Zamolxis, Sabazius, or Gebeleizis, what you will, for he has later names in Rome and Greece.

The Roman festivals of mid-winter, called Brumalia because they fell upon the shortest day (bruma or breuissima) of the year, and also those called Rosalia[2] for the midsummer-night of perfect blooming roses, all these maintained themselves with astonishing persistence on Thracian soil. Their centres lay just where the ancient cradle of Thraco-Macedonian[3] Dionysus-worship was to be found. The

[1] Herodot. iv. 94.
[2] Tomaschek, "Brumalia und Rosalia," Reports of Vienna Acad. Phil. hist. Class., 1868.
[3] The Macedonians had no distinctive religion. As soon as they appear in history they are in most respects Greek, but imbued with Thracian religious ideas, as were also other tribes of Illyrian origin. These ideals from Thrace they never abandoned, and modified only by degrees as Macedonia allied itself with the glories and greatness of Greece. Accordingly the distinction between Macedonia and Thrace, Thracian and Macedonian, may be ignored in treating of the history of Thracian

districts are two, the first of which lies among the snowy mountains and the mountain spurs of Olympus. This district is extensive if it be understood also to include Emathia, the heart of early Macedonia, and to take in Mount Bermius and the fabled roses of the gardens of Midas. This district, contiguous to Greece, may be conveniently called Pieria. Distinct from this, and farther to the north, lies, near the river Strymon of Orphic fame, the second centre of this worship, which bears the name of Pieris.

Not far from Philippi, which lies in this district of Pieris, was found an inscription belonging to a Roman epoch, but in the spirit of its piety towards Bromius can be detected the ancient and lingering worship of the Thracian Dionysus:[1] "*Hercules shed tears,*" the mourner says, "*then why not I, for Venus marks thee all her own by beauty less than by thy loving heart of excellence? Now whether the mystic maids for Bromius' service sealed chose thee on flowery meads their*

Dionysus. Only we may have reason to think that the constant and close communion between Greece and Macedonia reinforced all along the line certain cruel and crude Thracian aspects of the god which, without Macedonia, might have been more completely softened by native Greek ideas and observances. As to a fusion between Illyrians and Thracians as far as matters religious are concerned, this is made more than probable by the fact that, apart from their share in Thracian rites, the Illyrians cannot be found to have had a traditional religion. Their rudimentary observances were early absorbed in the wild Thracian cult, just as were certain local cults of early Greece. See in the Fragments of Olympiodorus (Dindorf, § 27), an account of Valerius in Thrace during the reign of Constantine. Hearing of treasure-trove, he got orders from the emperor to take possession. He found the ground was sacred, dug there, found three silver statues, upon whose removal by him Thrace and Illyria were overrun by Goths, Huns, and Sarmatians. Connected with these statues and their holy ground were mystical observances which protected both districts : ἐν μέσῳ γὰρ αὐτῆς τε Θρᾴκης καὶ τοῦ Ἰλλυρικοῦ κατέκειτο τὰ τῆς τελετῆς. One of the statues was to keep Goths out, the second kept out the Huns, and the third was a bar against the Sarmatians.

[1] *C. I. L.* iii. 1, 686.

mate and Satyr-friend to be, or whether the Naiads require thee to join their torch-led bands and hold with them high festival, wheresoever thou art, dear boy, and whatsoever . . ." and here the marble record ends, yet not before bearing its testimony to the persistence through Roman days of Dionysiac customs inherited from those unremembered Thracian tribes who lent their god to Greece. Dionysus in Thrace, accordingly, must be looked upon as the head of a world hereafter, but not of such an Elysian realm as that commonly thought to have satisfied Greek religious belief. The hereafter presided over by Thracian Dionysus was the world of worlds, the real life, far better and brighter than this. The reality of this Dionysus world and Dionysus worship is witnessed to by the many and vain struggles made by Christian bishops to eradicate from Christian merrymaking certain heathen practices derived from ancient Dionysiac festivals. We hear repeatedly of these practices in Christian documents, especially in the decrees of councils.[1] The

[1] Ralli and Potli, Σύνταγμα, etc., *Athens*, 1852-59, ii. p. 450. Having failed to find any trace of this monumental work in the catalogues of the British Museum, the Bodleian, or the Taylorian Libraries, I applied to my distinguished and learned friend Mr. Panagiotes D. Kalogeropoulos, Librarian of the Greek Parliament Library in Athens. In his answer he gives me the full title of the six volumes; I quote from the second. The general title is: Σύνταγμα τῶν θείων καὶ ἱερῶν κανόνων τῶν τε ἁγίων καὶ πανευφήμων ἀποστόλων, καὶ τῶν ἱερῶν οἰκουμενικῶν καὶ τοπικῶν συνόδων, καὶ τῶν κατὰ μέρος ἁγίων πατέρων, ἐκδοθὲν σὺν πλείσταις ἄλλαις τὴν ἐκκλησιαστικὴν κατάστασιν διεπούσαις διατάξεσι, μετὰ τῶν ἀρχαίων ἐξηγητῶν, καὶ διαφόρων ἀναγνωσμάτων ὑπὸ Γ. Α. Ῥάλλη καὶ Μ. Ποτλῆ, ἐγκρίσει τῆς ἁγίας καὶ μεγάλης τοῦ Χριστοῦ ἐκκλησίας, Ἀθῆναι, 1852. The title of the second volume, from which I quote, is: οἱ θεῖοι καὶ ἱεροὶ κανόνες τῶν ἁγίων καὶ πανευφήμων ἀποστόλων τῶν ἐν Νικαίᾳ, ἐν Κωνσταντινουπόλει, ἐν Ἐφέσῳ, ἐν Χαλκηδόνι, ἐν τῷ Τρούλλῳ τοῦ βασιλικοῦ παλατίου, ἐν Νικαίᾳ τὸ Βʹ. οἰκουμενικῶν συνόδων, καὶ τῶν ἐν Κωνσταντινουπόλει, τῆς τε ἐν τῷ ναῷ τῶν ἁγίων ἀποστόλων πρώτης καὶ δευτέρας, καὶ τῆς ἐν τῷ τῆς ἁγίας Σοφίας, γενομένων ἱερῶν συνόδων, μετὰ τῆς ἐξηγήσεως Ἰωάννου τοῦ Ζωναρᾶ, Θεοδώρου τοῦ Βαλσαμῶνος, καὶ Ἀλεξίου τοῦ Ἀριστηνοῦ, καὶ Πίνακος ἀναλυτικοῦ ἁπάντων τῶν ἐν τῷ δευτέρῳ τόμῳ κανόνων μετὰ τῆς συμφωνίας αὐτῶν, Ἀθῆναι, 1852.

Rosalia is described as a "wicked and reprehensible holiday-making"—πανήγυρις ἀλλόκοτος—celebrated at Easter in remote country districts through the persistence of an evil traditionary custom. This occurs in a note on an order of the sixth council at Trullo,[1] commanding the suppression of various heathenish festivals, including also the Brumalia. Again, in the tenth century, there was a decree against these festivals; but they apparently kept their hold upon the peoples inhabiting the Balkan peninsula even unto modern times.[2] There is a curious record of what seems very much like an adaptation to Albanian peasant life of the Athenian festival of Dionysus, and is probably a survival of the Thracian festival called Rosalia.[3] During the first week of May a festival is held, when the people

[1] January 15, A.D. 706.
[2] The earlier custom fixed the Rosalia at or about Whitsuntide.
[3] Arabantinos, χρονογραφία τῆς Ἠπείρου, Athens, 1857, vol. ii. p. 191 : Τότε φαίνεται τοῖς (Παργίοις) παρεχωρήθη καὶ τὸ δικαίωμα τοῦ κροτεῖν τὴν καλουμένην ἑορτὴν Ῥοσαλίαν ἢ Ῥουσάλια διαρκοῦσαν ἀπὸ τῆς Α μεχρὶ τῆς Η´ Μαΐου, ὅτε ὁ λαὸς ἐκλέγων πολίτην τινὰ ὡς ἀρχηγὸν εὐθύμει διὰ διαφόρων κωμικῶν σκηνῶν· μεταξὺ δὲ τούτων ἐκρότει καὶ πλαστήν τινα μάχην, σχηματιζομένων δύο στρατιωτικῶν σωμάτων, τοῦ μὲν χριστιανικοῦ, τοῦ δὲ ὀθομανικοῦ ἀρχηγουμένου ὑπὸ πλαστοῦ Πασσᾶ ὅστις συνελαμβάνετο αἰχμάλωτος, μετὰ τὴν γενομένην ἐν τῇ τελευταίᾳ ἡμέρᾳ τῆς ἑορτῆς ψευδομάχην. See in Folk-Lore for December 1890, p. 518, some interesting notes on May-Day observances in North-Western Greece, especially the Ionian Islands. If Mr. J. G. Frazer's informant had known more of the festal rites of antiquity, he would no doubt have carried the origin of actual customs far beyond the days of Venetian supremacy. As it is, he has enabled Mr. Frazer to give a most graphic description of the flower festival as celebrated in medieval times at Corfu and elsewhere. After all, the best authorities on such a point are the Greeks themselves. I have my kind friend Mr. Kalogeropoulos to thank for the following references. He writes : " As for *Roussalia*, you will find in the fifth number of Ἀνατολικὴ Ἐπιθεώρισις (January 1873) a dissertation of *Politis* περὶ Ῥουσαλιοῦ. This periodical was published in Athens. Kampouroglous wrote also about *Roussalia* on the 241st page of his *History of Athens*. Kampouroglous has also written something about *Roussalia* in the Ἑβδομάς (a weekly periodical published ¦in Athens). *Pandora*, another periodical, contained another dissertation of Politis rather shorter than the article of the *Epitheorisis*."

choose them a leader and give themselves over to pleasure in various comic performances, and among these they especially applaud a sham fight between two champions, one a Christian soldier and the other a Turkish pasha. It is needless to say that the pasha is worsted and carried off prisoner in this patriotic Punch-and-Judy show.

But now the main features of Dionysus in Thrace must be brought into comparison with Dionysus as he was worshipped in Greece. From being the god of the only real world, he comes further to underlie all that is most real, all that in nature arrests the eye, startles the ear, or awes the mind.[1] The two views of the god's nature lay confused in the childlike stories and rites of Thrace and the Thracians. To gather a complete, an early, and a plain record of the second and more obviously poetical view of the god, not Thrace, but Phrygia and Thrace together,—the larger Thrace, —must be applied to. Out of Phrygia, as has been intimated, came in part the ancient Thracians, and in Phrygia dwelt of old cousins of theirs who had fundamental beliefs practically the same with theirs. From the dim traces which are still preserved in Thrace and Phrygia may still be read a conception of Dionysus, which is that of later Greece reduced to simpler terms.

In this disentangling process it will be convenient to forget the so-called infernal character of the god, to forget, that is to say, the otherness of the world where he was thought to rule, and to remember alone its reality. To the tribes of Thrace these two qualities were no doubt dimly identical. Dionysus the god of reality soon becomes an incarnation of the elements. Wine was, in those early days

---

[1] Also as a god of the underworld he would be conceived of popularly as sending up trees and plants and as the author of springs.

of story-making, quite as much an element as water.[1] Wine was in fact regarded as a perpetual source of miracles, and came to be looked upon as a *tertium quid* in whose essence the natural and the supernatural met together, sometimes for good and sometimes for evil. It was at the same time an elixir of life and a draught by which men lost their senses and their lives; it represented and incarnated as it were the sterner as well as the more charming aspects of Bacchic power, for Dionysus was not only, as Homer[2] calls him, a "spring of joy for mortal men," but he was also the "angel of the darker drink."[3] He came offering his cup and inviting the souls of men "forth to their lips to quaff," and thus, beguiled by wine, they accomplished his will, following after him through madness and the gates of death. On the other hand, one of the streams with which Odysseus filled that trench, out of which the flitting ghosts had to drink before he could get speech of them, was a stream of sweet wine. And so it seems that wine had some power to lead back for an instant to the gates of life the very spirits swept forth by its spell into darkness and death. Elsewhere in the Homeric poems we hear again of the power of wine to awaken and make glad the anguished spirits of the beloved dead,[4] and a modern voice has uttered for the Persian Omar[5] the same belief that wine makes glad the dead—

> And not a drop that from our cups we throw
> For earth to drink of, but may steal below
> To quench the fire of anguish in some eye
> There hidden,—far beneath, and long ago.

---

[1] See, for instance, the way in which the Pramnian wine given by Maron to Odysseus is praised in the ninth *Odyssey*, vv. 196-213.
[2] *Iliad*, xiv. 325.   [3] Fitzgerald's *Rubaiyat*, quatrain xliii.
[4] *Iliad*, xxiii. 220.   [5] Fitzgerald's *Rubaiyat*, quatrain xxxix.

The worship of unusual brightness, of motion and flash, attached itself to the four elements of wine, fire, water, and gold. Dionysus was, accordingly, not the god of any one of these only. He was a god of flush and flame, made manifest in all flashing and flowing. It is not by making distinctions between the various elements, but rather by translating each into terms of the others that he is best understood. Gold was his especial element, hidden in the bowels of the earth or flowing in the fabled floods of Phrygian Pactolus. Chrysopator was his traditional epithet used by a Christian poet of Egyptian birth, Nonnus, who endeavoured to sum up the legends of Dionysus in forty-seven books, each consisting of a large array of Greek hexameters. Father of gold Dionysus really was from the first in Thracian Pieris. There is a hill near Philippi where the mountain tribes of Thrace used to get gold. They called it Dionysus' own. Then there is the story of King Midas,[1] which belongs to Thrace as well as to Asia Minor. Midas turned all he touched to gold; and the story is in reality a blurred record of Dionysus as Father of Gold where Midas stands for Dionysus. From Dionysus, as a mark of gratitude for hospitality received, was lent to Midas, by his own choice, the power of transmuting all he touched to gold, and when, because of it, he was brought near to starvation, his prayer for deliverance was to Dionysus. Dionysus bade him wash in the floods of Pactolus, and from this bath of Midas that river derived its fabulous richness in gold. In Thrace Midas had miraculous rose-gardens on the flanks of Mount Bermius. There he sought to take

---

[1] See Herodot. viii. 138, and also i. 14 and 35; Pausanias, I. iv. 5; Xen. *Anab.* i. 2, 13; and Hyginus, whose 191st fable gathers nearly all the threads of the story together.

the elusive Silenus. Long his efforts were in vain, but Silenus at last drank of a spring with which the wily Midas had mixed wine. Heavy with the unknown fumes, Silenus was seized, and Midas never loosed his hold until he had heard prophecies about things to come. This legend, in which Dionysus is both Midas and Silenus, both captive and captor, couples itself with the abundant record of Dionysus as a god of prophecy. But this power of prophecy came to him chiefly if not solely as the god of wine. In wine lurks truth, the adage says, and this is why no one was answered by the Thracian oracle on Mount Zilmissus,[1] before he had taken much pure wine. Wine belonged to Dionysus as the good gift that freed man's soul from man's self and made way for the power of the god to speak his will.

Fire belonged to Dionysus, partly no doubt from causes which made other divinities of the hereafter who were also nature gods most easily appeased by torch-bearing worshippers, and which gave rise to various fire-festivals. Furthermore, traces of sun-worship may also be detected in this aspect of the cult of Dionysus, but beyond this the violent and all-possessing power of flooding fire marked it as his own. However this may be, Dionysus was looked upon as *leader of the band of fire-breathing planets in the sky.* The *wielder of fire,* the *fire-faced,* the *sower of fire seed,* the *fire-begotten,* the *fire-thunderer,* or the *spirit that roars in high flames,*—all these epithets bestowed on Dionysus mark him as the mover and maker of fire. Aristotle tells an anecdote that attaches this aspect of the god also to Thrace. There was, he says,[2] a

[1] Macrobius, *Saturnalia,* i. 18, 1.
[2] περὶ θαυμασίων ἀκουσμάτων, cxxii. 133.

well-known place of Thracian assembly where Dionysus promised good crops for the coming year by a miraculous manifestation of flame from the top of his holy hill hear by.

Water again, which like wine was one of the streams of the draught poured out by Odysseus for the dead, is the element of the Thracian Dionysus, as is shown by his ancient Thracian name of *Dyalos, god of springing water.* In countless stories traceable to Pieria and Pieris, the god had for his nurses the spirits of flowing waters, his childhood's companions and woman-helpers were nymphs and naiads of the mountain sides. These were but one company of all the elusive troops of water-folk that flood the whole career of Dionysus. To water-nymphs must be added innumerable Satyrs and Sileni. Nothing is plainer than the meaning of those curious representations where Satyrs are pictured in the act of smiting the ground, whence obedient to their stroke a nymph arises. Here is water calling forth water, and the bubbling up of a mountain spring is the gist of these beautiful picture-poems.[1]

Silenus, companion of Dionysus' revels, sharer of his adventures in early and in later days, was an incarnation of fluid, a water-man who might at any time change again to the fluid from which he sprang. This being true of Silenus and all Sileni, it is in a measure true of Satyrs also, who are a more youthful repetition of the type of Silenus. A Silenus is an Asiatic Satyr, just as the Curetes are the Satyrs, the Sileni, the Tityi, and the Corybantes of Crete.[2] Without at all pressing this statement, we may learn from it that the attendants of Dionysus are as elusive as the god

---

[1] This interpretation was first given to them by Carl Robert.
[2] Strabo, X. ch. iii. pp. 463–474. This whole chapter is of the utmost importance for understanding Dionysus and allied divinities.

himself, and as each of the four elements in which his power was chiefly manifested. You no sooner begin to see what Dionysus and his creatures are than they are instantly something new. Each melts into another when you try to single him out in the whirling dance of Dionysus. Nonnus tells at length the following tale of Silenus.[1] Having danced his best in eagerness to win a prize, Silenus overreached himself. So swift became his motions, so numberless the undulating curves and swerves of his limbs, that all at once he was himself no more, but swiftly flowed as a river onward to the sea. His paunch became the river-bed, his hair showed upon the stream in guise of bulrushes in the shallows near the shores, and the pipes he played on resumed their ancient stand and grew once more as reeds. Through his attendants the Sileni, the god has been abundantly identified with water. But the Thracians and the Phrygians did more than this, they frequently identified the god himself with the watery element. As the representative of resistless water's flow, Dionysus was in their conception bull-shaped. The usual art-type of a river is the bull, oftentimes a man-headed bull, as may be seen on many ancient coins. Horace was not unmindful of this when he wrote:

>   Sic tauriformis volvitur Aufidus
>   Qui regna Dauni praefluit Apuli.[2]

There was a notion that in the bull resided exhaustless vigour, and thus the bull-form represented flowing and falling waters as the cause of growth and abundance. The bull serves in many mythologies along with the cow to represent any sort of a river and water in general, and even the later Greek artists remembered this, so that the beautiful

---

[1] *Dionysiaca*, xix. 261 ff.   [2] *Odes*, iv. 14, 25.

Dionysus of later days is sometimes represented with the horns of a bull.

Thus Dionysus in Thrace at last stands forth well-nigh complete, moving in all that makes real the world that is—water, fire, wine, and flashing gold. Moreover as dwelling in the land of the real he knew the truth, and would declare it when rightly approached by the use of his element, whether of wine or of water.[1] He was the giver of oracles in Thrace.[2]

Other features still remain for a necessarily discursive consideration. The Thracian Dionysus was a fierce and a pitiless hunter, a man-slaying power that would rend all creatures in sunder, an eater of raw flesh. This feature is undoubtedly Thracian and only survived in Greece. The Thracian Dionysus appears also to have been the god of lovely song and the leader of rhythmic dancing; but perhaps this was really added to him in Greece. The understanding of both these aspects requires first of all the observation of those minor and less constantly heeded persons who form his countless following.

Muses, Hours, Graces, Seasons, mountain nymphs, Oreads or hill spirits, Dryads or forest maidens, and Hamadryads, —these beautiful emanations from the central divinity of Dionysus dance around the triumphant god, and mourn him when he departs from them. But there are figures more intimately belonging to him, a numerous band of so-called Bacchae, Bacchants, or Bacchanals. Just so in early Thrace and Phrygia the wildly roaming woman votaries of Sabazius were called Sabae.[3] It is the god in them, not they themselves, that prompts their cries,—even when with loud lament

---

[1] Macrobius, *Saturn*. i. 18, 1.   [2] Euripides, *Hecuba*, 1267.
[3] See schol. on Aristoph. *Birds*, 874.

they mourn Dionysus dead they are still possessed by him. Through them he cries aloud and seeks with shouts and wizard motions to break the spell of death and call to life the spring — his quickened self. The great Thracian originals for these Bacchanals or Bassarids, as they are also named, were called Mimallones and Clodones.[1] These were women nerved to more than woman's work, who were much feared, and who followed the god through the valleys of Thrace. They all did nothing of themselves, but the god in them cried aloud, as they darted through the wilderness, the well-known Bacchant cries "evoe" (*eu hoi* or *eu soi*) and "saboi." Here, in the myriad women possessed of the god, we have a personification of the passive side of nature,[2] that into which the god as motion, as moisture, enters to make it wholly his.

Turning to the male figures that swarm continually about him, there is such confusion that no discrimination can at first be made. Satyrs and Sileni, already spoken of, men of the water and the wood; Telchines, those workers of metal from Rhodes; Corybantes, attendants given to Dionysus by his Phrygian mother the great nature goddess Cybele; Curetes from Crete,—all these and others have their function. Some of them, as the Satyrs, represent ever and anon the coarser aspects of wine-drinking; some, like the Telchines, have to do with Dionysus as father of gold, and naturally associate themselves with one who at Eleusis is almost identified with Plutus, or rather Pluto,[3] the god of nether

[1] Plutarch, *Alexander*, ch. ii.
[2] See T. A. Voigt's article "Dionysus" in Roscher's *Mythological Lexicon*, where this is made very plain in an admirable presentation with which Mannhardt himself would not have found any fault.
[3] According to Hesiod *Plutus* was a *son* of Demeter, and therefore not her son-in-law. His father was Iasion, and he was begotten in Crete (*Theogony*, 969 and ff.) This *Plutus* was an errant and elusive god,

gold and nether realms. In these figures who can rush into excesses unworthy of the god himself his majesty is so far saved. Another group of Dionysus' male followers must now be sought to represent his most darkly cruel aspect. Those curious and elusive beings, called Pans or Aegipans, swarm in every Bacchanalian rout, and though they make less noise perhaps than the Corybantes with their drums, not the shouting Bacchanal women themselves do such savage deeds as the Pans when they are roused. Aegipans and Bacchanals, therefore, are often possessed with the native savagery of the barbarous man-eating Dionysus.

Pan or Aegipan was originally capable of better things,[1] and in fact a pure and sweetly simple worship of Pan was cherished at Athens. He was originally a shepherds' god, and could not withstand successfully the superior claims of greater gods not confined, like himself, to the hamlets and haunts of lonely shepherds—rocky places on the very summits of mountains. Hence he surrendered his independence and is found in many shapes, both large and small, swarming in Dionysus' train. All Pans have goat's legs and horns, but not all are made utterly savage by contact with the Thracian god. Some Pans are young and graceful,

---

a wanderer whom the lucky would fall in with and straightway become rich and glorious. The Hesiodic conception of him bears a striking resemblance to the poetic notion of *Dionysus*, to meet whom and feel whose power was to be forever blessed, only the typical element of Plutus was only gold and never wine. Hesiod's Plutus is certainly not yet identical with the brother of Zeus and Demeter, Hades (*ibid.* 455), who was also Persephone's husband (*ibid.* 769). The Aidoneus who robbed Persephone from Demeter (*ibid.* 913) was apparently thought of as dimly identical with Hades. *Pluto* was a *daughter* of Oceanus and Tethys (*ibid.* 355), of those who with lord Apollo and the rivers take in hand the bringing up of men from their boyhood, according to the allotment of Zeus, ἄνδρας κουρίζουσι σὺν Ἀπόλλωνι ἄνακτι | καὶ Ποταμοῖς, ταύτην δὲ Διὸς πάρα μοῖραν ἔχουσι (*ibid.* 347 and f.)

[1] See Preller's *Greek Mythology*.

spending the time piping on reeds, and in the end this type of dear little Pan loses his goat's legs and becomes a civilised and harmonious young Satyr.

The fiercer type of Pan or Aegipan is distinguished from the Satyr by courage. For the Satyrs personify among other things the aspect of Dionysus which made Aristophanes lampoon him as a weakling and a coward. "Always drunk with wine, the Satyr kind is insolent through and through. Their brawling threats are loud, but war drives them in headlong flight. Of plentiful readiness they in the dance, and skilled beyond others in draining the widest cups and the deepest to their very dregs."[1]

A savage god had need of courage in his deeds of grim and reckless cruelty, and this quality was neither in Satyr nor in Silenus, but only in Pan. All three had horns and tails and pointed ears, and all seem at times to be nearly the same, since all represent the frenzy of the god superficially called drunkenness, yet in a crisis your Satyr is a tearful drunkard, your Silenus—in spite of all his wisdom—is a maudlin drunkard, while your Pan is always fighting drunk. The Aegipans of Dionysus did not wear horns and hoofs for naught, since they appear to have bequeathed these appendages to the devil of many a modern legend. With these Pans were associated all panic terrors inspired through them by Dionysus.[2] These savage and sudden inroads of terror form a counterpart to those equally mysterious and equally sudden ecstasies and bursts of reckless joy sent most frequently by Dionysus to his women votaries the passive Bacchanals. There is just this difference: the Bacchanals

---

[1] Nonnus, *Dionysiaca*, xiv. 120 ff.
[2] Eurip. *Rhesus*, 36; *Bacchae*, 303 ff.; Pausanias, II. xxiv. 6; see also Nonnus, *Dionysiaca*, x. at beginning.

feel the Bacchic bliss, whereas the Pans inspire the panic fears. And here begins the second stage of this short inquiry into the savage Dionysus, the rending god, the power from the world underground that directs the earthquake and its various attendant catastrophes of fire, of water, and of endless panic fears. The Bacchanals and Pans associate themselves even in Grecian story with frenzied rendings of men and animals. The frenzy prompting these acts is so plainly from the god that such rendings may be called acts of worship—features of his ritual. From this we may argue backwards to a considerable degree of cruelty and savagery in the worship of the Thracian Dionysus. Human sacrifice was assuredly not uncommon in the earliest worship of Thracian tribes, and it is likely to have been begun with an effort, like that described by Herodotus, to send a messenger to the god in his world beyond. A thirst for blood of some kind is very universally attributed to the dead by early legends. This thirst for blood is no doubt often a thirst for substantial life, as, for instance, was that of the shades who flocked around Odysseus, but it allies itself to cruelty, and its wildest fullest realisation is in the Bacchic *Thiasos*. This is but a much-needed collective name covering all followers of the god, all who are so full of him that they know not what they do—the Bacchanals or Maenads on the one hand, and the Aegipans on the other.

When this mysterious frenzy seized his Thiasos, woe betide man or beast whom they found on their way; the god possessed them utterly, and they wrought his miracles unarmed. The warlike excesses of horns and hoofs into which Dionysus hurried his outrageous Pans beggar description. In these tales the god is revealed in his most awful aspect. He was named *Anthroporraistes* or *man-*

wrecker on the island of Tenedos, while the Chiotes spoke of Dionysus *Omadios, glad of raw flesh*. For this last savage trait another epithet elsewhere used was *Omestes, devourer of raw flesh;* and these names may serve to indicate the dark background of the Thracian legends concerning the god. "Dionysus Omophagus, the eater of raw flesh, must be added," says Mr. Pater,[1] "to the golden image of Dionysus Meilichius, the honey-sweet, if the old tradition in its completeness is to be ... our closing impression; if we are to catch in its fulness that deep undercurrent of horror which runs below this masque of spring, and realise the spectacle of that wild chase in which Dionysus is ultimately both the hunter and the spoil." Indeed, what the same gifted writer says of the *Bacchanals* of Euripides may be applied to the legend of Dionysus as a whole: "It is itself excited, troubled, disturbing, a spotted or dappled thing like the oddly shaped fawn-skins of its own masquerade, so aptly expressive of the shifty, twofold, rapidly doubling creature himself." Truly "the darker stain" of the gloomier Thracian legend is always "shining through"; no matter what cheerful aspect of the Hellenised Dionysus you may choose, he is always a god of tragedies more than in name. This is exemplified in the old Attic legend of Icaria as well as elsewhere.

Before taking up that legend, however, a further consideration is desirable of what the god whose power it exalts came to represent for religious-minded Greeks. Already in proving that Dionysus stood for wine, water, fire, and gold, and in telling of his savage aspect, it has been impossible entirely to exclude points that are surely of later growth; so now in speaking of Dionysus as the com-

[1] "The *Bacchanals* of Euripides," *Macmillan's Magazine*, May 1889.

peer of Apollo, leader of the Muses, and himself the god of song, it will not be possible to exclude the earlier germs and signs of this later transformation, this translation of Dionysus from the depths of the Thracian wilderness and the world of the dead to the peaks of Grecian Parnassus.

All the elements of Dionysus associate with themselves a notion of swift brightness, of inevitable sparkle. The ecstasy that words cannot utter finds a near escape, its native utterance in song. Hence the pious Pindar sings in a famous prelude that "water is best, but gold is like a beacon blazing through the night, while songs that celebrate Olympian glories shine pre-eminent even like the flaming noonday sun."[1] In another prelude[2] the same poet sings of three things most useful to man: "Winds that blow and waters that fall in fertilising showers,—showers that are the children of the clouds;" and then as a climax, song, in which no doubt he would have us feel the swiftness of fresh winds and the richness of glad rain: "But if any show bravery in deeds, honey-sweet song shall spring forth and fly from tongue to tongue a pledge assured of glorious achievements to come."[3]

The many familiar phrases connecting poetic inspiration with springing waters and pure flowing streams, or with wine,—as when we hear that Alcaeus, Anacreon, Sophocles, and others could write and sing their best only when under its influence,—all these fancies group themselves around Dionysus as an incarnation of the swift flashing power and resistless beauty that attaches both to wine and water, but finds its fullest utterance in the changeful cadences of

---

[1] So begins his first Olympian Ode.
[2] Twelfth Olympian Ode, beginning.   [3] *Ibid.*

perfect song, the graceful undulations and fitful variations of an ordered and yet wayward Bacchic dance.

The worship of song and dance implied in their association with Dionysus came as an afterthought, or rather as a climax, for in this worship his diviner essence was most made manifest. In these, at last, were fused and expressed all the elements in which the power of Dionysus moved. The elemental force in wines and waters, in gold and fire, had been rudely associated and yoked together in the Thracian and Phrygian notion of Sabazius. Whence came the further step which made Dionysus-Sabazius the god of harmonious songs and rhythmic dances? This may be left in doubt, though tradition and the story of Thracian Orpheus indicate that this transformation was thought of as beginning far back in Thrace.

Thracians, we are told, established on Mount Helicon the worship of the Muses,[1] and one of the sayings at a Boeotian festival, which had other features of Thracian origin, shows how close a bond united Dionysus and the Muses. At this wild and Thracian-seeming festival, appropriately named the Agrionia,[2] the Boeotian women searched long and anxiously for the god with many lamentations; then, as at a sudden flash of light, they said each to her neighbour,—"He is not here but hath fled away to hide him with the Muses." The Muses, as known to their earliest adorers, were emanations, so to speak, from Dionysus the god of song. The higher and least earth-born of his qualities required the same separate incarnation and impersonation which was given in Satyrs and Sileni to his coarser strain. The history of the worship of the Muses, how they came to be nine instead of three, their original

[1] Strabo, X. iii. 17, p. 471.   [2] Plutarch, *Sympos.* viii. Proem.

number,[1] would lead too far afield. It appears that both the Muses and the Graces were adjuncts to Dionysus and Apollo when these divinities appeared as representatives of idealised song and dance. Dionysus was called Melpomenos in this capacity, and under the same aspect[2] Apollo was surnamed Musagetes. As before[3] in speaking of the more catholic and benign aspects of Apollo, so now, in penetrating into the higher regions and more inspiring features of Dionysiac worship, in treating of the perfected Dionysus, you come face to face with the perfect unison, the flawless concord of the two great gods of poetry, dancing and song. Not only did Apollo share with Dionysus his mountain of Parnassus and his Delphian temple, but Dionysus freely gave room for a temple of Delphian Apollo, "the Pythion of the Icarians,"[4] in his own first Attic home, close to the flanks of high Pentelicus.

Thither we now must go. Having examined closely the aboriginal Dionysus in Thrace, and having considered the prime factors in the Bacchic godhead from various points of view, we turn to that stage in the history of Bacchic worship which our own countrymen have done so much to illuminate—the first worship of Dionysus in the highlands of Attica at Icaria.

In this legend[5] traces of old Thracian savagery survive

[1] See Oscar Bie, *Die Musen in der Antiken Kunst.*
[2] The Muse Melpomene may be regarded as an emanation from this Dionysus, who is the Dionysus of Eleutherae. See Pausanias, I. ii. 5.
[3] Introductory Lecture, at the end.
[4] See Mr. Carl Buck on this and other discoveries (p. 174, *Am. Journal of Archaeology*, June 1889). The worship apparently came up to Icaria from the Marathonian tetrapolis, where there was a *Delion* whose rites were connected later with the Athenian Delia. See chap. viii. below.
[5] See Otto Ribbeck on the whole subject, *Anfaenge des Dionysoskults in Attica*, Schriften der Univ. zu Kiel, 1869. Also F. Osann in the sixth meeting at Cassel, October 1843, of the Verein deutscher Philologen und Schulmaenner.

in spite of transformations wrought by the Attic instinct, which always seeks to observe measure. The Thracian legend thus moderated to suit Attic taste, and brought into parallelism with the Eleusinian Demeter-legend, runs as follows[1]: "Under King Pandion—the fifth since Cecrops—Demeter and Dionysus came to Attica. Dionysus was entertained by Icarius, in Epacrian Icaria, while Demeter was the guest of King Celeus." Icaria comprised an upland valley hemmed in on one side by Mount Pentelicus[2] and separated from Marathon[3] by a huge mountain wall, which is cleft by the stream that flows from Rapendosa. Two other forest cantons, Plothea and Semachidae, formed the triple confederation of mountaineers to which Icaria belonged. The three bore a collective name, Epacria. An especial bond between Semachidae and Icaria—like that between Eleusis and Celeae—is suggested by the existence of a parallel legend to the effect that Semachus at Semachidae first entertained the god.[4] Icarius, who has been truly called "the heroic type of the Athenian farmer, devoted to his trees, his crops, and his only daughter Erigone," was so irresistibly hospitable that to the latest days the worshippers of Dionysus were fond of seeing him sculptured in the act of entertaining their god, a bearded and portly presence, who arrives noisily and numerously attended.[5] He is pictured in the act of having his sandals removed. This office is deftly performed by an obsequious dwarf of a

[1] Apollodorus, *Bibl.* iii. 14, 7.
[2] For a view taken from Icaria and looking toward Pentelicus, see Appendix XI. i. 49.
[3] For the view toward Marathon, see *ibid.* 48.
[4] See Stephanus Byzantinus, *s.v.* Σημαχίδαι. See Appendix II.
[5] A doubt has been raised whether this might not be anybody entertaining, rather than Icarius in particular. See Professor Gardner, *Journal of Hellenic Studies*, v. p. 137.

Satyr. So overcome is father Dionysus with the journey upward from Marathon,—where no doubt his Thracians landed him,—and by copious draughts of retzinato[1] on the way, that he requires a second Satyr to lean upon. In one bas-relief a palm shows upon the right, and a fig-tree on the left, symbolising, both of them, that epithet of Dionysus which is least certainly Thracian, Dendrites[2] or the spirit of growing trees. Here perhaps is a something added to the incoming god, which came to him from a primitive worship of trees,[3] inherited by the Icarian shepherds from remote and fetish-worshipping ancestors.

Dionysus proved no ungrateful guest, but rewarded Icarius

[1] Plut. *Quaest. conviv.* v. 3. My attention was called to this passage by the much lamented Dr. Schliemann. Plutarch (or whoever speaks under Plutarch's name) discusses the dedication to Poseidon and Dionysus of the pine tree, accounting for it by their common element of moisture and productivity: καὶ Ποσειδῶνί γε φυταλμίῳ, Διονύσῳ δὲ δενδρίτῃ, πάντες (ὡς ἔπος εἰπεῖν) Ἕλληνες θύουσιν. Then he accounts for Poseidon's especial claim on the pine by its use in shipbuilding, adding τῷ δὲ Διονύσῳ τὴν πίτυν ἀνιέρωσαν, ὡς ἐφηδύνουσαν τὸν οἶνον· κατὰ γὰρ τὰ πιτυώδη χωρία λέγουσιν ἡδὺν οἶνον τὴν ἄμπελον φέρειν· καὶ τὴν θερμότητα τῆς γῆς Θεόφραστος αἰτιᾶται . . . οὐ μὴν ἀλλὰ καὶ τῆς πίτυος αὐτῆς εἰκὸς ἀπολαύειν τὴν ἄμπελον, ἐχούσης ἐπιτηδειότητα πολλὴν πρὸς σωτηρίαν οἴνου καὶ διαμονήν· τῇ τε γὰρ πίττῃ πάντες ἐξαλείφουσι τὰ ἀγγεῖα, καὶ τῆς ῥετίνης ὑπομίγνύουσι πολλοὶ τῷ οἴνῳ, καθάπερ Εὐβοεῖς τῶν Ἑλληνικῶν, καὶ τῶν Ἰταλικῶν οἱ περὶ τὸν Πάδον οἰκοῦντες. Thus the Greek peasant of to-day need not be too much abashed when the vials of Occidental scorn are poured upon him because he likes still the resinated wine of antiquity—a high-bred taste, hard for some to acquire.

[2] *Ibid.* and also iv. 6, where a curious attempt is made by the Athenian Moeragenes to prove that the god of the Jews is none other than Dionysus. The season and also the manner of their chiefest feast is appropriate to Dionysus: τὴν γὰρ λεγομένην νηστείαν ἀκμάζοντι τρυγητῷ τραπέζας τε προτίθενται παντοδαπῆς ὀπώρας, ὑπὸ σκηναῖς καὶ καλιάσιν ἐκκλημάτων μάλιστα καὶ κιττοῦ διαπεπλεγμέναις. Little as Moeragenes convinces by his argument, he yet supplies interesting touches in a picture of countryside and greenwood festivals in honour of Dionysus.

[3] With this same primitive worship may also be connected the ceremony of "Aiorai," or the hanging of effigies on trees which characterised the Icarian festival, and was accompanied by the song Aletis. See for the facts Miss Harrison's *Mythology and Monuments*, p. xl. and ff.

by showing him how to plant and tend the vine, and how to make wine. Till then, shepherd-like, Icarius drank water chiefly and milk sometimes. Dionysus held forth to him a goblet crowned with foaming wine, and said, according to the gist of Nonnus'[1] report: "Lo, thou art blessed, for men shall sing in future days thy praises thus: Icarius rather than Celeus himself be praised, and Erigone, his daughter, beyond the praises of Metanira, Celeus' spouse. Triptolemus gave the wheaten ear, but from Icarius we have the wine-flashing clusters of summertide. Compared to these, what are the gifts of Demeter? Corn brings not, as wine, a sweet release from grief." This comparison is taken from Nonnus,[2] but it meets us in every version of the story, and doubtless represents the typically Attic way of regarding the boons of corn and wine,[3] and it foreshadows the ultimate union at Eleusis and Athens of Demeter and Dionysus.

The story of Icarius may now be continued in borrowed words: "The vine is carefully tended and reared; but a

[1] See the forty-seventh book of his *Dionysiaca*, from which details have been borrowed in the following account.
[2] See *Dionysiaca*, xlvii. 47 and 99.
[3] "There are no traces of a local Icarian attribution of Demeter's gift to Dionysus, but Pliny (*Nat. Hist.* vii. 59) says that Eumolpus introduced the cultivation of the vine and trees. Here then is the trace of a local Eleusinian legend attributing the Icarian gift of Dionysus to another Thracian figure in early legends. But this variation had no hold upon the imagination of religious men. In fact, as Dr. Merriam has abundantly shown, "the legends of Eleusis and Icaria were so closely connected in the minds of the mythologists that the one naturally suggested the other. Not only has Statius linked Icaria with Eleusis, but Apollodorus (iii. 14, 7) has done the same; as also Schol. Aristophanes, *Knights*, 697 (here Icarius welcomes Dionysus who is a fugitive from outrageous Pentheus); Philostratus, *Epist.* 39; Gregory Nazianzen, *Orat.* iii. p. 100 c; and Lucian, *De Saltatione*, 39, 40, where he speaks of both stories being represented in full by the dancers of the day. In some writers they were even confused, as in the *Etymologicum Magnum*, 62, 11, where Erigone is interchanged with Persephone. In *Servius ad Virgilii Georgica*, i. 19 Triptolemus is called the son of Icarius. Nonnus links the two stories, *Dionys.* xxvii. 283-307."

he-goat breaks into the enclosure and injures it with characteristic voracity. Icarius in anger slays the goat, offers him in sacrifice to the god, blows up the skin, oils it, and gives it to his companions to dance about, thus originating the sport of *askoliasmos*, a usual accompaniment of the Dionysiac festival. The divine gift is not destroyed by the goat[1]; but Icarius is soon enabled to follow the injunctions of the god, to travel about the country with a waggon loaded with wine skins, proclaiming the joys of the vine, with practical applications, and without water."[2] The Epacrian shepherds marvelled at the glorious gift. "Whence comes it?" they cried, "for it is not from the Naiads, their waterstreams are not sweet." Furthermore, as Nonnus, with rather frigid elaboration, makes them proceed, "it cannot be oil from olives, that is not for man to drink. It is not honey, for that begets a most swift and strong surfeit."

But the shepherds abused the gift and were made drunk with too much wine. Just here the more awful significance of Dionysus and his worship shows through the transparent innocence of these shepherd-simpletons. Ignorant of what drunkenness was, the legend goes on to say, they thought themselves undone. In fact it was the savage god who entered in and possessed them wholly. Dionysus required

[1] κἤν με φάγῃς ἐπὶ ῥίζαν, ὅμως ἔτι καρποφορήσω
ὅσσον ἐπισπεῖσαί σοι, τράγε, θυομένῳ.
—Evenus of Ascalon, *Anthol.* ix. 75.

[2] I quote from p. 65 of Dr. Merriam's "Report to the Committee of the School of Classical Studies at Athens," a monument of brilliant and accurate scholarship which does honour to the American School. To this Report I refer for an exhaustive account of the Icarian legend in all its bearings, with full enumeration of all the sources. It is fortunate that the singularly interesting relics of the country deme Icaria have found such an able interpreter. This great contribution to our knowledge of old Attica is contained in the same publication of the American Archaeological Institute with the seventh Annual Report of the Managing Committee of the American School, Cambridge, 1889.

the sacrifice of what was most prized and best beloved, and so, crazed by him, these shepherds slew Icarius, their benefactor and their friend, and then they swooned away, wholly overcome by the power of the god. When sense returned they woke and saw what they had done. The repentant murderers buried Icarius after washing him in a mountain stream on the edge of the forest, the very stream perhaps which all visitors of Icaria see to-day flowing through a glen near by. It is shaded by mighty plane trees so gnarled and hoar that it would seem as if no antiquity could outstrip theirs. Not far below these trees the stream plunges down a steep and reaches the valley of Rapendosa, whence it flows past Marathon into the bay towards Euboea. Near the plunge made by this stream is a cave still inhabited during the heats of noon by shepherds as simple as those in our old Icarian story.[1]

Icarius having been slain and buried, a terrific vision of him—so says Nonnus, and it is by no means sure that he invented this episode of the ghost [2]—clad in a blood-flecked garment, the "dappled herald telling of a murder to which none living bare testimony," appears to Erigone. The daughter wildly seeks his grave. Search is long in vain. Tired of her own way, at last Erigone follows her faithful dog Maera, whose instinct leads her to the place. Then, fordone with horror, she hangs herself beside her father's grave.

At this point Nonnus is truly pathetic in his account of the lament over Icarius and Erigone. "Wine, gift by my own Bromius, given to make men cease from care, sweet wine hath brought but bitterness to Icarius. Gladness it

---

[1] For photographs see Appendix XI. i. 46, 47.
[2] The dog Maera is made into the messenger in some versions, *e.g.* Apollodorus, above cited.

gave to all mankind, but death to him. Sweet wine was a foe to Erigone; for truly Dionysus, who comes to chase dull care away, hath pursued to her death and slain with grief our own Erigone."

As if to leave no doubt that Dionysus wielded a power of possession which drove men to madness and despair, and was not solely a god of wine and jollity, the last episode of the Icarian legend gives a woful account of how Erigone's death was atoned for. A mania laid hold upon all the maids of Icaria. With one accord, stung by a consciousness of guilt for what their fathers and brothers had done, they flew to the mountain-side and hanged themselves upon the forest trees.[1] Apollo's oracle, questioned in extremity, could only urge the punishment of the guilty murderers of Icarius. These slayers slain, a respite came at last. Ever afterwards the shepherds of Epacria worshipped Icarius, Erigone, and Maera (the faithful dog whom she had tenderly reared), and kept their memory green at a yearly festival. On these occasions small effigies were suspended from the branches of forest-trees,[2] to commemorate—so at least the story ran—Erigone's manner of death. Meanwhile the father, his daughter, and the sagacious Maera were translated to the firmament.[3] Icarius with his waggon becomes Boötes with his Wain; Erigone, the Virgin;

[1] A similar mania for hanging is recounted as overtaking the maidens of Miletus; see Gellius, xv. 10; and Plutarch, *De Anima*. For an extraordinary array of similar epidemics of suicide, see E. Bachut, *Histoire de la Médecine et des Doctrines Médicales*, Paris, 1873, vol. i. p. 56 and ff., where several curious modern parallels to this feature in the legend are given.

[2] For an admirable discussion of this practice, see Miss Harrison on the "Mythology of Athenian Local Cults," pp. xxxix. and ff. of the *Mythology and Monuments of Ancient Athens*.

[3] Hyginus, *Fab.* 130, end: "Erigone signum virginis, quam nos Justitiam appellamus; Icarius Arcturus in sideribus est dictus, canis autem Maera Canicula."

Maera, the Dog-star; and the Cantharus of Dionysus appears close at hand as the Crater.[1]

As to the legendary epoch to which this visit of Icarius and this old Attic legend should be assigned, the whole question hangs together with similarly insoluble ones,—with the date, for instance, of Demeter's arrival at Eleusis. King Pandion—himself of most elusive date—under whose rule Demeter and Dionysus came, is said to have had dealings with Thracians. These, however, were Thracians already established south of Thrace at Daulis, on a spur of the Parnassus,[2] toward the confines of Boeotia. All this favours at least the supposition that Thracian influence made itself felt in very early times on Attic ground. Accordingly the Icarian legend of Dionysus is likely to be as old as other tales told in Boeotia or on the islands of the Archipelago, such as Naxos and Icaros, both of which claim the glory of having given birth to the god of wine. In fact the mountains of old Attica gave to the Thracian god a home no less his own than the islands conquered by Thracians. Icaria became to him in Attica what Pieria was in Thrace; and the shape which tragedy took in Attica, and with it the course of the history of poetry even to the present day, was determined by the way in which Icarian shepherds understood the worship and the power of Dionysus. No doubt their manner of taking the whole story was a far simpler one than that familiar to Sophocles, yet it was sufficiently complex to make Icaria the cradle of tragedy and comedy.[3]

[1] To this Dr. Merriam adds (p. 67): "The bright star ε, near the right wrist of Virgo, was called *provindemiator* (προτρυγητήρ, Aratus, *Phaenomena*, 138), as rising shortly before the vintage. Icarius is Boötes, as *vindemiator* (τρυγητήρ, Schol. Arat. *Phaen.* 91).

[2] See Appendix II. at the end of this chapter, on Dionysus of Eleutherae.

[3] Athenaeus ii. 40 A: ἀπὸ μέθης καὶ ἡ τῆς τραγῳδίας εὕρεσις ἐν Ἰκαρίῳ τῆς Ἀττικῆς εὑρέθη, καὶ κατ' αὐτὸν τὸν τῆς τρύγης καιρόν· ἀφ'

This momentous beginning associated itself with the two mountaineer festivals celebrated by the Icarians—with their thanksgiving and fast-day observances, so to speak. Little or nothing definite is known of the former of these. It must have been a May-day festival like the Thracian festival afterwards called the *Rosalia*; the other corresponded to the *Brumalia*, in so far at least as it was celebrated in the bitterest cold of the bitter month Lenaeon.[1]

Their joy was in Dionysus revealed in streams flowing free and fast, no longer bound in wintry fetters of ice, revealed also in the plenteous foliage and brilliant blossoms of their native woodland home. The masses of yellow narcissus, found at their ancient home to-day, painting whole mountain-sides with their bright yellow, gleaming in the sunshine, and spreading fragrance near and far, may fitly give ocular demonstration of their old time gladness.

Their sorrowing was lament for Dionysus, loved and lost. They mourned when nature's flash and flow and all her lively colours seemed to vanish from their eyes. Partly to lament the loss of Dionysus' presence, partly to recall his life, they sought in winter time bleak and storm-swept summits. There tarried those upon whom came compulsion from the god. There Maenads and Bacchanals vied in wild dances and loud cries, which they thought would have power to bring back growth and life to trees and plants and streams. Dionysus slept or was among the dead. It was as though

οὗ δὴ καὶ τρυγῳδία τὸ πρῶτον ἐκλήθη ἡ κωμῳδία. See the last volume of Bergk's *Griechische Litteraturgeschichte* (*Aus dem Nachlass*, pp. 7 and 8).

[1] Dread are the days of the month Lenaeon, the flayer of oxen,
Under the blasts of the north wind, of ice that Boreas sharpens,
Scouring o'er Thrace and her pastures of horses to breadths of the ocean.—Hesiod, *Works and Days*, 504 ff.

they thought each winter would last for ever if they did not beat the ground and summon spring.

The sincerity with which they made these desperate forays into winter's fastnesses is best shown by hardships actually endured. The incident in point which has been preserved relates, not to the festival at Icaria, but to that on Mount Parnassus. This matters little, since both were centres of Dionysus worship, strongly influenced from Thrace in early days. On Mount Parnassus we hear that a band of frenzied votaries were blocked upon high levels above Delphi. In the midst of their incantations to revive the life of spring,[1] snows imprisoned them. Those who climbed the steep from Delphi for their rescue suffered from the utmost rigours of the cold. Their raiment grew stiff, and—so the unknown narrator declares—became absolutely brittle and friable.

Though it may safely be said that of the two peasant festivals celebrated in conjunction with Dionysus worship at Icaria and elsewhere one was sad and the other glad, no more definite account can be safely given. With the sad festival glad features were associated, and the glad festival was not without its mourning. Thus are the inherent contradictions of Dionysus in his very nature mirrored outwardly by his festivals.

It is reasonably certain that the whole observance which spread all over Attica and called itself the Rural Dionysia took its characteristic shape in Icaria. Wonderful to relate, the Attic salt of moderation and due measure came from

[1] See the Plutarchian *De primo frigido*, xviii.: ἐν δὲ Δελφοῖς αὐτὸς ἤκουες, ὅτι τῶν εἰς τὸν Παρνασὸν ἀναβάντων βοηθῆσαι ταῖς Θυάσιν, ἀπειλημμέναις ὑπὸ πνεύματος χαλεποῦ καὶ χιόνος, οὕτως ἐγένοντο διὰ τὸν πάγον σκληραὶ καὶ ξυλώδεις αἱ χλαμύδες, ὡς καὶ θραύεσθαι διατεινομένας καὶ ῥήγνυσθαι. In the light of recent events this passage gains new interest as the earliest circumstantial account of a *blizzard*.

the unaided taste of a community wonderfully aloof from all the rest of Attica. Icaria is deserted now, and lay far from the course of travellers until the American excavations unearthed fragments[1] which claim a visit from all interested in Greek antiquity. And truly the visitor is well repaid, finding how beautiful is the spot where highest art had its first outset, and earliest took shape.[2] Near its ruined church[3] begin the forests, the very "wilderness of Marathon," through which, the poet Statius says, Erigone once wandered seeking wood to place upon Icarius' funeral pyre. Here, in recent days, but fortunately past, were secret haunts of brigands now unknown to Greece. The lovely vale of Rapendosa is not far, for it belonged to Icaria's demesne.

This is the setting of the earliest legend of Dionysus in Attica; here were celebrated his Icarian festivals. Their importance is shown, and also their unusually noble character, by the fact that Susarion was first invited there, and that there was performed the first comedy, unless it be premature to give the name of comedy to Susarion's great invention. The requirements of the Icarian holiday-makers must have been raised amazingly by a gradually purified and elevated taste to lead them to invite Susarion from

[1] See Appendix XI. i. 52-55.
[2] This was tacitly recognised when a sculptured scene, representing Icarius, Erigone, and the dog Maera, was used to adorn the stage of the Athenian theatre of Dionysus. This scene, together with Hermes carrying the infant Dionysus to Zeus, is still admired at Athens by those who visit the ruined theatre. An examination of these sculptures has satisfied many that they were not originally made for the comparatively inconspicuous place into which they are now crowded, for they are really too high suitably to adorn what may be called the parapet of the raised stage built by Phaedrus where they now are. They originally decorated a stately façade upon the stage itself, which was probably built by the munificence of Nero, mindful of his duty as Apollo in the flesh.
[3] See Appendix XI. i. 50, 51.

Megara. Report had reached them of his new scheme of methodised revelry jocosely acted before the festive worshippers, and he had perhaps heard of the observances at Icaria, which were certainly his great opportunity. This happened, it appears, while the great Icarian Thespis was still a youth. Perhaps from seeing Susarion's first performance in his native place Thespis received the fruitful thought which prompted him later when he became the father of tragedy. And yet the invention was his very own, springing from the legends which had surrounded his childhood.

It was an Icarian custom to sing a mournful song named "Aletis, *the Wanderer*," in honour of Erigone, and relating her sad fate. To these songs Thespis had listened no doubt, and also to the strangely sad and wildly joyous Dithyrambus wherein were mirrored the contradictions involved in the nature of Dionysus. These recounted the poetic vicissitudes of the great divinity—his sufferings and his triumphs. Filled with a higher and a new apprehension of the scope of all these sad stories, Thespis transformed the Aletis and the Dithyrambus. 'He had heard, perhaps, of the wonderful performances of tragic choruses at Sicyon,[1] which so exercised the mind of royal Clisthenes that he interfered with the subjects represented, for fear of their strong hold upon the people who heard them.[2] Of Thespis Dr. Merriam[3] has truly said : "The sad story of the father of his gens (Icarius), the rites attendant upon the festival, the dithyrambic choruses in vogue predisposed him to this end (progress in tragedy), and gave him a nucleus to which he added the

---

[1] As Bernhardy says (*Litteraturgeschichte*, i. p. 417), the connection between early tragedy in Attica and these events at Sicyon has been overstated. Perhaps Bentley was right in saying there was none.
[2] Hdt. v. 67, end.   [3] Report, pp. 71 and 72.

actor, the prologue, and speeches between the choral songs, and he employed different masks to enable him to take the parts of several persons consecutively in the same play. This proved him the Columbus of a new world,—a mimic world, but one calculated to excite the interest, as it is said to have engaged the hostility, of the great law-giver. It must have been a few years only after Susarion's advent in Icaria that, as Plutarch tells us,[1] the novelty of the invention was attracting many, and Solon in his old age, being fond of amusement and music, also went to see Thespis acting in his own play. It is a legitimate inference from the language of Plutarch that the play was produced at some distance from Athens—in other words, in Icaria; for we can hardly imagine Solon, a true Greek, to have remained away from a festival of importance, with novel features, celebrated at his own door. Later than this event fell his censure of Pisistratus, for the latter's bad acting in the game which he played in winning his first tyranny."

The Dithyrambus, we may suppose, was so modified by Thespis that its calmer course allowed interruption; nay, even required it.[2] Out of the most lawless and wayward of lyric strains Thespis made tragedy, no doubt, by requiring both singers and holiday-makers to leave their uncouth ways of wildness and listen while the glorious sufferings of Dionysus came before them, recited by a single man (for it is not right, as yet, to call him actor) standing for and speaking for the bacchanalian concourse. He spoke, no doubt, in much the same spirit in which a speaker addresses

---

[1] *Solon*, 29.
[2] Bernhardy (*Litteraturgeschichte*, i. p. 417) quotes Themistius' dissentient citation of Aristotle, who plainly thought tragedy was built up on the Dithyrambus: τὸ μὲν πρῶτον ὁ χόρος εἰσιὼν ᾖδεν εἰς τοὺς θεούς, Θέσπις δὲ πρόλογόν τε καὶ ῥῆσιν ἐξεῦρε.

a Quaker meeting. It was he whom Dionysus chose for speaking. While he spoke he only was the living god made flesh. This advance towards full-fledged tragedy was made as early as the second[1] quarter of the sixth century B.C.

Upon this one step all others depended, and they were soon taken; for the perfection of Attic tragedy came early in the fifth century B.C. Before long, in fact, Icaria was no more the centre of the Attic worship of Dionysus,[2] and Dionysus was brought in triumph to take his place—last come but not the least of all the gods in Athens.

[1] The Parian Marble fixes Susarion's advent, with the first comedy performance, about the beginning of this second quarter. Icaria no sooner gave Attica its comedy than Icarian Thespis commenced tragedian and tragedy as well. For the various authorities, see Dr. Merriam's Report.

[2] But Icarians played an important part in Athenian history, contributing a great comedian, Magnes, who died not long before 424 B.C., as well as many pious and generous men of note. See Dr. Merriam's Report, pp. 80-93, where they are all enumerated and characterised. This account closes as follows: "We still seem to have enough to draw some conclusions as to the characteristics of the people who dwelt in that picturesque mountain-hemmed spot, and traced their ancestry back to Icarius, who entertained the god. We find no generals of renown, no statesmen active in moulding for good or ill the affairs of Athens, no orators of power, no one especially active in proposing and pushing laws in the public assembly for public weal or private gain, no historians, no philosophers, no artists. They are distinguished by two traits, which claim our respect and admiration. These are a deep devotion to religion and a sound and sturdy integrity."

APPENDIX II

DIONYSUS ELEUTHEREUS

A WHOLE cycle of stories touching the first arrival of Dionysus in Athens ignores Icaria, and centres itself around Eleutherae, a Boeotian town on the Athenian frontier, much claimed by Athens.[1] Eleutherae may be visited with immense profit to-day by those desirous of gaining the unforgettable impression which a strong Greek fortification built in the days of superb workmanship can make. On the high road from Athens to Thebes it lies not far from the point where the road dips down from the mountain spurs of Cithaeron into the level Boeotian plain. Its wonderfully preserved battlements are not seen well except from the Boeotian side; but he who turns back from the right point in the road will understand what is meant by saying that the Greeks could build nothing that was not subject to the laws of harmony and proportion. Go closer, and the symmetry with which square stones are here grouped together into a massive wall makes you wonder why so many strong walls in the world have been made so uninteresting.

But to return to Dionysus. That this Dionysus of Eleutherae played an important part is sure, since the beauti-

[1] Strabo, IX. ii. (p. 412). The Dionysus of Eleutherae was considered to be a later arrival than the Lenaean god at Athens, and the old Icarian Dionysus of course was thought of as having preceded him. See the article *Dionysia*, in Pauly's *Real-Encyclopaedie*, by Preller.

ful seat of honour still standing in place at the theatre of Dionysus in Athens is by inscription marked as belonging to the priest of Dionysus Eleuthereus. Moreover, in the older of the two temples, close to this Athenian theatre, was an image of Dionysus, said to have come from his temple at Eleutherae; and custom required this image to be borne once a year to a small outlying temple upon the road which led to Eleutherae.[1]

Furthermore, the coming of Dionysus-worship to Athens from Eleutherae is associated with the reign of King Amphictyon. Now the common version of the coming of Dionysus into old Attic Icaria goes back only to King Pandion, when also Demeter came to Eleusis. Without pretending to assign such a thing as a date, it is roughly true that Amphictyon belongs, according to Attic tradition, to an earlier time than Pandion. Too much importance need not, however, be attached to this matter of precedence, since the coming of Dionysus to Semachus and Semachidae is assigned[2] to the reign of Amphictyon. This story of Dionysus coming first to Semachidae—one of the three Epacrian demes, of which Icaria and Plotheia were the other two—is probably an attempt to mediate between and combine the Icarian and the Eleutheraean legends. The chief differences between Dionysus of Eleutherae and of Icaria are accounted for if we consider that he came more immediately from savage Thrace to Icaria than to Eleutherae. At Eleutherae, Eleuther was the one who taught his right worship, and fashioned his first image.[3] Now Eleuther was no less a personage than the son of Apollo by Aithusa,[4] who was herself a daughter of Poseidon by Alcyone, one of the seven Pleiades, daughters of Atlas.[5] Eleuther stands for a

---

[1] See Miss Harrison's account at pp. 254 and 571 of *Mythology and Monuments of Ancient Athens*.
[2] Syncell. p. 157 (125): κατὰ Ἀμφικτύονα τὸν Δευκαλίωνος υἱὸν τινές φασι Διόνυσον εἰς τὴν Ἀττικὴν ἐλθόντα ξενωθῆναι Σημάχῳ καὶ τῇ θυγατρὶ αὐτοῦ νεβρίδα δωρήσασθαι. ἕτερος δ᾽ ἦν οὗτος ἐκ Σεμέλης. The next king was Erichthonius. [3] Hyginus, *Fab.* 225.
[4] Pausanias, IX. xx. 1. [5] Apollod. III. x. 1.

softening or Hellenising influence, which Dionysus had submitted to before he reached Athens from this quarter—an influence emanating from Eleuther's father, Delphian Apollo. Voigt, in Roscher's *Ausführliches Lexicon*, thus sketches the legend of Eleutherae: "The daughters of Eleuther saw Dionysus clad in a black goat-skin. For scoffing at this vision they were visited with madness. To cure them Eleuther was commanded by an oracle to worship Dionysus *Melanaigis, of the black goat's fell.*" Accordingly, Hesychius describes Dionysus Eleuthereus as a god who gives release from the madness that comes upon Dionysiac revellers, and Pegasus, the Eleutheraean priest, stands for a moderate use of wine not unmixed with water.

IV

DIONYSUS AT ATHENS

IN the last chapter Dionysus was brought from Thrace, and found an Attic home in Icaria. Now he must be brought to Athens, and accompanied thence to Eleusis, where his power has already been recognised while we tarried in Icaria. The last and fullest presentation of the perfected god, at the moment when the widest reach of religious thought and richest depth of religious fervour attached to his worship in Athens and Greece, has been given us in the *Bacchanals* of Euripides. It only remains, therefore, to connect what we know of Dionysus in Thrace and Dionysus in Icaria with this worship of Dionysus at Athens. The culminating truth about the god will be revealed to us after attentive consideration of the most perfect play of Euripides, and then we shall in the next chapter close our consideration of the Eleusinian divinities with a concluding if not a final word about the Eleusinian ritual, and some account of the monuments of Eleusis.

The cult of Dionysus was not adopted at Athens as a matter of course. Patrician traditions firmly rooted at the capital long resisted popular pressure in favour of the peasant divinity from Icaria. There was evidently far less disposition in early Athens to meddle with Icarian merry-making than there was to take part in Eleusinian mysteries, with which at a very early date Athenian family traditions connect themselves.[1] Still the political fusion of Attica, which was associated with the glorious name of Theseus, could not in the long run be maintained without such broadening of religious observance in Athens, and in Attica at large, as should more completely make one the heart of Attic and Athenian religion. The exclusiveness of local or township ritual had to disappear, and some sort of religious fusion had to be brought about.

Fortunately this needed fusion tended to accomplish itself in spite of official discouragement. The spontaneous impulses of a people, religious without being superstitious, accomplished many large-hearted alterations, and among them the triumph at Athens of Eleusinian Demeter and

---

[1] Pausanias, I. xxxviii. 3, gives the terms of peace concluded between Athens and Eleusis after the war in which were killed King Erechtheus of Athens and Immarados of Eleusis, a son of the Thraco-Eleusinian Eumolpus. The Eleusinians were to submit to Athenian supremacy, saving only that they were to regulate the mysteries in their own way. Eumolpus and the daughters of Celeus were in immediate charge of τὰ ἱερὰ τοῖν θεοῖν, *the sacred observances in honour of the two goddesses.* But Pausanias names as successor to Eumolpus, Ceryx, a son, not of Eumolpus, but of Hermes and the daughter of Athenian Cecrops, Aglaurus. The same belief in an early intervention of purely Athenian families at the rites of Eleusis is shown by Strabo's explanation, XIV. (p. 633), of certain existing privileges attaching to the so-called βασιλεῖς at Ephesus. They represented a remote Athenian ancestor, Androclus, the son of Codrus, who founded Ephesus and assumed control of the Eleusinian rites transplanted thither at that early date. The most convincing authority for an early fusion in some sort of Athenian and Eleusinian observances is perhaps Herodotus in his account of Solon's answer to King Croesus, who wished him to tell of the happiest man he knew (i. 30). Tellus the Athenian was his man, for after a life otherwise completely happy Tellus died most gloriously fighting for his country against near neighbours (the Megarians). He fell at Eleusis, and was buried where he fell with all possible honours. Such burial of an Athenian on Eleusinian soil suggests more or less complete fusion of Athenian and Eleusinian rites and customs.

Icarian Dionysus. Here was indeed one of the earliest of many brilliant victories gained by Athenian democracy. Solon's actually visiting, or even a commonly credited report that he visited, the rustic play at Icaria or elsewhere in Attica, marks a turning-point in the history of Athenian state religion.

It is abundantly evident that in the earlier ages of their worship Demeter and Dionysus were alike divinities of the common people. Consequently we are not surprised to find either that the earliest recorded enlargement of the official religion at Athens was a recognition of Eleusinian Demeter, or that there is a still more complete record of the later official adoption of Dionysus forced by popular discontent. The people failed to win power under Cylon's leadership, but they succeeded in altering the state religion. Epimenides, a wise man of Crete, was called in, after Cylon's attempt had been suppressed, to devise means for allaying popular disaffection.[1] The gratitude felt for Epimenides

[1] The date of this purification of Athens by Epimenides was about 596 B.C. That a humanising change did come over Attic religion and its officially constituted observances is beyond the possibility of a doubt. What in general terms this change was, and that it was definitely associated with Epimenides, appears from Strabo, who says (p. 479): ἐκ δὲ τῆς Φαιστοῦ τὸν τοὺς καθαρμοὺς ποιήσαντα διὰ τῶν ἐπῶν Ἐπιμενίδην φασὶν εἶναι,—and Plutarch's *Life of Solon* (12, § 4 and ff.), where we read of Epimenides substantially what follows:—He was reputed a friend of the gods, with especial skill and knowledge touching mysteries and enthusiastic rites (τὴν ἐνθουσιαστικὴν καὶ τελεστικὴν σοφίαν). He did much to prepare the way for Solon's legislation by reducing to simplicity (εὐσταλεῖς ἐποίησε) the official sacrifices, and by softening down in them the observances of mourning. He introduced certain sacrifices into funeral rites, and thus banished harsh and barbaric usages to which most women had previously clung. But above all, by certain propitiatory and purifying rites, and by instituting new observances and sanctuaries, he made the city ready for sacred orgies and hallowed it for the service of justice, bringing it to a readier obedience of the promptings of concord. See Bernhardy, *Griechische Litteraturgeschichte*, i. p. 409. Since the above was written the newly-discovered Aristotelian *Constitution of Athens* has gone far to justify the importance here attached to the intervention

at Athens was commemorated by a statue,[1] and we may conclude that his reforms were made in the interest, not of concord only, but of the maintenance of the state religion on a broader and therefore a more universally acceptable basis.

In the month which was afterwards selected for the flower-festival of Dionysus, when that also was officially

of Epimenides, by briefly mentioning it as follows : 'Επιμενίδης δ' ὁ Κρὴς ἐπὶ τούτοις ἐκάθηρε τὴν πόλιν. This comes at the very beginning of the newly-discovered MS., and is preceded by an account of Myron's arraignment of the Alcmaeonidae and of their perpetual banishment carried out even upon the buried remains of their dead. This was all done in expiation of their outrageous suppression of Cylon and his faction. When the grateful Athenians, marvelling at his work, pressed riches and honours upon him, Epimenides took for his guerdon a branch of the sacred olive, and went his way.

[1] Pausanias says (I. xiv. 3 and 4) :—"I intended . . . to give such account as is possible of the sanctuary at Athens called the Eleusinion, but was prevented by a vision in a dream. I will turn to what may lawfully be told to every one. In front of this temple, where is the image of Triptolemus" ["We are undoubtedly justified," says Miss Harrison in her admirable commentary (p. 93 of *Mythology and Monuments of Ancient Athens*), "in supposing that the two temples" (one of Demeter and Kore, the other of Triptolemus) "went by the name of Eleusinion"], "is a bronze bull, apparently being led to sacrifice, and a seated figure of Epimenides of Cnossus." [Strabo (as well as Plutarch) tells us more accurately, X. iv. 14 (p. 479), that Epimenides came from Phaestus in the Cnossian district.] "Epimenides is said to have gone into a field and to have fallen asleep there in a cave, and the sleep did not depart from him for forty years ; and after his awakening he wrote poems and purified various cities, among them Athens." I have been quoting from Mrs. Verrall's excellent translation, p. 86 of *Mythology and Monuments of Ancient Athens*. The statue of Epimenides would naturally be placed in the Eleusinion, if Osann is right, as I have thought him, in attributing to him the official recognition of the Lesser Mysteries and their whole definite organisation. Whether the actual place of its erection should be in front of one temple or the other was a matter of chance or momentary convenience. I venture, therefore, to believe in the literal accuracy of Pausanias, both as regards the place of this statue and the person whom it represented. Indeed the witness of Pausanias confirms Osann's views adopted below. The name of Epimenides was indissolubly associated in the minds of religious Athenians with their Eleusinion and its Lesser Mysteries. Not to have raised his statue in just that precinct would have been like denying to Browning his place in Westminster Abbey.

recognised at Athens, Epimenides caused a new festival to be celebrated. This was a specifically Athenian observance in honour of Demeter and Persephone, but especially of Persephone, called the Lesser Mysteries, as distinguished from the older-established Greater or Eleusinian Mysteries to which it served as a prelude.[1] In the Lesser Mysteries Dionysus became associated with Demeter, the mystery of his birth under the name of Iacchos being duly commemorated. This was all the more natural because Dionysus had already found his way to Eleusis.[2] Not until nearly a century later is there record of a second step taken in the occupation of Athens by Attic Dionysus. This time the changes were conclusive and effectual; they were the result not of the people's disaster under a Cylon, but of the triumphs of the enlightened friend of the people, a native of the Attic highlands. The famous tyrant Pisistratus and his family appear to have been the providential defenders of the faith in Dionysus.[3] Before passing to the

[1] Diogenes Laertius, lib. I. cap. x. sec. 6: ἱδρύσατο (sc. 'Ἐπιμενίδης) δὲ καὶ παρ' Ἀθηναίοις τὸ ἱερὸν τῶν σεμνῶν θεῶν, ὥς φησι Λόβων ὁ Ἀργεῖος ἐν τῷ περὶ ποιητῶν.
[2] See the first note on chapter v. below.
[3] The evidence connecting Pisistratus with the revised and enlarged Bacchic worship at Athens is sufficient, due regard being had to the sort of evidence which is at all possible in a matter of the sort. What the evidence is Ribbeck has not stated adequately. I will here try to give a suggestion of it :

(*a*) The only positive evidence connecting Pisistratus with Dionysus is a somewhat inconsequent utterance of Athenaeus (p. 533 C): ὁ δὲ Πεισίστρατος καὶ ἐν πολλοῖς βαρὺς ἐγένετο, ὅπου καὶ τὸ Ἀθήνῃσι τοῦ Διονύσου πρόσωπον ἐκείνου τινές φασιν εἰκόνα. Some one will be sure to see in this a mere bit of invention springing from the well-known latter-day habit of making statues of living potentates with the attributes of various divinities. But this objection, if well taken, leaves still more assured the certainty of an especially close relation between Pisistratus and Dionysus. The story could not otherwise have got itself invented.

(*b*) Pisistratus is indirectly but very really connected through Onomacritus with the whole reshaping by the Orphic school of the religion and the mysteries of Dionysus and Demeter.

new festivals that were then instituted, the new features now discernible in the myth of Dionysus must be given. These are said to have been shaped and codified,

(c) Plutarch, Theopompus, and Athenaeus never tire in relating anecdotes to show how Pisistratus befriended the tillers of the fields. The newly-recovered *Constitution of Athens* (see chapter 16) re-enforces this point. Pisistratus did everything in his power to make the country people industrious and keep them in the fields rather than allow them to congregate anywhere and agitate. He instituted τοὺς κατὰ δήμους δικαστάς, made frequent country visits of inspection, and settled disputes. Then comes the brief story—well told, as Aristotle's pointed stories always are—of the labourer in the Hymettus district accosted at Pisistratus' command while digging with a (?) "spike." Asked what crops he grew, the countryman promptly answered, "Curses in plenty and abundant distress, and Pisistratus is sure of his tithes." In spite of the burning question of tithes, Aristotle goes on to say of Pisistratus: οὐδὲν δὲ τὸ πλῆθος οὐδ' ἐν τοῖς ἄλλοις παρώχλει κατὰ τὴν ἀρχήν, ἀλλ' ἀεὶ παρεσκεύαζεν εἰρήνην καὶ ἐτήρει δι' ἡσυχίαν· διὸ καὶ πολλάκις [παρῳμιάζ]ετο ὡς [ἡ] Πισιστράτου τυραννὶς ὁ ἐπὶ Κρόνου βίος εἴη. In spite of oppressive taxation the countryman of Attica believed in Pisistratus, who conciliated all his prejudices. Among these was a childlike belief in the bodily intervention of the gods skilfully flattered and practised upon by the return of Pisistratus with Athene Sotera to guide him,—some say she was a Thracian girl named Phye (cf. Athen. p. 609). Since there was a reshaping of the worship of Dionysus in his day and by his friend Onomacritus, can we suppose Pisistratus to have stood aloof from such an incomparable means of currying favour with his agricultural constituents, and satisfying his own religious impulses?

(d) That there was this new departure under Pisistratus is abundantly shown by the facts and dates in the career of Thespis. Furthermore, Plutarch's anecdote (*Solon*, 29) of Solon railing at Thespis for his play-actor's trick of manifold lying goes with his account of how the same law-giver jeered at Pisistratus' bad acting in the *rôle* of Odysseus (*Solon*, chap. 30), and manifestly associates Pisistratus with the new-fashioned play-acting.

(e) One striking fact is added to the above from Aristotle's *Athenian Constitution*, 15. Pisistratus spent his second exile in the district where Dionysus was earliest worshipped: περὶ τὸν Θερμαῖον κόλπον . . . ἐκεῖθεν δὲ παρῆλθεν εἰς τοὺς περὶ Πάγγαιον τόπους ὅθεν χρηματισάμενος καὶ στρατιώτας μισθωσάμενος . . . ἀνασώσασθαι βίᾳ τὴν ἀρχὴν ἐπεχείρει. See Mr. Kenyon's note.

(f) Aristotle mentions the tyranny of Pisistratus and the Pisistratidae as among the longest of duration known to him (*Politics*, v. 12). Generalising from his facts in the previous chapter (11) with an especial eye to the career of the Pisistratidae (*e.g.*, ἔτι δὲ μὴ μόνον αὐτὸν φαίνεσθαι μηδένα τῶν ἀρχομένων ὑβρίζοντα, μήτε νέον μήτε νέαν, ἀλλὰ μηδ' ἄλλον μηδένα τῶν περὶ αὐτόν), he says that a tyrant "should appear to be particularly earnest in the service of the gods; for if men think that a as it were, by Onomacritus.[1] However this may be, the connected story that got itself together at this time in Athens and Attica explains the aspect of Dionysus upon which the name Iacchos was bestowed. Iacchos is the Dionysus whose mystic birth came into the Lesser Mysteries long since instituted by Epimenides, whose Cretan birth had much to do with shaping the popular conception of this new aspect of the god.

This story had been in the air, and was only recorded, as it were, by Pisistratus and Onomacritus, who were encouraged by the Delphian oracle to do this. It is evidently made up of a motley and legendary material, ultimately Thracian perhaps, but immediately contributed from the islands of the Archipelago, and most especially from Crete.

ruler is religious and has a reverence for the gods, they are less afraid of suffering injustice at his hands, and they are less disposed to conspire against him, because they believe him to have the very gods fighting on his side. At the same time his religion must not be thought foolish" (Dr. Jowett's translation, pp. 181 and ff.)

[1] Onomacritus (see Herodotus, vii. 6) was on confidential terms with Hipparchus, but had to leave Athens because he introduced into the oracles of Musaeus one of his own, wherein the imminent destruction of an island near Lemnos was predicted. Lasus of Hermione, Pindar's teacher, detected his fraud. When the Pisistratids were in exile he appears to have been reconciled with them, and to have joined them in their visit to the court of Xerxes, whom he incited to war against Athens by various prophecies. Herodotus calls him χρησμολόγον τε καὶ διαθέτην χρησμῶν τῶν Μουσαίου. He was one of the codifiers of the Homeric text, into which he introduced various interpolations. What is thus known of his treatment of Musaeus and Homer makes it regrettable that we do not know the Orphic materials out of which he wrought what was possibly an officially sanctioned account of the Zagreus-Dionysus myth. But so far are we from knowing his sources that our means of knowing what was made of them are very scanty. It is only from comparatively late authorities that we hear of his dealings with Orphic materials. The Orphic brotherhood first showed itself in his day and at Athens. See for a sufficient account the articles "Onomacritus" and "Orpheus" in Pauly's *Real-Encyclopaedie*, both by Dr. G. F. Bähr. See for a yet fuller account Bernhardy, *Litteraturgeschichte* (i. 419-421, and ii. 425-440), and Lobeck's *Aglaophamus*.

Onomacritus, let us say, striving to weave conflicting accounts of Dionysus into one, hit upon the idea (or else finding it ready to his hand made skilful use of it) of a succession of births each one of which was a reincarnation of the one god.

Zagreus, or Dionysus, under his more savage and uncomforting aspect, Zagreus the wild Huntsman, an incarnation of the pitiless harms and blasts of winter-time, was the son of Zeus and Persephone. This Persephone was not the flower-faced maiden fair and sweet, but the threatening queen of death. Her son, this Dionysus-Zagreus, was mightily favoured by his father Zeus. So true was this that Zeus was about to give the child his throne, and to surrender with it his thunders and lightnings. But this plan, like so many others of Zeus, was defeated by Hera's jealousy. Hera set the Titans upon him, and they were his undoing, although he shifted into many shapes to get free. The Titans, fourteen in number, took Zagreus while he was under the shape of a bull. They tore him into fourteen pieces, which Apollo buried at Delphi. Only his heart was not buried there, for Athena took it and gave it to Zeus, who swallowed it and then brought forth to new birth the babe Dionysus, specifically named Iacchos. A favourite subject for sculptured bas-reliefs was this mystically-born babe Iacchos, wildly swung by a Maenad and a Satyr in the mystical sieve to which he owed his Orphic epithet of *Liknites*—Iacchos or Dionysus of the mystic sieve.

And now the necessity of understanding the definite official form into which this newly-recognised worship fitted itself brings up the more or less chaotic mass of Athenian festivals in honour of Dionysus. The following attempt to deal with it shall be at least characterised by a certain neglect of complicated and subordinate questions.[1] It goes without saying that Pisistratus and his advisers did not invent anything new when they instituted the Athenian festivals in honour of Dionysus. This was equally true, no doubt, of Epimenides and the Lesser Mysteries. They merely reorganised existing popular usage, and by official recognition gave it permanence, and secured its orderly observance. Pisistratus would naturally feel that he would tighten his hold upon his enthusiastic highlanders,[2] and that his power could thereby be more secure, if only he gave legal sanction to their favourite worship of Dionysus. He accordingly organised in the god's honour the most brilliant national ceremonies, and by instituting, as it were, a yearly triumph of Dionysus at Athens, he made his partisans sure of his and their supremacy.

The accomplishment of all this led him to make a series of religious innovations, which completed the work begun a century before by Epimenides, and by this great addition to previously recognised religious observances the religion of the Attic people in the broadest sense was finally established as the Attic state religion. Pisistratus, to put the gist of the matter shortly, introduced into the official calendar the two peasant festivals long observed in Dionysus' honour by the people in Icaria and elsewhere.[3]

---

[1] In attacking this much debated theme, I shall not attempt to arm myself in all cases with my sources. I have followed Ribbeck in many, though not in all, material respects.

[2] Aristotle's *Constitution of Athens*, 13: ἦσαν δ' αἱ στάσεις τρεῖς . . . τρίτη δ' ἡ τῶν διακρίων ἐφ' ᾗ τεταγμένος ἦν Πεισίστρατος, δημοτικώτατος εἶναι δοκῶν. Cf. Herod. i. 59, and Aristotle's *Politics*, v. 9.

[3] The whole problem of these festivals is complicated by a third set of *autumn* festivals celebrated specifically for the vintage. These assumed an enormous importance at all centres of Dionysus worship, and probably shifted the dates of the chief celebrations in his honour. It is even rash to say that these were not as old as any observances which I call

In doing this, however, he was careful to make such splendid additions and gorgeous modifications as gave the incoming god a great pre-eminence, and caused his newness to be forgotten. And now a brief account of these two festivals, the Anthesteria or flower-festival and the Lenaean festival, is requisite.

As Pisistratus found the flower-festival of Dionysus, it was apparently an occasion for greeting gladly the return of spring. There were children garlanded, and garlanded worshippers young and old. There was tasting of wine newly opened, and there was competitive potation, ending no doubt in some sort of wordy row like that which assails the ear to-day near frequented pot-houses of the cheaper sort in Greece. This flower-festival, as Pisistratus left it, was all that it had been, with the addition of a triumphal entry of Dionysus into Athens. Furthermore there was instituted a symbolical marriage of Dionysus, the idea of which was cleverly borrowed from the yearly marriage rite of Dionysus and Ariadne, celebrated on the island of Naxos in the Archipelago.[1] Cleverly borrowed, I say, because the Attic rite of marriage was only dimly connected with nature worship. Ariadne represents the spring, and her annual wedlock with Dionysus symbolises the yearly renewal of

Dionysus-festivals. It has, however, seemed suitable to leave them out here. For a full but rather confusing account of all festivals of the one kind and the other, see Preller's article "Dionysia" in Pauly's *Real-Encyclopädie*. The confusion is certainly not in Preller's admirable presentation, but rather in conflicting and insufficient information which alone is available.

[1] The merit of first seeing this connection belongs to Dr. Thiersch, who speaks of it in his introduction to Pindar, p. 156. Speaking of the archons Aristotle says, *Constitution of Athens*, 3: ᾤκησαν δ' οὐχ ἅμα πάντες οἱ ἐννέα ἄρχοντες, ἀλλ' ὁ μὲν βασιλεὺς ε[ἶ]χε τὸ νῦν καλούμενον Βουκόλιον, πλησίον τοῦ Πρυτανείου (σημεῖον δέ· ἔτι καὶ νῦν γὰρ τῆς τοῦ βασιλέως γυναικὸς ἡ σύμμιξις ἐνταῦθα γίνεται τῷ Διονύσῳ καὶ ὁ γάμος). . . .

nature's vivid powers of growth. But the wife of the King-archon at Athens did not necessarily suggest the spring. Dionysus' yearly marriage with her, celebrated in the Bucolion, was certainly witnessed at Athens with feelings much the same as those entertained by Venetians who witnessed the annual espousals of their doge with the sea. In the one case the bridegroom and in the other the bride represented the body politic, and the espousals in both cases proclaimed most loudly the existence of a tie between each member of the body politic and a power which all regarded as assuring safety to the state. Only for Venice the power was of this world and material, while for Athens it was the glorious divinity, the mysterious grandeur and intensity,[1] that transfigured the Attic Dionysus.

Such were the important and significant ceremonies added in Pisistratus' day to the flower-feast of Bromius, and they made of it a festival which later on Thucydides[2] calls "the older Dionysia," and which coincided with the summer feast of joy observed in the country, particularly at Icaria. Another phrase applied to it, also in Thucydides' day, is the "Lesser, or the Rural Dionysia." For this Mr. Browning has a shorthand phrase taken directly from the Greek: he has called this holiday the "Little-in-the-fields." These various names of Older and Lesser served evidently to distinguish the feast of Pisistratus from the Greater

---

[1] It should be mentioned (simply by way of showing what a puzzling mixture of life and death, gladness and grief, all Dionysus worship was) that the last day of Pisistratus' reformed flower-festival was a commemoration of funereal kind. Fourteen women took a solemn oath of purity and obedience to tradition. Then they made due sacrifice at fourteen altars, one for each of the fragments into which the fourteen Titans rent Dionysus-Zagreus. Possibly these were of the nature of those humanised funereal rites whose institution Plutarch attributes to Epimenides of Crete.

[2] ii. 15.

Dionysia which came into existence long after his day and generation.

And now for the second festival of Dionysus as instituted by Pisistratus. Remarking, no doubt, the great and growing importance of the Icarian mid-winter celebration, he legalised the popular winter holiday of Dionysus at Athens, and made various innovations in the direction of the new Icarian fashion of representing plays. And here we come to an important and more or less certain date. In 535 B.C., eight years before Pisistratus died, Thespis of Icaria brought out his first play, at the winter or Lenaean[1] festival in Athens.[2] Thus the Icarian Satyr-play and tragedy were brought to Athens just at the time when Dionysus came into power, so to speak. In fact their introduction was his triumph.

This renovation and new consecration of their immemorial merry-makings, and of the time-honoured rites resorted to for ensuring a fruitful year on the Attic countryside, gave immense satisfaction to the people at large. It lifted a load of apprehension and discontent from their hearts, and the echo of their longing, made less mournful by

[1] Ribbeck maintains with good arguments that the Icarians held to the old name for Gamelion, which was Lenaeon (see Plutarch's fragments on Hesiod, No. 29). That Athens once used this name for the month of the winter-festival of Dionysus-Lenaeus (for this name see Hesychius) and of the biennial processions of the Lenae (Strabo, x. 468) or Lenides (Eustath. on *Iliad*, vi. 132) to the mountains, especially to Parnassus (Pausan. X. iv. 3), is proved by its survival in Asia Minor, whither Athenians early transplanted it (see the inscriptions cited by Pape in his *Dict. of Proper Names*). The Boeotians possibly had the same name for the same season (Hes. *Works and Days*, 504), though Plutarch (fragments on Hesiod, No. 29) denies it.

[2] The precise date depends upon the Parian Marble, but not the fact, which is very widely vouched for. It is noteworthy that the trustworthiness of dates given on the Parian Marble has received confirmation, here and there, by the newly-recovered *Athenian Constitution* of Aristotle. See Mr. Kenyon's note on Damasias, p. 33.

trust in the coming of the god, is still heard in a prayer written by Sophocles, and uttered for luckless Antigone at a time of breathless crisis in her fate.[1]

"Come, for all the people tremble at the threatened harm. Pass thou with purifying footsteps down Parnassus' slope, ay! or cross the booming gulf of waters. Help! Leader thou of fire-flaming planets in the dance. Help! Overseer thou of cries men make through sleepless watches of the night. Show thee now, son of Zeus begotten! Come and bring from Naxos in thy train the frenzied Thyiades thy handmaidens, who all the livelong night dance thee, thee Iacchos, O dispenser thou and steward for mankind." The peculiar and startling locution here may be supposed to represent the acts of the dancing Thyiades, as a sort of materialisation of his power in them, their dancing is the god in them made manifest. The invocation which introduces this same prayer well shows the wide tolerance which gathered into Athenian worship epithets and rites from every home of the god in Greece; for many are his homes, and numerous indeed were the places of his birth. "Thou who bearest many names, Semele's delight, who watchest over far-famed Icaria[2] and rulest where all are welcome, in the sheltered lowlands of Eleusinian Deo. O dweller in Thebes of the softly gliding Ismenus, in Thebes the mother of Bacchanals. Thou hast shown thee amid the smoky glare of flaming torches, arriving on Parnassus—mountain of twin peaks. Near these two peaks live nymphs close to the cave Corycian, and there flow Castalia's fountain springs.

---

[1] *Antigone*, 1115-1152.
[2] That this is the right reading can hardly be denied by any one who has read pp. 96 and 97 of Dr. Merriam's Report. The conditions upon which Professor Jebb said he would read *Icaria* (see, in his 1st edition, note on line 1119) are now fulfilled, and he is half convinced (cf. his 2d edition).

Yea, the ivy tangled in the folds of Nysa's[1] hills, the tender green of lofty promontories covered with luxuriant vines send down to Thebes the Saviour God, and her streets are filled with the heavenly clangour of his echoing name. Thebes, dearly of him and of his thunder-smitten mother dearly loved!" Truly the ring of a most genuine piety sounds in many a passage of the Attic tragedians, but here Sophocles has certainly surpassed himself. The anxiety felt by Dionysus' peasant worshippers was that their god should be duly propitiated. They wished to conciliate his favour for Athens and Attica. Nothing could accomplish this unutterably desirable end but the official celebration of his festivals.

In satisfying this demand by his two feasts, the *Anthesteria* and the *Lenaea*, Pisistratus called Thespis and Tragedy from Icaria. But this performance of plays, once transferred to the broader horizon of the capital, soon grew to such proportions that it threatened to crowd out the indispensable and immemorial religious acts required to be done by all worshippers for the health of the state. Thus the deep religious purpose for which Dionysus and his worship were honoured at Athens would have been unfulfilled. To remedy this came the later institution of the Greater Dionysia, by which the most important representations of tragedies and comedies were relegated to a third and almost exclusive theatrical occasion made for the worship of Dionysus. The month of March was fixed upon for this festival, which seems to have been wonderfully free from the trammels of mystic nature-worship. It was indeed a new institution made in the spirit of the democratic reforms

---

[1] On Nysa, see Appendix III. at the end of this lecture, upon the second birth and eastern affinities of Dionysus.

of Clisthenes to honour the people's most beloved god. The name by which it was sometimes called was the *City Dionysia*, but its commoner name was the *Greater Dionysia*.

The gorgeous pageants of Venice in all her glory seem unspontaneous and almost insincere when compared with this great Athenian glorification of Dionysus. Patriotism intensified, exultant freedom, delight in beauty, delicate skill in all graceful arts, animated and adorned this World-Exhibition of high thoughts and melodious speech. There Dionysus shone, a leader of the Muses, and the Graces moved in his train. So transfigured was the Thracian god that all the savagery of his ancient worship now became a unison of speech and song and dance, a dazzling manifestation of all concordant arts, wherein there shone the blithest and the best that sculpture ever shaped or poetry conceived.

And now it is time to contemplate the god himself in all his Attic and comprehensive majesty. The enlightened Attic worshipper of Bacchus sought at the Athenian Dionysiac theatre, in the presence of the older gods, solemnly represented by their priests, a relief from that sense of spiritual oppression from which the human conscience has never been entirely free. As an analogy to the idea that "in Adam's fall we sinnéd all," may be found underlying this Attic ceremonial the idea of a vicarious complicity in the old-time murder of the Icarian king,[1] and of a predestined responsibility for the sad fate of Erigone.

All the great Athenian tragedies were acts of worship

[1] To speak of Icarius as a king is to use the language of the later and Athenian version of the legend which makes him king of Athens. This seems to be the version alluded to by Hyginus, *Fab.* 130, and by Pausanias, I. ii. 7, end.

dedicated to Dionysus,[1] but one of them is called the
Bacchanals, the last but one of all plays written by the
latest born of the three great tragedians, Euripides. The
Bacchanals enacts and explains as its sole plot and plan,
utters as the burden of all its choral songs, the fulness of the
power of Dionysus. Here no aspect of the Bacchic godhead is forgotten. Nowhere in all literature is the strange
baffling quality of Dionysus presented with such completeness and consistency as in this play of Euripides. Here is a
tragedy written with the sincerely pious intent of revealing the
spirit and the will of the god—a veritable Gospel according to
Euripides. A gospel truly, and of Dionysus; but of what
Dionysus? Is the god of this marvellous play—the vision
of him, that is, which was granted to Euripides in the fulness of his powers—a revelation from the purely Attic
worship of Dionysus, or a reminiscence of the fiercer
Thracian god, or is he a philosopher's fiction argued about
and reduced to consistency until he has lost the wild-wood
tang attached to his native self? The answer must be that
he is not one but all of these in one. Euripides no doubt
would be the first to feel that a poet could only gain by a
seeming inconsistency in an attempt to interpret the most
inconsistent of all divinities.

Hence the many aspects of the *Bacchanals*. It may be

[1] This fact needs frequent reassertion in answer to those who are
inclined to put a poet like Euripides in the position of a modern assailant
of religion. The circumstance that he wrote tragedies at all ought to clear
him of any such charge. As Bernhardy has most truly said, "People are
sometimes oblivious of the fact that the whole structure of Greek religious
service and their whole scheme of nature-worship remained wholly unshaken and intact until the Peloponnesian war or thereabouts. Accordingly such fault-finding or doubt as poets and thinkers express relates to
morals and to certain misrepresentations of the divine nature, and did not
come near the heart of their national religion." *Litteraturgeschichte*, i.
p. 420.

called the Passion-play of Attica, and it has been compared to the Medieval *Morality*. And yet a certain loftiness of religious tone does not here exclude the most unmistakable reminiscences of the fierce and awful god of ancient Thrace. The philosophic and discerning reader may see in the mother who rends her own son—in Agave and all her Maenad train—a spirited personification of the power in a roaring mountain torrent, and of the fury of lapping flames; but he will not press the point too far if he remembers that Euripides wrote his play while he was staying at the court of Archelaus in Macedonian Pieria, that very portion of Thrace whence Dionysus issued. It is as if a pilgrimage to the land of his birth were required by the god himself of a poet whose presentation of the Bacchic godhead was to perpetuate its undimmed memory.[1]

Something wilder than religious Athens knew surrounded Euripides and every Athenian who visited Macedonia in those days. Such visitors "would hear, and from time to time actually see, something of a religious custom in which the habit of an earlier world might seem to survive. As they saw the lights flitting over the mountains, and heard the wild sharp cries of the women, there was presented a singular fact in the more prosaic actual life of a later time, an enthusiasm otherwise relegated to the wonderland of a distant past, in which a supposed primitive harmony between man and nature renewed itself."[2] It is

---

[1] It has already been noted above that Pisistratus, during his second exile, spent most of his time in Thrace. On returning—this was his second restoration—he was enabled to encourage the innovations of Thespis, and give official sanction to the peasant worship of the Thracian god. See Aristotle's *Constitution of Athens*, 15, and Mr. Kenyon's reference there to Herodotus' allusion to supplies drawn by Pisistratus ἀπὸ Στρυμόνος ποταμοῦ.

[2] Here, as below, I quote from Mr. Pater's essay.

well known that the women of the house of Philip and Alexander were carried into measureless excesses by the possession of the god. They were Bacchanals with a vengeance, and all the dreadful deeds attributed by Euripides to his Bacchanals would therefore be looked upon by them as a poetic amplification only of what lay within their own experience. "Later sisters of Centaur and Amazon, the Maenads, as they beat the earth in strange sympathy with its waking up from sleep, or as in the description of the messenger, in the play of Euripides, they lie sleeping in the glen revealed among the morning mists, were themselves indeed as remnants — flecks left here and there, and not quite evaporated under the hard light of a later and common day—of a certain cloud-world which had once covered all things in a veil of mystery."

It is indeed marvellous that our poet in this very play, so well fitted to please a semi-barbarous Macedonian taste, so full of the proto-Thracian spirit of Dionysus, has been able to remain true to the loftier teachings of Anaxagoras and Socrates. The fact nevertheless remains that a leaven, half of philosophy and wholly religious, so pervades this play that it not only sums up the past but prefigures the future. It contains, revealed here and there in brief flashes, what may be called a Messianic vision. Less manifestly perhaps than Virgil, and yet perhaps more deeply, Euripides is moved by a vision long beforehand of religious truth to come. In the sorrows and the joys of Dionysus and his train, touches come here and there which are, it would seem, the outcome of a Dionysus-granted power of prophecy. Euripides had vision long beforehand of the mysteries of faithful sorrowing, the ecstasies of Christian joy. This is no new discovery, for in the days of the early Church the Christian poet Nonnus devoted his energies to a long and most loving work, chronicling with minute and pious care, often in most sweetly flowing verse, all that has ever been sung or said of Dionysus. Still more striking was the appreciation of Dionysus shown by the pious compiler of a curious work called *Christus Patiens*. To this devout Christian's uncramped and unpremeditated piety was given the vision of a real analogy between the passion of Christ and the passion of Dionysus. Moreover we owe, strangely enough, the preservation of some important lines in the play of Euripides to his curious cento.

And now before analysing the *Bacchanals* one caution must be given. None must suppose that the personage named Dionysus, who proclaims himself to be the god disguised in mortal form, is the only presentation of the godhead. This disguised Dionysus is in some ways still what we may suppose the one speaker used by Thespis in his earliest Icarian ventures to have been. He is not Dionysus but only a focal point around which gather, with endless and flickering play of change, the constantly shifting figures in the plot. The Maenads who followed the Dionysus-man from Asia, and who form the chorus of the play, are themselves the god. The Dionysus-driven women of Thebes who against their will are dashed from home to revel on the mountain side, these are but passive receivers of the Bacchic godhead—" Impotent pieces of the game he plays."

King Pentheus, though he loudly proclaims himself the foe of Dionysus, is only possessed by the mad frenzy sent by Zagreus-Dionysus, the wild Thracian huntsman who has found his furious way through Cretan legends. Dionysus, in some of his many phases, is manifested by any and every personage in the play. Even the scene of its enactment is full of the god, for it is the holy spot in Thebes[1] where Semele died in bringing Dionysus prematurely to his birth. We see the thunder-smitten ruins where Semele was slain. Their smoking embers are hallowed by a fitful flame. This is the god of fire actually present, and to him the spot had long been made consecrate by order of Cadmus, when Cadmus still was king. To mark them twice his own, Dionysus has covered these smoking ruins with his cherished vine.

The play opens with the arrival at this place in Thebes of the youthful god who soliloquises: Behold Zeus's son arrived at Thebes, where fire consumed his mother Semele. He surveys the scene, and proclaims his own presence marked by flame and by the vine. Then our Dionysus, in mortal disguise, looks out upon the world and sees the same godhead made manifest on every side, and recognised everywhere as pre-eminent. Nature with her floods and flames and all her luxury of green is his, for his power has made it; and man also, up to the present moment, has been prompt to pay him homage. The Lydians on their fields flooded with gold, the Phrygians and Persia's burning plains, the forts of Bactria and the snow-swept reaches of Media, all Araby the blest with the swarming cities of Asia Minor, have acknowledged the god. Now Greece must bow the knee before him. His night-long revels must be loved; and the reveller, in order no doubt to keep before him a sign of the star-flecked sky at eve, at midnight, and at dawn, must adopt the garb beloved of Dionysus—a dappled fawn skin.

The god made man proceeds to tell what brought him to Thebes. The madding impulses that Dionysus sends invited

---

[1] Cf. Pausanias, IX. xii. 3: φασὶ δὲ οἱ Θηβαῖοι, καθότι τῆς ἀκροπόλεως ἀγορά σφισιν ἐφ' ἡμῶν πεποίηται, Κάδμου τὸ ἀρχαῖον οἰκίαν εἶναι· θαλάμων δὲ ἀποφαίνουσι τοῦ μὲν Ἁρμονίας ἐρείπια καὶ ὃν Σεμέλης φασὶν εἶναι· τοῦτον δὲ καὶ ἐς ἡμᾶς ἔτι ἄβατον φυλάσσουσιν ἀνθρώποις.

by the insults heaped upon his dearest mother Semele at Thebes, and by an impious resistance there offered to his worship, have seized and carried away the womankind of all the town. The men are slower, more stubborn and prone to fight, though the battle be a losing one. The women of Cadmus' house have gone stark mad and have left their homes to revel in the wilderness of Cithaeron, and, lest they should not be filled enough with his power, Dionysus in the flesh now goes to them, and leaves those other Dionysus-driven creatures,—his Maenad followers who came to Thebes with him from far-off Asia. With his exit toward Mount Cithaeron ends the opening and introductory scene of the play—its prologue.

In the act of going Dionysus makes a sign at which the Asiatic Maenads, the Bacchanals from whom the play is named, troop wildly into the theatre; and the street around Pentheus' royal palace resounds with the beating of drums and Bacchic cries. The disguised Bacchus, the man-Dionysus, their youthful captain, is gone, but the god Dionysus still is there, and his voice is heard in the strains now sung by this Bacchanalian throng.

They tell of their weary journeyings made sweet by Dionysus' love. They warn the polluted and the profane to beware and give way, for the god is to speak in them. Then comes a divine song which tells of blessed mysteries. Blest is he who hallows his manner of life, and cleaves with his soul most straitly to the Thiasos fulfilled with the god, the Thiasos madly scouring the mountains; for thus shall his soul be purged and made most clean. Yea, and with the worship of the god must be joined reverence for the great mother goddess Cybele. "Then on, Bacchanals, on! ye Bacchants, lead ye Dionysus home to Thebes."

The next strain sings of thunder-smitten Semele, of Zeus, who snatched her babe to his thigh, whence it came in due season to full and fated birth.[1]

"Thebes," so shouts the Maenad throng, "Thebes, the nurse of Semele, deck thee now and yield to Bacchic promptings—

> Branches of ivy or of oak
> Take thou, a very Bacchanal;
> Nor let the Bacchant's dappled cloak
> Of fawn-skin from thy shoulders fall,
> White-fringe it all with wool-tufts small;
> The ferule wield with reverent care,
> And of its wantonness beware."

And now the risen surge of song beats higher still, and higher rises the quickening pulse of the inflowing god, for they cry—

> Soon shall the country rejoice in the dance,
> Soon with his revellers Bacchus advance,
> Into the hills, the hills shall he fare.

Then for a time not Dionysus, but a peculiar aspect of Zeus is the theme of the sacred song. They sing of the Zeus of Crete, who is after all not the father of Dionysus but Dionysus himself. Euripides certainly was conscious of this, and he means at least to suggest that Crete was a debatable ground, where the legends of Dionysus and Zeus met and overlapped. The Curetes in their Cretan haunts, the wildly dancing Corybantes so picturesquely sung of here, surrounded the birth and protected the rearing of

---

[1] Dr. Sandys, in his excellent note on this passage, refers to the epithet ἡμιτέλεστος, *half-matured*, used of Dionysus by Nonnus, *Dionysiaca*, xlv. 99; see also i. 5, and he also cites Ovid, *F.* iii. 717, *puer ut posses maturo tempore nasci, expletum patrio corpore matris onus*. See upon this curious feature of the myths the Appendix at the end of this lecture.

this Cretan Zeus-Dionysus. The mother goddess Rhea is associated with him in Crete, just as Cybele is united with Dionysus in Phrygian worship. Moreover the Maenads of our chorus immediately pass to a song of the invention of various Bacchic instruments—the drum, the flute, and the cymbal. We hear that all these were instruments for praising Cybele and Dionysus, or, if so you choose to say it, of Rhea and of Cretan Zeus.

That this whole song was profoundly religious is no doubt sufficiently evident, but the religious intent is nowhere more undisguisedly present than in its closing strain, where the ecstasies of pious revellings are wildly sung with the cry, "Evoe, Bacchus leads on and hearts are thrilled," which comes from promptings of the god himself. After this the miracles worked by Dionysus are touched upon. Here and elsewhere in the play the poet tells of the miraculous flow of milk and honey[1] that springs from the ground at the bidding of his Bacchant revellers. On they go, beating drums, singing

---

[1] In this and other passages of the play where Dionysus' followers show miraculous command over honey, Euripides indicates his familiarity with an out-of-the-way legend of Dionysus at home in the island of Euboea, which lay near by, under the jealous governance of Athens, and which was largely occupied in the poet's day by Athenian colonists. According to these legends Dionysus was reared in Euboea (anciently called Macris, or Long-island) by Aristaeus, the giver of honey, who was his constant instructor. His nurse in Euboea was a nymph, who is sometimes said to have been named Macris. Nysa, a name familiar as applied in many Dionysus-stories to the moist and wooded place where the fiery god came to birth, was a second name given to this Euboean nurse of Dionysus. Whether her name was Nysa or Macris, this Euboean maiden was Aristaeus' daughter. The remarkable point to remember from these Euboean legends is the prominence in them of milk and honey, two good gifts from which Dionysus is dissociated in the earliest Attic story. Furthermore, it is noticeable that Euripides, in weaving these bright Euboean strands into his play, made it plain that he regarded himself as a religious interpreter for the whole of Greece and not for Attica alone. For an account of the wider scope of the legends of Dionysus' birth at Nysa, see Appendix III. at the end of this chapter.

Evoe to the Evian god. Phrygian shouts they shout, while flutes trill in their revels to thrill them with rippling joys. But while we look, as with a flash from many white limbs darting forward, they have passed ere has died on the ear their shout, "On, Bacchants, on!"

Now the plot begins to thicken, and the three central acts, courses, or periods—what you will—now begin. The whole play has five parts, of which the introductory one is already over. At the end comes the fifth and concluding part, a winding-up of the play.

In the three central acts now beginning is portrayed the Passion, as it were, of Dionysus. In the first act, Reason fails to turn the enemy, King Pentheus, from his impious purposes against the god. Here, at the very outset, the flutter of frenzy to come hovers over Pentheus the arch-sinner, and he already belongs to Dionysus. In the second act comes the consummation of blinded Pentheus' sin. The man-Dionysus, the vicar of the god in Thebes, is seized and thrown into prison. The Maenads from Asia are threatened with violence, and the Theban revellers on Mount Cithaeron are hunted, and some of them taken and thrown into prison. But close upon the heels of sin treads punishment. The third act sets forth the nature and the manner of an awful chastisement inflicted upon King Pentheus, on all his house and on the land of Thebes. An earthquake comes first to reveal the wrath and majesty of outraged Dionysus. Out of the midst of the earthquake the man-Dionysus emerges from his dark prison, reminding Eleusinian hearers of Persephone restored from the realms of Hades to Demeter and the day. He comes to foil and flout his half-crazed persecutor, as appears in the next event on the stage. Madness seizes

Pentheus, madness and the judgment of flood and fire, those attendant ministers of the earthquake which are personified in the Theban Maenads. These finally rend Pentheus and reduce him to a shapeless and dismembered heap of fragments. The wages of sin is madness first, and finally death. So ends the Passion of Dionysus in the destruction of his persecutor in whose dismemberment we see rehearsed the tragic fate of Dionysus-Zagreus. The conclusion or Exodus of the play sets forth a moral that recalls the purifying ritual introduced with Delphian Apollo's sanction from the border town of Eleutherae.[1] The moral in point is, that there is need of Dionysus' help in recovering from harms brought about by his own power, and with it is coupled an urgent representation of the folly of all resistance to the god.

Such is a brief outline of the central acts and conclusion of the play, whose noble introduction has been examined already at length. It now remains to take an equally careful view of these four main parts. To begin with the first scene, where the intending sinner is still on his probation. The transgressor in question is Pentheus the son of Agave, Semele's sister, into whose hands his grandfather Cadmus has resigned the royal power at Thebes. Tiresias the seer is first seen upon the stage. His name is Tiresias, but he has suffered a Bacchic change into something not himself; and his gospel is the method of Bacchic madness. This Tiresias is not the dread shade that defies in Homeric song the power of darkness and seems to live in death. Nor is he the Tiresias of Sophocles, that majestic incarnation of wisdom whose mighty wrath and burning scorn cowed even the spirit of Oedipus the Great. Tiresias in

[1] See above, Appendix II., on Dionysus of Eleutherae.

the *Bacchanals* is grotesque, if we forget that Dionysus has entered into him and possessed him, when he comes upon the stage attired in a Bacchic garb, ill-suited alike to his years and his priestly office. He is bent upon taking his part in Bacchic revellings, and is in the act of seeking another—a companion old like himself, and like himself ill-suited for the dance. This companion appears; he is the royal Cadmus, and shows at the outset eagerness even greater than that of Tiresias for gambolling in the wilderness of Cithaeron, saying:

> Where leads the dance, where must we take our turn
> And toss our gray-haired heads? Interpret thou,
> Aged Tiresias; lead my old age,
> For thou art wise. The livelong day and night
> Untiring with my thyrsus I'll smite earth.
> 'Tis sweet for us when we our age forget.[1]

Tiresias ends by seeming the less grotesque of the two; it is he who turns apologist for Dionysus, and very skilfully his argument begins:

> "We reason not o'er nicely of the gods,
> They are the heirlooms by our fathers left,
> As old as time; no logic shall destroy them,
> Not though the keenest wit should prompt the thought.

Scoff not at old men dancing, mock not at these ivy crowns on our silvered heads," he says,—

[1] The merit of having established, by changing one letter in the MS., the undoubted reading here belongs to Milton. See Dr. Sandys on this line. He says of Milton's emendations, "They were written in the margin of his copy of the edition of Euripides printed by Paul Stephens at Geneva in 1602, 2 vols. 4to, now in possession of Henry Halford Vaughan, Esq., of Upton Castle, Pembroke. Milton bought it in 1634, the very year in which he wrote *Comus*, which was acted at Michaelmas of that year, and shows in several points special familiarity with this and other plays of Euripides. Cf. especially *Comus*, 297-301 with *Iph. T.*, 264-274.

> The god hath not distinguished if the young
> Or if the older man should join the dance,
> Claiming from all alike service and honour.

But look, Tiresias and Cadmus cease their talk and retire up the stage. Hurrying footsteps interrupt them, and they see from afar Pentheus; he comes breathless, and quivers from head to foot when he pauses. This sort of tremor is a well-known sign of approaching madness. The tie is close that binds the aged Cadmus of Sidon to this new-comer. Pentheus is twice over Cadmus' grandson; through Echion his father earth-born, sprung from the dragon's teeth which Cadmus sowed near the spring of Dirce at Thebes; and through his mother Agave, Cadmus' own daughter. Accordingly in this scene where Pentheus is most nearly his native self he shows a certain affection for Cadmus, the only gladness in him, for he was otherwise all grief, even as his name implied.[1] Tiresias and Cadmus moved our laughter when they first entered; contrasted now with Pentheus they take on the semblance of calm and almost of dignity.

Words chase each other out of Pentheus' mouth. He was abroad. News came of Theban women revelling on Cithaeron, wild with that strange impostor Dionysus. "It is a shame! these women cloak impure desires with professed piety. But," he screams, "I have caught some of them"; and then adds, with a cruel sneer, "I am after the others. Agave my mother, and her sisters Ino and Autonoe, are of the band, and all shall be prisoned." Thinking of the Dionysus-man, he adds:

> To us a being strange is come, they say,
> From Lydian lands, a wizard and a cheat,

---

[1] His name is a Greek equivalent for *Tristan, the man of sorrow*.

With golden curls and fragrant flowing hair.
His wine-flushed glance hath Aphrodite's charm,[1]
And day and night he wanders with them there.

Here Pentheus refers to the revellers on Cithaeron. Soon, losing all self-control, he says blasphemously:

I'll end the thumping of his thyrsus-wand
And all the tossing of his locks: his head
Shall fall, by this hand from his body sundered.

Sneers at Dionysus' fire-birth and Semele's fame and fate; scoffs at Dionysus' second birth from Zeus's thigh,[2] coupled with insults heaped upon the memory of Dionysus' well-beloved mother, now follow quickly, and the blasphemer is so wholly engrossed in his blaspheming that he fails to see the two old men who have been hovering in the background awaiting opportunity to address him. Now, with a wild start at their Bacchic trappings, Pentheus whirls a torrent of angry words upon them. He fairly goes mad with rage. Tiresias is responsible; Tiresias must be gaoled with the women captured from Cithaeron. A gleam of moderation revisits him just here; after all, Tiresias is too old for such treatment, he says. Those women, though, must and shall be kept from wine. "Wine-bibbing is no meat for womankind!" exclaims the tumultuous-minded king. The quality of Tiresias, as Sophocles portrayed him, now shows in his wrathful answer to the king.

[1] Dr. Sandys is very happy in quoting here two lines of the *Comus*, 752, 753, which very probably were inspired by this passage:
 What need a vermeil-tinctured lip for that,
 Love-darting eyes, or tresses like the morn?

[2] Here as in other blasphemies of Pentheus we have a picturesque statement of the doubts and difficulties felt by reasoning men concerning certain grotesque features in the myth of Dionysus. See Appendix at the end of this chapter.

> Sham wisdom oils and glibly wags thy tongue,
> But all thy argument is foolishness.
> A bold man skilled in overmastering speech,
> If sense abides not in him, harms the state.

And here Tiresias, inspired less by the god perhaps than by the over-subtle reasonings about gods and men which he so eloquently scorned earlier in the play, subjects the tale of Dionysus' second birth to a treatment half meant in earnest and half intended as an answer to the fool according to his folly.[1] To understand the subtlety of his argument here, it must be understood that měros is the Greek word meaning piece or part, while mēros means thigh.

"Scorn not," says the subtle seer Tiresias, "but reverently repeat the tale how Zeus plucked to Olympus the babe unborn. Thence Hera strove to fling him down, but she was foiled. To defeat her Zeus took a piece,"—a měros—"from earth-encircling ether. This phantom babe was abandoned to Hera. The real Dionysus babe, meanwhile, was firmly sewed with golden needles into Zeus's thigh"—his mēros. After this sophism Tiresias ends his justification of the ways of Dionysus by telling Pentheus of the god's miraculous power. "Bacchus," he says, "is a prophet and a warrior. The radiant peaks of lofty Parnassus are redolent of the god by day and night—

> Thou shalt descry him still: on Delphi's rocks
> He bounds torch-dancing o'er their twin-peak'd alps,
> Flinging and whirling the leafy thyrsus-wand."

Another phase of Tiresias' defence of the god is an answer to the king's wild accusation taxing the Bacchanals with wantonness. This passage is worth remembering, because,

---

[1] For further discussion of this curious defence of the faith, see Appendix III. at the end of this chapter.

taken with a passage from the messenger's speech,[1] it contains our poet's pious understanding of the revels of Bacchanalian women, and because Milton admired it, and expanded it in a well-known passage of his *Comus*.[2] It runs as follows:[3]

[1] The other passage is one of the most wonderful in the play, vv. 677-688 :

> Late as to pasture forth I led my kine. . . .
> While gleaming sunrise sped its warmth to earth,
> I saw three bands of women-revellers :
> The first Autonoe ruled, the second band
> Thy mother Agave. Ino led the third.
> Lapped all in slumber lay their limbs relaxed,
> Some couched on heaped-up twigs of silver fir,
> Some pillowed on oak-leaves, their heads low laid
> Reclining where they might, yet as they should ;
> Not right thy word, that, overcome with wine
> And with the sounding flute, they left their lords
> To hunt for Cypris through the wilderness.

[2] Directly inspired by vv. 314-318 which follow in the text, indirectly by the ones quoted in the last note, and by the wildwood spirit of the *Bacchanals* which he has woven in a wonderfully original fashion into the whole of his masque, are Milton's justly celebrated lines in praise of chastity, *Comus*, 418-475. The process of picturesque expansion to which the most classical of English poets has thus subjected the most romantic of the Greek classics has its parallel in Goethe's expansion of *Iph. Taur.* 1401, 1402 :

> A sister's love thou feelest, goddess, too ;
> I yielded but to that, I love my kin,

into the following, where the terseness of the original is sadly lacking :

> Du liebst, Diane, deinen holden Bruder
> Vor allem was dir Erd' und Himmel bietet,
> Und wendest dein jungfräulich Angesicht
> Nach seinem ew'gen Lichte sehnend still.
> O lass den einz'gen Spätgefundnen mir
> Nicht in der Finsterniss des Wahnsinns rasen.

It is curious to find Milton and Goethe playing so decidedly the part of romanticists as compared with Euripides ; it is equally curious to find in these instances so complete an exemplification of Mr. Sidney Colvin's definition of classical and romantic writing : "in classical writing every idea is called up to the mind as nakedly as possible, and at the same time as distinctly ; it is exhibited in white light and left to produce its effect by its own unaided power. In romantic writing, on the other hand, all objects are exhibited as it were through a coloured and iridescent atmosphere." Preface to *Selections from Landor*. [3] Vv. 314-318.

Not Dionysus' strength, when Cypris calls,
Shall make a woman chaste. Inborn and bred,
Bone of her bone, is thorough chastity
Where she is chaste. 'Tis worth our weighing well:
She that is chaste may not corrupted be
For all her Bacchanalian revellings.

Finally, despairing utterly of converting so blatant a sinner as Pentheus, the prophet shows a sad foreknowledge in his closing words:

Thou art crazed to death, nor hast thou drugs,
Nor findest none to cure thee, drugged with folly!

Now Cadmus seconds his companion's urgent reasonings and beseeches Pentheus not to persecute Dionysus, not to neglect the mountain revels, but, by leaving Thebes for Cithaeron, to stay at home with righteousness. After the plea of wisdom has failed, the voice of pleading love still sounds: "My son," says Cadmus, "stay at home with us; cross not the threshold into outer lawlessness." Here Cadmus strives by an ingenious way of putting his thought to humour in words the dangerous frenzy of Pentheus while he really contradicts him. Pentheus is all for staying at home, and therefore Cadmus talks of going out to the wilderness as the only real way left open for staying at home, a novel way of presenting the gist of the adage *ubi bene ibi patria*.[1] But Pentheus is obdurate, and Cadmus humours him still more; granting that he may be right in scorning Dionysus' godhead, there are considerations of family policy which ought to make Pentheus wink at the divine pretensions of his cousin—the son of Semele, the sister of his mother Agave.

But all arguments and all management are vain. Pen-

[1] Or, as Menander puts it, τῷ γὰρ καλῶς πράσσοντι πᾶσα γῆ πατρίς.

theus can no longer contain himself. He fairly foams
with rage at the end of Cadmus' expostulation. Fiercely
he turns away, and despatches men to the holy places
where Tiresias practises augury. These must be entirely
destroyed. Against the cheating stranger, the Dionysus-
man, he sends guards saying:

> That girl-shaped vagrant, bringer of this pest
> We know not of, the man-shaped Dionysus,
> The worker of abominations—Stone him!

Thus cries frantic Pentheus, and Tiresias bodingly murmurs to Cadmus as they go,

> May Pentheus never bring
> His namesake Grief, O Cadmus, to thy home.

This first act of the play now closes with a lyric cry
from the Maenad worshippers of Dionysus.

Holiness with her pinions of gold is summoned to
earth that she may record the blasphemies of Pentheus.
Dionysus is praised as the god of garlands and feasts, of
dancing, thyrsus in hand, and of sweet shrillings from flutes.
His gifts are wine and riddance of lingering sadness, with
sleep that closes great joy. "Lawless folly ends in harm.
Peace and soundness of mind under the watchful gods bring
concord and happiness. But," the song and its singers maintain, "there is wisdom and wisdom. Man's wisdom can
bring him to folly:

> No true wisdom comes from being wise
> In dizzy thought that past man's level flies."

But enough of calm reasonings, the lyric song now
breaks away from contemplation, and revelry is its theme.
Revelry and some place not curst like Thebes with Pentheus'

sin. "Oh for Cyprus, Aphrodite's isle! Lead on to Pieria and high Olympus' steep, great Bromius!" The course of song finally grows more calm. Through jollity of feasts, through prosperity and peace that breeds stout men, the lyric ode goes on its way, showing the mercy of Dionysus and his loving-kindness.

> To him whose fortunes rise,
> To him whose hopes decline,
> He gives glad gifts alike; to none denies
> The painless joys of wine.

At the end comes a prayer which is partly an argument:

> Through every night and day
> To live through life the happy way
> From froward men withdrawn apart!
> For me the throngs of lowlier men; their creed,
> Their way of life, be graven on my heart!

Thus closes the first great act, which we may call the *Probation of Pentheus*. The second great act which now begins gives an account of the *Sin of Pentheus*, which is the *Passion of Dionysus*, and the third and last great act depicts the *Perdition of Pentheus*.

At the opening of the second act a guard leads in the Dionysus-man, the Asian reveller whose unresisting ways had won his captors' hearts, and awed them into recognition of his godhead. This prisoner is welcomed by Pentheus with blasphemous exultation, although a warning comes with him. The guard who leads Dionysus prisoner reports the first of the miracles that foreshadow the awful judgment of Dionysus. The women from Cithaeron, in whose capture Pentheus so exulted, have been freed as by enchantment from their bonds. Self-loosened, their shackles fell away and invisible hands have burst their prison bars. Pentheus hears all this unmoved, and scorns the pressing appeal of the rough and ready guard to change from his wilful impiety. Turning to the prisoner, the king pays an unwilling tribute to his loveliness in words that well describe the latter-day Dionysus, a type with which we are most familiar—

> Thy frame is not unshapely, stranger,
> Not wrestling made this hair of thine so long.
> Its gracious flow half hides thy very cheek;
> Thy skin is white to help thy scoundrel schemes.
> Not sunburnt thou, but pampered in the shade.

Then begins a strange duel of words between Pentheus and the god. "What is thy name?" King Pentheus harshly asks. "Not hard to know, for I was born in flowery Tmolus," is the answer. "What are these new rites of thine?" the king then asks. At the answer, "They are of Dionysus," Pentheus loses all self-control, and pours out abuse upon Zeus and Semele and the night orgies in honour of Dionysus. "What shape," the king again asks, "do these precious orgies take?" "That may not be told to men unholy; the revellers have gifts well worth the knowing, though thou shalt not hear." Flurried by the god's unwavering tone of reprimand, Pentheus nevertheless puts a bold face upon the matter, and, after sneering, invites still sterner reproof by asking how the god looked when he showed himself to the faithful. "Even as he willed," the answer comes, "not shaped by my command."

After this the king crazily dashes out with wild attacks upon the Bacchic ritual, but at each onset he is checked and checkmated by stern reprisals from the inflexible god whose human representative stands before him. Gradually

Pentheus loses his head so completely that he has to be guided, so to speak, towards his own iniquitous purpose. His sin approaches consummation when, in answer to Dionysus' words "Tell me my fate, thy threatened terrors name," he declares that he will shear off his prisoner's soft and silken locks.

"My hair is consecrate, I wear it for the god," the beauteous stranger answers. In spite of this and repeated warnings, Pentheus snatches away the thyrsus-wand, and is for putting "the insolent fellow" in prison.

At this point the possession by Dionysus of the Dionysus-man culminates and gradually becomes complete. Till now he distinguished between himself and the god, but now he declares confidently that the god will free him, and to silence Pentheus' sneers, he says of Dionysus—

> Now present, he now sees what I endure!

Soon after this the culmination comes, and he is completely the god when he says—

> He is in me: wicked and blind thou art.

Pentheus, worsted in argument, is about to carry the day by an appeal to brute force. He has Dionysus bound and prepared for imprisonment, each step being in spite of solemn warning. The most solemn of these is where the god says—

> Thy life, thy name, thy sin thou knowest not.

At this Pentheus' spirit cowers, and all in a tremor he cries in a dazed way—

> Pentheus, Echion's son and Agave's I am.

And then he hears with terror from the prisoner whom his men are leading to confinement—

> Thou and thy name are meet for deep disaster.

"Coop the fellow in the stables," he cries in fear and anger, "let him dance there with dumb beasts." Speaking of sure requital to come speedily, the disguised Dionysus disappears at last with the threatening words addressed to Pentheus—

> Though thou declarest Dionysus is not,
> In binding me thou art confining him.

Now the Bacchanals sing a song of fear and woe. This is the winter of their discontent, and truly this darkest point in the play mirrors the sadness and the longing of those mysterious winter festivals on Mount Parnassus and in Attica which were always attached to the worship of Dionysus. The analogy of this festival, which included rejoicing for the new and mystic birth of the god lamented so lately, accounts for one theme of this song, a glad welcoming of the birth of Dionysus.

"Achelous' daughter Dirce makes Theban lands yield abundantly. Dirce, whose waters welcomed the new-born Dionysus and bathed him that the flames from his father's bolt might leave no scar,"—Dirce is now unfriendly to the revellers in whom dwells the fulness of Dionysus.

Pentheus and his sin soon engross their song. He is a fierce-glaring monster fitly spawned by earth from dragon's teeth. They close with a prayer to Dionysus for help. As it proceeds this prayer becomes an incantation in the spirit of rude magic charms used by peasants to bring forth nature's power and ensure full crops.

"Dionysus, dost thou leave thy prophets here to strive

in vain? With brandishings of thy most golden thyrsus come down Olympus. Where in Nysa's wilds or on the heights Corycian art thou, Dionysus? Art thou near the Thracian realm of singing, whose forests followed Orpheus, marshalled with all wild beasts in his wake? Lo! he comes over Axius. He comes with whirling Maenad train across the Lydias, father of plenty in the Thracian land of good horses."

This is the frantic prayer for help of "captive good attending captain ill," transmuted in the Bacchic fires of faith so as to become an invocation which reshapes itself at the close into a song of thanksgiving and praise. It ends with the strains of Bacchus' triumphal march in order to usher in the Lord of Vengeance whose coming with requital is at hand.[1]

"Make way," so runs the burden of this song of the judgment of Dionysus,

> Let justice be shown and be dread,
> For justice make way and her sword;

---

[1] I cannot do better than quote from Professor Tyrrell's Introduction to the *Bacchanals*, where I have found, just at the moment of going to pre s, a presentation of the deep religious significance of the whole play from which my too belated knowledge of his admirable work has prevented me from profiting sufficiently. Of the various choral odes Professor Tyrrell most truly says: "The *parodos* and the four *stasima* not only are suitable in a degree rare in Euripides to the parts of the action at which they are respectively introduced, but form a whole in themselves and an elaborate picture of the Bacchic cult. The parodos (vv. 64-169) describes the outward form and ritual of the Bacchic worship; the first stasimon (vv. 370-431) describes its sacred joys, the second stasimon (vv. 519-575) refers to the birth of the god, the third (vv. 862-911) breaks into tumultuous enthusiasm and anticipations of triumph, and the fourth (vv. 977-1024) urges on the 'hounds of frenzy' against the violator of the rites of the Maenads." Professor Tyrrell refers to Pfander's *Die Tragik des Euripides*, Bern, 1869; and also to Schöne's similarly striking account of the choral odes of the *Iphigenia at Aulis*, the very last play written by Euripides.

To his throat shall she set it and smite off the head
Of Echion's earth-spawned offspring untoward,
The godless, the lawless, the froward.[1]

With this song ends the *Passion of Dionysus*. Now comes the third and last great act, a veritable *Vision of Judgment*, which treats of the *Perdition of Pentheus*. It begins with the first revelation which this play contains of Dionysus in his terrific might. The god comes to the rescue of his suppliants, and to give judgment against the evildoer. Forth from the earthquake, which is Dionysus' might,[2] steps smiling and unharmed the prisoner of a moment since. The veil of the palace of Pentheus has been rent, but Pentheus, more and more dazed and crazed, is still unabashed. He is for further harm to Dionysus, but ere he attempts it he listens to a messenger from Cithaeron. There the might of the god has shown itself in a judgment as it were of fire. Crashing down the hills and spreading terror and ruin far and wide the lava-stream of Maenad women has proclaimed their lord's resistless might. This appears next in the coming of madness which enters the guilty soul of Pentheus. Crazed by his own rising frenzy and mocked by the disguised Dionysus, who leads him towards death, Pentheus goes to spy out the Maenads at their revels on Cithaeron. He is himself madly accoutred as a Bacchanal.

Off there on Cithaeron comes the final execution of the will of Dionysus upon the luckless king. Perched high on a pine tree, by a mad freak of his own which the disguised

---

[1] Vv. 1010-1013. This is the last song of the chorus.

[2] The chief authority for this statement is in this and other passages of the *Bacchanals*, and in the identification of Dionysus with fire. Cf. also a fragment—relating to Bacchic orgies—from the *Edoni* of Aeschylus, Dind. 55: ψαλμὸς δ' ἀλαλάζει ταυρόφθογγοι δ' ὑπομυκῶνται ποθὲν ἐξαφανοῦς φοβεροὶ μῖμοι, τυπάνου δ' εἰκὼν ὥσθ' ὑπογαίου βροντῆς φέρεται βαρυταρβής.

Dionysus made haste to gratify before disappearing in a pillar of fire, Pentheus is spied by the Maenads. They whirl the tree to the ground and, mad themselves with Dionysus, they look on the king as a mountain-ranging lion.[1] Thus these frenzied women surround him, now darting and dancing light as flickering flames, and now in mass resistless whirling like a torrent down the mountain side. Here is the devastating flood that comes with an earthquake springing upward from unseen sources terrific in its might.

[1] In this wild scene Euripides glorifies and does a sort of poetical justice to country customs which still subsist and have often been fraught with the shedding of human blood. See Mr. Frazer's interesting chapter on "Killing the Tree Spirit" (pp. 240-253 of vol. i. in his *Golden Bough*) where he gives—following Mannhardt and others—an account of the Lower Bavarian custom of various mock executions at Whitsuntide. The *Pfingstl* thus executed is like Pentheus here a king of the wood, and "his defeat and death at the hands of another proved that his strength was beginning to fail, and that it was time his divine life should be lodged in a less dilapidated tabernacle." See also F. A. Voigt (article "Dionysus" in Roscher's *Mythological Lexicon*, p. 1061). There was a legend (Pausanias, II. ii. 5 and 6) concerning two most sacred Bacchic images at Corinth, one of Λύσιος and the other of Βάκχειος. They were made, not of the wood of the true Cross, but of the wood of the very fir tree upon which Pentheus was placed by Dionysus, as we read in this play. Moreover a command had come from Delphi to worship the tree as the very god himself—τὸ δένδρον ἴσα τῷ θεῷ σέβειν. From this Voigt rightly concludes that the Maenads must have worshipped the tree before felling it. There was a still more primitive and Asiatic custom in the Thraco-Phrygian home of Dionysus. There they felled a fir tree once every year, and carried it in solemn procession to its home—the god's temple. Thus in the Corinthian tale preserved by Pausanias we have record of the ancient transfer of worship and allegiance from the tree, which was the older incarnation of Dionysus Dendrites, to the graven image which eventually attached to itself all worship. Strabo, a wonderfully acute observer of the broadest aspects of Greek religion, groups together (X. p. 468) Dionysus, Apollo, Hecate (Proserpina?), the Muses, and Demeter, and ascribes to their worship τὸ ὀργιαστικὸν πᾶν καὶ τὸ βακχικὸν καὶ τὸ χορικόν, καὶ τὸ περὶ τὰς τελετὰς μυστικόν. Then he adds what is of especial interest in conjunction with Pentheus and the fir tree: δενδροφορίαι τε καὶ χορεῖαι καὶ τελεταὶ κοιναὶ τῶν θεῶν εἰσὶ τούτων. After this he seems to grow confused and to take Apollo and the Muses out of this group, where of course, viewed under certain aspects, they are not at home, though by right of descent and through ties of early ritual they are indissolubly bound to it.

The tall fir tree of Pentheus sways and yields, it crashes to the ground overborne by these flames and floods of Dionysus. Pentheus himself, when once he touches earth, is seized by the women. Flames they are no longer, and they are not floods, but of a sudden they become the many-handed earthquake which has shaken Thebes, and so they rend and hideously mangle Pentheus' limbs. His head is plucked from his body, his feet are wrenched from his legs, his thighs are forced from their sockets, and his sides are flayed and lacerated foully. Tossed into the air, his limbs deface the leafage of the trees, and his head is spiked on a spear to be carried off in triumph by his mother Agave. The earth was his father's mother, and Agave his own mother with her three Maenad bands impersonates the mysterious and wrathful powers of nether earth.

Here, perhaps, if the line is to be drawn at all, comes the division at which the *Perdition of Pentheus* ends, and the fifth part of the play begins.

Filled with the spirit of fierce Dionysus, the wild huntsman, Agave cries aloud, still madly thinking that she bears in triumph a lion's head, "Bacchus led on in the chase wisely, for wise he is. He made the Maenads dart and hunt this quarry to its lair." With mystical significance the chorus of Bacchanals from Asia make answer, "Yea, for our king is a huntsman." Dionysus, plainly, is a jealous god, visiting the iniquities of Pentheus on his mother Agave, and his power is so strong that those whom it has once possessed cannot lightly find returning sense. So it is that Agave, glorying in the slaughter of a lion—the unwitting murder by her devoted hands of her own and only son, grows impatient under her father Cadmus' vain efforts to restore her mind, and harps upon grievances against her son.

"How age turns men to crabbedness," she cries. "Would that, like his mother, my son were a lucky hunter; but heaven-fighting he is fit for, and good for nothing else." Then she turns again to Cadmus, saying, "Father! rebuke him roundly. Bring him here to me." Her mind is bent on having the head, her glorious hunting-prize, fastened trophy-fashion on the palace front. She waits for Pentheus to do it.

Wondrously true, wondrously sad is the moment when Agave ceases to be the god, and comes back to herself at last.

Cadmus has waited for a pause in his daughter's ravings, and when it comes he suddenly says, à propos of nothing, "Look up and scan the sky."[1] Surprise seems to still her frenzy, and she asks, "Why bid me look at the sky?" Disregarding this question, he asks if the sky seems altered. Now Agave finds that she sees it more clearly. "Its light is brighter, things seem to stand more firmly in the world." "Art thou restored to sense?" finally asks Cadmus, and his daughter answers—

> I know thy meaning not, and yet somehow
> Sense comes, and from my former mind I change.

Skilfully Cadmus pursues his advantage, and awakens the slumbering memories of calmer days in Agave's mind. Finally she turns questioner, and presses him with inquiries about her own mad doings. With a shriek of despair she finally recognises the head of her own son in her own hands, and sees at last that she has murdered him in Bacchic frenzy, and cries, "We're Dionysus-slain, I see it now."

[1] Those who have experience in cases of mental aberration must admire the truth to fact in this representation of a recovery of sanity under wise guidance.

Cadmus, speaking for the god,[1] makes answer, "Outrage breeds outrage, you denied his godhead."[2]

The winding-up of the *Bacchanals* in the last one hundred lines has little further bearing on the divinity of Dionysus and needs no comment here. It is sufficient to have had a glimpse in this sublime play[3] of the god as he was conceived by the Athenians, who worshipped him in the fulness of his Thracian and Old Attic godhead. From this ruder and earlier conception much that was not divine but cruel and barbarous had been separated, but enough of proto-Thracian harshness and pitilessness, as of the untamed powers of nature, still attaches to him even in the *Bacchanals*, to make it once more plain that not he, but rather Apollo his brother, must always represent the most purely Hellenic ideal of a righteous and beneficent god.

[1] In this wonderful scene Cadmus represents the god—he incarnates Dionysus the saviour from Dionysiac madness. It is significant that this most merciful aspect of Dionysus is the last one presented in the play. After this Dionysus appears as the *deus ex machina*, and formally justifies his dealings with Thebes and the house of Cadmus by appeal to Zeus. See the Appendix (II.) to the foregoing lecture for an account of this Dionysus Eleuthereus. Cf. also for a very complete presentation of the cheerful and beneficent aspects of the Bacchic godhead, the Orphic Hymn to *Dionysus Lysios*, No. 50, in Hermann's Collection (Leipzig, 1883). The invocation is:

κλῦθι, μάκαρ, Διὸς υἱ', ἐπιλήνιε Βάκχε, διμήτωρ,
σπέρμα πολύμνηστον, πολυώνυμε, λύσιε δαῖμον.

[2] V. 1298. After the speech of Cadmus immediately following, at v. 1325, Professor Tyrrell says a modern play would have ended.

[3] For the presence of the sublime in Euripides, denied by some, we have the authority of Goethe, who knew well and well appreciated the *Bacchanals*. See his translation of the great scene between Agave and Cadmus written in 1826 (vol. xxix. of Cotta's 1868 edition, pp. 34 and ff.) In his conversation with Eckermann of the 18th February 1831, he said: "Alle, die dem Euripides das Erhabene abgesprochen, waren arme Häringe, und einer solchen Erhebung nicht fähig; oder sie waren unverschämte Charlatane, die durch Anmasslichkeit in den Augen einer schwachen Welt mehr aus sich machen wollten und wirklich machten als sie waren."

APPENDIX III

SECOND BIRTH OF DIONYSUS—HIS EASTERN AFFINITIES

IN Euboea, as in other Aegean Islands such as Naxos and Icaria,[1] the legends of Dionysus became entangled with a mass of tradition which belongs to the far Eastern world. With this is closely connected a record of prehistoric changes in the tribe and family which survives in the curious story of the second and only real birth of the god from Zeus's thigh. This complex snarl of variegated tradition is perhaps most plainly recorded in the first of two fragments of a hymn to Dionysus.[2] "Some there are who say 'twas on Draconus,[3] 'twas in Icarus, some say; and some say in Naxos, son of Zeus who wert sewed in with needles, some say 'twas on the banks of Alpheius, the deep eddying river, that Semele went with thee and brought thee to birth for Zeus who rejoices in thunders; others there are, my king, who relate that at Thebes thou camest to birth, —all of them speaking falsehoods. For verily the father of men and of gods brought thee to birth where men were far away, and in secret from white-armed Hera. A certain spot there is called Nysa, a lofty mountain covered with

---

[1] Not the Attic deme Icaria.   [2] *Homeric Hymns*, xxxiv.
[3] A promontory on the Aegean island of *Icaria*, or *Nicaria*.

blossoming forests, in the uttermost parts of Phoenicia it lies close to the streams of Aegyptus." [1]

Two things are here attested, for only one of which— his second birth — we are prepared by the ordinarily accepted accounts of Dionysus. For the birth of Dionysus in the far East nothing in the Icarian legend, and little in the Theban legend, save the importance of Cadmus of Sidon,[2] and certain Thraco-Phrygian features of the tale, have prepared us. Moreover, the second birth of Dionysus as it stands in the purely Grecian legends is not only a most mysterious but a seemingly grotesque episode. The idea of taking this episode out of the more or less purely Greek story of the god, and of connecting it with his fabled birth in the far East, is certainly suggested by the Homeric fragment above quoted, but it had never occurred to me until I received some very valuable information in answer to a request which I addressed to my friend Mr. Clinton Dawkins. I had asked him to make inquiry about the habitat of the cinnamon tree, wishing, if possible, to determine by that means what sort of place Nysa, Dionysus' birth-place, was thought to be, when it was identified by Herodotus with a place where the cinnamon grew. I wished to know whether cinnamon trees grew in dark low-lying meadow-lands or on rugged mountain sides. The information so kindly provided by my friend came from no less eminent and learned a source than Sir George Birdwood, K.C.I.E. With his kind permission I reproduce it here, since it gave the right clue and has helped me towards a very fair solution of the difficulties concerned.

"Herodotus (iii. 111) says—'Some relate that it [κιννάμωμον] comes from the country in which Dionysus was brought up'; and (iii. 97)—'The Aethiopians bordering upon Egypt . . . and who dwelt about the sacred city of Nysa, have festivals in honour of Dionysus'; and again

---

[1] This fragment was found in the same Moscow MS. where the *Hymn to Demeter* first came to light. It is also known through Diodorus.
[2] Herodotus, ii. 48 and 49.

(ii. 146) he says—'But Dionysus was no sooner born than he was sewn up in the thigh of Zeus, and carried off to Nysa, above Egypt, in Aethiopia.' Now there are several Nysas. Herodotus meant Nysa in Aethiopia, that is the Troglodytic country beyond the Soudan; for the Soumali country is the cinnamon country. On the other hand the story of Dionysus, 'the Assyrian stranger,' is, *inter alia*, a myth of the development of Phoenician commerce, of which wine was everywhere throughout the Eastern Mediterranean (Levant) the staple; and the Greek myths associating the wine god with Mount Meroe[1] in Aethiopia probably arose from the fact that in the original Phoenician myth he was not a 'child of the womb' but 'of the thigh' ($\mu\eta\rho\delta\varsigma$). That is to say, these myths probably arose at the time when kinship among men had ceased to be traced through their mothers and had already begun to be traced through their fathers. Similarly the association of the wine god with 'Nysa above Egypt' was presumably due to there having been a Nysa near Meroe, and to his Greek name being $\Delta\iota\delta\nu\nu\sigma\sigma$; this Greek form of his name being probably a folk corruption of his Phoenician name, which would almost certainly end in *nisi* 'man.'

"Of course the cult of the vine and the manufacture of wine did not arise in Aethiopia but on the slopes of the Indo-Caucasus, and hence Mount Meroe [Meru] and the Indo-Caucasian Nysa have been identified as the seats of the education of the young $\Delta\iota\delta\nu\nu\sigma\sigma\varsigma$."

It is evident most abundantly from the Homeric Hymn and from Herodotus that the notion of Dionysus' second birth was often connected with *thigh mountain, Mount Meroe*, and it is equally plain that this connection might involve rejecting more or less consciously—according as the matter was more or less reasoned out—the current reports of his birth at Thebes, or Naxos, or elsewhere in Greece, or Thrace,

---

[1] Cf. Eustathius (fol. p. 310, l. 6) on *Iliad* ii. 637: ὄρος δέ τι Ἰνδικὸν Μηρὸς ἐκλήθη, Διονύσῳ ἀνακείμενον, ὅθεν Μηροτραφὴς μεμύθευταί, φασιν, ὁ Διόνυσος.

or Phrygia. Perhaps the whole story identifying Nysa—that elusive place, which never stays quite where you put it, but has a trick of moving far East if you seek it in Greece, and of lurking in Thrace if you seek it in Egypt or Arabia—with Mount Meroe and the far East may have been called into being by the epithet of Dionysus μηροτραφής, *nursling of the thigh*, which goes hand in hand with that other one εἰραφιώτης, *sewed in with needles*. Perhaps some mute inglorious Euhemerus could settle the difficulty quite comfortably by saying that the epithet should be translated *nursling of Mount Meroe*, and then he could say that the other epithet was a mistake produced by a stupid tale regarding the thigh of Zeus. This is, however, a too convenient way of meeting the difficulty, nor is that adopted by Euripides in the *Bacchanals* in the least more satisfactory, although it was made with a certain Jesuitical sincerity, and in its day probably satisfied many religious minds in difficulty about the patent incongruity of the tale. For when Euripides wrote the *Bacchanals* the best intellects of the time, and he was among them, still clung to a belief in the efficacy of a subtle analysis of words.[1]

Tiresias, a holy man, utters the apology, explanation, or—if you chose to call it so—the sophism[2] by which Euripides

[1] Cf. Mr. Tyrrell's admirable note (p. xxx. of the Introduction to his *Bacchae*): "The reason of this etymologising"—he speaks of that at v. 520 of the play—"is to be found, as Schwalbe well observes, in the deep conviction with which Greek antiquity was imbued, that between the word and the thing denoted by it there was some secret bond or hidden affinity."

[2] For an equally curious sophism which Sophocles puts into the mouth of Antigone, see his *Antigone*, 904-915. Both of these passages are alien to modern taste, and are prompted by the rhetorical training enjoyed by Sophocles and by Euripides. Goethe, *Conversation with Eckermann* of 28th March 1827, says he would give a great deal if a "tüchtiger Philologe" would prove that the passage from the *Antigone* was spurious. The chief reason why this desire of his has never (*pace* Jacob) been gratified is found in Aristotle's citation of lines 911 and 912, and in Herodotus, who has put the same rhetorical commonplaces into an episode of Persian history (iii. 119).—Since writing the above, I have read Professor Jebb's Appendix, where he rejects lines 904-920 as interpolated by Iophon or as due to the actors. I am not, however, inclined to take this view.

shames the blasphemies of Pentheus and other scoffers at the second birth of Dionysus.[1]

Him dost thou scorn, and mock to hear the tale,
How in Zeus' thigh he was sewn up. Give ear
And learn of me that this is as it should be.
When Zeus from flames and lightnings plucked him out,
And bore Olympus-ward a god unborn,
Then Hera sought to fling him down from Heaven,
Zeus foiled her plot with counter-plots divine.

---

[1] *Bacch.* 286-297. Dindorf rejects these lines because of their "dictio inepta confusa omninoque non Euripidea," which amounts to saying, Euripides did not write them because they are not by Euripides. This seems to be Wecklein's view. Professor Tyrrell makes out a better case: "It seems hardly too much to say that vv. 286-297 must be interpolated, because they explain away a story taken as literally true by the chorus, vv. 520-530, and also in the second strophe of their entrance song." Theirs, he maintains, was the orthodox version opposed by Euripides to the sceptical one given by Pentheus. "It can hardly be maintained, therefore, that Euripides would have assigned to Tiresias (who, as well as the chorus, is all along the exponent of the views of the believers) a theory explaining away the myth in which the chorus express their belief." Here Professor Tyrrell seems to me to apply essentially modern standards of faith and orthodoxy to the side of Greek religion which is most absolutely turned away from them. To me, and I suppose to many, such a divergence is far from inconceivable between Tiresias and the chorus,—both of them equally authoritative, both of them equally orthodox, if such an alien word may be used where it has no real application. It would be indeed marvellous if the god of transformations, illusions, and contradictions did not often inspire his votaries to contradict each other. No one phase of the elusive manifestations of Dionysus, and no one's account of any feature in his story, must be treated as final. It must, furthermore, be remembered that these offending verses can be taken as a very clever answering of the fool according to his folly, an attempt to mediate between the blasphemous scepticism of Pentheus and a story which he was incapable of accepting as the true believers did. Regarded in this light the *sophism* of Tiresias is a Jesuitical concession made for the salvation of Pentheus' soul as a last and desperate move. Cadmus follows with the last appeal of all, which is characterised by the same spirit. He allows that Dionysus is a man. These concessions form part of the plan which shows in Pentheus the self-deluded and self-devoted victim of wanton wickedness. "No one can ever convince every one that this passage is spurious," says Professor Jebb of *Ant.* 904-915. Change *spurious* to *genuine*, and the remark applies to *Bacch.* 286-297. Every one can, however, be convinced that both passages, *if spurious*, were the earliest of interpolations. Thus, in any case, *Bacch.* 286-297 retains its religious significance.

> A piece[1] torn off from earth's encircling ether
> He framed to be a pledge of peace[2] with Hera,
> With Dionysus' semblance cheating her.
> But men report that for a time the god
> Grew in Zeus' loin,[3] contriving all the tale,
> Exchanging terms because a changeling pledge
> To Goddess Hera was conveyed[4] by Zeus.

The temper in which all these difficulties, so far as it may be said that they are still difficulties, in the legend of Dionysus are now met is a very different one from that in which Euripides wrote the above. As for the Nysa placed in the far East, and Dionysus' eastern birth, that goes to prove the probable infusion of a strong Phoenician, Egyptian, or Arabian strain into the habit of Dionysus as known among the Aegean islands in early days. Add to this the apparently Phoenician character and derivation of his name, and the whole setting of the beautiful Homeric Hymn wherein we read how sea-robbers tried to carry off the god, and how they were punished for it. Then the outlines for understanding Dionysus as "the Assyrian Stranger," and for interpreting certain touches in his story as "a myth of the development of Phoenician commerce," are complete.

The mystery of his second birth remains to be cleared up. In the fragment of a Homeric Hymn quoted at the outset it is noticeable that the writer rejects all maternity in the case of Dionysus, puts poor Semele entirely out of court, and maintains that Zeus only, and Zeus alone, brought the babe to birth. Backofen,[5] in his *Mutterrecht*, first had a glimpse of the fact that here was a Greek parallel to the more primitively grotesque assertion made by implication in the curious practice known as the *couvade*, that a child's father is both parents in one, and that he is most

---
[1] μέρος.
[2] Literally *a hostage* (ὅμηρον), and this is part of the play upon μηρός and μέρος. [3] μηρός. [4] ὡμήρευσε.
[5] See F. A. Voigt on "Dionysus" in Roscher's *Ausführliches Lexicon*, p. 1046.

particularly and especially its mother. Curiously enough not Dionysus only, who proves it in his own person, but also Apollo, here again his ally, maintains this strange doctrine. Aeschylus, with a deep insight into the mysterious background of his own faith, makes Apollo say, in the *Eumenides*, οὐκ ἔστι μήτηρ . . . τοκεύς, . . . τίκτει δ' ὁ θρώσκων. The great principle exemplified in the second birth of Dionysus is a triumphant justification for Orestes, the slayer of Clytemnestra, and the same intense belief that the mother has no relation to her child, which is all its father's, leads certain savages to eat children born to their own wives of fathers who are slaves captured in war.[1] In fact, the story of Orestes represents a more primitive and unflinching assertion of the nullity of the mother's motherhood and the reality of the father's than does that of the second birth of Dionysus. In this last common sense has asserted itself, and the child is partially matured in Semele's womb.[2] Then when she has been destroyed before the full period for Dionysus' birth has come, the *half-formed babe*, ἡμιτέλεστον, as Nonnus calls him, is transferred to the thigh of Zeus.

And now, since the testimony of cannibal customs has been referred to, it is high time to put the whole question at issue in the hands of the anthropologists, who are alone competent. Fortunately Dr. Tylor has dealt with the matter in one of his most recent papers.[3] Indeed this very point, *i.e.* the place and the function, in the early stratification of family customs, to be assigned to the violent assertion that a child's father is his all, and his mother has no part in him, is taken by Dr. Tylor as his especial theme. Out of scattered materials strewn like glacial boulders upon the

[1] For the fact and a most instructive account of the *couvade*, see Dr. Tylor's *Early History of Mankind*, vol. i. pp. 287-297.

[2] A further proof of the reassertion of the mother's natural rights which plays its part in shaping this myth is found in the beautiful affection of Dionysus for his mother Semele. This lovely trait is omnipresent in his story. Mr. Pater has been particularly happy in his account of it.

[3] "On a Method of Investigating the Development of Institutions applied to Laws of Marriage and Descent." *Journal of the Anthropological Institute*, February 1889.

path of civilisation he builds up a wonderfully well-founded and solidly based structure of scientific demonstration. This is in fact the topic which he has chosen for a treatment so strict in method that he may well hope that its elucidation shall "overcome a certain not unkindly hesitancy on the part of men engaged in the precise operations of mathematics, physics, chemistry, biology, to admit that the problems of anthropology are amenable to scientific treatment."

A more precise description of the "quaint custom" called the *couvade* is now desirable, since it is here contended that the same explanation will account for that and for Apollo's vindication of Orestes as guiltless though he had slain his mother, together with the episode of Dionysus' second and only real birth from the thigh of Zeus his father. In the *couvade*, to quote from Dr. Tylor,[1] "the father, on the birth of his child, makes a ceremonial pretence of being the mother, being nursed and taken care of, and performing other rites such as fasting and abstaining from certain kinds of food or occupation, lest the new-born should suffer thereby. This custom is known in the four quarters of the globe. How sincerely it is still accepted appears in a story of Mr. Im Thurm, who on a forest journey in British Guiana noticed that one of his Indians refused to help to haul the canoes, and on inquiry found that the man's objection was that a child must have been born to him at home about this time, and he must not exert himself so as to hurt the infant. In the Mediterranean district it is not only mentioned by ancient writers, but in Spain and France, in or near the Basque country, it went on into modern times; Zamacola in 1818 mentions, as but a little time ago, that the mother used to get up and the father take the child to bed. Knowing the tenacity of these customs, I should not be surprised if traces of *couvade* might be found in that district still."

The place of this custom in the early history of man-

[1] P. 254 in the journal above quoted.

kind hangs together with the more or less well-established fact that there were three stages of successive development in family and tribe organisation. In the first and earliest of these, sometimes called the *matriarchal* stage, descent and inheritance had only to do with the mother.[1] Here then was the absolute contradiction of Apollo's dictum in the *Eumenides* of Aeschylus. Here the child is as solely and exclusively his mother's as afterwards was maintained to be solely his father's. Between these two strata there was an intermediate stage wherein both customs struggled for predominance.[2] Now the most startling confirmation of this order for the development of early customs is given by Dr. Tylor's discovery—which he makes doubly impressive by a sort of geological diagram— that the *couvade* is unknown in the lower or *matriarchal* stratum, begins after the middle of the transitional stratum, and spends itself early in the upper or *patriarchal* stratum. Thus the *couvade* was a visible symbol, a practice by the adoption of which the father's authority was finally and definitely asserted. As soon as this victory was won the custom by which it gained the day became a mere curiosity, a survival.

The curious thing is that the Greek power to transmute all things and to beautify whatever came into the Greek consciousness should have conquered even the stubborn material afforded by this graceless struggle for mastery within the primitive human family, and should have associated its dimmed and mysterious record with those masterpieces of the high poetic genius of man, the *Oresteia* of Aeschylus, and the *Bacchanals* of Euripides.

---

[1] See in the seventh annual report of the trustees of the Peabody Museum, Cambridge, Mass. (1884), Mr. Lucien Carr's able paper on "The Social and Political Position of Woman among the Huron-Iroquois Tribes." These tribes and many of those of the Pueblos in Arizona are still at the *matriarchal* stage.

[2] It is perhaps fanciful to suggest that the rival pretensions of Clytemnestra and Agamemnon to dispose of Iphigenia are a record of this middle stage.

Indeed I cannot more suitably bring to an end these notes upon a survival in Greek tragedies themselves of primeval customs than by referring to a thoughtful though a brief account recently given [1] of the manner in which the Greeks performed their tragedies as a similar survival—I mean their use of masks in acting. "No one of the early tragedians . . . did in fact invent masks, but . . . these existed as survivals of the paraphernalia of the Greek rites from remote and uncivilised times. . . . Indeed the use of masks is widespread among uncivilised peoples; it begins apparently with a dim notion of terrifying or deceiving demons, and soon becomes a formula of worship. It was from this state that the custom appears to have entered the Greek drama. . . . While the mask is common among nearly all savage races, we may find it surviving in the dramatic performances of the Chinese and Japanese." [2] Interesting though the Chinese and Japanese drama is, and not devoid of the genuine power that belongs to an art which has its definite traditions, the difference between its appointments—not to speak of essentials—and those of the Greek stage is very great, and on the score of beauty of course is all in favour of the Greeks. Starting apparently from the same or practically the same barbaric ritual which is the background of Chinese and Japanese theatrical performances, the Greeks were guided to beauty by an instinct which was all their own, and which has made them the sponsors of all that is best in dramatic literature. As Mr. Perry has admirably said, behind the perfected Greek drama "was a past that had triumphed successfully over the barbarism which left its rites, so to speak, as the raw material to be worked by art and enthusiasm into a thousand charming forms. The savage survivals were, like the physical geography of the land, tamed, smoothed, cultivated, made inhabitable, not destroyed." [3] In the realm

---

[1] *A History of Greek Literature*, by T. S. Perry: New York, Henry Holt and Co., 1890.
[2] *Ibid.* pp. 229, 230.   [3] *Ibid.* p. 224.

of the drama, as in all other regions of literature and art which the Greeks knew, they and they alone possessed the art and the enthusiasm which could deal with stubborn and primitive materials—the only ones at hand. Accordingly each newly discovered trace in Hellenic work of prehistoric man and his ugly ways is but a new occasion for marvelling at the transcendent genius of Hellas.

V

THE GODS AT ELEUSIS

IN the previous chapter it has been assumed, according to abundant testimony,[1] that Dionysus in some shape or other very early associated himself at Eleusis with the

---

[1] The presence, as an object of early Eleusinian worship, of a mystical δαίμων is denied by none. But because there is no mention of Dionysus-Iacchos in the Homeric *Hymn to Demeter*, and because the Zagreus legend, which finally summed up the nature of the specifically Eleusinian Dionysus, emanated from Onomacritus and the new Orphic sect at Athens, some maintain that Dionysus was an utter stranger to the Eleusinian cult until the days of Pisistratus. This interpretation of the facts, which are unfortunately too few to speak very clearly for themselves, fails to correlate with the mystical δαίμων of early Eleusis, the Zagreus-Dionysus who, in the later Mysteries under the surname of Iacchos, yearly visited Demeter and Persephone, and who was variously represented as a brother and a son of Persephone. The traditional connection between Thrace and the mythical Eumolpus, whose very name has a touch of the music of Apollo and Dionysus in it, and the theory among late Greeks that Eumolpus had to do with the worship of Iacchos at Eleusis, lead towards the conclusion that, after all, the early mystical δαίμων is a proto-Thracian Dionysus under some sort of Eleusinian disguise—the old netherworld god of Thrace, brought by that early influence from the north, represented by the name Eumolpus to complete the group of divinities worshipped at Eleusis. The characteristically Eleusinian epithets of Pluto and Eubouleus suit well this primitive divinity when once he is far from Thrace and under the softening influences of Demeter. As for the absence of any mention of Dionysus-Iacchos in the *Hymn to Demeter*, it must be remembered that neither is the great Eleusinian hero Triptolemus there mentioned, except among others represented as of equal importance with him in the establishment of the Eleusinian rites. In spite of this circum-

two goddesses of the Mysteries. So far as chronology applies, it is evident that this first of his comings to Eleusis was thought of as having taken place not long after the day of Demeter's arrival at Eleusis and of Dionysus' visit to Icarius. We may safely take it for granted, however, that his status in those early days was far inferior to that to which he subsequently attained through the reforms and innovations made first by Epimenides and Solon,[1] and then by Pisistratus and Onomacritus, whereby he was enabled to participate in Eleusinian observances from the vantage-ground of an independently organised Athenian ritual in his honour. After Epimenides had suitably organised the Lesser Mysteries at the Athenian Eleusinion, the god could in due time become the leader of the *mystae* in their yearly procession to Eleusis, and under the name of Iacchos, which perhaps had not attached to him in his early days at Eleusis, when he was merely a πάρεδρος—an associate divinity, was there welcomed as the coequal of the two great goddesses.

In a sense therefore the coming of Dionysus, as an independently recognised divinity, to take his share in the worship of those who thronged to the Greater Mysteries, was prepared by Epimenides and brought to pass by Pisistratus and Onomacritus; and the first move

stance testimony from other sources assigns a prominent place to Triptolemus in the local cult. Indeed we may consider the presence of a representative of Dionysus in the early legend a thing assured, since there was anciently more than one version of the story of the *Hymn to Demeter* (see Pausanias, I. xxxviii. 3, where Pamphos is followed as to the number and names of the daughters of Celeus), and since the Demophoon incident, the only point where Dionysus-Iacchos-Triptolemus could be concerned, plainly does not hang together with its surroundings. See note 1, p. 194.

[1] I thus couple Solon with Epimenides, because Plutarch (as quoted note 1, p. 123) says that the latter prepared the way for Solon's legislation, and also because one of Solon's laws distinctly applied to the concerns of the mysteries set in order by Epimenides. Andocid. *de Mysteriis*, 110-112.

was brought about from Athens. But had not earlier influences already made some place for the new-comer at Eleusis, the great Eleusinian alliance of three coequal divinities would not so easily have come to pass. It is an undoubted fact that the popular legends and unauthorised observances at Eleusis began to recognise the Thracian god at some earlier time while he still bore plain marks of being king of the underworld. This view is in agreement with the traditions of Eumolpus and the Eumolpidae, while any other makes it difficult to understand why Dionysus attached himself in just the way he did [1] to a group of gods where Hades played a part not unimportant, though to us obscure. The coming of Dionysus to Eleusis evidently enhanced the importance of Hades, and took away something [2] from Demeter's overpowering predominance. But by this limitation she apparently gained in effectiveness what she lost in exclusiveness.

[1] See F. A. Voigt (art. "Dionysus" in Roscher's *Lexicon*), where various epithets of Hades are shown to belong to Dionysus, particularly that of Εὔβουλευς. The *name* Eubouleus is especially connected with the Hades legend at Eleusis, both in the Athenian and the Argive tale. There was undoubtedly a more or less definite distinction drawn, in the Eleusinian and cognate worships, between two male divinities worshipped in conjunction with Persephone, one of which may have been more especially identified with Dionysus than the other; but it is more than likely that they represented the two types of Dionysus-Dendrites and Dionysus-Hades. The chief authority for this distinction is hardly earlier than the fourth century B.C. It is an inscription found on a tablet in a tomb near the ancient Sybaris. The deceased, one of the καθαροί, *i.e.* initiate, writes: "Ἔρχομαι ἐκ καθαρῶν, καθαρὰ χθονίων βασίλεια Εὐκλῆς, Εὐβουλεύς τε . . . See Pausanias, I. xiv. 1-4, and Miss Harrison (*Mythology and Monuments of Athens*, pp. 95-101). See also Chr. Scherer (art. "Hades" in Roscher, pp. 1783 and ff.), where the euphemistic epithets of the god are discussed, and the softening of the sterner aspects of Hades through contact with the cult of Persephone and Demeter is noted.

[2] She lost a touch of vindictiveness, which in the legend at Hermione led her to burn Colontas in his house (Pausanias, II. xxxv. 4), and a gloom which gave her the surname Erinys at Thelpusa (Pausanias, VIII. xxv. 4).

Like the worship of Apollo at Delphi, that of Eleusinian Demeter did, however, owe its increasing importance to a hospitality, which welcomed new-coming divinities with no thought of curtailing their traditional powers. Dionysus came to Eleusis and took his place there by the side of Hades,[1] so that Heraclitus in one of his dark words declares this identification to be a proof that life and death are one.[2] The original Thracian conception of Dionysus, based as it was upon the belief that death was life, was in this manner reasserted.

Besides the bond of kingship in the netherworld, Hades and Dionysus were affiliated by their relation to the treasures concealed in the bowels of earth. Control over these came by right—so ancient piety argued—to the lord of the world below. Hence Hades and Pluto,[3] the god of riches, were

---

[1] See Voigt (art. "Dionysus" in Roscher's *Lexicon*, p. 1047) on Dionysus' bringing of Semele from Hades to Olympus, which he compares to the Assumption of the Virgin Mary. Certainly Pindar's tone (in the third Pythian) about Semele justifies some such parallel. Enthusiastic worshippers of Dionysus attributed to him power over the life to come, and welcomed his use of it to lead Semele into the assemblage of gods on Olympus.

[2] Heraclitus, quoted by Clement of Alexandria, *Protreptica*, p. 30: ὡυτὸς δὲ 'Αΐδης καὶ Διόνυσος ὅτέῳ μαίνονται καὶ ληνάζουσιν. (Cf. Ritter and Preller, *Hist. Phil.* I. 39 a, who say, after quoting, as of Heraclitus, the celebrated φάος Ζηνὶ σκότος 'Αΐδῃ, φάος 'Αΐδῃ σκότος Ζηνί· φοιτᾷ καὶ μετακινέεται κεῖνα ὧδε καὶ τάδε κεῖσε, πάσην ὥρην διαπρησσόμενα κεῖνά τε τὰ τῶνδε, τάδε δ' αὖ τὰ κείνων, "'Αΐδης, quem eundem deum esse cum Libero Patre dicebat [*scil.* Heraclitus], significat vim humidam tenebricosam telluris, Iupiter lucidam et ignitam coeli.") See also Scherer (as above) on a relief found at Locri.

[3] It might be hazarded as a conjecture that the coming of Dionysus to Eleusis brought with it for Hades the surname Pluto. Certainly the epithet Πλούτων first appears for Hades in the Attic poets of the fifth century. Aeschylus, *Prom.* 806; Soph. *Antig.* 1200; Euripid. *Alcestis*, 360, *Herc. Fur.* 808; Aristoph. *Plut.* 727. See also at the beginning of the eighth book of Plato's *Laws* a passage where Pluto is named alone for all the Chthonian gods. Preller, commenting on this fact, attributes the epithet Pluto to the Eleusinian worship. Chr. Scherer (art. "Hades" in Roscher, p. 1786) inclines to agree with Preller as to the epithet Plouto, but objects that the other euphemistic names must have come from tradi-

one, and hence Dionysus, to the extent that he was originally a netherworld god, was in his own person called Father of Gold, and to him were dedicated the gold-bearing floods of Phrygian Pactolus. Demeter, Persephone, Aidoneus-Pluto, Iacchos-Dionysus, and Rhea-Cybele—these, the five divinities of Eleusinian worship, become three before the eyes, as it were, of their worshippers. Iacchos-Dionysus and Aidoneus-Pluto mysteriously melt into one, while Rhea-Cybele and Demeter are similarly fused. This would leave just three—one Demeter-Rhea-Cybele gave the feminine element. The second, Hades-Iacchos-Dionysus, represents the male element, and finally the third is Persephone. It has been abundantly shown how Demeter and Persephone were regarded as one, being so filled with mutual love that all barriers between them melted away. A similar identification of Dionysus and Persephone is shadowed forth by legends of their marriage. Hence what we may call the first of the Eleusinian mysteries,[1] since it deals with the hidden nature of all the gods at Eleusis, is not without a modern parallel. It presented itself to the pious mind in terms and with difficulties, most of which recur in one statement or another of the mystery of the Holy Trinity. Eight names, four of goddesses and four of gods, came finally to stand for two persons in whom was presented one great fact—the course of nature. Demeter was Persephone; both and each were Rhea, who was Cybele. Aidoneus

---

tions preserved among the people. Suppose that Dionysus brought this golden contribution, and that the other mild epithet of Eubouleus came from Greek, and especially Eleusinian, tradition, then the softening influence which gathered these kindly qualities around forbidding Hades belongs still to Eleusis.

[1] I am intentionally using the word Mystery in the modern sense, because it is noticeable that a religious conception very nearly approaching it is characteristic of the Orphic writings, and was familiar to Euripides.

was Pluto; while both and each were Dionysus, who was Iacchos, and also, in some sense, Triptolemus.

The two divine persons around whom these abundant names and attributes gathered at Eleusis were in the highest sense not two but one. They were one as concave and convex are one; they represented the active and the passive aspects of the great and universal all. Nor is it fanciful to add that they represented two typically Greek ways[1] of understanding the world and all that is therein; the one way was that of Demeter and Xenophanes, the other way was that of Heraclitus and Dionysus.

Dionysus all flash, all heat, all motion flowing and growing, living and dying, dancing and flying,[2] was a fit incarnation of the philosophy of those whom Plato laughingly calls the "Streamers," men who with Heraclitus, the dark philosopher, talked of the course of nature as being that of a swift and shifting stream or a fitfully burning conflagration.

[1] For a somewhat fuller account of these, see sections 3-7 of my Introduction—based upon Dr. Crons's—to Plato's *Apology*: Ginn and Heath, 1886.

[2] See Pausanias, III. xix. 6, for Dionysus worshipped at Amyclae as ψίλαξ, or winged, and cf. E. Thraemer (art. "D. in der Kunst," Roscher, p. 1152). Dr. Braun (*Kunstvorstellungen des geflügelten Dionysos*, Munich, 1839) first called especial attention to this. Speaking of the winged Dionysus at Amyclae, Pausanias makes a somewhat forcible-feeble remark, to the effect that the god of wine may well have wings, since under wine's influence men flutter, and are uplifted as by wings. There is a merry French song in praise of Dionysus,—"Vive Denis notre bon père!" is the gist of it; but the last verse gives to *Dionysus Liber* both wings and song, as follows:

"Ce Liber père des repas
Qu'on adore au siècle où nous sommes,
En trépassant ne mourut pas
Ainsi qu'on voit mourir les hommes ;
Un assoupissement vineux
Poussa son esprit lumineux
Dans un doux repos de vingt heures,
Après quoi ce dieu s'envola
Dans les eternelles demeures
Chantant ut ré mi fa sol la."

Certainly the poetic genius of man never conceived any personality better suited than that of Dionysus to represent the ever-moving stream, the ever-living and ever-dying fire of Heraclitus. Those minds whom this doctrine confused and alarmed could take the very different view of nature and divinity presented by Xenophanes; and Demeter's personality gives most admirably the aspect of divinity which they would chiefly worship. Demeter is peace bought with the price of sorrow, love mingled with sadness; hers is a constant soul, unswerving and unselfish in her boundless love for sweet Persephone. Let Demeter then stand for the new aspect of divinity proclaimed and justified by Xenophanes.

Tired of the tales that the charming Homer told, shocked and pained at the wickedness of gods who were human at heart and only superficially divine—magnified men freed from death and age but not from sin—Xenophanes declared that god was one, even so Demeter and Persephone were one; he said that god was infinite, even so was the love and longing of Demeter for Persephone. Indeed it has been often remarked that a new spirit came into Greek religion and life with the new worship of non-Homeric divinities at Eleusis; and this new spirit was just what Xenophanes longed for.

In the unknown, or at most half-known, spirit of the Eleusinian mysteries, one virtue reigned with living power, which some think has in our days vanished from all Christendom. This virtue is much lauded by the pious Plutarch; it is the virtue of silence. Indeed all the rites of Eleusis would have been in vain if it were possible to describe minutely the Eleusinian ritual after the confident fashion of the author of *The Divine Legation of Moses*.[1]

[1] Warburton, Bishop of Gloucester.

Worshippers were bound by every fear, and lured by every hope, touching their fate after death[1] to reveal no word of what was said, and to withhold the least hint of what was done in the Eleusinian Holy of Holies. What is

[1] The scholiast on line 158 of the *Frogs* of Aristophanes says: "The opinion prevailed at Athens that whoever had been taught the Mysteries would, when he came to die, be deemed worthy of divine glory. Hence all were eager for initiation." This would sometimes take place when a man was near his death. See Aristoph. *Peace*, v. 374 f., where *Trygaeus*, sure of approaching death, tries to borrow three drachmas to buy a bit of a porker (for an offering to the gods below), and says, "You know I've got to be initiated or ere I die." A curious ray of light is thrown upon the whole question of the mysteries, and the comfort which they gave by assuring to the initiated especial privileges in the life beyond, by four Orphic fragments found in Southern Italy (three at Sybaris and one at Petelia). The date of the tombs wherein they were found on thin plates of gold is the third century B.C.; but Comparetti, in his account of them (*Journal of Hellenic Studies*, vol. iii. p. 112), says the Orphic fragments go back to the time of Euripides, and he refers to the well-known passage in Plato's *Republic* about the *Orpheotelestae* (ii. 364 B). In the preceding chapter I have spoken of the first Orphic doctrines promulgated by Onomacritus at Athens; Mr. Cecil Smith, "Orphic Myths on Attic Vases" (*Journal of Hellenic Studies*, vol. xi. p. 346), gives the following summary of doctrine (derived from the three inscriptions in question) from later Orphic poems, and from a vase-painting of great and almost unique interest that goes back to a date earlier than 480 B.C.:—

"In the cosmogony of the Orphic teaching there are two great cosmic elements—Zeus, the omnipotent all in all, and his daughter Kore, who combines in her personality the characteristic features of Persephone, Artemis, and Hekate; from the union of Zeus in serpent form with Kore, Zagreus is born, and to him, essentially in his character of χθόνιος, the kingdom is given of this world. Zagreus is the allegory of the life and death and resurrection of Nature. In the generally accepted version, he is brought up as the Zeus-child, and from fear of Hera, is sent on earth to be warded by the Kouretes. Hera sends the Titans, who surprise Zagreus at play, tear him in pieces, and eat him all except the heart. Zeus destroys the Titans with his thunderbolts, and out of their ashes the human race is born. Since the Titans had swallowed Zagreus, a spark of the divine element forever permeates the human system. The heart is carried by Athene to Zeus, who either gives it to Semele in a potion or swallows it himself, and thus is born another Zagreus, the 'younger Dionysus,' ὁ νέος Διόνυσος." For the initiated death is a piece of good luck, and on one of the Sybaris tablets the departed soul exults, saying to the gods: καὶ γὰρ ἐγὼν ὑμῶν γένος ὄλβον εὔχομαι εἶναι. Having atoned for the sin of the Titans by mystic ceremonies, the initiated claim the heritage of Zagreus, which is life everlasting. He is in their members, and through his death their immortality has been won.

sometimes, with a too ineffable self-complacency, called the "modern mind," might learn a lesson from the novices at Eleusis; and it is perhaps good for us all to ponder over this ancient recognition of the unutterableness of the unutterable. This ground of holy reserve, not always respected to-day, was kept intact both in Greece and at Rome by the Mysteries.

If silence is the chief lesson and culminating grace[1] derived from Eleusis, it may be asked why there is more to say? But even the secret of those Mysteries has been in a certain fashion laid open, and their noble spirit breathes from many masterpieces of the Greek genius. Such was the speaking power of Greek art, that the sculptors and the poets have almost revealed the secret in the beauty of their work. Certain statues of Eleusinian divinities bear the impress of the Mysteries, as do indeed the eyes of many a saint pictured by Christian art. Even in Botticelli's awkward and mysterious grace we read this same unnamed and unnameable constraint and mystery.

The first and most delicate manifestation of this shows in the peaceful and enigmatical beauties of Demeter and Persephone. Give to this constraining power something of manly force, and it constrains no longer to repose. The universe whirls onward then in Dionysus' wake. The trees are drawn to follow Orpheus and his Thracian lyre. With Dionysus all nature floods forward and onward to a

[1] For fear of having been misled into a one-sided statement, I give the following graphic summary of the spirit in which the faithful were invited to the Mysteries, which I abbreviate from Mannhardt's Demeter essay: "Come, whosoever is clean of all pollution, and whose soul hath not consciousness of sin. Come, whosoever hath lived a life of righteousness and justice. Come, all ye who are pure of hand and of heart, and whose speech can be understood." Almost every Athenian sought out the celebration, and from time to time communed with the gods of Eleusis for the ease of his soul.

goal, which is neither named nor known, and yet is the first cause of an irresistible impulse. The intensity of calm which is sometimes to be seen in Demeter's grief, and sometimes even gives to her joy a sober hue, allies itself with one aspect of the annually recurring tragedy of life decaying, and of growth on earth. Forsaken in her grief she is the spirit of loneliness, the genius of home-sickness; and even in her appeasement she still seems alone. Persephone, her joy, is with her truly, but she brings to her mother that nameless tremor, half of peace and half of unutterable oppression, which comes to a lingerer musing in the fields of spring.

The more boisterous joy of Dionysus is this tremor raised to a higher power, and contains its oppression and its gladness both intensified. The promise written, half in sadness, first upon the hesitating face of spring comes to its uttermost fulfilment in an ecstasy of joy which is near to downright madness and fraught with death. The crescendo of growth and vigour drives away and utterly dispels the outward show of mystery, because the mystery itself lies hidden. It is the god himself who enters in and fills his worshippers and all the world with his constraining power. He is in all things, and he leads all things on the way of his choice. From flash to flash, from flame to flame, the scale of bright and fluid being is run through with the whirl, as it were, of a devouring fire that darts across fields of yellow grain. Demeter is no longer there, nor yet are we who have been swept along by Dionysus in his fluid train. Yet this is not the last word of the mysterious power that shapes the varying course of nature. The learned and truly pious Strabo somewhere says that it was but right for the Eleusinian worshippers to guard most jealously a mystical secret. How otherwise could their ritual have shown forth the nature of the gods at Eleusis? Their secret always eluding inquiry was like their godhead for ever eluding the grasp of our senses,[1] for ever streaming on beyond reach of our straining eyes. The Streaming philosopher, Heraclitus, declared solemnly that you could not twice step into the same river, and Strabo would have us apply this to divinity, and mark how the same Dionysus is never met with twice. This may be called, and was sometimes meant as, a Pantheistic doctrine; but sometimes it was of higher import, and Dionysus was thought of as a spirit moving in all things, whose worshippers must not attach themselves to any one manifestation of him, but must worship him in spirit and in truth.

And yet this fast and furious race from shape to shape was thought of only as a final paroxysm, like the fortissimo that comes near the end of a musical composition. Then nature reaches fulness, fruits are shining where lately were the buds of spring, while the dancing Maenads whirl across the face of the earth, moving in Bacchic revelry their gleaming feet, tossing their necks into the dewy air. This is the Maenads' hour of triumphant freedom. Now let them sing while they may the victorious refrain in Euripidean numbers. "What is the wisdom, what among mortals the boon of heaven that is fairer than waving the hand victorious over a fallen foe? What is glorious, that is always dear."[2]

Dearly bought indeed is this Bacchanalian victory, for there is a mystery revealed in sadness when the ecstasy

---

[1] Strabo, X. iii. 9 (467): ἥ τε κρύψις ἡ μυστικὴ τῶν ἱερῶν σεμνοποιεῖ τὸ θεῖον, μιμουμένη τὴν φύσιν αὐτοῦ φεύγουσαν ἡμῶν τὴν αἴσθησιν.
[2] Euripides, *Bacchanals*, 877-881, and 897-901.

of joy is past. A frenzied impulse overtakes the revelling Maenads, and lo! their nearest and their dearest lies before them hideously slain. In overpowering their foeman they have unspeakably harmed their own. The huntsman from whom they thought to escape was none other than their own Dionysus, the pitiless huntsman Zagreus. They thought to be swift and go from him free when he had really entered in and possessed them utterly. Winter is at hand, there are no buds, no blossoms, no fruits, and no joys. The sad awakening comes—Dionysus is dead. Is he not buried within the temple of Apollo at Delphi? And now the worshipper is left alone! And yet not quite alone, for he has for his comrade in grief Demeter, the all-welcoming—Demeter, in her lonely trial longing and grieving, seeking and finding not—Demeter whose only comfort is in doing deeds of sweet and unpremeditated love.[1]

Let us now, while we still are under the spell of Demeter's sorrowing godhead,[2] enter into the holy place at Eleusis and consider reverently its broken stones and buried walls. Here is a place consecrated by eight hundred years of pious usage and spoiled by centuries of neglect. At last

[1] The way in which allegiance to the spirit of the Mysteries begins with Persephone and Demeter, transfers itself for a climax to Iacchos, and then dies down to a calmer loyalty again, chiefly to Demeter and the high standard of right living associated with her, is best seen in the passage of the *Frogs* of Aristophanes summarised at the end of this chapter. See vv. 372-459.

[2] This phase of Demeter is characteristic when her divinity stands in contrast to that of Dionysus. Dionysus also when taken alone has his sad and subdued aspects. For both these divinities alone were conceived of as covering the whole ground more completely but not less really occupied when they each supplemented the other, and both made room for Persephone. Demeter as the productive Earth (Eur. *Bacch.* 274-276) was conceived of as going through in her own person all the stages and phases of vegetation, and of the husbandry by which earth was cultivated. See Lenormant, art. "Cérès" in Daremberg and Saglio.

a time for the re-awakening of glorious pagan memories has come at Eleusis, since the present condition of its site is the result of much careful excavation.

From Athens to Eleusis is not far, though it is more than a Sabbath day's journey. In more accurate measurement the distance to Eleusis is slightly over twelve miles. The first excavations at Eleusis were made early in this century by the London Dilettanti Society.[1] From these labours came a good account of the site and of the two ceremonial gates or Propylaea—both of the latter belonging to the days of Roman supremacy at Eleusis. Of these first excavations an account is given in the *Unedited Antiquities of Attica*, published in 1817. The Dilettanti Society could not cause the modern village of Levsina to be removed from the site most important for excavation, and therefore obtained little or no knowledge of the Hall of Initiation. This forced omission, and nearly all others, have been made up for by Greek excavations which were ended only in 1887. At the request of the Greek Archaeological Society, Dr. Dörpfeld made out in 1887 the full ground-plan of all buildings whose foundations were left on the site when the village houses had been removed. The plan published in 1888 will never receive any important modifications, though details may still be forthcoming; and I desire to give my warmest thanks to my friend Dr. Dörpfeld for allowing me to publish it here. The enthusiasm and ability of Dr. Philios, the commissioner

---

[1] This chapter is so especially concerned with Eleusis rather than with the approach to it from Athens that François Lenormant's admirable work in excavation and publication has no great prominence in my presentation of Eleusinian religious antiquities. His work, however, and his account of the Sacred Way, demand the fullest recognition, and his *Grande Grèce* also contains much invaluable information about Dionysus in Greater Greece. From his articles in Daremberg and Saglio's *Dictionary* I have constantly derived enlightenment.

for years in charge of the Eleusinian excavations, have abundantly justified the confidence reposed in him by the Greek Archaeological Society, and earn the gratitude of all students, who may now see in Dr. Dörpfeld's plan a record of the results due to Dr. Philios' learning, energy, and ability.

Eleusis lies upon and around a group of rocks which separate the south-eastward breadths of the Thriasian plain from the smaller Rarian plain, which is north-west of it. Towards the south and east spreads the beautiful Bay of Eleusis, and beyond rise the purple heights of Acamas[1] on Salamis—Salamis looming up as if to shut out all view of the Gulf of Aegina and distant Cyllene. The best description of Eleusis is perhaps that given in the *Unedited Antiquities of Attica*, as follows:

"The south-eastern extremity of a low rocky hill about 300 yards from the sea was chosen by the Eleusinians for their citadel—their acropolis. The declivity of this hill facing the south-east being formed into an artificial terrace, and the rock having been cut away from the front to the rear, a level area was obtained for the sacred enclosure of the mystic temple. This magnificent structure, built by Pericles, stood a bold and prominent feature in a picture whose background was formed by the walls and towers of the impending acropolis. In front the villas and gardens of the Eleusinians complete the picture, spreading themselves around the foot of the rock and along the borders of the Bay of Salamis—called also the Bay of Eleusis, since Eleusis is on its northern shore—while the sea-girt heights of Salamis lock it in towards the south. As accessories in

---

[1] For the authority upon which I use this name for the Salaminian mountains, see Appendix VIII. end, on "The river Bocarus and John Meursius," after chap. vii. below.

the composition of this grand design, the lofty gates or Propylaea, with the temple of Artemis Propylaea, were worthy of admiration."

Such is the picture of ancient Eleusis skilfully drawn in 1814. In it we see, vaguely indeed but really, something of the later magnificence at Eleusis. This was the Eleusis of Roman days, for the great Propylaea—not to speak of the upper gateway or Lesser Propylaea of Appius Claudius Pulcher[1]—were built in Roman days and not visible to the eyes of Ictinus. This was the Eleusis which came to destruction in the year of our Lord 396 at the hands of monks who followed in the wake of Alaric and his Ostrogoths. Eunapius calls these worse than Ostrogoths "the black-robed crew," and their iconoclasm, no doubt, merited his most "vinegar epithets"; but still even these zealots did less harm probably than the poverty and sloth caused by the intolerable and continuous oppression weighing heavily upon generations who afterwards lived near and on the site. Various churches and a whole village got themselves built within the boundaries of the holy precinct by a process utterly destructive of all manner of architectural remains, and particularly of the precious statues left in fragments, but still no doubt left by those Ostrogothic monks who would hardly have been able to demolish everything of the kind. Heads, arms, and

[1] Cicero to Atticus (vi. 1), "Unum etiam velim cogites. Audio Appium προπύλαιον Eleusine facere. Num inepti fuerimus, si nos quoque Academiae fecerimus? Puto, inquies. Ergo id ipsum scribes ad me. Equidem valde ipsas Athenas amo. Volo esse aliquod monumentum. Odi falsas inscriptiones statuarum alienarum. Sed ut tibi placebit." Very interesting remains of this ceremonial gate of Appius still lie upon its site. A certain originality is shown in its composite capitals and in the decorative use of wheaten ears and the vaguely known instruments of the mysteries upon its entablatures. For photographs of these remains see Appendix XI. i. 43, 44.

beautiful draperies fashioned delicately in marble seemed to the clumsy and half-barbarised Albanian builders of Levsina to exist for nothing else than the fire whose burning gave them lime for building their unsightly huts. After these devastations no hope could be entertained that any full knowledge of the temples and statues of the gods at Eleusis should ever be rescued from its ruins. We are forced in fact to make many a conjecture before the results of the most patient and painstaking excavations will yield any clear notion of that unique structure the Eleusinian Telesterion or Hall of Initiation. This was called in the description quoted above the Mystic Temple, but is more accurately designated by Aristophanes as the " Home that welcomed the Mystae," Strabo's phrase for it being ὁ μυστικὸς σηκός, *the holy enclosure of the Mystae.*[1] It was in fact not as other Greek temples were, for, as Strabo directly implies, it was not the dwelling-place of any god, and contained therefore no holy image. It is unique because on no other Greek site has there been found a meeting-house built, as this one was, for the celebration of a definite ritual. The Thracian worship of one of the Eleusinian gods, Dionysus, seems to have required meeting places or houses of some kind, but there is only the vaguest record of them. The truth therefore is that the Eleusinian Hall of Initiation is the only known *church* of antiquity, if by church we mean not so much the house of the deity as the meeting-house for worshippers, a place where they may congregate for worship.

This Hall of Initiation, if we would know it as it stood

[1] He plainly distinguishes it from the temple of Demeter. See IX. i. 12 (395) Εἴτ' Ἐλευσὶς πόλις, ἐν ᾖ τὸ τῆς Δήμητρος ἱερὸν τῆς Ἐλευσινίας καὶ ὁ μυστικὸς σηκός, ὃν κατεσκεύασεν Ἰκτῖνος ὄχλον θεάτρου δέξασθαι δυνάμενον.

in the days of Athenian greatness and power, must be shorn of the Roman façade and the porch of Philo. These must disappear with the walls that go with the lower or most northern Propylaea, a ceremonial gate built in the Emperor Hadrian's day.[1]

Suppose, then, Hadrian's grand gate of entrance is removed; take away also the outer wall (indicated by salmon colour on the large map) that this gate pierced. Then you have thrown open a considerable space between a sacred building—the temple of Artemis Propylaea (Artemis *at the gate*)—and an older gateway piercing an older outside wall. This is the gateway, already talked of above, built by Appius Claudius Pulcher. The report of it moved Cicero to propose that he and his rich friend Atticus[2] should build something of the kind for the Academy. Supposing ourselves in Eleusis before Appius Claudius and his workmen, then in place of his gate we should have found something of wholly Greek antiquity—something to show forth the earlier history of the shrine and sanctuary. Here anciently was a strong gate which, with the wall that it pierced, could be defended against all enemies of the gods and of Eleusis.[3] Having passed through this gate and hastened to the Hall of the Initiated, we might, supposing our visit fell

[1] It was the irony of fate which afforded money and to spare in Hadrian's time for completing at Eleusis an imitation of the masterpiece of Mnesicles, itself left unfinished for the lack of moneys in the coffers of imperial Athens.

[2] The passage at the end of the first letter in the sixth book of their correspondence is given above, p. 188, note 1. Atticus apparently did not encourage Cicero, perhaps because he reflected that Cicero would have contributed more beautiful discourse than hard cash to any joint undertaking of the kind.

[3] That there was fortification in the early days cannot be doubted, in view of recorded attacks. Certain remains of old-time masonry, together with the fixed position of the Sacred Way, make it practically sure that here was a fortified gate.

after 310 B.C., find an important feature which was not known to the worshippers in the days of the Peloponnesian war—I mean the porch of Philo, built at the expense of Demetrius the Phalerean in 310 B.C. Ictinus must have planned either this porch or something like it, but it certainly was not built in his day. And finally, if we returned to the site four centuries or so later, we should discover an enlargement and remodelling of the Hall as built by Ictinus. The site as it existed before 310 B.C. was enclosed by a defensible wall, and approached by a fortified gate on the site of the ornate and unfortified Propylaea of Appius. The Telesterion or meeting-house consisted of two narrow rooms, had no front porch, and was not quite so large as Roman reconstruction subsequently made it.

It is very easy to forget the little or nothing known about certain small temples and treasure-houses of uncertain date. These grouped themselves about the great meeting-house of the Mystae, and like it had the living rock of the Eleusinian Acropolis as their background. This rock towards the north exhibits two remarkable cave-like arches in the living stone. Such was the site before 310 B.C.—six hundred years, that is to say, before the sanctuary was ravaged and destroyed.[1]

---

[1] Cf. Strabo, quoted above, p. 189, note 1, and Vitruvius, *Praef.* vii. 16, 17, Schneider. Plutarch (*Pericles*, xiii.) gives a rather detailed account of the various architects and builders who apparently carried out the plans of Ictinus, though the words of Plutarch alone might lead one to think he did not connect Ictinus with the work, but rather considered its building to have been, like the Parthenon, under the general supervision of Phidias. He says that Coroebus began to build it, proceeding so far as to set the columns up on the foundations, and adding the architrave. Coroebus died, and Metagenes of the deme Xypeta continued the work, adding the διάζωμα (is this to be translated *frieze*, or has it the meaning of *praecinctio*, a *narrow upper gallery*, for access to upper seats, which at Eleusis would mean *a ledge hewn out of the rock*, to allow access to the upper story?) and the columns of the upper story. Xenocles of Cholargia finished the ὀπαῖον, whatever that may here be supposed to mean.

Now let us approach the remains as they are. Neglect the Roman remains of triumphal arches on your left; look for a moment at the site of the temple of Artemis at the gate; consider the intense misunderstanding of the Doric capital that led Hadrian's builders to give such a stiff and lifeless curve as that shown in huge examples that cumber the ground on the site of Hadrian's gate of Ceremony. There is, if only it were worth the looking at, a monstrous lump of white marble here. It was a huge medallion tastelessly injected into the gable or pediment of the Propylaea aforesaid.[1] Some think a mysterious person figured here—a priest, say; but others more prosaically claim that Hadrian himself somewhat awkwardly presided over this rule-of-thumb Doric architecture for which he is responsible. But let us get inside this gate and forget everything about it save only that it faced north-east. Following now the Sacred Way which trends to the left and ascends, we may now pass the remains of the smaller gate of Appius, which faces due north. To those who think they can solve the riddles of all religions by accumulating facts about the orientation of temples it will be of importance to note that the four corners of the great meeting-house at Eleusis point respectively north, south, east, and west. Before reaching this northern gate of Appius we are not yet on the ground of old deemed holy; but this gate once passed, we are where the yearly procession from Athens first felt that its goal was reached. A long journey it was for those burdened with offerings—this twelve miles, the last nine of which were without shade, if one may rashly suppose the distribution of trees always to have been what it is to-day.

---

[1] See for the photograph of it published by the Hellenic Society, Appendix XI. i. 43.

Here we are at last within the sanctuary ταῖν θεαῖν, *of the goddesses twain.* Before looking about us within, let it be stated, for the benefit of geometers, that this sacred ground enclosed by walls and rock is in shape an irregular pentagon. Of the five enclosing sides, the longest is the line of overhanging rock—the Acropolis. At the northern end of this rock wall, which runs from west to north, are the two caves. Just north of the northernmost of the two caves this longest side meets the shortest side—a wall running north-eastward from the Acropolis rock to the gateway just entered. Of the three remaining sides one is a wall parallel to the Acropolis rock, and the other two, also walls, connect this parallel side respectively with the gate of Appius and the western end of the Acropolis side. Such are the boundaries, through the ruins of which we suppose ourselves to have walked.

And now we may well begin with a curious examination of the ground we tread, over which so many pious feet have passed. Beyond the lesser or Appian gateway traces appear of the Holy or Processional Way, but under the disappointing guise of a Roman pavement—slabs of stone made fast with mortar upon the native rock. In Grecian days the bare rock was probably not improved upon either here or in the much and piously travelled roadway leading up to the Athenian Parthenon through the Mnesiclean Propylaea. Various traceable pedestals indicate that many monuments lined this processional road, which so far resembled many others. Between the gate of Appius and the overhanging Acropolis rock is the small precinct of Pluto, which is approached by a step or two and an entrance-gate. This small corner, belonging to Demeter's self-constituted son-in-law, is remarkable rather for the striking configuration of the natural rock that shuts it in on the west than for the slight traces of a very small temple which it contains. The finding here first of a bust representing Eubouleus,[1] the Eleusinian Hades, and then of a bas-relief representing Demeter, Persephone, and Hades, establishes the proprietary right of Aidoneus-Pluto to this spot, included though it be within the sanctuary walls of the dread twain goddesses.

Within this small precinct facing north, and just south of the intersection of the longest (or Acropolis) side with the shortest side of the sacred pentagon, is a hole in the rock, raised higher than man's stature above the general level. In the rock below, and north of this aperture, are steps[2] roughly hewn leading to a height, and a foothold from which it is easy for any one to climb through the hole and enter the arched cave-like space beyond. This cave, as it may be called, together with a larger one much resembling it just south of it, would have seemed, and apparently did seem, in myth-growing days, the very spot where Aidoneus on his chariot might have swept with Persephone into his nether abode. The rock overhanging the Cnidian[3] precinct

[1] See note 3 above, p. 177; note 1, p. 174; and Chr. Scherer, article "Hades" in Roscher's *Ausführliches Lexicon*. I hear of an article (not procurable before going to press) in the *Mittheilungen*, wherein Dr. Kern successfully maintains that this beautiful head represents not Eubouleus but Triptolemus. This would tend to confirm my contention (see chapter ii. above) that Demophoon is an interloper in the story of Demeter, and that Triptolemus was the real nursling. Furthermore, it would tend to connect Triptolemus with this precinct of Pluto, and to affiliate his worship with that of Hades and Iacchos. Cf. *Daremberg et Saglio*, p. 634, col. 2.

[2] Dr. Dörpfeld kindly calls my attention to the possibility that these very roughly cut steps may have belonged to the arrangements for a modern house.

[3] What Attic tradition records as the coming of Demeter to Eleusis gains in significance if we find reason to suppose this new departure of nature-worship in Attica to have been prompted from the north,—if Demeter came from Thessaly as did Aesculapius and as Dionysus came from Thrace. A very definite tradition asserts that the Cnidian sanctuary of the two goddesses was founded from Thessaly, as were the Coan and the Epidaurian rites

of Demeter and Persephone was found by Sir Charles Newton to have similar peculiarities to these of the Eleusinian Acropolis.

But, to return to the precinct of Hades-Pluto, nearly in front of the two caves are unmistakable traces of a very small "cella" or temple of Pluto. The foundations show it to have been ten feet broad by sixteen feet long. The head of Eubouleus-Triptolemus,[1] found near it, very closely resembles one which was long called Virgil, and which is to be found in the Capitoline Museum. It is none the less beautiful because Professor Benndorf is almost alone in attributing it to the Phidian age.

Emerging from the Plutonian precinct, and passing a few steps southward on the Processional Way, turn again westward, and there find the more or less uncertain foundation-stones to which probably corresponded two buildings. These are identified respectively, but only the farther one confidently, with the two treasure-houses mentioned in Eleusinian inscriptions. One may have been the treasure-house of Demeter; and if this be so, the other, in case it was anything, was that of Persephone. The importance of the treasuries which these foundations may represent is abundantly shown in the accounts of the temple-funds so plentifully forthcoming of late years, and so well

in honour of Aesculapius. See above, ch. ii. and below, ch. vi. The coming of Demeter from Pyrasus and the Dotian plain of Thessaly is by no means inconsistent with an aboriginal Eleusinian nature-worship and nature-goddess. So too the Thracian Dionysus coming to Icaria absorbed, and was absorbed by, an indigenous worship of a kindred nature to himself. The known facts plainly require such an explanation. See above, ch. iii.

[1] For a very good reproduction of it, see Miss Harrison and Mrs. Verrall's *Mythology and Monuments*, p. 105. Brunn has it in his *Monuments of Ancient Art*. It gains much in interest and importance if Dr. Kern can show that it represents Triptolemus.

edited. The reason why such scanty foundation remains were here found is that the solid rock lies close to the surface, and, accordingly, all traces of such buildings as existed were most readily obliterated.[1] Therefore very little concerning these would-be treasure-houses can be ascertained.

Whether each of the two goddesses had an especial temple for her own abiding can also never be ascertained with certainty from anything that has been discovered on the spot, and accordingly what may possibly be traces of two small temples are only doubtfully to be described as such. The facts, such as they are, may be stated as follows: traces of a smaller temple, which might be attributed to Persephone, are near the northern angle of the Hall of Initiation to the east. The plainer traces of a temple, larger, though still small, are visible at the northern end of the raised terrace which runs between the Hall of Initiation proper and the overhanging north-westward rock. Here may conceivably have stood Demeter's temple on a higher level, to the north of the same north angle.[2]

And now I have mentioned the chief among the lesser buildings, about none of which, excepting perhaps the first, there can be reasonable certainty. (1) The small precinct and small temple or "cella" of Plutus; (2) and (3) the supposed treasuries, one for each goddess; (4) the very problematical temple or cella of Persephone; (5) the equally doubtful temple or cella of Demeter. Besides

---

[1] The poor Albanians, in giving themselves and their animals various rudimentary comforts, have played fast and loose with the rock here.

[2] Strabo's words (see note 1, p. 189) make it certain that a temple of Demeter formed one of the conspicuous features of the sanctuary; and the comparative insignificance in size and prominence of the remains on this site leave the whole matter in doubt.

this there was in some place, not determined, within the precinct a Neocorion, *i.e.* quarters for the neocoroi—those in executive charge of the buildings and minor concerns of the sanctuary.[1]

As for the great Initiation Hall, the most interesting by far of all the features on this site, let us admit to start with that its study is a matter of great perplexity, in spite of an absolute certainty with regard to the most important leading facts.

Your first feelings, as you wander up and down across this Eleusinian wilderness of stones, are confusion and helplessness. Before you lies what seems to be an incongruous crowd of foundations for the bases of columns, no two of which seem to be part of one scheme. A closer examination shows in effect that there are many kinds of foundations, bases, and traces of columns belonging by their manner of construction to many epochs of building. These puzzling and overlapping traces are multiplied especially at the eastern angle of the Hall. That quarter of the ground occupied by the whole Hall which lies nearest this eastern angle contains fifty-six bases or traces of columns, while upon all the remainder only thirty-seven can be found.

This curious fact leads to a closer examination of the column-foundations where they are most numerous, and here a wishing-cap is necessary. Put on this cap, while looking at these shapeless-seeming ruins, and wish for all the knowledge of the various masonry of various epochs possessed by Dr. Dörpfeld, director of the German Institute at Athens, or by Dr. Philios,[2] the indefatigable excavator at

---

[1] See Appendix I. above, for some account of the later history of this word νεωκόρος.
[2] See his pamphlet (Athens, 1889, Ch. Wilberg) *Fouilles d'Éleusis*, 1882-87.

Eleusis. Then you would note how the various traces gradually group themselves as follows: (1) twenty-five small square foundations, coloured red on the plan, about 10 feet apart, these being wholly confined to this eastern quarter of the site; (2) twenty places for round columns 15 feet apart, requiring (in the northern corner) one more, of which no trace can be found, to make up the symmetrical tale,—twenty-one; (3) six large square foundations requiring the addition of two more than the remains found to complete the necessary eight. Besides these three fashions, there is a fourth fashion of column foundation. These are distributed very curiously over the whole space,—forty-two bases in a square of a hundred feet more or less.

To the smaller hall, destroyed by the Persians, belong the first mentioned square-column foundations, discoverable exclusively within the eastern quarter of the site, and coloured red on the plan. This smaller hall may be called the Hall of Pisistratus, though what is certainly known about it is that it was destroyed by the Persians after Xerxes' defeat at Salamis.[1] Traces of their destructive fire have come to light, giving the confirmation of our own eyes to what Herodotus reports in general terms. In the year 479 B.C. Mardonius burned and overturned the Initiation Hall of Pisistratus. Its building is attributed to the age of Pisistratus because the foundation walls of it are practically identical both in the materials used, the order of their

---

[1] Before the Persians, King Cleomenes of Sparta seems to have devastated the sanctuary (Herod. vi. 75, cf. 64, and v. 74 and ff.) Here is a confirmation of the notion suggested by the nature of the remains of the earlier Greek walls enclosing the precinct. They must have been a fortification, otherwise a King of Sparta would never wantonly have attacked them, or the sanctuary which they enclosed.

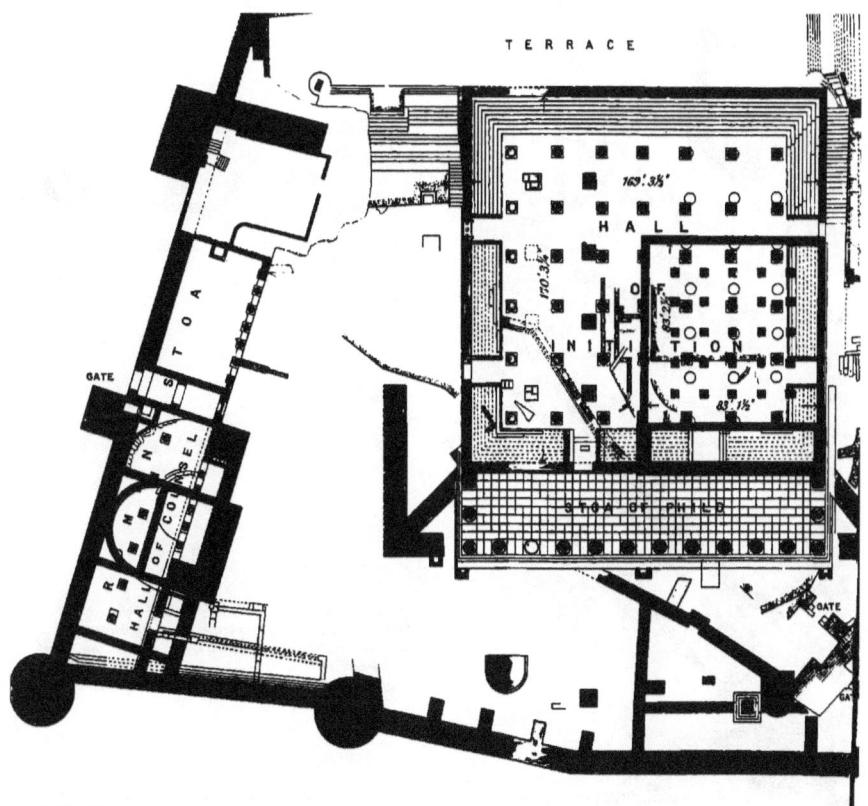

After Dr Dörpfeld's Plan in the Journal of the
Greek Archaeological Society 1887 and reproduced here
by kind permission

PLAN OF EXCAVATIONS

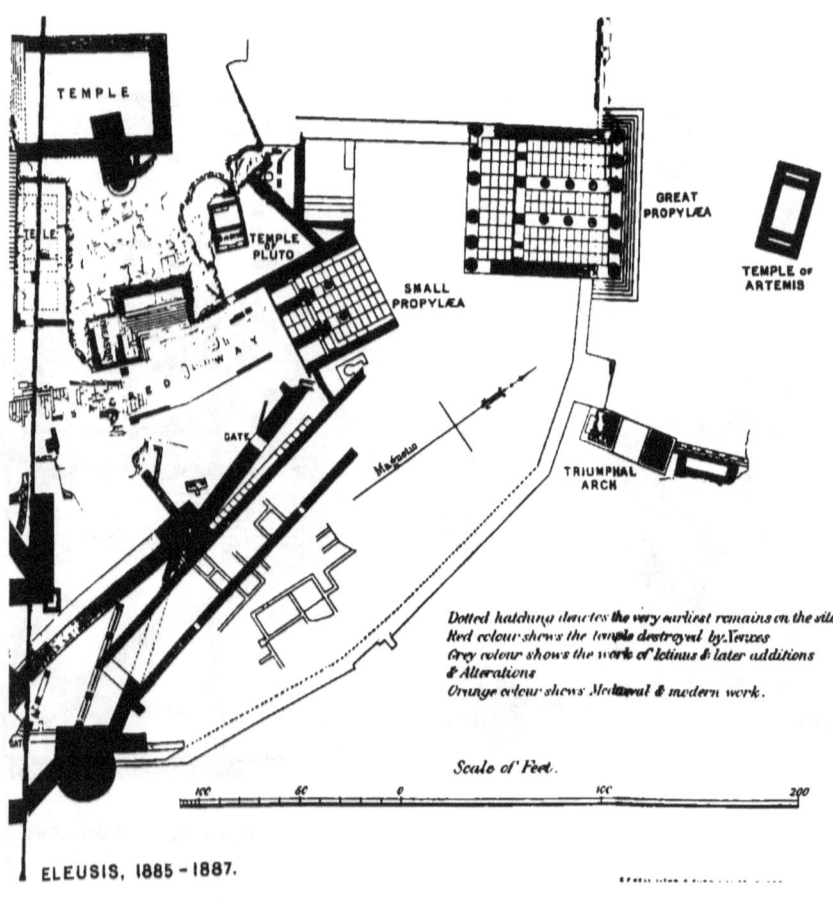

superposition, and the manner of their putting together, with buildings known to have been built by Pisistratus, the great advocate of Dionysus, the defender of faith in the gods at Eleusis. The ceiling of this Hall was supported by twenty-five interior columns, it was entered from the south-east through a portico, and it can hardly have failed to justify the twenty-five supporting columns by a large upper-story room approached no doubt from the level of the upper terrace. The Acropolis-rock had not of course been cut away at that time.

After this Hall of Pisistratus a Hall of equal frontage but twice as deep was built, by cutting into the rock for more room. This Hall was supported by twenty-one interior columns. To this important structure (which we may call the Hall of Cimon, since it was built in his day) must be allotted those twenty columns 15 feet apart, more than half of their number being hopelessly entangled among the older remains of the Hall of Pisistratus.

Now, therefore, the wilderness at the east angle of the hall—the columns, bases, and traces, fifty-six in number—perplexes us no longer. The eastern angle of the Hall proper, in Ictinus' plan, was the eastern corner of the porch of the earlier Hall of Pisistratus. This early building with its porch covered slightly more than one-fourth of the ground allotted to the Hall of Ictinus, and about half of that occupied by the Hall of Cimon. Of the fifty-six bases and traces huddled together in this corner of the whole space, twenty-five belong to the Hall of Pisistratus, fifteen to that of Cimon, and sixteen to the last and Roman refashioning of the building. There are no columns or bases of columns here which belong to the Hall of Ictinus, for the Hall of Ictinus consisted of two chambers, a new one added by Ictinus to the already existing Hall of Cimon. This will be made clear by consulting the small plan here given and by comparing it with the large one.

Before turning to a consideration of the Hall of Ictinus, it is worth while to seek confirmation for the facts in the architectural history of the spot thus far obtained. Corresponding to some, if not to all, of these successive temples, there must have been various walls of enclosure. Around the wilderness of column bases, at various distances and in various directions, extend foundations of walls built in the most various manners of masonry. There is the old fashion of wall called Cyclopean, there is the wall which belongs to the day of Pisistratus, built after the manner of the upper foundation-courses of the building just south of the Erechtheum, between it and the Parthenon at Athens.[1] Then come walls of later and better Greek workmanship, belonging to the days of Cimon and Pericles. Finally there are abundant traces everywhere of Roman building.

The upshot of competent examination here gives us traces of a building earlier even than the Hall of Pisistratus, of some building dating back perhaps beyond history,—a building too around which ran a protecting wall. What remains of it is indicated by the dotted hatching on the plan. The whole space thus pre-historically pre-empted was much smaller than the later precinct. All this may be conveniently named the Cyclopean Hall, if it be remembered that Cyclopean means almost anything, and that there is nothing to show whether this early building was a hall or a

[1] For photographs showing this foundation, see Appendix XI. i. 14. Cf. Mr. Leaf's photograph of Eleusinian foundations, *ibid.* ii. 40.

fortress simply. This phrase shall commit us only to the vaguest recognition of the antiquity of building upon Demeter's Eleusinian place of worship, and will give as a background for the successive Halls of Pisistratus, Cimon, Ictinus, and the Roman Hall, the dim vision of a primitive place of refuge, and perhaps of a worship primitively lodged after the fashion of the so-called "cave temple"[1] of Apollo on Delian Cynthus.

But after these Cyclopean remains and the three Halls above mentioned came the Romans and their buildings and repairings. They enlarged the space occupied by the Hall of Ictinus, especially towards the Acropolis-rock; apparently they tore down the wall by which Ictinus separated his addition from the Hall of Cimon, and they suppressed the eight heavy columns (represented on the large plan by six large square foundations, and two dotted squares) of Ictinus' Hall, as well as the twenty-one columns of Cimon's Hall. In place of these they put in forty-two columns of their own more or less symmetrically distributed over the whole space. Upon the Greek walls enclosing the whole sanctuary traces of Roman repairing are tolerably clear. The restoration of the upper and lesser ceremonial gate by Appius Claudius probably amounted to a rebuilding, and the lower wall, joining the Lower and Greater Propylaea to the Greek fortification walls, is wholly Roman. To sum up the history of building on this spot: Behind everything we have (1) the Cyclopean Hall; next came (2) the Hall of Pisistratus; then, after (3) the Hall of Cimon, came (4) the Hall of Ictinus, which was succeeded by (5) the Roman Hall.

And now it becomes necessary to give such account as

[1] For some account of this, see below, chap. viii.

may be possible of the Hall of Ictinus. I owe to the kindness of Dr. Dörpfeld the sketch-plan here given.

OUTLINE-SKETCH OF THE GROUND-PLAN OF
THE HALL OF ICTINUS

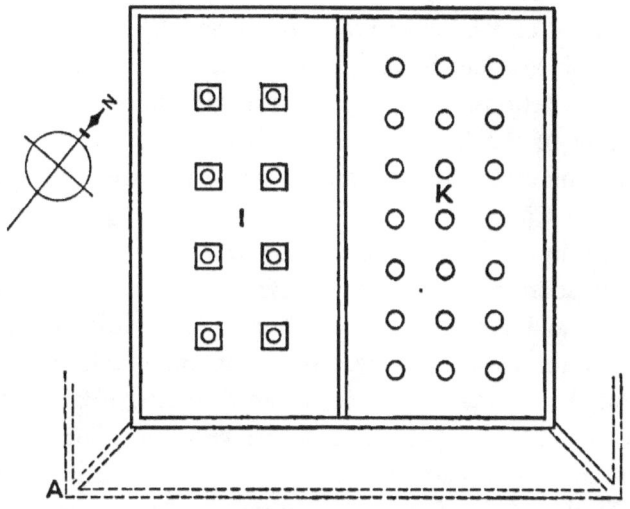

I. Chamber added by Ictinus.
K. Hall of Cimon.
A. Foundations which later served for Philo's Porch.

This Hall of Ictinus was really two Halls, the old one of Cimon, which it was apparently necessary to respect, and the new one of Ictinus doubling the available space. It seems likely, however, that the new was separated from the old by a wall which was changed when Ictinus built from the north-west outside wall of Cimon's Hall into a partition wall between the two large chambers. The forty-two foundations in the Roman refashioning of the whole form so conspicuous a feature on the large plan that it is difficult to disentangle from them the work of Ictinus and Cimon. The late character of these forty-two bases is proved by the comparative poorness of their construction and by the presence of a Roman inscription among materials built into the most easterly of these forty-two bases. The Romans made a slight gain in size by hewing a few more inches out of the native rock, and hence their Hall was upwards of 170 feet in length by about 169 in width. The Hall of Ictinus, including both compartments, was apparently of the latter dimension both ways. That it had a partition wall is made probable by the necessity of respecting what Cimon built, and still more nearly certain by the survival in the Roman plan of two front doors of entrance. These doors were necessary before they remodelled the interior and removed the partition. Afterwards one large one would have been in every way more effective and useful, but so serious a departure from the original plan was not made. Nothing is definitely known, however, of what and where were the doors used in Greek days. Since the Hall of Ictinus had this partition, its lower story would not have been suited for the largest meetings. Hence the necessity of an upper story where the space, divided below, was thrown into one large square room. In this room, entered from the upper terrace where lay the larger Temple —supposably that of Demeter—we imagine services to have been held in the greatest days of Athens.

There is no room for doubt as to the existence of an upper story, because Plutarch's testimony is explicit,[1] and is confirmed by various features of the site. The numerous columns of the lower hall require it, as before said; and moreover a carefully wrought terrace,[2] hewn out of the

[1] See above, note 1, p. 191.   [2] Plutarch's διάζωμα.

rock high up, on the level probably with its ceiling, calls for it. Ictinus, following no doubt the practice used in building the Hall of Cimon, utilised the receding configuration of the rock-hill, for the first story, by hewing from a point high enough above the level of the Hall of Pisistratus to give his ground floor sufficient height, and thus placed its north and west corners in the solid rock; he was, in beginning again from that high point, so near the rounding top of the hill that he could easily cut out this upper ledge from which to step into the second story of his great hall. To this ledge broad rock-cut stairs lead up from a point near the western angle of the lower hall, while narrower steps are found at the north angle. Mount these stairs and you are on the artificial terrace just described, and find that it is a continuation, beyond the outer walls of the Hall, of the floor of the upper story. More than the fact of its existence at the level of this still existing ledge we do not know of Ictinus' upper chamber or hall, except that Metagenes of Xypeta, who fashioned the outside ledge, set up the upper story columns. There is, of course, very little doubt that a similar upper chamber existed in the Hall of Pisistratus, all of whose essential features were reproduced four times as large by Ictinus, who here, as at Bassae, included the site of the ancient sanctuary in his new building. At Bassae the old temple of Apollo, facing east, was incorporated by Ictinus into the great Temple facing north and south. The configuration of the Eleusinian Acropolis did not force the architect to make any change in orientation, and Ictinus faced his hall south-east just as the smaller hall of Pisistratus, its predecessor, had faced. Only by a skilful use of new space and of the upward slope of the rock Ictinus made his Hall look far longer in proportion to its width than it really was, and therefore his building assumed something more near the ordinary proportions of such a temple as the Parthenon. The device above alluded to was the suggestion that the back of the building was hidden in the rock, which was in fact to some extent the case. Something in the finished surface of a vertical course of rocks along the north-west or Acropolis side of the raised ledge (or διάζωμα), already talked of, makes it seem probable that this impression of a temple to the gods of nether earth, partly hid by that jealous element and partly showing in the light of day, was still further enhanced by the suggestion of a portico towards the Acropolis. It is conceivable that the roof of the upper story should have covered more than the space above the lower hall, by the extent of this ledge. Thus would the demands of symmetry, always listened to by Greek artists, and heeded by none more than by the architect of the Parthenon, have been satisfied. This single story would have looked like the top of a larger porch whose lower parts were concealed. This would have been such a counterpoise to the porch of Philo on the opposite or front end as was allowed by the requirements of the ritual and the configuration of the precinct of the gods at Eleusis. Other considerations of proportion make this notion that a porch was suggested at the back seem plausible to me. One of these is that the space between the front wall of the initiation chamber and the front of the colonnade of Philo's porch is just about the width of the upper ledge extending from the back wall of the same chamber (the wall hewn out of the rock) to the point where the hill unhewn resumes its natural upward slope. The second argument from proportion is simply the Greek habit, and especially that of Ictinus, which would seem to have abhorred undisguised and unblushing squareness in a building. Ictinus was willing to increase at Bassae the difference between length and breadth which he had made so markedly in the Parthenon (as compared with previous buildings), and there was still more reason for him to do something of the kind at Eleusis, since the total height of Philo's portico—some equivalent to which was contemplated in Ictinus' plan—must have been that of the two stories behind it. This must have seemed to come dangerously near [1] the dimensions of the hall itself. Therefore, without some such device he would have had a building of very obviously monotonous proportions, not far from a cube in the effect of its mass upon the eye. With the aid, however, of Philo's porch and of the corresponding porch suggested at the back, the whole building viewed from without gains the appearance of a lofty structure about half as long again as it is wide. The back of this building showed only indistinctly because its base was wholly entangled and involved in the hill out of which the front portion had completely disengaged itself, standing forth with its portico of fourteen lofty columns. Nether earth clung to her fraction of this Hall of the Eleusinian gods, just as she claimed her fraction of fair Persephone's life.

Such then was the Telesterion, the great house of worship at Eleusis, the enlarged and embellished substitute for that once built according to the commands given by Demeter to Triptolemus, and to his father and brethren.

[1] I do not of course mean to suggest the possibility of its really having been even half as high as the hall was long. But the height was of course exceptional, and to it—so far as the eye of one approaching Philo's porch, or the building as Ictinus left it, was concerned—had to be added that of steps leading up to it.

She commanded that it be built above the well—Callichoros by name—where Celeus' daughters found her sorrowing as she sat. This well and the Agelastos Petra or Laughless Stone close by it, upon which the goddess sat, cannot now be found. Such was not the case in ancient days, as is shown by the following record found in one of the inscribed temple accounts unearthed upon the spot.

"Paid for the transport of 25,000 bricks to the Eleusinian temple in Athens from the (Agelastos) Laughless Stone, 120 drachmae." From these same accounts it further appears that the Rarian plain—memorable because it was there that Triptolemus first taught men the cultivation of grain—was owned and farmed by the Eleusinian temple administration. One entry shows that the grain from this field came to the priest at Eleusis, and another entry runs: "To Nicon, for removing a corpse from the plain and for its purification." An especial item allowed in this account is for a pig used in the cleansing or purification just mentioned. The account above alluded to, of 25,000 bricks transported from Eleusis to the Eleusinian precinct in Athens at the expense of the administrators of the sanctuary at Eleusis, indicates that the two holy precincts were under one management, and recalls the story of the institution of the Lesser Mysteries at Athens and their close affiliation with the Eleusinian festival.[1]

This lesser and affiliated festival was celebrated at Athens in the month of flowers (February-March), and the Athenian precinct where these Lesser Mysteries took place was appropriately called the Eleusinion. Of this and of its two temples, one of Demeter and Persephone, and one of Triptolemus, I have already had occasion to speak, and

[1] See above, ch. iv.

also of the statue which it contained representing that great religious mediator, Epimenides of Crete, who consecrated this Eleusinion, and through the Lesser Mysteries made of the worship at Eleusis a bond of union between those old-time rivals, Athens and Eleusis. To the former and more or less exclusively Eleusinian and patrician worship of Demeter, Persephone, and Hades, a new and popular feature attached itself in honour of the Icarian and Athenian Dionysus, and the yearly visit of Dionysus Iacchus to the gods at Eleusis was made a cardinal and carnival feature in the Eleusinian Mysteries, which thus became a pledge of brotherhood and equality for all the tribes of Attic-born men.[1]

The Lesser Mysteries at Athens were a sort of preface to the greater ones of Eleusis,[2] and the time of their celebration was earlier in the year. The Greater or Epoptical Mysteries did not come until the month Boedromion (August-September), six months later than the flower-month (Anthesterion) of the Lesser Mysteries.

The ordinary progress of initiation was as follows:—In the flower month at Athens an applicant could become a mystes—a novice, let us say—by participation in the Lesser Mysteries at the Athenian Eleusinion. Thus, and apparently only thus, was a man qualified to take part, six months later, in the Greater Mysteries at Eleusis. But even then he appeared at Eleusis only as a mystes or novice, and could not join in all the acts of worship or see all the ceremonial. After a year had elapsed, however, our mystes became an

[1] Mannhardt very truly says that the inspiration drawn from initiation at Eleusis by the noblest spirits of Greece has illustrated the sanctuary there as a place where humanity made one of its most ennobling forward steps (*Posthumous Essays*, "Demeter").

[2] The ἄρχων βασιλεύς with four commissioners (ἐπιμεληταί) appears to have controlled the whole cult at Athens and Eleusis.

epoptes, and as such saw with his own eyes and heard with his own ears all that the Greater or Epoptical Mysteries afforded. The religious privileges of the completely initiated are reached at Eleusis by two qualifying stages, as who should say by baptism at the Lesser, and confirmation at the Greater Mysteries.[1] The vague and unprecise terms in which the full ceremony is described are terms of sight. The Epoptes or Viewer is said to have Autopsy, or sight with his own eyes—Real Vision. These hints, with others, such as the connection between showing light and the title of the leader of the mystic ceremonial who was called Hierophant, persuade some that after a period of darkness the initiated saw a great light.

Little as we know of the unrevealed ceremonial that took place within the Eleusinian precinct, we know that enormous numbers, as many perhaps as 30,000,[2] gathered from various parts of Greece went from Athens, and we know something in detail of the preliminaries at Athens and of the observances on the Sacred Way to Eleusis. The whole festival lasted about twelve days. Several days before it began there was a preliminary meeting at Athens. Just one day before it there was also at Athens the day of puri-fication. All the mystae[3] and every creature and thing

[1] Plutarch in his life of Demetrius Poliorcetes (26) says of Demetrius: τότε δ'οὖν ἀναζευγνύων εἰς τὰς 'Αθήνας ἔγραψεν ὅτι βούλεται παραγενόμενος εὐθὺς μυηθῆναι καὶ τὴν τελετὴν ἅπασαν ἀπὸ τῶν μικρῶν ἀχρὶ τῶν ἐποπτικῶν παραλαβεῖν, τοῦτο δ' οὐ θέμιτον ἦν οὐδὲ γεγονὸς πρότερον . . . ἐπώπτευον δὲ τοὐλάχιστον ἐνιαυτὸν διαλείποντες. The intimidated governors at Athens did not dream of refusing this unparalleled demand, but resorted to a juggle with their calendar that the letter of the sacred law might be observed.

[2] See Herod. viii. 65, where the visionary procession on the Sacred Way is seen κονιορτὸν χωρέοντα ἀπ' 'Ελευσῖνος ὡς ἀνδρῶν μάλιστά κῃ τρισ-μυρίων.

[3] See *ibid.* the account of the freedom of all to be initiated. Dicaeus there describes the Eleusinian festival for the benefit of king Demaratus,

that was to play a part in the great ceremonial underwent purgation by washing in the sea.

Sea-surges dash all human harms away, says Euripides somewhere,[1] expressing a belief well-nigh universal in ancient Greece. Truly the sea entered into Greek worship, with its suggestions of infinite space and calm, of limitless motion, its mighty and tumultuous heart-beat. At Eleusis and elsewhere the ever-sounding sea, whose surge still echoes through the most beautiful and pious masterpieces of the tragic, the lyric, and the epic muse, was present with worshippers whose frequent footfall reverberated through the precincts and the dwellings of the gods in Greece.

The first two days of the Eleusinian-Athenian festival were spent in Athens after these ceremonies of purgation.

Solemn preparations were there and then completed for the great ceremonial procession from Athens to Eleusis along the Sacred Way and through the sacred gates into the precinct and its Great Hall of Initiation. By means of all this pomp Dionysus-Iacchos was associated with Demeter and Persephone at Eleusis, and Dionysus became one of the gods at Eleusis, under the name of Iacchos which was chanted by the mystae all through the day while they brought him to Eleusis, and again during the day spent in bringing him back to his home in the Athenian Iaccheion,[2]—within the Eleusinion already much spoken of.

Underlying all the light-heartedness shown by those who

---

saying : τὴν δὲ ὁρτὴν ταύτην ἄγουσι 'Αθηναῖοι ἀνὰ πάντα ἔτεα τῇ Μητρὶ καὶ τῇ Κούρῃ (the regular phrase for Demeter and Persephone), καὶ αὐτῶν τε ὁ βουλόμενος καὶ τῶν ἄλλων 'Ελλήνων μυεῖται· καὶ τὴν φωνὴν τῆς ἀκούεις ἐν ταύτῃ τῇ ὁρτῇ ιακχάζουσι. This last word describes the cry "*Iacch*', *Oh Iacchos*," and thus brings into prominence the part of Dionysus in these yearly observances.

[1] *I. T.* 1193.
[2] Plutarch, *Arist.* 27. See above the citations from Herod. viii. 65.

joined this procession was an incommunicable solemnity shadowed forth in that strangely awe-inspiring chapter where Herodotus tells of a vision of floating dust and of echoing cries from a ghostly choir of disembodied celebrants on the Sacred Way from Athens.[1] This host from the world beyond led Iacchos to the rescue at a time when Attic sanctuaries had been devastated and Athenian altars overturned, when none dared longer to walk in the deserted streets of Athens or visit her ruined temples. By this portentous apparition the doom of the Persian invader was foreshadowed and the coming of a brighter day was assured by the gods at Eleusis. They sent forth in the darkest hour of danger and despair a rescuing band of hope to lead fainting Hellas from martyrdom to peace. After the dust and the sound as of many voices, a mist arose and floated off towards Salamis, foreboding the destruction of the Persian fleet. Thus in the eyes of Herodotus—a fit spokesman here as elsewhere for all the faithful—the Holy Alliance at Eleusis of Demeter, Persephone, and Dionysus —the Mother, the Daughter, and the Son—was the comforter and the saviour. Through it were assured knowledge and maintenance of Greek laws and religion, progress in learning, and union of heart with all the divinities of Hellas.[2]

No wonder then, if the yearly procession of the living mystae was often thought of as a foretaste of the life beyond, a dim vision of happiness to be hereafter in the islands of the blest, a rehearsal or promise in this world of the performance in the world to come. No wonder that

---

[1] The first reading suggests that Herodotus is thinking of a procession from Eleusis to Athens ; that is not, however, necessarily the case. For the passage, see above, note 2, p. 209.

[2] τὸν τροφέα, τὸν σωτῆρα δι' ὃν εἶδον νόμους "Ελληνας, ἔμαθον γράμματ', ἐμυήθην θεοῖς.

Aristophanes puts away for a moment his cap and bells when, having brought down into the world below his caricature of the god Dionysus accompanied by Xanthias, a type of the boisterous clown in old comedy, he suddenly confronts these two jesters with the march, the music, and the song of a mystic chorus of the initiated, who are repeating in the world below the yearly procession from Athens to Eleusis. They are bringing home the god Iacchos. Here is a striking and unstudied homage paid to the solemnity of Eleusinian worship in the sudden cessation of boisterous fooling at the approach of the mystae.[1] Breathless and all in a tremor they finally hear the mystic cry from afar: "Iacch', oh Iacchos! Iacch', oh Iacchos!"[2] Then they know that the band of the faithful is coming, and are abashed, and for the first time they hold their peace.

Meanwhile the mystae draw near and enter the orchestra with a song to the god in their midst:[3] "Stir thou the fire-flakes of torches, whirling them with thy hands, Iacch', oh Iacchos, fire-bearing star of night and of our mystic rites. Look, the meadow is aflame with fire; old men's knees are lithe for dancing now, they shake off all their pains and all the time-long weariness of hoary years in the rites of holy observance; but thou, flaming with thy torch, lead on the forward march to the blossoming meadows by the stream."

Here, as a preface to the solemn invocation of each of the three gods at Eleusis in turn, the Hierophant bids the profane and uninitiated to depart: "I forbid them, I forbid them again, and again a third time I forbid them; let them make way for the initiated." Turning to the latter, he then

[1] Aristoph. *Frogs*, 312, cf. 154 ff.
[2] *Ibid.* 316-459.
[3] Only the substance is here given, except where every word has its important bearing.

says: "Raise ye the voice of song, begin your night-long revels that beseem the festival we keep."

Then follows a solemn processional song in honour of Persephone, which is full of the cheer of glad spring. Manfully each is advancing towards the flowering nooks of fair meadows, dancing, gibing, frolicking, and railing cheerily. For verily each has had his fill of fasting and purification. "March on in cadence, and take care to exalt right heartily the saviour goddess with your voice in song uplifted, for she it is who saith that she is the country's salvation forever assured."

Now the Hierophant bids them invoke and give thanks to the harvest-queen Demeter, and thus their song begins: "Demeter, queen of hallowed services, join now in help of thine own to save them. Suffer me to dance the livelong day in unendangered jollity, and let me utter much in jest, and much in earnest too. Make my doings worthy of thy festival, and when my frolic hour is past, and all my fooling done, victorious let me crown my brow."

And now the Hierophant calls for a song in honour of the last of the three, the last-come god at Eleusis, who is first in the hearts of those whom he has led and who have brought him to the Eleusinian merry-making mysteries. "Iacchos," they fervently sing, "most precious to my heart, make this the sweetest moment of the feast, follow along with me to the dwelling of the goddess, and show thee a stranger to weariness though long is the journey that thou art making. *Oh Iacchos, lover of the dance, come thou with me to help me on the way.* Yea, in merrily tattered garb with thy sandals recklessly torn thou canst discover the way to let us dance and play and pay no penalty. *Oh Iacchos, lover of the dance, come thou with me to help me on the way.* For verily I gave a sidelong glance at a bit of a girl just now, and through a rent in her bosom's array I caught sight of my beauteous playmate's charms. *Oh Iacchos, lover of the dance, come thou with me to help me on the way.*"

The unruly element, associated chiefly with a certain phase of the cult of Dionysus, has asserted itself more and more in this last song, and at the end it reaches such a pitch of license that the two jesters quite recover their balance of mind, while the chorus of the initiated yields wholly to a headstrong impulse. Trusting in Iacchos for impunity, they fling wide the floodgates of ribaldry, raining alike upon the unjust and the just their jibes, sacred and profane, mentionable and unmentionable. "Now if you choose," they say, "let us join one and all in scoffing at Archedemus. Why, he has lived to be seven years old before he cut a single Athenian grinder,[1] you know, but still he's in business in the demagoguing line up in the world among the living corpses,—a captain in the knavery of the world."[2] And so the mud-throwing goes merrily from bad to worse and worst, giving a wonderfully telling and ideally realistic picture of scenes that were yearly enacted by the real procession from Athens to Eleusis. This feature in the day's doings was connected with a bridge over the Attic river Cephissus. Just out of the gates of Athens, just after various solemn preliminaries at the city shrines had ended, the mystae halted, and took their revenge for days of purification and fasting. Here they let their pent-up jollity have its full fling, and these *jibes at the bridge* have also to take their part in the netherworld celebration described by Aristophanes.

[1] οὐκ ἔφυσε φράτερας. [2] τὰ πρῶτα τῆς ἐκεῖ μοχθηρίας

At last there is a pause, the Hierophant bids them resume their march, and gradually as they go the thought of the woes of Demeter shows itself first in their choice of words, and finally in the return of serious thoughts and solemn aspirations' which form the pious burden of their closing strain. "Onward we go to the flower-faced meadows where abundant roses grow. On we go, in our own merry fashion dancing, dancing more than well¹ the measure led off by the glorious Fates. On us alone in very truth the sun doth shine, we only know the light of gladness, as many of us as have passed through the rites of the Mysteries, and lead our lives in piety among the native born and the strangers within our city's gates."

Here we have a case where all the essentially religious features of the yearly holiday-making in honour of the gods at Eleusis were enacted before the eyes of those who under ordinary circumstances would yearly take part in the celebration themselves—the whole Athenian public. But the circumstances were extraordinary; and although the scene is in a comedy, there is throughout a pervasive seriousness which alone would require us to assign a religious motive for its performance—that motive was the satisfaction of a fervent desire to propitiate the gods at Eleusis felt universally at Athens. The play was brought out in January of the year 405, just after the dearly bought victory of Athens at Arginusae.² Ever since the Spartans had taken the advice of the exiled Alcibiades and maintained a garrison in Attica at Decelea, the merriment of the yearly

---

¹ τὸν καλλιχορώτατον (τρόπον) has an unmistakable reminiscence in meaning and sound of the Καλλίχορον φρέαρ, where Demeter sat until she was comforted there by dances. Homer, *Hymn to Demeter*, 272; Pausanias, I. xxxviii. 6.
² See Kock's introduction to his edition of the *Frogs*.

procession to Eleusis had been greatly interfered with, even though it be supposed to have had the protection of a sacred truce.[1] Thus at a time when the Athenians were in a gloomy and thoroughly discouraged state of mind, the religious consolations and assurances of salvation gained by the normal celebration at Eleusis and the processions before and after it were so curtailed that, instead of expecting help from Eleusis, the pious Athenian must have feared that the Eleusinian Alliance of gods was offended by years of comparative neglect. Then it was that Aristophanes, inspired perhaps by the story recorded in Herodotus of a visionary celebration held by the departed in the upper world, hit upon the idea of having something like it celebrated by his living mimes in a stage counterfeit of the world below. The resulting success of his play was overwhelming and unexampled. The *Frogs* was acted a second time without alteration that same year, and over and above all the ordinary marks and rewards of victory, the poet had given to him a branch of the sacred Athenian olive-tree. This last honour was a rare and high mark of popular gratitude for great help to the State, paid afterwards to Thrasybulus. It was equivalent to the public bestowal of a crown of gold, which fell to the lot of Demosthenes. Only the propitiation of the favour of the gods at Eleusis, a thing quite independent of the merits of the play, could have warranted such a mark of favour to Aristophanes.

To his audience the presentation which Aristophanes gave of the procession and the rites before and after up to the moment when the real and most unutterable mysteries began was in fact eminently consoling, for the poet, without

[1] The willingness of Sparta to interfere with Eleusinian worship had been amply shown by the conduct of Cleomenes referred to above.

dwelling upon details known familiarly to all, reproduced the spirit and the truth of the observance. Indeed as the mystae leave his stage they are proclaiming the justice and loving-kindness of Athens to all within her gates. In order to complete in detail the picture given by our poet, certain facts familiar to his audience, or else presented to them visually on the stage, must be rehearsed and heeded. Some of them are as follows: The Hierophant or leader and marshaller of the procession had other names such as Iacchagogos, the Vauntcourier or Leader of Iacchos. Through the Holy Gate they passed crowned with parsley and with ivy where fruits were intertwined. In their hands they carried Bacchus' lighted torches or else Demeter's sheaves, and thus their mere array was eloquent of harmony between the goddess and the god. Many were the stations required by immemorial custom for this procession. Harvest usages observed in the intervening villages naturally grouped themselves around the passage of these pilgrims, who formed the annual escort of the farmer's god, Dionysus, to Eleusis.[1] Before the Attic Cephissus was reached the district of Lakkiadae required a pious pause. Phytalus there had played host to Demeter, and his reward had been the gift of figs. With jibes and jollity the Eleusinian band crossed the memorable bridge and approached the altars of most gentle Zeus beyond the Cephissus. Reminiscences of heroic Theseus detained them then, and after this they halted at the shrine of Cyamites, giver of beans. Much as the Bean-giver was here revered, the beans which he gave, and all beans, were strictly excluded from the Eleusinian precinct of Demeter.

[1] For a more complete account see F. Lenormant's *La voie sacrée* already alluded to.

This, says Pausanias, is a mystery known to those initiated at Eleusis.[1]

In the pass where stands the modern cloister and church of Daphne they stopped at a temple originally Apollo's, but where later on Demeter and Athena shared the sanctuary with Apollo. Then, just after a forward glimpse of the bay of Eleusis, halt was made at Aphrodite's temple, and the tomb of Eumolpus was reached. This great Eleusinian hero welcomed them and Iacchos to the Eleusinian plain, all the more heartily perhaps because, like Dionysus himself, he was from Thrace.[2]

A whole book was written in antiquity by Polemon on this processional progress, and Pausanias repeats from this source many interesting details, willing all the more to give information on the preliminaries of the great Eleusinian festival because divine warning has sealed his lips about the Mysteries themselves.

It does not suit the present theme, however, to dwell further upon details; enough has already been said to show how great a complexity of ritual, what an enormous variety of local customs, attended the annual progress of Dionysus to Eleusis. If the ceremonial used upon his arrival were known to us, we should doubtless marvel still more at the power of growth and of fusion inherent in the local religions of Attica, at the way in which Demeter and Persephone tamed the wildness of Thracian Dionysus, while all three counteracted the bloodless gloom of Hades and were united with him at Eleusis in the time-honoured observance of eight hundred years.

[1] The bean seems by long familiarity to have fallen into contempt, so that we no longer shudder at it, and are only amused at Pythagorean scruples which led men to die rather than pass through a field planted with this tragic vegetable.   [2] Strabo, VIII. vii. 1 (383).

VI

AESCULAPIUS AT EPIDAURUS AND ATHENS

ONE of the great features of the Greater Mysteries commemorated the Eleusinian initiation of the god Aesculapius. In the fabulous past this god of healing had crossed the Saronic gulf and associated himself and his Epidaurian worship with Athens and Eleusis, and this mythical arrival prefigured, as it were, the introduction of Aesculapian worship at Athens, and the renown of his Athenian shrine founded from Epidaurus in historical times.

In the days of his widest influence Aesculapius, the god of healing, was looked upon—in spite of various records making him a son of Zeus—as the son of Apollo. So completely was he associated at one time or another with his father Apollo Epicuros or Epicurios,—the supporter of health,—that we may if we choose look upon him as Apollo's plenipotentiary in the comparatively late legend that connects him with Eleusis.[1] A tie of more than com-

---

[1] The influence of Pythagoreanism upon the beginnings of medicine is not less abundantly proven than the close tie that bound Pythagoras and his school to Apollo. Seven of the Alexandrine doctors (see Daremberg's list) bore the name Apollonius. This denoted one whose spirit was under Apolline guidance. Such a son of the healing spirit of Apollo was Aesculapius, the divine exemplar to whom Greek doctors looked up.

mon strength seems to attach him to Demeter and Persephone, for he is associated with them in certain bas-reliefs. His connection with Dionysus is vaguer by far, but not less real.

Ultimately it may be possible to make out with some clearness the precise nature of this tie binding Aesculapius to the gods at Eleusis. But, in the present state of knowledge, the closest scrutiny of Aesculapius and his worship only reveals uncertain associations and resemblances. Like the gods at Eleusis, Aesculapius was not recognised in the fulness of his subsequent godhead by the Greeks of Homer's epoch. Aesculapius, like those same gods, but far more vaguely and uncertainly, is a nature-god. Like Dionysus and Demeter he, or at least his characteristic element, came to an ultimate and more southerly birth-place from the north.[1] Perhaps he may be looked upon as a netherworld nature-divinity, the same in many respects with Dionysus, but without his tragic intensity. To this residuum add something of the Olympian mildness of Zeus, and you have a being who may with equal appropriateness be classed with the netherworld brother of Zeus or be called a son of Zeus. Dionysus came from Thrace

---

In later days Apollonius of Tyana (see Appendix IV. below), the favourite of Aesculapius, stood for the same Apolline perfection. In prayers and offerings at Aesculapius' shrine Apollo was commonly named first and then Aesculapius, and furthermore, according to the rule of Hippocrates, every doctor qualified as such by an oath "in the name of Apollo the healer, and of Aesculapius, of Hygieia and Panacea, and of all the gods and all the goddesses."

[1] I have not found it either possible or advisable to go into the theory, a plausible one, that the Thracians may have been the Pelasgian predecessors of what we call the Greek civilisation, and that we should not talk of an invasion from the north, but rather of a survival or inheritance. According to this view the most ancient traces of building on the Acropolis, whether of Eleusis or of Athens, might be attributed to these Pelasgo-Thracians.

and from Macedonia just beyond the range of Mount Olympus, Aesculapius came from that part of Thessaly which is closest to these mountains, and Demeter's Thessalian origin was from Pyrasus not far away. At Pyrasus was Demeter's first home, and among the mountain tribes near by Aesculapius originated. He was the tribal god of the half mythological people called Phlegyae and Lapithae. In the wake of northern tribes this god Aesculapius—a more majestic figure than the blameless leech of Homer's song—came by land to Epidaurus and was carried by sea to the eastward island of Cos. With him perhaps was borne from her Thessalian home the goddess Demeter, who found her Cnidian shrine not far from the Coan home of Aesculapius. This southward journey is the counterpart of that by which Dionysus is supposed to have reached, with bands of Thracian invaders, Attica and Boeotia as well as his island home on Naxos. Our knowledge of these invasions, Thracian and Thessalian, is so misty that it is well-nigh absurd to attempt to say which preceded the other, or indeed to maintain with any vigour that all these various divinities cannot have been brought in by one and the same southward movement of mountain tribes; for the boundary line separating Thessalians from Macedonians, and the distinction—never clear—between Macedonians and Thracians, are not strictly applicable to these prehistoric days.

Arrived from the north, Aesculapius grew in importance with the growth of Greece, but may not have attained his greatest power until Greece and Rome were one. At all events every stage of his power and prestige connects itself so closely with the various phases of secular medicine that, in order to understand the results of recent excavations at

Athens and Epidaurus,—made at both places in sanctuaries of Aesculapius,—something must be said about the position of Greek doctors and the history of Greek medicine, sacred and secular. This last distinction was certainly not made until after the fabled siege of Troy, as is shown by the earliest record of Greek opinion about doctors which is to be found in the *Iliad*. One of the sons of Aesculapius, Machaon, was seriously wounded in a *mêlée*. When he fell disabled, consternation seized the Greeks until Nestor's timely aid was invoked. Nestor, the personification of respectable tradition in those days, bears off the healer Machaon, declaring roundly, as he does so, that a doctor is far better worth saving than many warriors unskilled in leechcraft. Plainly a doctor, as Nestor understood the word, meant not a secular but a sacred person, and medicine was both sacred and secular. Here is a half superstitious and wholly generous admiration for skill in medicine that may be called a typically Greek sentiment; since it never has died out in Greece, and is found intact among the Homerically simple-minded peasants of to-day.[1]

It will eventually be necessary to analyse this typically Greek sentiment of Nestor's and to appeal to the Homeric poems at large about doctors and medicine. Thus we shall understand on the one hand the worship of Aesculapius as a wonder-worker, and on the other the non-miraculous professional skill possessed by Greek doctors who pursued the art of healing and perfected the science of medicine independently of the god. Let us begin our survey at a time when doctors had a considerable knowledge of medicine. This unmiraculous and scientific profession may be traced

[1] See Appendix V. on the status of Greek doctors in modern times.

back to a correspondingly positive and unsuperstitious aspect of Homeric medicine.[1]

Let us consider the condition of Greek medicine as it was in the days of Hippocrates of Cos, ordinarily miscalled the father of Greek medicine. A casual glance at Littré's complete edition of all works handed down under the name of Hippocrates shows that among them are monuments of sound medical labours carried out before his day. Indeed Hippocrates dealt with a large body of ascertained medical facts, and Greek medicine was far advanced when he began. To make this apparent we need only consider the career of Democedes as related by Herodotus.

Two generations before Hippocrates, in the second half of the sixth century B.C., this Democedes lived, and enjoyed an Asiatic renown, equivalent in those days to what our doctors call a European reputation. Starting from the far west, Croton in Italy, where Pythagoreanism had given a great impetus to the study of medicine,[2] the alert and ready-witted Democedes went to Aegina and distanced all competitors in the race for appointment there. This was the more brilliant, says Herodotus, because he was, when he entered the lists, without the instruments freely used by his fellow-candidates. A year's service on Aegina as public

[1] Daremberg, *Histoire des Sciences Médicales*, I. ch. iii.
[2] The influence of many philosophers may be traced in the method and opinions of Hippocrates, but probably no school affected the beginnings of medicine so much as that of Pythagoras. See, among the letters attributed to Apollonius of Tyana, number xxiii., "Pythagoras said that medicine came most near to divinity, and inasmuch as this was the case, medicine should care for the soul as well as for the body; or else the whole living being would fail of full health from having his higher element diseased." The Pythagorean Alcmaeon of Croton was addicted to anatomy —he dissected animals; and these studies contributed to give a specially useful bent to the school of medicine at Croton, of whose renown Herodotus makes admiring mention. It must be remembered that Croton was the centre of Pythagoreanism.

practitioner paid by the state so increased the reputation of Democedes that Athens offered him the same duties and an increase of salary. He was no sooner settled at his work in Athens than Polycrates, the too-fortunate tyrant of Samos, succeeded in getting him by doubling his salary. A call still further east soon came to Democedes,—a promotion under the disguise of complete disaster. The flood of fortune that had so long upborne his patron Polycrates ebbed suddenly away. Democedes, captured and enslaved during the sack of Samos, was hurried into the far interior, to the palace of Darius. Long a despised and unnoted captive, he was at last terrified by a summons to the king. The rest of the story, beginning with his refusal to acknowledge his own skill, repeated itself at the court of the Duke of Savoy in the sixteenth century,[1] and is travestied in one of Molière's best farces. Threats overcame the great doctor's scruples; and Darius' sprain, which had only been aggravated by the treatment of the accredited Egyptian doctors, was quickly and completely cured.

The story of Democedes' career proves at least that Herodotus, writing and living early in the days of Pericles and Hippocrates, believed that skilled doctors of Greek training had been in request as such for a century and a half at least. To show how advanced was the condition of medical science in the day of Herodotus, there is all manner of undoubted testimony. Socrates for instance, who was only eight years older than the great Coan doctor, throws light upon this point in his chaff of a friend named Euthydemus, who undertook to make a stir in the world by having many books. "Of course you who have so many

[1] See Malgaigne's *Chirurgie grecque avant Hippocrate.*

books are going in for being a doctor," says Socrates, and then he adds, "there are so many books on medicine, you know." Euthydemus repudiates this inference with indignation. Whatever the quality of these books may have been, their number must have been great to give point to this chaff. Xenophon is nearly contemporary though somewhat later, and his testimony may be added. The liberal provision of medical care for his retreating army, the matter-of-course way in which the most suitable remedies get themselves promptly applied on occasion—all this tells of an established system of military practice,[1] and proves again how little sense there ever was in saying that Greek medicine began in 460 B.C. with Hippocrates of Cos. There can be no doubt that Hippocrates was not bred under the shadow of the great Coan temple of Aesculapius for nothing. His own writings prove that he heeded well the lore of the priests at Cos. For, although he is not the author of the compilation made from materials accumulated at the Coan temple and included among his supposed work, he plainly used that compilation, and was guided by the traditions which it embodies. It is equally certain that he gathered in the fruits of many generations of zealous labour in surgery, and it seems possible that much of the surgery before his time had been developed quite independently, without knowledge, so to speak, or connivance of Aesculapius, the god of medicine. There is at all events little or nothing to show that Aesculapius was worshipped in Magna Grecia and at Croton, while Democedes, who was trained there, certainly was specially qualified as a surgeon. Malgaigne

[1] See in the *Gazette Hebdomadaire de Médecine et de Chirurgie* for June 20th 1879, Dr. Corlieu's "Étude médicale sur la retraite des 10,000 precédée de considérations sur la médecine militaire dans les armées grecques."

goes too far if he claims that Democedes had not a full acquaintance with the remedies in use when he flourished.[1]

It is best, however, not to linger over the question whether or not the surgery known to Hippocrates had become as intimately associated with the shrines of Aesculapius and the guild of the Asclepiadae as the other traditions and practices which made up early Greek medicine.[2] One thing at least is certain, that necessity was the mother of this invention; it had a secular origin in constant warfare. To the bickerings of earliest Greece science owes a greater debt than is often recognised. The fullest record of the way in which this debt was incurred is found in the *Iliad*, that poem of glorified bloodshed. Here is the positive, the secular, the scientific aspect of Homeric medicine. There can be no reasonable doubt that all the minute descriptions given in the *Iliad* of wounds, thrusts, and contusions were listened to by men of Homer's time with a breathless interest. Everybody finds them more or less trying now. To know in one of these battles just where the man was struck, just how far the weapon went, and exactly what was the behaviour of the striker and the struck when the blow was given, seems of slight interest or of none at all to-day. The wonderful thing to us is that there should ever have been a

[1] Malgaigne and Daremberg are at variance here. See Ch. Daremberg, *État de la Médecine entre Homère et Hippocrate*, p. 52.
[2] For an astonishingly unsubstantiated claim that Democedes and the medical school of Croton were absolutely outside the domain of Aesculapius and uninfluenced by his worship, see Guardia's *La Médecine à travers les Siècles*. This book would perhaps not be one to mention if it had not given the authority of its writer's scholarship to the useless theory that in ancient as in modern times there was a recognised conflict between "science and religion." A particularly misleading reproduction of Guardia's arbitrary and baseless account of the worship of Aesculapius and its relation to sound medicine can be found in an essay read before the Birmingham Speculative Club by Balthazar W. Foster, M.D., and published in 1870.

popular interest in these slaughterous minutiae of the human frame. But, for all that, Homer's careful accuracy is better art, and of more enduring interest, than the loose and laughable anatomical absurdities, the braggart atrocities so frequently admired in *chansons de gestes* and in various utterances of the age of medieval chivalry. The tiresome minuteness of Homer has always the merit of accuracy and truth. Competent judges in matters medical have pronounced Homer a marvel of clearness and precision. That his account should be trustworthy was absolutely required by his hearers. They had a personal knowledge in the matters whereof he sang, and demanded of him not simply such precision as they could attain themselves, but hoped no doubt also to glean from his descriptions hints for future combat. They knew anatomy chiefly that they might, when fighting, put in each blow where it would do the utmost harm. They wished to kill rather than to cure; and yet, like the heroes in whose life the poet mirrored their own, they had some knowledge of surgery—enough to help a wounded comrade in danger of his life.

With the incentive supplied by a breathlessly interested audience it is not surprising that Homer, or the Homeric bards, should have been extraordinarily painstaking in matters anatomical. Among scores of wounds described by him, only seven, it is said,[1] are given so vaguely that the skilled anatomist cannot determine very nearly where, and in some degree also how serious, a wound is meant. As for the defects in Homer's anatomy they are few, and such as may more fairly be cloaked with the poet's mantle than

[1] For a competent specialist's account of the facts upon which this appreciation of Homeric anatomy, surgery, and medicine is based, see Charles Daremberg in the *Revue Archéologique* for September, October, and November, 1865. "Etudes d'archéologie médicale sur Homère."

the shortcomings discoverable in *Amadis de Gaule*, or even in our own Spenser's *Faëry Queene*.

The same detailed knowledge of anatomy which Homer possessed, and which was possessed by his most critical audiences, is very naturally attributed to his great heroes. To be convinced of this, hear Odysseus when a desperate situation prompts the thought of suicide. He does not think vaguely of self-destruction, he knows the exact and most vulnerable spot where he will strike himself; and it is the same when he has the giant Polyphemus in drunken sleep before him. You can fancy a warrior of Homer's day teaching his son by Odysseus' example the duty of knowing the human frame in every least detail. You can fancy the same anxious father taking the miserable case of Pandarus to bring home to his boy the fatal consequences of incompetence and inaccuracy. Foolish Pandarus thought that a mere shoulder-wound inflicted by his arrow on Diomede had killed him, and not brought him merely to a faint. Therefore the reappearance of Diomede, after recovery, so unmans this ignorant would-be slayer that he loses nerve and is slaughtered ignominiously.

A second and strong impulse to this minute anatomical knowledge of Homer's day was, as already said, the need of such knowledge to succour a wounded comrade. This further involved a rough knowledge of surgical aids and of certain simple remedies. A good man of war, a real hero, was bound to know the surgery of his day. Rough and rudimentary as this was, it involved a knowledge of bandaging, the respectability of which is proved from early pictures representing the process. Combined with this heroic surgery was a certain familiarity with drugs. Powdered herbs, for instance, were used to staunch the flowing blood, and also to ease pain. It may in fact be said most truly that the reader of Homer, to be ideally qualified, so far as medicine is concerned, must know anatomy rather well, should have seen some simple processes of surgery, and should know the medical properties of several common herbs.

Thus it gradually grows plain that the anatomy of Homer had a very considerable bearing on the subsequent development of medicine. To the Homeric infatuation for minutely clear accounts of the give and take of sword-thrusts, spear-thrusts, arrow-wounds, and of all the awful bruises, fractures, and contusions caused by such jagged stones as still cover the fields of Greece, modern science owes tools without which its early course would have been hampered and its vision constantly befogged. The Homeric heroes won more than their own victories where they fought and conquered with such desperate skill; they won a victory for us as well. They fought strenuously that we might think clearly, since a vast proportion of the anatomical terms in scientific use to-day are words whose meaning became definite as those heroes grew more skilful in fighting, and learned to use their weapons with a deadlier knowledge.

The chief inheritors of the almost scientific and wholly unmiraculous surgery and surgical skill of the Homeric age were professional doctors, such as those who competed at Aegina and Athens with the skilful Democedes. These men, often in the employ of the state, made possible, and kept in successful operation, large public establishments which really deserved the name of hospitals.[1]

This must be insisted upon, because there is a growing danger of calling by the name of hospitals institutions

---

[1] On this difficult question see Dr. Vercoutre, "La médecine publique dans l'antiquité grecque," in the *Revue Archéologique*, 1880.

which, in spite of certain resemblances to hospitals, have a very different character—the temples of Aesculapius. A severance, gradually indeed but very early, took place between secular and Aesculapian healing. It is not easy to recognise this fact, because anciently there never was in any field, least of all in the field of ancient medicine, the modern antagonism between science and religion. Let those who wilfully misinterpret the past in order the more completely to misunderstand the present say that this was so because science was unscientific, or because religion was an empty show. The fact remains that, in spite of the severance above-mentioned, the doctors kept in touch with the worship of Aesculapius, and the priests in his temples did not scorn such secular knowledge as they could gain from lay practitioners.

Perhaps the difference in temper between these two schools, if the word school may be so far misused, is best understood by a backward glance. Let us again apply to Homer and—forgetting this time that he had facts to deal with—let us ask him for fancies. In contrast to what I have said concerning the definite knowledge implied by the Homeric anatomy, there was a fairy-land in the medical world of the heroic age, and within its borders ruled a spirit which knew not accuracy, and was but faintly and distantly acquainted with facts. The two sons of the noble leech Aesculapius, named Machaon and Podalirius, together with an unspecified number of doctors, not only had in a more perfect degree the knowledge of anatomy which the Homeric heroes possessed, but also a general claim to infallibility was popularly made for them. They were, as has been abundantly shown, surrounded by a deference not shown to ordinary men. A superstitious regard for Aesculapius and his two sons allied itself to a child-like belief in the existence of miracle-working drugs. These drugs were either, like the *moly* given by Hermes to Odysseus, procurable only by an immortal god, or, like Helen's Egyptian *nepenthe*, they came from some far-off and unvisitable place. Just so it was with the miraculous *lotus blossom*. Such too were the herbs of marvellous and uncanny effect known to Circe and Medea, who both had learned of them from their father Aeëtes, to whom the knowledge descended from his father the Sun. From Paean (who came later to be identified with the Sun and Apollo) were descended, so Homer says, the Egyptians, and all Egyptians had wonderful knowledge of herbs. Aesculapius himself was, as his worshippers finally agreed, the offspring of Apollo, who was Helios, this same Paean, the sun-god. One more touch of Homer's must here be mentioned. His Aesculapius, although Apollo is his father and protector, had Coronis, a mortal maiden, for his mother, and had to gain by mortal means his more than mortal skill in medicine. This brings us to a whole cycle of early legends, touched upon more or less fully by Homer, where medicine becomes further involved in the mists of uncertain mythology and early superstition.

The schooling of Aesculapius in medicine was not different from that of many other heroes. The master common to them all was Chiron, in whose nature the irrepressible bestiality of his fellow-centaurs has been transformed into a wise and genial power of sympathy. The gentle Chiron possessed a power of insight into nature, was so at one with the hearts of men and beasts, that although by nature he was below, by knowledge he was above mere human kind. Chiron's strange name and nature, half human and half of lower origin, may stand as a link between the spirit of man and the useful essence of plants, just as the lower animals connect man's bodily frame with the shapes of the vegetable kingdom.¹ Chiron embodied for the Homeric understanding what we prefer, after our more abstract fashion, to call the earliest of all early stages of medicine. This prehistoric medicine consisted of a well-defined though superficial knowledge of the human frame, by no means equal to that which may fairly be attributed to Odysseus, and of a limited acquaintance with nature's most obvious simples. So far as this last point is concerned, Chiron embodied all the knowledge of Homeric days, which was by no means incompatible with that superstitious belief in the efficacy of certain unprocurable roots and herbs of which Homer is full, and the like of which survives to-day in various tales of the mad-dog stone. This skill of Chiron the centaur in the medicine of herbs is medicine reduced to its simplest terms, and in this were versed those who bore the greatest names upon the Heroic roll of honour—Aesculapius and Amphiaraus, the Boeotian Aesculapius about whom much has been recently discovered at Oropus in Attica, Achilles and Theseus, Jason and Aeneas, Castor and Pollux, Nestor and Odysseus, Peleus, Telamon, Meleager, and many others. Hence it is that all of them are spoken of as pupils of Chiron.

The fact that Aesculapius, although under the especial

¹ Just here the distinction, much insisted upon above, stands within the danger of confusion and threatens to break down, for Chiron ends by representing the reasonable and unmiraculous aspect of early medical lore. We find in the fantastic centaur a spirit of serene science and right reason which defies every attempt to draw a sharp line dividing the fanciful and fairy-like from the positive and practical in Homer's poetical account of heroic medicine. Here in a new case we feel the incommunicable charm and subtle creative power of Greek fancy.

favour of the god of healing, was yet classed among the other illustrious pupils of Chiron, shows that the Homeric age was hardly more appreciative of the divinity of Aesculapius than of the divine character and importance of Demeter and Dionysus. Aesculapius and his sons are thought of by Homer as divinely perfected men—leeches whose skill is human, though of an excellence all but divine. Plainly this Homeric Aesculapius is not the great god of the Thessalian Lapithae and Phlegyae. Only an echo of his power and helpful kindness reached the early Greeks, sounding through the *Iliad* and the *Odyssey*. In order that the divine pretensions of Aesculapius might ally themselves to the gentler and more human aspect which he wears in Homeric story, a radical change was required. All this is brought to pass in the story of the birth of the god at Epidaurus, where Coronis, a daughter of the Thessalian king Phlegyas, brought him to birth. The accident of Phlegyas' temporary sojourn in Argolis and Epidaurus, so the Epidaurian legend runs, made Aesculapius an Epidaurian; but upon this accident his latter-day majesty depends.

But, before pursuing this Epidaurian theme, let us summarise the early course of medicine in Greece. Even in Homer's account, where the whole field of medicine is small, and where there are no clear subdivisions, certain divergent tendencies may be dimly distinguished. There is the positive practical tendency, and this is perhaps the preponderating one. There is also the poetically superstitious tendency, which shows itself in tales of marvellous cures by Aesculapius and others, of wonderful drugs procured by heroes under the especial protection of heaven, and of wonderful skill and knowledge possessed and taught by Chiron. From the former and more positive tendency sprang Greek anatomy and surgery, the medicine of Democedes, Hippocrates, and the school that sprang up under the shadow of the Coan sanctuary, together with a fair proportion of the sayings and doings of conscientious priests in the sanctuaries of Aesculapius scattered over Greece. From the less positive and more superstitious aspect of medicine as known in early legends, Homeric and others, nothing perhaps would have come without the help of the Thessalian deification of Aesculapius. When the Thessalian cult of the god of healing came into contact with the conceptions of medicine embodied in the *Iliad*, it apparently exercised little or no influence upon the positive, but absorbed into itself the vague and the miraculous. All the wondering terror with which Chiron's skill, Circe's sorcery, and Medea's knowledge of simples had been regarded was soon garnered into the treasure-houses of Aesculapius. His temples became centres of miracles, as well as places for the practical study of medicine. Of course there was this latter side to the worship of Aesculapius, or else Hippocrates would not have spoken as he did, and in later days Galen would not have had such close commerce with the priests of Aesculapius. Indeed, superstitious as the worship of Aesculapius was, the most irrefutable proof that it was neither wholly nor intolerably so is the more than toleration of it by the most admirable men of Greek and Roman medicine.

There is one point of view common to the most marvellous of Homer's fairy tales, to the practice of medicine by the priests of Aesculapius, and to certain most and least approved aspects of modern medical procedure. This is the notion of affecting the mind through the body. That wonder-working Egyptian drug, Helen's nepenthe, and also the fatal flower of the lotus, cast a spell upon the mind.

In like manner, after the worship of Aesculapius had run its course through centuries and reached its final, perhaps its most useful, form in the days of Galen and the Antonines, this same belief was most vigorous. "It was an age of valetudinarians," says a competent authority, "in many cases of imaginary ones; but below its various crazes concerning health and disease . . . lay a valuable, because partly practicable, belief that all the maladies of the soul might be reached through the subtle gateways of the body."[1] The man who understood drugs was, in Homer's day, and during the age of the Antonines, as he is now, a healer of all curable illnesses whether of body or mind. Then as now power through the body over the mind was attributed to him.

The priests of Aesculapius, however, were far from taking a materialistic view of the soul. They supplemented the notion that an unsound mind can be cured through the body by another to which they attached every importance, *i.e.* that the sound mind can and should completely control the sound body. The prescriptions of Aesculapius were sometimes given to the purified and expectant sufferer in dreams. Often Aesculapius himself appeared in a dream and touched the sick; sometimes a messenger came, a voice as it were through the gateways of sleep would tell what herb or what treatment was necessary. Sometimes healing came from the nocturnal touch of serpents or of dogs sent by the god to his suppliants.

The prescribed process by which the possibility of dreaming an inspired dream was attained was one which

---

[1] *Marius the Epicurean*, by Walter Pater, M.A., chap. iii. The whole of this admirable chapter well repays careful study. I know no other adequate modern presentation of the sweetness and sanctity of the service of Aesculapius.

necessarily stilled the mental alarms of the sufferer. His condition had to be one of passivity, such as doctors sometimes impose upon those who suffer from nervous prostration. Not in a moment of excitement, but during the calm hours of unstirred sleep came these divine dreams. They might visit men anywhere, but for the most part they came only in the hallowed seclusion of the Aesculapian Sanctuary. Since all who were at the point of death and of child-birth were rigorously excluded, panics and excitements were the less possible; the patient had to conform to the law of purification prescribed in the temple, and then to lie down within the temple itself or a porch[1] near by, and within the precinct. This process of lying down in the temple for the purpose of dreaming gets itself called by a Latin name which means literally sleeping in, and we hear much of the practice of Incubation in the ancient temples of Aesculapius. Men of pious minds resorted to it in order to hatch out dreams whereby knowledge of needful remedies came to them. The dream was more or less consciously thought of as having a being apart, like the dream in the *Iliad* sent by Zeus to Agamemnon,—only the dream in the temple of Aesculapius came to enlighten, not to deceive. What such dreams were supposed by the pious to accomplish is best shown by the prayer which Aristides addressed to them. "Endue my body," prays the grateful worshipper of dreams, "with such measure of health as may suffice it for the obeying of the spirit, that I may pass the day unhindered and in quietness."[2] The body was cured in order that through it the spirit might gain self-command and rule the whole man.

[1] The word *stoa* or *porticus* is strictly required. Neither of these being English, I have preferred to stretch the meaning of the word porch.
[2] Mr. Pater's translation.

I have said that Greek secular medicine sprang from the more positive and surgical side of the earliest pursuit of medicine. I have also said that all the extravagances and miracles believed in from the earliest days centred gradually around the worship of Aesculapius. But in fact the line between secular and sacred is hardly more easy to draw for these later days than for Homeric times. Surgery, of all things, ought to have been the exclusive province of the secular practitioners, and yet inscriptions[1] found at Epidaurus within the precinct of Aesculapius show that operations were sometimes performed by the servants of the god and under his inspiration, though, to be sure, the particular cases there described would appear to have been most unsurgically dealt with. On the other hand, if the distinction in question is pressed too far, or too sharply drawn, a secular practitioner like Herophilus ought to have been quite free from the Homeric point of view about the superhuman efficacy of drugs. And yet this Herophilus, a celebrated physician who flourished during the first years of the third century B.C., speaks of all medicines as gifts from the gods, and calls them, when rightly used, "the hands of the gods."[2] This appeal to the healing hands of the gods in everyday practice is a beautifully enlightened modification of Homer's

---

[1] The best concise account of these inscriptions known to me is Dr. Merriam's referred to below. Their discovery and elucidation is one of the first of the useful achievements of the distinguished M. Kabbadias, Ephor-in-chief of Antiquities. Strabo speaks of them, and adds that similar ones were to be found at Cos and Tricca: *i.e.* inscriptions that give record of the manner of each cure, VIII. vi. 16, p. 375.

[2] See the first sentence of the dedication addressed by Scribonius Largus to Caius Julius Callistus. Compare the use of this quotation by Erasmus in his ingenious comparison of the Gospel of St. Luke to a healing medicine. This is in the dedication of his paraphrase of that Gospel, and contrast the sense attached to an analogous expression in the *Philoctetes* of Sophocles : speaking of Philoctetes writhing with pain, the chorus cries out ὦ παλάμαι θεῶν (177).

notion that the root *moly* could only be digged from its secret hiding place by a god. And indeed this utterance of Herophilus was quite in agreement with the view of Hippocrates, who said long before the day of Herophilus, with reference to divine intervention and healing, "Medicine inclines to do honour to the gods as concerning symptoms or sickness, and doctors give way before them, since medical lore has no superabundance of power."[1]

And yet this harmony between science and religion, this pious deference of physicians to the god of physic and their respect for the miracles worked in his name, left a difficult question for the decision of laymen. When should there be appeal to the god and his divine skill, and when should the counsel of human doctors be resorted to? The doctrine of Socrates may well be taken to represent the mind of the most enlightened men. "Seek as far as you may to help yourself before asking the gods for help and counsel." This was the view of Socrates about consulting oracles in general, and no doubt he would have applied it to the most primitive and wide-spread of all Greek ways of consulting oracles, the dreaming of dreams in the sanctuary of Aesculapius, as well as to other appeals to Aesculapian skill. "Exhaust human skill and resource before appealing to the god," he would have said. Theoretically this view of

[1] See the sixth paragraph of the treatise on professional honour (περὶ εὐσχημοσύνης). This treatise is by some considered, though on purely negative grounds, of doubtful authorship. I am convinced with Daremberg that it is by Hippocrates; some doctor certainly wrote it, and it certainly represents a typical point of view. This spirit of pious deference to divine power is by no means confined to one treatise of Hippocrates. There is a solitary quotation upon which the ingenious Wilamovitz-Moellendorf founds his otherwise baseless assertion that Hippocrates was free from any belief in Aesculapius. The passage occurs in the treatise on airs, waters, and climates, and is a protest against a gross Scythian superstition. Moellendorf's very strained reading of it can be refuted by other undoubted sayings of Hippocrates.

duty was above reproach, but practice was another matter. Many motives led the faithful to consult Aesculapius more frequently than this principle, strictly adhered to, would allow; and among them the most decisive one was his approachability. A feeling of familar comradeship was inspired in all his worshippers by Aesculapius, and in this Socrates certainly shared, since his dying words were: "Crito, we owe a cock to Aesculapius." The meaning of this solemnly smiling farewell of Socrates would seem to be that to Aesculapius, a god who always is prescribing potions and whose power is manifest in their effects, was due that most welcome and sovereign remedy which cured all the pains and ended all the woes of Socrates—the hemlock, which cured him of life which is death, and gave him the glorious realities of hereafter. For this great boon of awakening into real life Socrates owed Aesculapius a thank-offering. This offering of a cock to Aesculapius was plainly intended for him as the awakener of the dead to life everlasting.

In the story which makes Aesculapius incur the wrath of Zeus in order to recall to life one who was dead, and further, in the minds of all worshippers, this god—standing before Zeus as divine yet also human—is, like Prometheus, a loving and indulgent friend of man even when other deities frown. Apollo intercedes for him with angered Zeus much as he might for a man. Something of the mortality attributed to him in the Homeric poems, a half-humanity, clung to Aesculapius throughout antiquity; and the latter Greeks never quite banished from their worship of this god the notion that he was a hero or demigod only. How natural it was in Athens to think of a healing power under this aspect is shown by the dim knowledge that we have of an

Athenian temple dedicated, not to Aesculapius, but to the "Hero physician." Even after his full divinity came into general recognition, therefore, Aesculapius bore marks of his previous condition. He was worshipped and besought not always under the name of a god, but most frequently under the designation, familiar to Christian ears, of the Son of God. *Filius dei* was in fact the habitual and unqualified manner of addressing Aesculapius in his temples at Rome. Partly human of birth, he was wholly so in sympathy; but, in his perfect power to help and heal, he was divine.

This halo of humanity, if the expression be allowed, was worn by Aesculapius with all the better grace because he was by no means foremost in the Olympian hierarchy—since our minds condemn us to talk of a hierarchy when there was none. The god of healing, with all his train of abundant divinities, Health, Panacea, Convalescence (Telesphorus), and the many others,—kindly presences all of them, called into being solely to ease men's pain,—may be thought of as dwelling somewhere midway between the gods above and men below. There they dwelt in order perhaps to be near at hand when the calamities of men required their instant aid. So human were the beginnings of Aesculapius that he depended upon the power and presence in Olympus of Apollo his father. Just as we may imagine, if we choose, that Aesculapius was the vicar of Apollo on earth to represent him at the Eleusinian Mysteries, so we know that Apollo was the heavenly presence whose Olympian power sustained and increased the divine efficacy of all the works of his son Aesculapius. The words *filius dei* apply to Aesculapius as the son of Apollo the god.

"Save me, and heal my grievous gout, O blessed and

most mighty presence, I adjure thee by thy father, to whom I loudly pray." Such is the prayer addressed to Aesculapius, "Son of Leto's son," by Diophantus, an attendant at his shrine, which has been lately uncovered on the southern slope of the Athenian Acropolis. This inscribed prayer is that of Diophantus born in the Athenian township of Sphettus. Its faults are many in versification, and it lacks poetic delicacy of phrase, but still—Diophantus having been an attendant in the Athenian temple of Aesculapius—it preserves for us an official view of the relation between Aesculapius the divine son and the divine father Apollo. In their eyes a prayer to Aesculapius was also a prayer to Apollo, and the god of healing was thought of by them as a pitiful and indulgent mediator between man and the Holiest and Mightiest. "No one of mortals," Diophantus continues in this same inscription, "can give a surcease from such pangs. Thou alone, divinely blessed one, hast the power; for the supreme gods bestowed on thee, all pitying one, a rich gift for mortals. Thou art their appointed deliverer from pain."[1] Thus Aesculapius was not mortal though he was under inspiration from above—he was the well-beloved saviour from suffering, the comforter sent by Apollo.

A curiously close relation between Apollo the father and the son Aesculapius is shown by the Apolline epithet Paean

[1] See in the May number of Gaillard's *Medical Journal* (vol. xi. No. 5), published in New York, an article on "Aesculapia as revealed by Inscriptions," recast from a paper read before the New York Academy of Medicine, 19th March 1885, by Augustus C. Merriam, A.M., Ph.D. Professor Merriam has there given the most concise account of all the facts bearing upon the worship of Aesculapius at Athens and at Epidaurus, and his account of the inscriptions is not only exhaustive but most entertaining. He also gives abundant references to more detailed accounts of the matter in hand.

which this same Diophantus bestows upon Aesculapius in his record, made in the same place, of thanks for recovery. He thanks "Paean Aesculapius," to whose skill he attributes his deliverance. This consummation devoutly to be desired was promised him by Aesculapius, who appeared in a dream. This whole episode in Diophantus' life is a most authentic and imperishable record, kept upon stone, of the mediating and human divinity of Aesculapius, who transmitted the kindly will of Apollo to suffering men, and lent them the means of grace. It may truly be said of this god of healing that he and his father are one, for even the dreams wherein Aesculapius himself appeared and wrought cure were addressed as the "children of Apollo." "Oh, ye children of Apollo, who in times past have stilled the waves of sorrow for many people, and lighted up a lamp of safety before those who travel by sea and land, be pleased in your great condescension . . . to accept this prayer . . ."[1] So opens the collect of Aristides already alluded to. The final source of power is Apollo; and the accomplishment of cure, no matter what natural means and medicines are employed, is at the bidding of Aesculapius, whose lovingkindness miraculously brings healing. Often, therefore, he was looked upon as a patron saint might be. He was a mediator and an elder brother—a being close to the divinity, with whom the worshipper need not always be on terms of the most ceremonious observance.

This nearness to man involved what we might call humility in some sort, or self-subordination in regard to the other gods; but both of these terms are far too exclusively modern to be used very strictly of any Greek divinity. Aesculapius was not a jealous god, and when his holy pre-

[1] Mr. Pater's translation.

cinct was set apart near to the ancient places of worship sacred to other and older gods, there was not room perhaps for showing him all due honour. Therefore Aesculapius, more than most of the gods in Greece, required for his cult a district all his own—a country sacred to him, where his worship should be the centre of religious and also of social life. Such a country, dedicated to his worship, was the district of Epidaurus.

On the eastern coast of Argolis, full in view from the islands of Salamis and Aegina, over against Athens and the Piraeus, lies the town of Epidaurus, with the volcanic and picturesque peninsula of Methana just to the south of it, beyond a fertile seaward plain. This plain and the mountain heights beyond it form the district of Epidaurus. In the town itself were minor sanctuaries of the god—not only a temple for himself, but one for his wife, *Gentleheart* or Epione they called her; but beyond this name, and the existence of her Epidaurian temple, which disappeared with the town of Epidaurus, little more is known about her. Fortunately it is otherwise with the great centre of all Aesculapian worship in antiquity—the Epidaurian *Hieron* or Holy ground. This lies higher up and farther inland than the town of Epione's shrine. From this Hieron of Epidaurus went forth to the east and west those who established the great centres of Aesculapian worship elsewhere. They claimed to have founded the Coan[1] temple, near which Hippocrates was born, and the sanctuary sacred

[1] Some sort of Aesculapian worship at Cos, of an earlier date than any possible foundation from Epidaurus, must be allowed. Indeed, success and pre-eminence at a comparatively late date probably made the Epidaurians claim to have founded various temples quite as old as their own. The Eleusinians certainly claimed the same sort of precedence over Peloponnesian shrines of less note than theirs, but of equal or greater antiquity.

to Aesculapius on the island in the Tiber at Rome certainly derived from them.

Suppose we have landed at ancient Epidaurus and are bound for this beautiful upland health resort. First our course lies southward till, at half a mile's distance, the inland road turns to cross the fertile but narrow Epidaurian plain, which is about a quarter of a mile in width. The way then follows a mountain torrent for a time, and goes inland two miles and more. Here at a crossways the pilgrim to the shrine of Aesculapius leaves the high road to ascend the side and cross the shoulder of Mount Titthion. Two downward miles, and you are at last on consecrated ground. A semicircle of gentle and, for those parts, well-wooded slopes hems in the Hieron to the northward, the southward, and the eastward, while towards the north-west the valley leans downward into a wider valley, through which extends the carriage-road that goes to Nauplia.[1]

The Epidaurian birth-legend of Aesculapius has already been alluded to. When her father, the Thessalian King Phlegyas, visited Epidaurus to spy out the land with a view to conquest, Coronis was with him. She, fearing discovery by him when her time came, caused the new-born babe Aesculapius, her son by Apollo, to be exposed on the upland slopes of Mount Titthion. The existence of this babe remained unknown of Phlegyas, and would perhaps long have been unheard of, had it not been for what befell a mountain-ranging shepherd, just when the babe was exposed. This shepherd missed a faithful dog and also one of his flock. Aresthanas—for such was the shepherd's name—hastened to make thorough search, and after wandering through many mountain places, found the missing goat giving

[1] The usual approach is by this excellent road.

sustenance to a new-born babe, while the faithful dog was keeping careful guard over the two. To commemorate this beautiful and miraculous episode the name of that mountain became Titthion—the mountain of the nursing-goat.

When Aresthanas sought to lift up the babe a great light streamed from it, as it were the flash of lightning. This was a sign from Heaven; therefore he left the infant god where he had found him, not lifting him up nor bearing him away. Soon the fame of this and other wonders that followed it was noised abroad over land and sea, and people knew that the infant Aesculapius was skilled in all manner of devices for the sick, and—most wonderful of all—people were made aware that in him was the miraculous power to raise from the dead whomsoever he would.

This later story just given from Pausanias is very different from Pindar's earlier one. When Pindar wrote, Aesculapius had not yet definitely changed his abode, and was still sometimes thought of as living in Thessaly. The general course of events, as well as the names Phlegyas and Coronis, are common to both stories, and prove them to be one; but on the whole the earlier[1] one—Pindar's, which knows not Epidaurus but unfolds itself in Thessaly—is the more tragical. There was on the part of Coronis, whom Apollo had wedded, a faithlessness so flagrant that it brought her destruction. The righteous indignation of Apollo, whose sister Artemis slew the guilty maid, made him forget the child that was to be, until Coronis, not yet a mother though a guilty spouse, lay stretched upon the flaming funeral pyre.

---

[1] See the XVIth Homeric Hymn, where the Dotian plain of Thessaly is given as Aesculapius' birthplace. "To Asclepios, healer of sickness, begins my song; to Apollo's son, whom heavenly Coronis bare on the Dotian plain, and she was Phlegyas' daughter."

Snatched from the flames, Aesculapius is given to the care of Chiron, of whom he learns the art of healing. Pindar's tale keeps Aesculapius near to Tricca, his most ancient and original place of worship, not far from Pyrasus, the earliest and Thessalian abode of Demeter. Homer's account of Aesculapius differs from both of the above legends in its more matter-of-fact tone. The miracles are fewer in Homer's version, but he agrees with Pindar in making Thessaly the birthplace of the god. As before insisted upon, Homer's Aesculapius was scarcely a god — he was the hero who came to parry and make unavailing the thrusts of all manner of diseases.

Turning now from the god Aesculapius to his chief dwelling place, from mythology to archaeology, let us go up to his holy place in the valley overlooked by his Epidaurian birthplace Mount Titthion, and also by Mount Cynortion, sacred from of old to his father Apollo. Once arrived there, we cannot fail to notice the health-giving purity of the air and a kindly cheerful smile that meets us in the landscape. But soon the most surprising, the only surprising, feature in the landscape lays hold upon the eye and engrosses the mind—the theatre of Polycletus. Many ancient theatres have been excavated in Greece, in Greater Greece, and Grecian Asia Minor, but the Epidaurian theatre is the most perfectly preserved and the most beautiful of them all. This theatre of Dionysus, and also the exquisite and unique Rotunda, which lies within the sacred enclosure of Aesculapius, are architectural masterpieces by Polycletus, a native of Argolis, where Epidaurus lies. Although there were two artists of this name, the elder and the younger, and there has consequently been a discussion of the point, the theatre and the Rotunda at Epidaurus are now generally credited to the younger Polycletus. Of the Rotunda I shall presently speak. Of the theatre Pausanias declares his high opinion : "Roman theatres may be finer," he says, "and those of latter-day Greece may be larger, but still the Epidaurian masterpiece of Polycletus is peerless for harmony of proportion and charm of aspect."[1]

From various sources, but chiefly from the minute pains given to results of excavation at Epidaurus and Athens, it appears that certain features characterised any and every precinct of Aesculapius in the days when his worship was finally organised. First a small temple for the god himself to dwell in was required. Aesculapius was too generously scrupulous about any curtailment of comfort for the sick who resorted to him ever to require a large temple for himself. In this modest building was the statue of the god, and there were hung or disposed in some satisfactory way the smaller and more valuable votive offerings made to him by grateful convalescents. The one thing needful was room for long and commodious porches with the right

[1] It was not accident which grouped together on the Athenian Acropolis as well as in the Hieron at Epidaurus the temple of Aesculapius and the theatre of Dionysus. Convenience certainly had something to do with it, and at Athens the comfort of the sick required just the exposure of the theatre. Moreover, the inspiration and amusement afforded to invalids by ready access to theatrical performances were numbered among their curative resources by the priests of Aesculapius. The well-known case of Aristides leaves no doubt on this point. Still, beyond these more prosaic reasons religious ones might be assigned. Aesculapius and Dionysus were associated in ritual by their connection with the Greater Mysteries at Eleusis. Their common origin in the northward regions of Thessaly and Thrace left its mark in certain touches common to the legends of their birth. There was, furthermore, a part assigned to the god Aesculapius in the festivals of Dionysus. What this was can only be guessed. Perhaps it may have connection with a need for Aesculapius, the upraiser of the dead to life ; for Dionysus, typifying by his yearly death the winter of each year, had to be quickened every spring, and thus could profit by the near presence of the healing god, the well-beloved son of his brother and ally, Apollo.

exposure. In these the wards of Aesculapius were housed. There and in the temple too they slept, awaiting visits of healing from the inspired dreams.

This feature is more clearly made out in the precinct at Epidaurus than in the Athenian sanctuary, though both of them certainly were amply provided with such accommodation for patients. The capitals of the Epidaurian porches[1] were Ionic, those at Athens seem to have been Doric. The Epidaurian porch was upwards of 120 feet long. The length of the porches at Athens is not easy to make out, since there appear to have been different buildings at different times. The long porch at Epidaurus was really two and not one. Though the two unite into one continuous stretch, one has a lower story which is absent from the other. This is largely due to a clever use of the natural slope of the ground. Both at Athens and at Epidaurus the god could, for the purpose of visitation by night, emerge from his temple and immediately find his expectant suppliants sleeping in the porch close by.

The temple at Athens has not been clearly made out. There seem to have been two temples not now easy to disentangle and attribute rightly to the right period for the building of each. Both were small; of that little we may be perfectly sure. The temple at Epidaurus was about eighty feet long and upwards of forty feet in width. It was of the Doric order, and fine fragments of its sculptured ornamentations are preserved in the museum, a farm-house close to the theatre of Dionysus. There was apparently a very fine frieze of lions' heads upon it, much like the one which we shall find upon the Rotunda near by. The

[1] Here again I am using the word porch to describe a *stoa* or *porticus*; in fact I plead guilty to doing this throughout this chapter and elsewhere.

eastern pediment contained a group representing the defeat of the Amazons, while the western pediment was filled by sculptures representing a Thessalian tale of the victory in Thessaly by the Lapithae (near friends of Thessalian Phlegyas) over the Centaurs. The three angles of the gables were surmounted by delicate statues of victory, whose more or less marred remains are visible now in the Central Museum at Athens. Within was the great statue of all-pitying Aesculapius wrought in ivory and gold by Thrasymedes. Of this statue coins were the only record until the beautiful bas-reliefs of Epidaurus came to light.[1] His brow, like that of Zeus, has all the serenity and unfathomable peace that glows upon the noonday firmament in cloudless summer time. There is no trace here of sternness; all that the face of Aesculapius discloses well behooves the gentle-hearted husband of (Epione) Gentleheart. Aesculapius sits not too majestic in benign repose. One upraised leg is resting on the other, and he gazes with eyes overflowing with health-giving wisdom not far away, and not upward but forward as if kindly to entreat with welcome all those who suffer and are heavy laden. To him let them confide their woes, on him let them lay their burdens of suffering and their forebodings of despair. He sits calm and most divinely competent to counsel and to guide. This attitude of reposeful capability was given to the god of healing on many a tablet inscribed with grateful names, and bearing on its sculptured surface a picture of the god at the moment when offerings and supplications were made to him. Many such have been found at Athens, and these votive bas-reliefs form some of the most interesting features in the too little

---

[1] See Brunn's beautiful photograph of the best of the two, *Denkmäler der antiken Kunst.*

frequented chamber on the Acropolis, which is devoted to fragments from the Asclepieium at Athens.

With the exception of the Rotunda, a temple of Artemis near the entrance was the only other important building in the Epidaurian precinct. Dogs' heads, which took the place of the lions' heads conspicuous on the temple of Aesculapius and the invalids' porch, ornamented the frieze of this temple of Apollo's twin sister. This interesting detail suggests that Artemis was here worshipped as huntress or, if you choose, as mistress of the hounds. The temple of the god Aesculapius being small, that of Artemis was smaller still; and as little is known of it in detail, we may with a clear conscience neglect it in order to devote attention to the most marvellous building of them all—the Rotunda or Tholos of the younger Polycletus.

This remarkable structure was famous throughout antiquity, for it was one of the most perfect examples of the graceful and efflorescent style which came into favour after the day of severely perfect architecture and sculpture. Its round shape invited flowery ornament, and the genius of the younger Polycletus showed itself here at its best. A new delicacy and life was given to traditional forms of ornamentation. They left the hand of Polycletus so quickened and transformed that they seem to have come to him fresh from the flowering meadows. He took the massive Doric column and lent to it for his purpose a delicate outline, while he preserved the significance and charm of modulated curves in its capital. Such was the external circle of columns which he placed upon triple steps of ascent. Thus we have a less massive seeming basement than the three steps of the stylobate of the Parthenon, three concentric circles, two within and one at the outermost verge. Footed upon the innermost round of this triple support a circle of twenty-six Doric columns arose to bear the most beautiful of burdens—an entablature composed of three harmonious parts. First, and resting directly upon the columns, came the architrave—a smooth marble beam running without interruption around the whole circumference. Resting upon this was the frieze, a very broad band of alternating rosettes and triglyphs. The triple vertical line in the triglyph framed most exquisitely the square slabs, each bearing a central rosette. Rosettes have been found on Mycenae vases, and are generally said to be an inheritance from Assyria; they appear on Egyptian monuments of the eighteenth dynasty. Still, in the hands of the younger Polycletus, they appear as something new. They seem to have been gathered by him from the fields of Greece in the loveliest meadows of spring. There they still grow to-day, and begem the tanglewood on every sheltered slope with dots of pure and incandescent red. The shapely form of that bright red anemone was commonly set upon memorial slabs above funereal inscriptions, and now we find it idealised and complicated but still the same simple flower-form taken to be the heart and essence of the frieze in Polycletus' entablature. The third and crowning portion of it, the last perfection surmounting this most exquisite of buildings, was its cornice. This was a band with beautifully sculptured lions' heads surmounted by acroteria, which in this case are flower-like points surmounting graceful leaf-like curves.

Pass now between the Doric columns on the eastward side where the doorway opened towards the temple of Aesculapius. There the door pierces the cella-wall, and beyond is the interior. The roof within was supported by fourteen of the most exquisite Corinthian columns that the mind of man has ever dreamt of. From the same meadows where grew the red anemones Polycletus took the delicate daisy—I have seen just such growing profusely upon the battle-field of Marathon [1]—and set it upon his capital above the acanthus leaf. The curving tendrils, not too profusely clustering around the summit of the column, seem with gladsome upward swing to tempt the eye still on until the delicate daisy crowns this creation woven together out of the graceful spirit of grasses that wave in the field, of tendrils that cling, and of flowers that bloom by the wayside. Here is the earliest existing and the best of all known Corinthian capitals.[2]

When the delicate grace of these exquisite architectural blossoms gathered itself into final form before his mind, Polycletus, the great architect, knew perhaps that Pausias [3] was to decorate the circle of its walls with paintings. Combining, perhaps for the first time, two great discoveries, perspective and encaustic, which were partly his, Pausias decorated the interior curves of the Rotunda with beautiful

---

[1] See a most beautiful photograph of it taken by Mr. Elsey-Smith and published by the Hellenic Society. A very beautiful enlargement of this is most opportunely published in the *Proceedings of the Royal Institute of British Architects*, vol. vi. New Series, 1890.

[2] Of this, Mr. Francis C. Penrose writes, see p. 67 of the *Proceedings* referred to in the preceding note. "To me the cap from Epidaurus is extremely interesting, because it is very similar to the capitals of the columns of the temple of Jupiter Olympius at Athens—a temple to which I have paid much attention. The forms of the leaves of the two examples greatly resemble one another, and the ornaments, namely, both the central flower and that figure somewhat resembling a *fleur-de-lis* which occupies the corner of the volute, have their counterparts in the central flowers of the caps of the Athenian temple, and thoroughly confirm my opinion that the columns of the latter are Greek and not Roman work."

[3] Not Pausias but Pauson is unfavourably compared by Aristotle with Polygnotus. His influence was the less pure because of his preoccupation with technical matters, partly too because of the subjects which he chose.

pictures. One represented Eros, whose weapons were flung away, while he grasped a lyre upon which he discoursed sweet music; another, of less high inspiration but most celebrated for its technique, was his allegorical figure of Methe or drunkenness. Like Benozzo Gozzoli, Pausias excelled in the painting of children, little boys especially, and none could rival his painting of flowers. Polycletus had already framed this building out of the glowing shapeliness of anemones and the delicate loveliness of the pale and golden daisies of the fields. Pausias, in the chaplet of Eros, no doubt justified the words used of his skill by Pliny, who says that "he brought the much practised art of painting flower-garlands to the climax of harmonious variegation." Here then was the gist of his flower-like building in a boy embowered with blossoms, who was in act of choosing the better part—music instead of mischief-making arrows. The lyre is better far, since music charms the highest, the deepest, and the inmost soul, and therefore best symbolises Eros, the awakener of unstinting and exhaustless love.

But we have not exhausted the wonders of the Tholos. The very centre of its beautifully tesselated floor had a downward exit. Here was most artfully constructed a labyrinth, traceable still in all its windings. These made it necessary to pass forwards and backwards, going three times completely around the circle before the lower door of the exit could be reached. The use of this subterranean labyrinth is no easier to make out than that of the whole building. Some think the harmless snakes sacred to Aesculapius had quarters here, and issued hence to play their part in healing visions. But this is pure conjecture, as is also the suggestion that the Tholos was built around a well or a spring whose healing waters have wholly disappeared.

Here is no room for speaking of the part in miraculous cures played at Epidaurus by the venomless serpents which still abound in those parts, and are made very prominent by Aristophanes in his famous burlesque account of a night in the Athenian sanctuary of Aesculapius. We cannot enter here into the history of the serpent impostures practised by that arch-mountebank Alexander of Abonotichus. The consideration of all the miracles commemorated by inscriptions at Epidaurus, and of the trial which they were to the faith of pious believers, would be too long. The distinction between Roman and Greek Aesculapia, as well as the whole question of the relation between sound practice and that of the priests of Aesculapius, of Serapis,[1] and of a host of divinities who sprang up in the latter days of paganism to cure all diseases, must be left without discussion here. It is sufficient to know that men of reasonable minds continued even in later days to resort to the various shrines of healing, and frequently found restoration and consolation by that means.

Pain of whatsoever kind moved the benign hero-physician, the divine Aesculapius. His aid therefore was granted to all those needing it if they only could receive it. The possibility of receiving it depended in one sense not upon

[1] Egypt, from which it is supposed many features of the earliest worship of Aesculapius were borrowed, sent forth in later times the healing god Serapis, a powerful rival to Aesculapius. How closely his original Egyptian character clung to Serapis even in his shrine at Delos may be gathered from an absurd story preserved by Aelian. We are told that Serapis granted the restoration of an eye to a horse who was brought in distress to his temple. The horse was of course a thoroughbred, and naturally made his appearance in the temple with thankofferings. This last touch recalls the sayings and doings of the deathless steeds of Achilles, and the whole episode, like the Homeric account of the wounding and fall of Nestor's horse, is based upon a commiseration for suffering beasts which finds expression in modern times more substantially but less poetically.

him at all but solely on them. They had to have faith, and such faith that it blossomed into purity. The preliminary laving, usually in sea-water, required before entering the porch to await the coming of inspired dreams, symbolised outwardly the inner obedience of the faithful to a command inscribed, as we well know, upon the doorway of entrance to the Epidaurian sanctuary—

"None but the pure shall enter here."

I have used the word faith because, in addition to purity, there was a deeper tie involved, a personal compatibility between the suppliant and the divinity supplicated: to be healed by the god it was needful to be pleasing in his eyes, otherwise he failed to appear.

Here was a religious idea capable of many abuses, but useful and right for controlling the self-indulgent who stood between themselves and health. An especial oracle from the god could not intervene at every meal prescribing each disobedient patient's meat and drink. For this duty as well as for an example some one especially accredited by the favour of the god and qualified by the rigour of his own life was needed. Such a divinely chosen guide for the weak and erring was young Apollonius of Tyana,[1] during his monastic seclusion in the temple of Aesculapius at Aegae. He was especially called to the Pythagorean life and discipline, his revival of which begins with his recourse to Aesculapius and his rejection of the teachings of Epicurus. "Wouldst thou but talk with Apollonius, thy relief is sure," said the oracle at Aegae to an unruly and self-indulgent youth whose much eating and drinking prevented his cure.

[1] See Appendix IV.

This idea of the necessity of some one whose life should be purity incarnate, and who should intercede with Aesculapius (himself thought of in Homeric days as an intercessor), became more prominent, and one of the very last glimpses given us of the persistent worship of Aesculapius upon the Athenian Acropolis is in the life of Proclus, of whom we hear as one of those holy men whose intervention was all-powerful with the god of healing.

Thus as we bid farewell to Aesculapius he seems himself in act of bidding farewell to earth and is withdrawing himself from men to the far-off dwellings of the careless Olympian gods.

APPENDIX IV

APOLLONIUS OF TYANA

THIS Tyanaean master of miracles attached his teachings and his philosophy to Pythagoras—a name to conjure by—and his miracles received a certain divine sanction from his acceptableness in the eyes of Aesculapius. In his early youth, at the age of sixteen, a sort of inner light irresistibly prompted him to leave Tarsus and his first master who was an Epicurean, and to resort to the temple of Aesculapius at Aegae, a Cilician town not far away. Neither Tarsus nor Aegae in fact was very far from Tyana of Cappadocia, his birthplace. During four years Apollonius lived in a monastic seclusion at Aegae, increasing in stature and in favour with the god, loving with unspeakable love and strictly living the ascetic Pythagorean life. An account of these years was written by his contemporary, probably also a sharer in his life of self-denial and self-devotion, Maximus of Aegae.

The more adventurous and most miraculous career of Apollonius upon his travels, and during his trial, was chronicled in rough notes by his companion Damis the Ninivite, a remarkably credulous person, who seems invented for the purpose of believing more than the uttermost possible. The Grammar of this Ninivite's Assent indeed makes exceptions into rules, and leaves nothing that can surprise except the normal and natural course of events.

A third account of Apollonius was written contemporarily by Moeragenes. Possibly this was the same Moeragenes who figures as an Athenian elsewhere,[1] but whoever he was, he wrote in four books a life of Apollonius of Tyana. These four books of Moeragenes were read [2] by that great champion of Christianity against Paganism, Origen, and his estimate of the Tyanaean ascetic and worker of miracles was evidently derived from them.

So far I have named writers on the career of Apollonius whose books have perished. The book which has not perished is that of a fourth biographer who, unlike Maximus, Damis, and Moeragenes, was not a contemporary. His name was Philostratus, and he has most aptly been called "Romancer-in-ordinary"[3] to her Imperial Majesty Julia Domna. When he had culled marvellous incidents from Maximus, and gathered in romantic adventures and incredible miracles from Damis, Philostratus found the narrative of Moeragenes—full of wonders though it apparently was—too tame, and therefore, choosing to think that it betrayed ignorance of his hero, he neglected the best material at hand.[4] In place of this he added to what was already untrustworthy popular rumours and traditional records of miracles—a mass of mythology which had gathered around Apollonius during the century separating his death from the day of Philostratus and his protectress, the Empress Julia. Among these tales were no doubt many, if not all, of the features which Philostratus' work has in common with the four Gospels and the career of St. Paul as set forth in the Acts of the Apostles. That nothing might be lacking, Philostratus contrived to use in one way or another various favourite passages of his borrowed from

---

[1] Pseudo-Plutarch, *Quaest. Conv.* book iv. end. It is to be hoped that he is no kinsman of the bandit Moeragenes who ranged the Taurus a few generations before. Cf. Cic. *Ad Att.* v. 15 and vi. 1.
[2] Origen, *Con. Cels.* vi. 41.
[3] *Essays and Studies*, by B. L. Gildersleeve.
[4] E. Müller, *Eine culturhistorische Untersuchung.*

Xenophon,[1] an author upon whom he formed his style, and to adorn the already overloaded travellers' tales of Damis with elegant extracts from such records of history and travel as were accessible to him. He is evidently indebted here and there to Lucian's *True Story*, a charming caricature of the marvellous-absurd yarns which had so long a vogue at Rome. The way in which this last indebtedness is contracted abundantly convicts Philostratus of an utter lack of humour. Indeed this weakness is the pith and marrow of the whole biography, as may most agreeably be revealed to readers of the delightfully humorous summary of the work given by Professor Gildersleeve in his essay on "Apollonius of Tyana."

Philostratus was not called to the office of writing the "Evangel of Apollonius" by an inner light, as Apollonius was to the Pythagorean way of living. The first suggestion of it came from the Empress Julia Domna, to whose remarkable literary circle Philostratus belonged. We know just enough of this circle to see that it contained many cleverer people than Philostratus, and it seems, from admissions in his preface to the book, that Philostratus wrote, or if you choose compiled, the life of Apollonius with a hampering desire to suit the tastes of this coterie. There was Moesa, Julia's sister, a particularly domineering person, as history was soon to show; and Moesa had two daughters who well knew their own minds. Supposing these ladies interested in having some one write an ideal presentation of the life of Apollonius, to whom could they turn? They might think of their legal friend Ulpian, like themselves of Phoenician descent, but he was out of the question; nor could they expect literary skill of Papinian, as they well knew, since he was a kinsman of theirs. Of their circle, however, were Aelian the honey-tongued, and Philostratus. The ridiculous credulity of Aelian makes it possible that he would have done worse even than Philostratus. Julia perhaps chose Philostratus because he represented Greek

[1] See a dissertation by C. von Wulfften Pathe. Berlin 1887.

culture and had no convictions of his own. It was his clever style that she especially appreciated. To him the empress gave, as he is careful to relate in beginning, the notes roughly made by Damis the Ninivite and entrusted to a kinsman from whom she got them in the process of collecting books, which occupied much of her attention. Out of these notes she thought the skill of Philostratus could fashion a record which should embody the Way, the Truth, and the Life. Being daughter to a Phoenician who was high priest in the temple of the Sun at Emesa, she naturally felt that impulse toward intensifying and reforming men's faith which characterised in those days her native corner of the world. Thence had come not only Apollonius of Tyana, but Paul of Tarsus and Simon Magus, as well as the beginnings of Christianity, and out of Julia's own house was soon to come Elagabalus, whose execrable reign was a Nightmare of Religious Reformation.

We may well shudder to think what might have been the result if our records of the life of Christ had fallen into the hands of a Philostratus. What if we had, instead of the four Gospels, a smoothed and would-be racy narrative written in the vein of your Parisian feuilletonist,[1] to suit the tastes of a circle far more definitely restricted than the modern "tout Paris"? An irritating impression of unreality, which forces itself upon the reader of Philostratus' *Life of Apollonius*, makes it hard to get through even one of its eight tedious books. No one has more pithily expressed the feelings of all upon this point than Erasmus in his preface to St. Luke addressed to Henry the Eighth. I quote from an old translation: "*Who readeth the lyfe of Apollonius Tyaneus any otherwayse then as a certayne dreame? Yea or rather who vouchsalueth to reade it at all?*"[2]

---

[1] G. Bernhardy applies this word to Philostratus in the *Allgemeine Litteratur Zeitung*, 1839.
[2] Quis Apollonii Tyanaei vitam non veluti somnium quoddam legit? Imo quis legere dignatur?

Indeed the surprising fact is that respect, veneration, and even worship should have attached to Apollonius after he had been so completely victimised by the journalism of his day. And this surprising fact is surely an argument for something made of solider stuff than dreams, something really admirable in the true Apollonius, if anybody ever disentangled him from the play-acting personage of Philostratus.

No one has the means of forming at the present day an independent opinion of Apollonius. We are obliged first to reject the picture of him given by Philostratus, and then, either to have no mind about him at all or to be of the mind of those who did know the facts. These may be separated into three classes: first come the religious-minded Christians who in spite of their prejudice against a reviver of paganism respected in Apollonius a man of saintly life and religious inspiration; second come the scoffers like Lucian and Apuleius, who did not take religion seriously, and thought such a man necessarily either a knave or a fool, or both; third comes—in a class all by himself—Dio Cassius the historian, who evidently never quite appreciated what he was talking about in mentioning Apollonius. In one place where he is irritated he says substantially, "Caracalla preferred the company of freedmen to that of men of my mark, and was given over to cheats such as was Apollonius the Cappadocian."[1] Dio forgets the tremendous endorsement with which he has previously accompanied a much clumsier account than is given by Philostratus of one of Apollonius' great deeds. "No matter how much men may doubt it, this story is as true as truth itself,"[2] he says after relating that while Domitian's assassination was in progress at Rome a certain man of Tyana named Apollonius went up to a high place and described the event before the people as if he were present, though he and they were in Ephesus "or some such place."

---

[1] lxxvii. 18.
[2] τοῦτο μὲν οὕτως ἐγένετο, κἂν μυριάκις τις ἀπιστήσῃ. lxvii. end.

Of the three classes above mentioned of those who had opportunity to know the facts about Apollonius, the third, which contains only Dio, need occupy us no further, because Dio plainly had never given any serious thought to the career of the Tyanaean, and did not know that his wonderful Ephesian clairvoyant, Apollonius, was Apollonius the Cappadocian, whom he scorned. The second class contains Lucian and Apuleius, each of whom mentions Apollonius just once.

Apuleius, in his self-vindication against the charge of using sorcery to win the hand of the heiress Prudentilla, says indignantly, after repudiating the charge: "If you can but prove the least colourable motive of self-interest in my suit for Prudentilla, then I grant you all. Then you shall call me a Carinondas, a Damigeron, a very Moses, an Apollonius, Dardanus himself, or any magician of vaunted repute since Zoroaster and Hostanes." Here murmurs interrupt him, and he turns to the magistrate, saying, "Maximus, you see the hubbub they make, because I named a few magicians' names. What can be done with people so low and uncivilised?" It does not suit Apuleius, for the purposes of his defence, to say more than this, but he plainly suggests that Apollonius, who had not been dead more than forty years at the time, was better than popular prejudice would allow.

Lucian of Samosata — a Voltaire capable of making merry over the burning of Servetus—bears, by his silence more than by what he says, a similar testimony to the quality of Apollonius, whom he dismisses with a sneer at the absurdity of the play-actor's part which he played. If the Apollonius known to him had been really the Philostratus-Apollonius, Lucian would have made merry over all his adventures and pretensions[1] instead of saying simply that

---

[1] For a forcible presentation of this, see Bishop Lloyd's letter to Bentley, who had consulted him about a proposed edition of the life of Apollonius. After printing one or two pages Bentley abandoned this project.

the first teacher and corrupter of the arch-impostor Alexander was a follower of the "tragic Tyanaean."

When it is remembered that Lucian believed fervently in the doctrines of Epicurus, against which the whole life of Apollonius had been a protest, an inclination to neglect any insinuations from this source will become irresistible. Accordingly we have left for our advisers only the Christian opponents of Apollonius, who seem the only persons that took the pains to understand him. The general impression which they had of him is borne out by the best of all possible witnesses—Apollonius himself. There remains an extract from a work written by the Tyanaean's own hand, which was so prized that it was engraved at Byzantium on pillars of brass.

This quotation is cited twice by Eusebius of Caesarea—whose date is 330 A.D.—once in his Preparation for,[1] and once in his Demonstration of,[2] the Gospel. "Even the well-known Apollonius of Tyana, whose name is upon all men's lips for praise, is said to write much in the same strain in his work on sacrifice about the first and the great God." Then follows a confirmation of the account in Philostratus of the new Pythagorean doctrine of his hero. Apollonius teaches that "there is one Highest God above and apart from the lower and many gods. Beyond the reach of the contaminating world of sense as he is, nothing apprehensible by any organ of sense, neither burnt offerings nor bloodless sacrifices, can reach him, not even uttered prayers. He is the substance of things seen, and in him plants, animals, men, and the elements, of which the world is made, have life and exist. He is the noblest of existences; and men must duly worship him with the only faculty in them to which no material organ is attached—their speculative reason." Eusebius quotes this with approval as coming from the most illustrious philosophers of Greece, and thus pays to Apollonius, by appealing to him against the baser sort of paganism, the highest tribute

[1] C. 12, book iv. [2] C. 5, book iii.

that a Christian could. This is the more significant, because Eusebius is the one who was at great pains to refute Hierocles on behalf of the Christians.

Hierocles maintained that Apollonius had lived a more exemplary and divine life upon earth than the Christ of the Gospels. His miracles were more numerous, Hierocles said, and better vouched for than those of Christ, and yet there was no pretence that he was god, but only one favoured of the gods. All this Eusebius attacks and refutes without pretending, as many carpers at the Philostratus-Apollonius have, that Apollonius was "a devil with bat's wings and a long tail."[1] He very rightly holds Philostratus responsible for many of the erroneous pretensions of Hierocles. Origen, who wrote his defence of Christianity against Celsus before this controversy between Hierocles and Eusebius took place, and before any attempt to put Apollonius on a par with Christ had been made, speaks with the same temperate respect of Apollonius, mentioning him, however, as a worker of miracles.[2]

Other authors confirm some of the better traits of the Apollonius of Philostratus. St. Augustin, for instance, commends him as exercising a larger measure of self-control than Zeus. Eunapius speaks of his life as proving him better than a philosopher. "He was something between the divine and the human, and his is not so much a life as the sojourn of a god with men." Eunapius, however, was a pagan, and his testimony is of very different weight from that given by Christian writers. Moreover Eunapius certainly had in mind chiefly, if not solely, the Apollonius of Philostratus. Concurrent testimony to the high standing of Apollonius may be accepted with all due reservations from various pagan sources. There was doubtless something in the facts about him known to the Empress Julia and her circle which singled him out as the best hero for a Pagan reformation. Less weight attaches to her son

---

[1] More the Platonist puts this phrase into the mouths of the detractors of Apollo and his oracles.   [2] *Contr. Cels.* vi. 41.

Caracalla's building of a temple in his honour, but the same is hardly true of the conduct of her great-nephew, the Emperor Alexander Severus. In his Lararium, says Spartianus, he had not only the statues of deified emperors, but also a choice of the most righteous—the more especially hallowed souls. Among these was Apollonius, and also, according to a contemporary writer, Christ, Abraham, and Orpheus, as well as his own ancestors. This is a particularly interesting passage, for it tends to show how the religious impulse which led men to deify the emperors, finding in their unsaintly lives its own corrective, was led on to the deification of any and all conspicuously noble characters.[1] Who shall say that the state of mind to which this led did not make men better able to reach the ideal of the *Imitation of Christ?*

Under the same category of pagan tributes to the character and sanctity of Apollonius falls the tale of how he saved his native Tyana from destruction by turning aside the wrath of Aurelian. Apollonius appeared, and by his bodily presence saved Tyana, just as Athena is said to have shown herself to the affrighted Alaric, who spared Athens in consequence. These latest results of the myth-making power in paganism bear a striking family resemblance to the earliest lives of the Christian saints. In them gods, demi-gods, and heroes alike are assimilated to the status of patron saints.

But to return to the most important, the only convincing, tributes to the excellency of Apollonius of Tyana, those from early Christian writers, the last, but not the least, which shall be mentioned is in a letter of the Christian Sidonius Apollinaris to a counsellor of Evariges, king of the Goths.[2] As Cudworth (writing in a rather prejudiced vein) says of him: " though a Christian, he (Sidonius) was

---

[1] The pinnacle of sanctity reached by Apollonius did certainly place his claims to reverence on a par with those of the emperors. This accounts for the well-known coins that bear his profile upon them.

[2] *Letters*, book viii., third letter.

so dazzled with the glittering show and lustre of his (Apollonius') counterfeit virtues, as if he had been enchanted by this magician long after his death." The following is a sufficient though not minutely accurate translation of the letter in question. "Read of a man (with reverence to the Catholick faith be it spoken) in most things like yourself, sought after by the rich, yet not seeking after riches; covetous of knowledge, not of money; abstemious in the middle of feasts, plainly cloathed amongst the sumptuous, severe amongst the luxurious, rough and unadorned in the midst of delicate nations, and shining with a venerable negligence amongst the wanton nobles of Persian kings. And when he made no use of the flocks either for food or apparel, he was rather slighted than envied in the kingdoms thro' which he travelled, and when the good fortune of kings favoured him in everything, he only asked those favours which he was more ready to give than to take."[1]

Surely we need not be more prejudiced against Apollonius than were his Christian antagonists in the days when more was known about him than we can know to-day. We may, at least, leaving momentarily out of account whether he was or was not in himself an impostor, be thankful that the idealised figure of Apollonius rallied around itself so much of the life and enthusiasm of departing paganism; for there were points of striking similarity between his life and teaching and that life the imitation of which is Christianity. We may safely see in the attempted reforms of Apollonius a preparation of the pagan world for Christianity, since "even Christians have thought reverently of him, and believed that he did his wonders by the power of God, or by secret philosophy and knowledge of nature not revealed to other men."[2]

[1] For this. version see Bayle's *Dictionary*, translated in 1735, *s.v.* "Apollonius."
[2] Meric Casaubon, alluding to words attributed to Justin Martyr.

APPENDIX V

THE STATUS OF MODERN GREEK DOCTORS

In almost any Greek village you choose, the man whom all delight to honour is pretty sure to be a doctor. The mayor, or demarch, whose courtesy I experienced at Thebes, was a medical practitioner, and in many other places—Kalamata, for instance—great kindnesses came to me from doctors, men of influence always. In one town of considerable importance the apothecary had been elected mayor.

What the Greeks have always admired is that men's intellects should unerringly hit the mark. Nowhere can this unerring insight be better shown than by the swift leap of a wise doctor's mind to the truth about disease. In the United States of America there was, at the beginning of this century, an admiration more than Greek for doctors, since they were credited with such artistic capacity that a Dr. Thornton was encouraged to compete with a professional architect for the honour of building the Capitol at Washington.[1] Special causes, however, brought Greek doctors into the forefront of intellectual life after the supremacy of the Turks.

"Under the Turkish rule and before the Greek revolu-

[1] See Mr. Henry Adam's interesting account of this matter in his *History of the United States of America during the first Administration of Thomas Jefferson*, vol. i. ch. iv. p. 111.

tion," my friend M. Demetrios Bikelas writes me, "most of the learned Greeks who were not clergymen were doctors. They could not pursue, with any chance of profit, any other branch of studies. Medicine sometimes opened the way to higher positions. Thus the celebrated Alexander Mavrocordato, grand drogman of the Porte (1636-1714), was a doctor of Padua. Italy was then the place whither such Greek students as could leave their country resorted. At the beginning of this century a great many of the learned Greeks who helped the revival of their country were equally doctors. Neither these nor those of the preceding centuries confined themselves to medicine; some were poets, such as Vilaras of Janina (1771-1823). Even Christopoulos, one of the best lyric poets of Greece (1772-1847), had studied medicine at Buda; Coray, the famous scholar, was a doctor of Montpellier (1748-1833). Colettis, who played a great part during the war of the revolution, and died Prime Minister of Greece in 1847, began his career as the doctor of Ali Pasha of Janina. The fathers of the Carathéodori — two cousins, one of whom (after having been minister of foreign affairs, and the representative of Turkey at the Congress of Berlin) is actually Prince of Samos, and the other Minister of Turkey at Brussels—were both distinguished doctors at Constantinople.

"The calling of a doctor was so honoured that custom had attached to it the title of 'Your Excellency,' ἐξοχώτατε. Doctors are no more addressed by this title in Athens, but I am not sure that there are not still Greek countries where they enjoy this title, generally applied to diplomatists. Since the revolution and the institution of the Greek university, medicine is so far from being the only branch of knowledge pursued in Greece, that the faculty of law draws the greatest number of students at the Athenian University. And yet there has been the natural increase, a very considerable one, in the number of Greek doctors. It would be invidious to choose names among the Greek doctors who have distinguished themselves in Greece of late years. I may, as an instance of the aptitude of Greeks for that science, mention the names of the late M. Damaschino and of M. Panas, who had both attained to the Professorship in the Faculty of Paris. I may also mention the well-known author, Dr. Paspati, who studied in America. Dr. Cavafy, too, one of the physicians of St. George's Hospital in London, is a Greek by birth."

VII

APHRODITE AT PAPHOS

The statue of Aphrodite found by excavation on ground sacred to Epidaurian Aesculapius represents that smiling goddess as the wearer of a sword.[1] Here is an ancient reproduction of that beautiful statue fashioned by the Athenian Alcamenes,[2] a statue whose cheeks and full front face were lauded by Lucian of Samosata. Of this early masterpiece the Epidaurian statue, though mutilated, gives a charming suggestion. But, alas! Lucian tells of a pulse of sweet harmony in its rounded and dainty wrist, and a light movement of charm and delicacy in the fingers. These perfections we shall never see, for the Epidaurian copy is bereft of hands.

But why should a statue of Aphrodite grace the sanctuary at Epidaurus? The same reason, though hard for us to give, suffices which established her worship at Athens on the south side of the summit of the Acropolis, not far above the Athenian precinct of Aesculapius.[3] There

---

[1] See a beautiful photograph in Brunn's Denkmäler series.
[2] See Furtwängler, in Roscher's *Ausfürliches Lexicon*, p. 413.
[3] Still nearer to this Asclepieium was a shrine probably of Aphrodite Pandemos, *i.e.* that aspect of the goddess which brings her into the worst company.

she was worshipped as Sosandra,[1] a rescuer of men, and there stood the wonderful and very ancient statue by Calamis. At Athens, furthermore, was the great original by Alcamenes just spoken of, the Aphrodite of the garden. Within the Cnidian precinct of Demeter, and not far from her own home at Cnidus, a head of Aphrodite was found, which, though mutilated, shows in its expression the influence of Demeter; and Aphrodite's shrine upon the pass near Daphne was one of the halting places of the procession to Eleusis. Thus was Aphrodite often associated in neighbourly fashion with Demeter and with Aesculapius.

At Corinth, Elis, Sparta, Delphi, in various places of Crete, on the island Cythera, in most centres of Sicilian life, all over Asia Minor — everywhere, in fact, where Greek religion had its footing, near Apollo's temple on Delos, on the Olympian hill of Cronos, high above the temple of great Zeus himself, the Greek goddess Aphrodite was worshipped, and statues of her were placed near the special shrines of all the other gods, while the very throne of Phidian Zeus, in his Olympian temple, was adorned with a sculptured representation of her birth at Paphos.

The influence for good and for harm of the ideal represented by this goddess was one of the most widely felt in antiquity, nor was her hold upon men's minds always superficial.[2] According to the ancient view of her power, Aphrodite swayed the fate of gods as well as of men.[3] This power she exercised not only to cover the earth with fair flowers and fruits, but also to bewitch men, to allure women, and to enchant the mind of Zeus himself, and high Apollo. The impulse of love which she inspired was stronger even than

---

[1] See Lucian, *Imag.* 4, and cf. Furtwängler as above, pp. 411 and 412.
[2] See below, p. 303.   [3] *Hom. Hymn,* iv. 247 ff.

Fate, or as her Athenian worshippers reverently put it, she was the oldest of the Fates.

It will repay us well to go and find this marvellously strong power in the place where, as an influence over Greeks, it had its birth. Let us therefore turn to the western coast of Cyprus, an island which is probably more Greek to-day than it ever was in the past.[1] Aphrodite rose from the sea at Old Paphos in Cyprus, and as a Greek goddess of strong power, she ruled Hellas from her Paphian precinct. This is significant, for the fact that Cyprus and Paphos were not originally of Greece prepares us for another fact, which the Greeks themselves well knew, that Aphrodite came to them from many parts of the world, but chiefly from Phoenicia, and, through Phoenicia, ultimately from Assyria.[2]

Having her home in Paphos, aloof from the centre or

[1] See F. W. Barry, "Report on the Census of Cyprus" (London, 1884). Of 186,173 souls in Cyprus (1881) 140,793 speak Greek, and 42,638 speak Turkish, while Arabic, English, Maltese, Armenian, and French are spoken by not inconsiderable groups. The Greek Church has 137,631 members, and there are 45,458 Mohammedans in Cyprus.

[2] If this statement be so worded as to exclude originally Greek characteristics from the early goddess, it is undoubtedly false. Aphrodite, daughter to Zeus and Dione, appears as an almost purely Greek conception (free from any oriental touch) every now and again in the early poets (Homer and Sappho), and there is an echo of such a report of her in Euripides; but after all that Holwerda and Engel have said to prove her to be Greek, and to derive, so far as she was not Greek, from Asia Minor, Aphrodite remains in her most characteristic qualities of Semitic origin. See Duncker's *History*, i. p. 274. As a learned authority says (Robert's *Preller*, p. 352) "Diese Verschmelzung der Leben gebenden und vernichtenden Macht in einer weiblichen Gottheit finden wir nicht nur in Babylonien und Assyrien, sondern auch bei den Semitischen Stämmen des Westens, bei den Syrern den Phoenizern und Carthagern, bei denen die Baaltis, die Astarte-Aschera, die Dido-Anna abwechselnd Segen und Frucht, Tod und Verderben sendet." See Plautus, *Mercator*, near the beginning : "Diva Astarte hominum deorumque vis, vita salus ; rursus eadem quae est | Pernicies, mors, interitus." On the theory of her Hittite origin, see Appendix VII.

Greece, Aphrodite was less transformed by Hellenism than any other of the figures and ideas brought to Greece from the East.[1] Here, then, in Cyprus, may be studied a visible contact between the Semitic and the Hellenic genius in religion. Aphrodite, as the Greeks knew and worshipped her, was neither Semitic nor Greek, but a curious complication akin both to Greece and to the East far and near. She bears traces of the armed Ishtar of Assyrian mythology, as for instance in the above mentioned Epidaurian copy from the statue of Alcamenes, where she has put on a sword, and again in statues known to have existed at Sparta, Corinth, and elsewhere. In fact under the smiles and blandishments of golden Aphrodite in her sunniest Grecian days lurked always the jealous wrath of a divinity who would have none other before her. Here for the first time in Greek mythology we have clearly set before us a jealous and revengeful[2] omnipotence asserting itself, not as in Dionysus' case over men only, but also over the gods.[3] Aphrodite is much more than a deified incarnation of the powers of growth and increase in nature, and although the same be true of the Eleusinian gods, yet in a certain oriental sense her power has a wider field than that either of Dionysus or of Demeter. No doubt her influence over typically Greek minds was the more superficial on this account. But where and while she ruled, her sway was absolute, and admitted of no questioning. Her will, whether for evil or for good, was always law, and the worshippers of her

[1] The Cyprians well knew and freely admitted that Aphrodite came from the East. See Herod. i. 105: τῆς Συρίης ἐν 'Ασκάλωνι πόλι τινες ὑπολειφθέντες ἐσύλησαν τῆς Οὐρανίης 'Αφροδίτης τὸ ἱρόν· ἔστι δὲ τοῦτο τὸ ἱρὸν πάντων ἀρχαιότατον ἱρῶν ὅσα ταύτης τῆς θεοῦ· καὶ γὰρ τὸ ἐν Κύπρῳ ἱρὸν ἐνθεῦτεν ἐγένετο, ὡς αὐτοὶ λέγουσι Κύπριοι.
[2] *Iliad*, iii. 413 and ff.
[3] Hom. *Hymn*, iv. 247 and ff.

predilection prostrated themselves before it, like slaves before a sultan. They all trembled and bowed down in fear of the dreadful visitation of her wrath. This is an aspect of the goddess of which those who try to understand her never must lose sight, but lest we dwell upon it so long as to forget the more genial and graceful traits in her character, let us rather contemplate Cyprus, her island home, her refuge in supreme moments alike of sorrow and of joy, Cyprus, the island made glad with dances—a mother of winsome loves.[1]

This is the isle of many names—called by the prophets of Israel Chittim; by the poets of Greece surnamed, from its many jutting headlands on the north, the Horned Isle; and, from the lowland flats upon its southern and eastern sides, the Hidden Isle. Approach the south-western coast, if you will—as did the Knights Hospitallers of old—from Rhodes. Let the morning be breezy and hazy so that clouds may rest upon the hills that cluster at the feet of the higher ranges behind, crowned by Mount Troödos, anciently Mount Olympus.[2] Then there will be a mist rising up from the sea and meeting these low-lingering vapours. At such a moment Cyprus is the hidden isle,[3]— hidden until, at the

[1] Insula laeta choris, blandorum et mater amorum, *Claudian*.
[2] Many modern maps put the Olympus elsewhere, but with no good reason. See Appendix VII..
[3] "Varia autem nomina illius erant, in quibus Cryptus, Plin. V. xxxi. Vocatam ante Acamantida tradit Philonides, Cerastin Xenagoras, et Aspeliam et Amathusiam; Astynomus Crypton, et Coliniam. Causam addit Stephanus, quod sub mare occultata fuerit. Ἀστύνομος δὲ φησί, Κρυπτὸν κεκλῆσθαι διὰ τὸ κρύπτεσθαι πολλάκις ὑπὸ τῆς θαλάσσης. Ita enim hic emendo: quippe perperam editur, Κύπρον, Cryptum . . . tum Eustathius, in Dionysium. οἱ δὲ Κρυπτόν ποτε κληθῆναι αὐτήν λέγουσι διὰ τὸ κεκρύφθαι ὑπὸ θαλάσσης. Aliam causam videtur assignare Phurnutus, *De nat. Deor.* ubi de Venere: ἐκ τούτου δὲ καὶ ἱερὰ τῆς Ἀφροδίτης ἡ τῶν Κυθήρων νῆσος εἶναι δοκεῖ, τάχα δὲ καὶ ἡ Κύπρος, συνᾴδουσά πως κατὰ τοὔνομα τῇ κρύψει, . . . *nomine suo occultationem referens.*" From an unpublished MS. (autograph) of John Meursius, *Cyprus*, Lib. I. chap. vi., in St. Mark's Library, class x. cod. sec. xvii. a, 214, 1, 156.

last moment, the view of it springs upon you. Then after crossing the tempestuous gulf of Sathalia [1] one may feel perhaps like shipwrecked Odysseus, who—

> . . . caught a glimpse of shore close at hand
> Giving a sharp glance forward upborne on the crest of a billow.

If, instead of landing at Limassol, the port lying nearest to the temple of Paphian Aphrodite, we had approached Cyprus from the north, a far more picturesque impression would have been received. Close to the northern coast-line from end to end runs a bold chain of picturesque peaks, of the same formation with, and parallel to, the Taurus range in Asia Minor. Cyprus consists first of these two mountain ranges, the northern and southern; and secondly of an alluvial plain, called Mesorea or Mid-mountainland, that stretches between and connects the two.

A geologist of the airy and positive-poetical [2] sort would say that this midmountain plain was but a film of yesterday,[3]

[1] Brother Stephen Lusignan describes it as "l'espouvantable gouffre de Sathalie," and the legend connecting St. Helena (the empress) with Cyprus tells of her stilling its stormy uproar by dropping into it a nail from the true cross. Curiously enough the cross upon which the penitent thief was crucified was discovered in Cyprus by Lazarus and St. Mary Magdalene! Meursius, *Cyprus*, cap. 28 of Book II.
[2] I need not say that a very different sort of geologist has been found in the gifted M. Albert Gaudry, to give an admirable account of Cyprus. See his paper presented to the Société Géologique de France, on November 14, 1853 (vol. xi. in the second series of that Society's publications); also his "*Recherches scientifiques dans l'Orient*," published with a beautiful geological map at Paris 1855.
[3] How far this is really the case largely depends upon the as yet undetermined age of the northern range of mountains. This whole question is dealt with by Dr. Oberhummer of Berlin in two most thorough papers "Aus Cypern" and "Die Insel Cypern," published respectively in the *Zeitschrift der Gesellschaft für Erdkunde zu Berlin* (xxv. Band 1890), and the *Jahresbericht der Geographischen Gesellschaft zu München* (Heft 13, 1890). Dr. Oberhummer speaks of the probability that Herr Alfred Bergeat will soon solve the difficult questions at issue by careful reports

and would tell you of a recent era when there was no visible plain, but only the submerging sea stretched between. Then Cyprus was not one but two islands—the northern and the southern. The northern island was, at that imagined and not impossible time, a mere backbone of bold peaks,—an outwork, so to speak, protecting the parallel mountains of the Asiatic coast in Cilicia or Caramania only fifty miles distant to the north. Look southward and, supposing yourself (always in company of the poet geologer) to have gone backward a few aeons,—you see first a gulf of thirty miles expanse, and then the southern or Troödos island of Cyprus. Of these two mountain parts of Cyprus the history has been as different as are their scenery and their climate.

On the southern side of the island the slopes of Mount Troödos are the one and only refuge from the fever-exhalations and terrific heats of the height of summer, and thither all fly who are able to do so, when the dog-days impend. Of this southern side of the island Martial's saying holds true, "*infamis calore* Cyprus,[1]— Cyprus is *decidedly hot.*" Such harbours as Cyprus boasts—there is not one on the island where an ordinary steamship can find safe anchorage—are with one unimportant exception on the southern side. This southern Cyprus is the Cyprus of history, and the midmountain plain[2] belongs to it. In

from the spot. The interesting and instructive account given by Dr. Oberhummer of the table-mountains in the midmountain plain of Cyprus, and his comparison of them with features in the Sahara, is one of his many contributions to knowledge of Cyprus. His papers came to me unfortunately as I was going to press, and I therefore profited too little by them.

[1] Infamem nimio calore Cypron
Observes, moneo precorque, Flacce,
Messes area cum teret crepantes
Et fulvi iuba saeviet leonis.—*Epigr.* ix. 91.

[2] This Mesorea, one end of which is fertilised by the Pediaeus,—a Cypriote river Nile, Gaudry, *Recherches*, p. 96,—M. Gaudry calls "un

what remains, the mountain backbone of northern Cyprus, no great centre either of religious, political, or commercial interests (unless Cerynia[1] be forced to do duty as such) has ever been established; and therefore this, its most beautiful and healthful portion, may be said never to have belonged to Cyprus in any real fashion. This whole northern reach is little more than an elegant extract from the obscurer portions of Asia Minor, whereas the great plain and the southern mountains of Cyprus had a physical character of their own. Here was a natural meeting-ground for all peoples of the East and West — where the tongues of Syria, Assyria, Phoenicia, and Egypt from the East, and the Greek and Roman vernaculars from the West, could be heard. Even when the centre of commercial exchange between the East and West had long passed away from Southern Cyprus, still the island remained a place of congress, a point of contact and impact for eastern and western religious influences.

The present status of Cyprus is in fact its whole history in a nutshell. Nothing for Cyprus and everything for all the world besides. Governed by the English on ordinary terms, Cyprus would have every chance of prosperity, if we may judge from the Ionian islands under British administration. But these western rulers in Cyprus are now administering Eastern laws, not English nor even Cypriote, but Turkish laws. The English in Cyprus have been described somewhat bitterly by one of themselves as Turkish tax-gatherers. And these taxes are not even levied for the Turk's own use, but go to assure a pittance to Turkish

des lieux les plus fertiles du monde." In the season when I saw it nothing of this richness appeared.

[1] Before the days of Cerynia (Cerines), Lapethus came very near to attaining a real importance.

bondholders in France, England, and elsewhere.[1] So it has
been always with Cyprus. Before the Turks, the more
rapacious Venetians exploited the island most mercilessly;
they got it by a trick the very nature of which showed that
Venice had lost every imperial instinct, and could only
oppress. Before the Venetians came the French dynasty of
the Lusignans,[2] who established a feudalism efficient perhaps,
but certainly corrupt and monstrously cruel from the first.
Lusignans, Genoese, Venetians, all these western potentates
and powers lost every moral quality the moment they
touched unhappy Cyprus, so that the islanders might well
regret the days when Rome and Byzantium[3] ruled with even

[1] In his paper (pp. 98 and ff.) "Die Insel Cypern" referred to above, Dr.
Oberhummer gives an extremely clear account of the financial impossibilities
under which the English administration of Cyprus is now and has been
labouring. The yearly tribute ultimately payable to the bondholders is
£92,686. This was fixed on the basis of an average account of revenues
for the five years preceding 1878. Those familiar with the incapacity
for administration possessed and prized by the unspeakable Turk will not
wonder that the calculations of 1878 were all wrong. Dr. Oberhummer
gives the following figures of yearly income and outgo in Cyprus, and they
speak for themselves—

	Income.	Outgo.
1879-80	£148,360	£117,445
1880-81	156,095	119,416
1881-82	163,732	157,672
1882-83	189,000	120,000
1883-84	194,051	111,685

[2] On this whole chapter in Cypriote history the greatest authority, as
well as the most entertaining, is the gifted M. de Mas Latrie. For a
most readable book on Cyprus in the Middle Ages, and in modern times
down to the English occupation, see his *L'île de Chypre*, Paris, 1879, which
is dedicated to Sir Henry Layard. See also his monumental *Histoire de
l'île de Chypre sous le règne des princes de la maison de Lusignan*, Paris,
1861.

[3] A flourishing condition of Cypriote industry and a high repute for
Cypriote stuffs in Byzantine days is implied in a letter written by the holy
Epiphanios to the Bishop of Jerusalem. In the midst of a tirade against
the heresy of Origen, Epiphanios alludes to a high-handed proceeding of
his own. He had entered a church and found there a rich cloth, with a
representation of the face of Christ or of that of some saint. He ordered

hand, assured protection, and moderate imposts over their ill-fated country. And to-day, when their rulers are the best and most upright of men, ready and eager to help, a fatality prevents the island from gaining what it should, and still the hardships of Cyprus win her no hope.

So far back as history reaches there has been no independence for Cyprus, and there never has been a Cypriote nationality or national enthusiasm. It is all the more surprising, therefore, that a Greek enthusiasm has seized upon the larger portion of the natives to-day. The vivacity and strength of the modern Greek nationality is nowhere more apparent than in this peaceful and almost complete conquest of the allegiance of Cyprus.

For the theatre of a religious evolution where the western spirit of Hellenic beauty and independence should meet the eastern spirit of blind submission and comprehension of divine omnipotence, and combine on equal terms, a place which belonged to no one and to every one—Cyprus—was required. I have enumerated the various occupants of Cyprus since the days of Rome only as a prelude to a similar enumeration which shall go back as far as, and perhaps a step farther than, the undimmed record of history may warrant. Such a backward survey is plainly needed in order that there may be some knowledge of the background upon which the composite international worship of Paphian Aphrodite was sketched.

Before the Romans were the Greeks, before the Greeks the Phoenicians. Before the Phoenicians were the Lycians—

this to be cut down, and gave word that a poor man should have it for grave-clothes. There were murmurs; the people thought he should have replaced it. This he promised, and now apologises for delay. He had delayed, "*wishing to get a good one from Cyprus.*" Now, under pressure he sends the best he can get.

or were they the Hittites?—and a Semitic race—so thinks Mr. Max Duemmler—was displaced by the Lycians. Perhaps these were the Hittites. The whole subject of the pre-Phoenician inhabitants of Cyprus is beset with unusual difficulty.[1] Were these Lycians, for instance, the writers of the strange Cypriote characters found all over the island? Or are these Cypriote letters to be attributed to Max Duemmler's Semitic aborigines? Other authorities declare that whoever first used these Cypriote characters—whether you call him Lycian or Semitic or aboriginal—was a Hittite of the Hittites.

Plainly we shall hardly escape without offending various people of various minds if we undertake to have an opinion about the earliest takers and makers of Cyprus. There are those who find traces in Lycia and Phrygia, throughout the modern Caramania, of an early invasion from Thrace and the West, and who claim that this invasion swept over Cyprus as well. Certainly these Hittites or Thracians or Semites or Lycians could easily cross the fifty miles of sea and come over from Cilicia. In fact the crossing has many times been made by invading grasshoppers,[2] feared to-day more than Hittites, Thracians, or Lycians.

[1] Mr. J. Arthur R. Munro writes me: "As to the primitive population I think the evidence is tending to show that there was a great immigration of a semi-Greek stock from Asia Minor where they had passed under oriental influences, and only a slight immigration (if any) direct from Greece. The connection with Arcadia in language (*v.* Meister) and traditions, names, etc., seems to me best explained not by colonisation, but by supposing the first tide of Greek peoples flowed southward in parallel streams (1) into Greece, and (2) over the Hellespont, the Arcadians being a remnant of the pre-Dorian people maintaining themselves in the Highlands."
[2] See Gaudry's *Recherches*, p. 147, also the excellent book, published in 1878, on Cyprus by R. Hamilton Lang of the Imperial Ottoman Bank. Chapter x. deals with droughts and grasshoppers. The very remarkable sympathy of Mr. Lang for the Cypriote peasantry

The Phoenician invasion itself was marvellously early, for their first Cypriote possession was apparently their first foothold on foreign soil. Anxious to enlarge the trade of their coast towns of Tyre and Sidon, they founded a trading post on the nearly opposite strand of Cyprus, at the place now called Larnaca, and used in modern and in medieval times as the sea-port of the inland cathedral-town of Nicosia, also called Lefcosia. The ancient name bestowed here by the Phoenicians was Kittim, preserved by the Greeks and Romans in the form of Citium. The site chosen first by the Phoenicians in Cyprus was wisely selected, for it remains to-day the important port of the whole island. Now its importance comes chiefly from relations with the West; anciently it was wholly identified with the fortunes of Phoenician Tyre and Sidon.

"The burden of Tyre, howl, ye ships of Tarshish,"— says Isaiah the prophet,—" for it is laid waste so that there is no house, no entering in; from the land of Chittim it is revealed to me. Be still, ye inhabitants of the isle, thou whom the merchants of Zidon that pass over the sea have replenished."

The other two places for colonising selected by the Phoenicians were Amathus and Old Paphos, neither of which has preserved a shadow even of that sometime glory. Even in ancient times it was apparently the religion rather than the commerce of Phoenicia that kept its foothold in these two places, which were never of any great extent or importance outside of their respective sanctuaries. Hence

makes his book an invaluable one, and its worth is increased by the appreciative use he has made of an unpublished report on Cypriote agriculture made in 1844 by M. Fourcade of the French Consular Service. Mr. Lang's book well deserved to be translated into French, as it was in 1879.

there is a plentiful lack of evidence[1] from the soil itself and its contents to show that Phoenicians ever found lodgment in either place.

The Phoenicians were the common carriers of antiquity, and their genius was so purely for expediting exchange and promoting commerce that they had, even in their great centres of commerce—let alone such places as Paphos and Amathus—little or no energy left for building. If this was true of Phoenicians in the country of their birth and preference, how much more true must it have been of the Phoenicians in Cyprus,—an alien land where no monuments of any epoch, saving tombs, have survived;[2] with the sole

---

[1] In his admirable publication *Devia Cypria*, Mr. D. G. Hogarth raises the whole question of Phoenician influence in Cyprus, saying "Indeed as research has tended more and more to minimise the part played by the latter (Phoenicians) in Cyprian economy, and to reject their claim to be the importers even of the great goddess, or the founders of her temples, so western influence must be relegated to the days of Evagoras." To this Mr. Hogarth adds in a note,—where he speaks with the utmost knowledge of the facts, since he superintended the excavations at Old Paphos—"It will be remembered that we found no Phoenician relics at Old Paphos at all; nor have any been found at Amathus, Salamis, Lapethus, or indeed (except in isolated instances) anywhere but at Citium and Idalium." This is all very strong negative evidence, nor is the late use of the Ionian alphabet more positive. Really positive evidence seems required to refute Herodotus and others who put Phoenician cults at Old Paphos, and who doubtless had before them avenues of information for ever closed to us. They constitute the only evidence at hand to show what intelligent men believed in those days about the origin of the worship of Aphrodite at Paphos. We are beginning to have a certain amount of evidence which they lacked, and it is becoming plain to me that Aphrodite united to the Phoenician strain, that fixes her character, peculiarities derived neither from the Phoenicians nor from the Greeks. The only possible way in which these new and important facts can eventually achieve due recognition is to have them stated at this stage of the investigation by one who denies the Phoenician origin of the goddess. Such a statement Mr. Hogarth, who inclines to that view, has been good enough to make in a letter to me full of valuable suggestions on many points. For his account of the Hittite origin of Aphrodite, see Appendix VII. below.

[2] The condition in which the ruins of the temple of Paphian Aphrodite have been found is so lamentable that it would be a mockery to speak of it as a surviving monument. See below, Appendix VI.

exception of a few bits from Roman times and some few very noteworthy medieval churches and ruined castles. A century will hardly be required, at the rate of dilapidation now observable; in less than that time even these will have disappeared, and there will be no reading of the past elsewhere than in tombs used many times and rifled by many generations of men who were for the most part ignorant and superstitious.

That the Greeks, who did so much building of durable sort, should have left no monuments in Cyprus worth mentioning is a matter of surprise, because of the early date of their first occupation of various parts of the island. But, in spite of this early occupation, it cannot be denied that the Greeks have never been justified at any time in the past as much as they are now in calling Cyprus a Greek island. The monuments in this land were sure to perish. They were never built by a people rooted in the soil, and some new master always came who did not know and had no care for the buildings left by those whom he dislodged. The site of Salamis and Famagosta best illustrates this curious state of things. Farthest north lay the Greek colony of Salamis. This was abandoned for the medieval walled city about five miles to the south of it, Famagosta—a town with churches innumerable and a cathedral, as well as the most wonderfully complete fortifications. Famagosta is now an untenanted simulacrum of the commercial glories of the days of Italian supremacy in Cyprus, and not quite a mile farther south lies Varoschia, where the living successors of the Salaminians and Famagostans of old now congregate. It is as if we found a ruined city at the battery end of Manhattan Island and deserted tenements at 23d Street, because the traffic of New York had been transferred to the neighbourhood of the Harlem River.

The moral to be drawn from this digression is that the circumstances of Cyprus, and the native pursuits of the Phoenicians there and elsewhere alike, will prepare us for the scantiest yield of Phoenician remains on sites where they are known[1] to have lived for many years.

I have said that Cyprus was just the place where Greek and Phoenician influences could meet and mingle without the interference of surrounding circumstances to give predominance to either. This is so true in essential matters that even the date of the Greek colonisation of Cyprus stretches far enough back to come near the earliest occupation of Cyprus by Phoenicians. Kittim (Larnaca-Citium) preceded the Greek occupation; but there are stories which

[1] This knowledge is neither derived from monuments nor confirmed in any appreciable degree, as regards Paphos and several other Phoenician abiding places, by archaeological discoveries. See above, note 1 p. 282, where Mr. Hogarth's striking testimony is quoted. But still undoubted traces of a Phoenician occupation have been found at Citium and Idalium, and their presence at this last place gives a trace of their close connection with the goddess there worshipped. Furthermore, the oldest portion of the temple of Aphrodite at Paphos (see Appendix) might perhaps prove to be of Phoenician construction, if we were fortunate enough to know anything sufficiently definite about Phoenician building. These slight clues derived from excavation and archaeological research help us toward certainty when the early traditions connecting Cyprus with the Phoenicians are duly taken into account. To begin with Homer, the *Odyssey* mentions Cyprus five times, and the *Iliad* only once; but Aphrodite is mentioned as Cypris—a name unknown to the *Odyssey*—five times in the *Iliad*. Thus Cyprus was well known to the Homeric mind; and Aphrodite, in spite of her Greek father Zeus and mother Dione, was habitually severed from her Olympian peers, and associated with Cyprus. Now Cyprus is plainly associated in the *Odyssey* with Phoenicia and Egypt (iv. 83), and in the Homeric Hymn to Dionysus, the Tyrsenian (Phoenician) pirate talks of taking his captive to Egypt or to Cyprus (v. 28), and thus bears testimony to the intimate home relations between Cyprus and the Phoenicians. Plainly if the Homeric mind had been as deeply interested in the history as in the worship of Aphrodite, we should have had from Homer what Herodotus finally gives us, a statement that the Phoenicians brought the goddess's worship to Cyprus. Homer knows nothing of the goddess's birth in Cyprus. This came in the Homeric Hymns and in Hesiod. The mention of Cyprus in connection with Aphrodite by Herodotus and later writers is familiar, and is often alluded to in other portions of this chapter.

leave it doubtful if Old Paphos may not have known Greeks as well as Phoenicians in its earliest days.

The Arcadian chieftain Agapenor — naïvely qualified by a Lusignan chronicler[1] as "Lieutenant-général des Navires du Roy Agamemnon," "King Agamemnon's lord high admiral"— founded Paphos on his way home from the sack of Troy. This Paphos of Agapenor is probably the later New Paphos,—a town commercially far more successful than the older and Phoenician Old Paphos on the hill not far away; but still, our confused informant Pausanias declares that Agapenor established the worship and the temple of Aphrodite at Paphos, and adds by way of making confusion worse confounded that this Paphian worship instituted by Agapenor had until then been maintained at Golgoi, another place in Cyprus. But testimony of superior weight to that of Pausanias tells us that the first worship of Aphrodite at Old Paphos was Phoenician. Only it evidently came very early and very closely in contact with the adventurous Greeks. Much or little as Agapenor may have done for the worship of the goddess at Paphos, he certainly did as much for it in Arcadia,—the temple of Aphrodite Paphia at Tegea in south-western Arcadia was of Agapenor's founding. It is worth noticing carefully how inevitable was the acceptance by Greece of this originally Assyrian goddess. Arcadia is at the centre of the mountainous Peloponnesus, and yet to this heart of the Highlands of Greece came from opposite quarters the same eastern and alien goddess. The

---

[1] Brother Stephen of Lusignan in the very much fuller French version published by himself of his villainously printed *Chorograffia et breve historia universale dell' isola di Cipro principiando al tempo di Noe per in-sino al* 1572, per il R. P. Lettore Fr. Stephano Lusignano di Cipro dell' ordine de Predicatori. Bologna, 1573. For a further account of this book see Appendix VIII.

temple at Tegea was founded from Cyprus (Paphos)[1] in the East, whereas in the opposite and north-western corner of Arcadia a temple of Aphrodite was founded in the inaccessible district of Psophis, and founded too from what then were the uttermost parts of the West. The Psophidian temple was due to the zeal of worshippers of the goddess at the ancient shrine on Mount Eryx, in north-western Sicily.[2] A third Phoenician foundation (where recent diggings[3] have discovered next to nothing at all) was far nearer to the heart of Greece than eastern Paphos or western Eryx,—the island of Cythera from which Aphrodite drew one of her sweetest names, Cytherea.[4] Strange to

[1] Paus. VIII. liii. 3 ; cf. *ibid.* v. 2.
[2] Paus. VIII. xxiv. 1 and 6.
[3] These were made with his accustomed skill by Dr. Schliemann.
[4] This epithet of Aphrodite has had a surprising effect upon the beautiful name of that beautiful corner of Cyprus named *Cythrea*. Brother Stephen of Lusignan and many others transform it by a slight change in its last syllable but one into *Cythera*. A more forbidding spot, Mount Cithaeron, has also attempted to usurp the place of Cythera in Aphrodite's affections (cf. Bartolommeo da li Sonetti on Cythera). See Boccaccio's *Teseide*, VII. stanza 43.

        O bella Iddea del gran Vulcano Sposa
        Per cui s'allegra il monte Citerone.

This is reproduced by Chaucer, *Knight's Tale*, 1363,

    Fairest of faire, o lady myn Venus,
    Daughter of Jove and spouse to Vulcanus,
    Thou goddess of the mount of Citheroun.

Again Dryden, in his *Palamon and Arcite*, following Chaucer, gives a description of beautiful paintings where the Cithaeron again does duty for Cythera,

    For there th' Idalian Mount and Citheron,
    The court of Venus, was in colours drawn.

Last of all, in a recent writer we find the old confusion reasserting itself in a description of Paris society : " It was a charming world of fancy and caprice ; a world of milky clouds floating in an infinite azure, and bearing a mundane Venus to her throne on a Frenchified Cithaeron." It is needless to say that no place less belongs to Venus Aphrodite than the gloomy wilderness of Boeotian Cithaeron where the Maenads tore Pentheus in pieces, and whither Oedipus was sent as a babe to be exposed.

say, there is no record of any considerable influence exercised from Cythera upon the worship of Aphrodite in Greece. From the West, beyond the foundation at Psophis and some probable influence upon Greeks in Sicily, little or no influence reached Greece, and therefore Paphos in Cyprus was the centre of the worship of Grecian Aphrodite, first and last.

Accordingly, if we would come under the Grecian spell of Phoenician Aphrodite, we must leave Greece proper and go to the southward Cyprus, which is neither in Europe nor in Asia; neither of the East nor of the West; not Greek nor yet Phoenician. There we must go from the harbour of Limassol by the shortest road to Old Paphos, for although not wholly Greek and not wholly Phoenician, Aphrodite is Paphian [1] always and entirely.

Let us approach the island and the way from Limassol to Paphos with no undue anticipations. Rifled tombs, broken fragments, foundations half effaced are the reward which students of Cypriote antiquity chiefly receive. Bearing this in mind, we may well linger a moment, when we are four miles from Limassol on the road to Old Paphos, at Colossi to admire a splendid square castle,[2] not utterly ruined as yet. Here the Knights Commanders dwelt for many years.[3]

[1] *Od.* viii. 363, *Hom. Hymn*, iv. 59 ff.; Eurip. *Bacch.* 385 and 406, etc.
[2] See a photograph of it published by the Hellenic Society, Appendix XI. i. 89.
[3] Nothing seems to me more discouraging than the attempt to photograph, or rather to *orthograph*, the shades of popular mispronunciation where a name has its established form. Accordingly, I adhere with M. de Mas Latrie to *Colossi*, leaving others to choose between *Colossois* and *Colossin*. The mystifying name of Colossi—given as *Colosso* on the unpublished map made by Leonida Attar in 1542, and now in the Museo Correr at Venice — is said to derive from the Colossos of Rhodes. This may be the case, but the name certainly has nothing whatever to do with the Rhodian Knights Hospitallers, through whom Colossi became

The character of the coast-shapes and landscapes as you journey on past Colossi to Old Paphos is noteworthy, because of a contrast with what comes when Paphos is reached. Around the monastery of St. Nicholas—on the promontory of Curias, before Colossi is reached—may be found vast low-lying areas close to the beach of the sea. Here the strangest shapes may be seen fashioned out of very soft limestone by the action of the rains sometimes, and sometimes of the waves. Vast arches reach out to dim and shapeless buttresses, while the sea dashes up under the arch and often covers wholly its seaward support. This is nature's architecture, and the like of it may be seen in various lands, as, for instance, on the Californian coast near Santa Cruz. So friable is the limestone of Cyprus that it

famous. The Knights Templars had the whole of Cyprus for part of a year, built the cathedral at Nicosia in part, and made strong castles at Larnaca and elsewhere, but they never held Colossi. Before its grant to the Knights of Rhodes, a Frenchman named *Nicholas Garin* owned it, and he adopted from it the feudal title of *Garin de Kolossi* or *du Colos*. The only analogy that suggests itself to confirm the derivation from the Colossus is an insufficient one. Padre Coronelli's book on Morea and Negroponte has on its title-page "Si vende alla Libreria del Colosso sul Ponte di Rialto." Nicolas Garin may after all have got the title "Du Colos" by trade associations, and then have named his estate in order to derive a feudal title from it. After purchasing all outstanding rights, Hugues I. of Lusignan was the final grantor to the Knights of these estates in entirety, his father or uncle having already given some portions. The Hospitallers finally appointed a commandery for Colossi, and made it the centre of management for all their rich possessions in the island. These they held for three centuries—until the Turks came in 1571. The Sultan appropriated most of the Hospitallers' lands. He had good reason to covet Colossi, for its *commandery* wine—so called from the Knights and their commandery (*preceptorery*) was the earlier polysyllable)—still enjoys a well-deserved celebrity. To be sure it is now made unpalatable to some by the tarred skins which serve for bottles. On this subject see Gaudry, *Recherches*, p. 330. See also in Mr. Lang's *Cyprus*, chap. ix., where he speaks of the *Commanderia* wine as used in France and Italy. Whoever has tasted a good old vintage of this wine will rejoice that Madeira has been restocked since the *phylloxera* from the district of Colossi. Nothing more like Madeira exists than the wine of Colossi.

seems ever ready to vanish away. There is, in fact, a melting process continually in progress all over the island. Hence vast caves near the earth's surface which invited the successive occupants of Cyprus to use them for places of burial.[1] Hence also the habit of hollowing out in the willing stone all manner of tombs and passages leading from subterranean vault to hidden chamber. The ground of Cyprus sounds hollow everywhere under the hoofs of the mules,—the whole landscape sometimes seeming but a mask covering over the bones of men long dead.

Close to Colossi and the castle of the Knights Commanders is Episcopia or Piscopia, associated with a branch of the Venetian Cornaro family and with one of Titian's masterpieces.[2] But it is time to draw near to Paphos, which is after all only a day's journey on muleback from Limassol. As we approach, the limestone hills cover themselves with a brighter green. Near Pissouri and Old Paphos, now called Couclià, are sudden whims in the surface of the soil. Green slopes lead more or less precipitously downward, sometimes to a field shaped like an amphitheatre, sometimes to a meadow nearly square. These lower places cover themselves with shrubs, and if the early day brought showers, as it did when we were riding that way, the golden slanting sun of eventide shoots pleasantly through their dripping leafage, making them sparkle, as it were, with the winning smile of golden Aphrodite. Cheered by this glimmering show of welcome, we turned around the jutting foot of a wooded hill, and came upon the last stream to be forded

---

[1] More than once I have seen daylight at the farther end of a cave near the top of a ridge, which had evidently been melting away by this process. These caves are often used for sheep-folds, which go by the old name of *mandra*.
[2] In the Frari Church at Venice.

U

that day. Then in a half-ruined castle called the Tschiflik or farmstead, which surmounted the upward swerve of the Paphian hill, we were most warmly welcomed by the English excavators, already beginning to wind up their business at Paphos, and preparing to hand over the site to the charge of Government.

The next morning we had before us the site of the temple of Aphrodite at Old Paphos, discovered and fully understood for the first time since the day when St. Barnabas[1] called down upon it the wrath of heaven, and by a judgment of earthquake and fire put an end to many abominations. To discover precisely what earthquake the saint inflicted would be vain; there have been so many before and since upon this luckless spot.[2] There is no lack of founders and builders for this home of Paphian Aphrodite; they are as numerous almost as are the writers who tell of the temple's

[1] The martyrdom of St. Barnabas took place in Cyprus. See in John Meursius' unpublished MS. revision of his well-known book on Cyprus, a note which refers to this at the end of chap. v. in book II.: Nec fecit tantum martyres Cyprus, sed et dedit. In his erat Barnabas apostolus de quo dixi.

[2] There was a serious earthquake here under Augustus, in the twenty-seventh year of his reign, cf. Eusebius copied by Abbas Uspergensis and Marianus Scotus. Meursius, *Cyp*. II. xx. and I. xviii., quotes Seneca, *Epist*. xci., *Nat. Quaest*. vi. 26, and also *Sibylline oracles*, III. and IV. Under Vespasian, in the ninth year of his reign, three towers of the temple fell. *Hieronymus* (note on the lost text of Eusebius, lib. II. *Chron*. given by Meursius, I. xviii.) quotes Bartholomaeus Saligniacus, *Itinerarii* iv. cap. 6 : Paphos ruinis plena videtur, templis tamen frequens. This is a century after the Acts, where see chap. xiii.; see also Bede on the Acts. Fortunately of late years there has been a cessation. In 1830 the unlucky Dr. Ludwig Ross was badly shaken while in Cyprus, and has given an account of the adventure. He was at Dalin at the time, and he says: "Am andern Morgen (February 21) erwachte ich schon um fünf Uhr durch ein langes anhaltendes Erdbeben das mit leisen zitternden Schwingungen anfing und mit einer heftigen Erschütterung endigte, und dessen ganze Dauer wohl eine halbe Minute betrug." Later, while at Hieroskipou (Strabo's ἱεροκηπία; see Hogarth's *Devia Cypria*, p. 41), two miles east of New Paphos, he says: "überhaupt soll dieser Theil der Insel bis Limissos den Erdstossen sehr ausgesetzt sein."

foundation. The first builders up of the Paphian sanctuary appear, in fact, to have been as plentiful as the earthquakes that shook the temple down.

With the legendary name of Cinyras—the most widely recognised of these first founders—connects itself the Eastern pedigree of Aphrodite. Aphrodite came originally from Assyria, and it is therefore no surprise to hear from one source that Cinyras, usually regarded as from Syria, was king of the Assyrians. This wonderful Cinyras was the great ancestor of the priestly family or guild that long ruled over the district and sanctuary at Old Paphos. The collective name applied here was that of the Cinyradae or descendants of Cinyras. The most interesting of the sons of Cinyras is the beautiful and ill-fated Adonis, who, among other things,[1] is the Assyrian Tammuz brought to the western coasts of Syria and Phoenicia. In various legends this son of Cinyras, Tammuz-Adonis, plays the part of Dionysus and Persephone in one. Around him gather the sorrow and the joy of the yearly death and yearly revival of nature's growth.

The beautiful legend of Aphrodite's love for Adonis— how he was wounded when engaged in the chase, and how Aphrodite, filled with grief on hearing the sad tidings, made haste to the Idalian fields of Cyprus and found there her dying love—appears to be a story of later growth. It was connected with the inland sanctuary of Aphrodite in Cyprus, having little or nothing to do with Old Paphos. Amathus, the third Cyprian centre for the goddess's worship, was, like Old Paphos, on the sea coast. There, we hear, was a temple where Aphrodite was worshipped in common

[1] I am well aware that it is quite possible to bear too exclusively in mind the eastern affinities of Adonis. He is as close to the Phrygian worship of Atthis and Cybele as he is to the Phoenician Ishtar and Tammuz, —closer perhaps.

with Adonis, the two forming a godhead, both male and female. Perhaps this dual worship at Amathus was of distinctly Phoenician origin, and it is possible that the Adonis of Amathus was an earlier aspect—nearer to what is found in the annals of Ninivite religion—of the charming and tragical Tammuz-Adonis.

But the father of Adonis, Cinyras, is by no means disposed of in the slight mention made above. Pindar speaks of "Cinyras whom the golden-haired Apollo dearly loved, the dutiful servant of Aphrodite." The men of Cyprus, so Pindar says, were never tired of telling various stories about Cinyras. This native tendency to tell anything that came into your head about Cinyras maintained itself even till late Christian days. Malevolence and fanaticism then combined with a justified reprobation of Paphian licentiousness to frame a story that Aphrodite was only a criminally beloved paramour of Cinyras. In honour of this mortal and misguided woman Cinyras built a temple at Old Paphos, where her tomb and his are still shown to-day. The only religious fact to be derived from this story is an important one, as will appear later, *i.e.* that in the precinct of Paphian Aphrodite at Old Paphos the tomb[1] of that goddess and of Cinyras were conspicuous.

In giving some idea of the medley of legends and tales that centred about the name of Cinyras we must resign all hope of gaining a consistent idea of his personality. Avalanches of mythology have swept down upon him from all quarters, so that he is but a remembered name and not

[1] On the various aspects of the Greek Aphrodite that make of her a goddess of the land of the dead, see Dr. W. H. Roscher, in his own *Ausführliches Lexicon*, p. 402.

a person. He is connected with the Trojan war, during which he was king of Cyprus. Thus Homer's conception of him lends him no preternatural powers, no divine attributes. He was Agamemnon's distant admirer and benefactor who sent him armour:

> Tidings he heard in Cyprus and fame that Achaeans
> Planned to set sail in their ships for Troy and its capture,
> Wherefore he gave the breastplate in order to please Agamemnon.

All this is creditable, but the tale which arose shortly after Homer's day was less creditable to Cinyras' heart than to his head. Bound by oath to supply a certain number of ships against Troy, the crafty Paphian monarch did supply just the number promised; only, as their size and equipment were not nominated in the bond, it pleased his royal thriftiness to send ships of microscopic dimensions fashioned out of clay.[1]

But after all the real Cinyras, founder of Old Paphos, lived long before the Trojan war, and was far more than the obsequious admirer of Agamemnon, far higher minded than this crafty evader of the solemn terms of a treaty. Ages before the Trojan war he lived, first founder, priest, and king, not only of the sanctuary of Aphrodite in Old Paphos, but of one at Byblus in Syria—Byblus, where the goddess was revered, as at Paphos, under the form of a cone of white stone.[2] Byblus is quite as closely identified in fact with the goddess in the history of Syrian religion, as is Paphos in that of Greek religion. A name well known

---

[1] Probably some primitive record of ritual observance lurks beneath this pointless tale.

[2] Maximus Tyrius, *Dissert.* viii. 7: Παφίοις ἡ μὲν 'Αφροδίτη τὰς τιμὰς ἔχει· τὸ δὲ ἄγαλμα οὐκ ἂν εἰκάσαις ἄλλῳ τῳ ἢ πυραμίδι λευκῇ, ἡ δὲ ὕλη ἀγνοεῖται.

of us all, that of Pygmalion, is connected with Cinyras. The two were kinsmen; and their bond of kinship, so far as mythology has worked it out, consisted in their both being originators of skilled processes in the various arts that adorn the mind and the life of man. Both play a Promethean part in dowering mankind. Cinyras, for instance, invented mining, bricks, and various agricultural implements,[1] and Pygmalion became celebrated for his skill in sculpture.

Cinyras is so closely identified with Cyprus, in spite of the tie binding him to Byblus, that he is spoken of as coming from almost every country which contributed to the early peopling of the island. He was from Cilicia as well as from Syria and Assyria, and he was beloved of Aphrodite. This glory he shared in legend with Adonis, and is half identified with him. Apollo delighted in him, and yet there was a rivalry in musical performances wherein Cinyras —taking for the nonce the *rôle* of Marsyas in the Thraco-Phrygian story[2]—was worsted by his protector Apollo.

As for this musical episode in his career, it has a greater importance, some think, than would casually be attached to it. The theory is that the name Cinyras thinly disguises that of a musical instrument, associated with the royal founder and priest of Old Paphos. This name and the proverbial wealth of a Midas, along with the story of his birth in Cilicia, have attached themselves to him from Asia Minor, the land of the Phrygian flute and the home of soft Lydian airs.

If it were possible to unravel aright all the legends of Cinyras, the whole early and unknown history of Cyprus

---

[1] Tegulas invenit Cinyras . . . et metalla aeris, utrumque in insula Cypro, item forcipem, martulum, vectem, incudem (Pliny, *Nat. Hist.* vii. 195).   [2] See p. 92 above.

might be understood. For just as the three touches above mentioned come from Asia Minor, so from Phoenicia in part, and largely again from Phrygia in Asia Minor, comes his close connection with Adonis. As the case stands we have only the tantalising satisfaction of knowing how many and of what divergent origin were the threads that time and the fruitful invention of story-tellers and poets have woven into the variegated yarns concerning Cinyras. Let the whole of them serve as a background for the worship and the presence of the goddess Aphrodite at Old Paphos. Let us fling upon the throne of Paphian Aphrodite the richly variegated web of early legends, and then when she shall have taken her seat, and with smiles shall be admiring her own loveliness in an upraised mirror-disc, we may call to her as burning Sappho called of old, "Immortal Aphrodite throned in many hues."[1] The hues lent by early legend are always pure of quality and soft in tone, and even Aphrodite's beauty is enhanced by them.

Now that we know the worst and the best of the first founder of the Paphian temple of Paphian Aphrodite, let us look at the site[2] where he builded her temple of old. He built it, after the manner of the Assyrians and Phoenicians, in a high place. The hill of Old Paphos is distant about one mile from the sea. Half of this mile is taken up by a gradual slope from the hill's summit to its base. The sea lies south-west of the temple-site, and in the far distance, at the end of a gradual but constant upheaval of range upon range of hills, rise the heights around Mount Troödos, itself not visible from here.

---

[1] ποικιλόθρον' ἀθάνατ' 'Αφρόδιτα.
[2] For a detailed account of the remains there discovered, see Appendix VI. below.

A gentle slope, strewn with bits of limestone ranging in colour from yellow to gray; close to its brow a small and uncleanly village, on the east and west of which are the beds of inconsiderable streams,—such is the Paphian site, and such the modern village of Couclià (Couvocles in Old French). The prevailing tint in early May, when we visited it, was a yellow which might have verged towards brown had it not been for a spare crop of grain that invisibly warmed the surface tint. The curious eye peering eastward is rewarded by a vision of palms. These and the peculiarly picturesque discomfort of the squalid village houses assure you that you are neither in England nor in New England.

Just here the friable limestone, beaten on other coasts near by into fantastic cliff-shapes, takes unnoticeable rounded forms or clothes itself with soil. A stretch of fertile bottomland reaches from the foot of the Paphian hill south-westward to the strand of the sea. At a distance of about three hundred yards from the water's edge there is a drop of ten feet, and again at half that distance a second drop of about the same number of feet. Thus was the sheer rock rounded and the higher reach of meadow-land terraced down to the verge of the sea for a gradual ascent to the high place of Aphrodite at Old Paphos. Across this green and flower-strewn meadow-carpet moved the new-born goddess from the surface of the wave. Thither, says Hesiod, she had been gently borne drifting eastward from Cythera; or, as others might say, westward from Syria. Whichever of these directions is assigned to the coming of the goddess, one detail all legends have in common, *i.e.* that Aphrodite was born here in Cyprus, and her name is Cypris or Cyprogeneia—Cyprus-born.

As a Greek goddess, swaying the gods on Olympus

and ruling according to her good pleasure the hearts of all mortals, Aphrodite was born at Paphos in Cyprus. Speculations about her history before her birth at Paphos did not enter into the devout minds of her worshippers. For them she was what the unhappy Phaedra calls her, Cyprian Aphrodite of the sea—Cypris Pontia. Nor was this Paphian birth without an enormous influence upon the larger world outside of Greece. There was a something in the Paphian Aphrodite that her eastern original lacked, and this something can by a process of exclusion be proved to have been a distinctively Greek aspect of her divinity. Aphrodite's birth at Paphos made her at last accessible to purely Greek influences, and qualified her to play a great part in the religious history of the world. It was perhaps a misfortune that Greek influences never wholly divorced her from the manners and customs that finally attached to her in the East, as a Syrian and Phoenician divinity. At all events much that was outrageously gross and uncivilising in her latter-day worship at Corinth and elsewhere in Greece is traceable to the direct influences exercised from the East by her later and unclean worship there. We can, therefore, agree with a gifted American scholar,[1] who, under the happy inspiration of words associated with Plato's name,[2] has said that "the Greek received nothing from the East that he did not make doubly his by the beauty with which he invested it, and the Aphrodite Urania is as far above the Oriental personification of the conceptive principle of nature, as the graceful image of Venus issuing from the shell . . . excels the clumsy merman Dagon whose hands and feet

---

[1] *Essays and Studies*, by Basil Lanneau Gildersleeve, 1890.
[2] *Epinomis*, 487 E, ὅτι περ ἂν Ἕλληνες βαρβάρων παραλάβωσι, κάλλιον τοῦτο εἰς τέλος ἀπεργάζονται.

were cut off upon the threshold of his temple when he lay a prostrate deformity before the ark of the Lord at Ashdod."

The something which stamps Aphrodite as a specifically Greek version of the often perverted Eastern goddess is certainly that which made her admirable above her eastern originals, and secured her the adoration of all the world.[1] The Greek strain in Paphian Aphrodite is almost at war with the sombre jealousy which never really left her because it attached itself to her Assyrian nativity. Greece gave to her a fresh and breezy sanity and an inborn grace that Euripides describes so perfectly, calling her peerless among the gods in just this her quality of qualities. *Eucharis*, he calls her,—gently, sweetly, gracefully charming. She had, as Euripides worshipped her, beyond all other goddesses the charm that wins and never loses, the grace that woos and wearies not, the beauty that waxes and never wanes, the smile that attaches and never repels.

Somewhere Euripides describes the only ray of hope left to lighten the darkness of despair as the Aphrodite of woes. That hold upon hope and help which leads a man in the midst of desperate flames to wait one precious moment longer before he flings himself headlong to destruction is the Aphrodite of his woeful state, whose power subdues the wildness of sudden impulse and saves his life. Here is the Aphrodite Sosandra, rescuer of men, the Notre Dame de Bon Secours, worshipped on the Athenian Acropolis, where her statue by

---

[1] The very transformation in meaning which Aphrodite's epithet Urania underwent before our very eyes, so to speak, is full of the Greek spirit which purified and ennobled. Herodotus identifies Aphrodite-Urania with Mylitta (i. 131 and 199), with whose coarse rites Plato's Urania has nothing in common. The real equivalent of Mylitta, so far as these rites go, would be Aphrodite Pandemos. See Robert's *Preller*, pp. 354 ff.

Calamis cheered and uplifted the sinking hearts of those who came to worship. Hers was a graciousness so bountiful and subtly winning that its spell cannot and never will be broken. To this degree of spiritual nobility had the Greeks at Athens in their pious meditations brought the charm of Aphrodite, known in simpler Homer's day as her charmed girdle, of which he says :

Broidered and fashioned therein were all means of enchantment,
Love-longing was there and commerce of love, and there was love's chatter,
Words and cajolements that steal away wits, even men's that are wisest.

The almost wholly physical charm of her Cestus was not, as Homer conceived it, absolutely inseparable from Aphrodite. She alone possessed it, but if she chose she could lend it, and so it was that Hera borrowed it of her. On the other hand, the later and more spiritual charm which shone through disasters and rescued sorrowing men was inseparable from her. No goddess, not even Hera, Queen of Olympus, could borrow this, or rescue as she could by the gracious subtlety of her smiling love. Not Euripides only but Pindar the sublime saw and spoke of the peculiarly Greek quality in Aphrodite. Only Pindar, as in so many other cases, beheld the more solemn and serious aspect of this great truth. That principle of measure and retributive compensation—which bids despair despair not, but lures a desperate man to hope, revealing in the very presence of woe glimpses of grace and showing the face of joy to come—assumes another and more solemn guise when men are glad and fortune favours them. A pang there is in fullest moments of supreme joy which prompts us to beware,—a sense of penalties to come which visits him whose joy might grow excessive, and whose pleasures make him lose the consciousness of duty to be done. This throb of pain in pleasure's midst, this pausing in mid-course of the forward fling of gladness, is perhaps but the negative pole that should be coupled with the saving graciousness of Aphrodite Sosandra's smile. She saves man from himself both in sorrow and in joy. And so Pindar, in his ninth Pythian ode, agrees with Euripides, telling how "Silver-foot Aphrodite tempered the loves of Apollo and Cyrene with awe," with a sense of some limit not to be exceeded. This awe-struck sense of shame at the thought of too great excess Pindar has called *Aidos*, and Euripides has personified the impulses which violate it in speaking of—

> Eager Loves that past all measure fling.

From these the chorus of women in the *Medea* of Euripides beg Aphrodite to deliver them. They pray to her for deliverance from jealousy such as has devastated Medea's life and happiness. They beseech her to "choose with critic glance" the "wedded happiness of women."

And so, with all the purity of her natal element, Aphrodite rises up before the high moods of imaginative meditation vouchsafed to Euripides and to Pindar. Yet Euripides does not forget her original function as a nature-goddess, as another beautiful song from his *Medea* well shows:

> Cypris, when from fair Cephissus' downward streaming wave
> Draughts of water, so 'tis said, to quaff she sometime drew.
> Breathed adown the countryside blithe winds that softly blew,
>   Crowned her locks with roses red that sweetest perfume gave,
> Sent to second wisdom, Loves all righteousness to save.

These are some of the higher notes, the more purely Grecian, and therefore the more beautiful and nobler aspects which made the cult of Aphrodite, when it spread over all the Roman world, a benefit to civilisation. Would that only her nobler part had ever found allegiance in the pagan world. For better for worse, for richer or for poorer, the Roman Emperors took Venus Aphrodite as their own and made her mistress of the world. Their veneration sprang from no idealised adoration of the highest range of inspiration derivable from her, they were prompted rather by considerations heraldic, genealogical, and theological. It was therefore not purely an accident that made Caesar's watchword on the field of Pharsalia "Venus victrix," for such an accident, without being deeply significant, reveals the presence of Aphrodite in the thoughts of those who fashioned Rome.

This being the case, it is no matter of surprise that one of the very noblest and broadest conceptions of the goddess in the plenitude of her imperial power should be that of a Roman poet,—Lucretius. For him she is more than the source of all joy on earth and in heaven. She is the principle of life; without her earth can have no flowers, the woods can have no foliage, and the birds sing only at her will. "Without thee," he cries, "nothing that is can ever attain existence."

This is really not very far from that simple and touching conception which was the very primal foundation of immortality for the goddess Venus Aphrodite, the pure and noble delineation of the Assyrian goddess Ishtar in a poem far older than that of Roman Lucretius. This poem was found stamped upon tablets of burned clay in the library of Sardanapalus or Assurbanipal at Niniveh. The goddess left this upper earth to seek among the dead below her Tammuz dearly loved and lately lost. No sooner had the wondrous Ishtar disappeared from earth than life in the upper air was brought to a pause, and the most unspeakable distress made the whole universe wail and faint. Ishtar, waiting at the dust-bestrewn portals of Urugal, laments her case in the most exquisite strains of the old Assyrian poem:

> All love from earthly life with me departed,
> With me to tarry in the gates of death . . .
> And chilled shall cheerless men now draw slow breath.
>
> I left in sadness life which I had given,
> I turned from gladness and I walked with woe.
> I search for Tammuz, whom harsh fate laid low.
>
> The darkling pathway o'er the restless waters
> Of seven seas that circle death's domain
> I trod, and followed after earth's sad daughters
> Torn from their loved ones and ne'er seen again.
>
> Here must I enter in, here make my dwelling
> With Tammuz in the mansion of the dead,
> Driven to Tammuz' house by love compelling,
> And hunger for the sight of that dear head.
>
> O'er husbands will I weep, whom death has taken,
> Whom fate in manhood's strength from life has swept,
> Leaving on earth their living wives forsaken,
> O'er them with groans shall bitter tears be wept.
>
> And I will weep o'er wives, whose short day ended
> Ere in glad offspring joyed their husbands' eyes;
> O'er them shall tearful lamentations rise.
>
> And I will weep o'er babes who left no brothers,
> Young lives to the ills of age by hope opposed,
> One moment's life by death unending closed.[1]

---

[1] For a more complete version of this with others, made from a literal version of the cuneiform text kindly supplied me by my friend and former colleague Dr. Lyon, see *The Story of Assyria*, where the gifted author, Mme. Ragozin, does me the honour of printing my versions in an appendix.

Here is a large and oriental luxury of grief, a tragedy and mystery of woe which is ill suited to the smiling Aphrodite of the Greeks, and which stirs far deeper down the hearts of men than even the Venus-Aphrodite of Lucretius.[1] The truth is that there is no parallel easily found to the tragical shudder that runs through every line of this Assyrian poem. Among Greek divinities Demeter[2] rather than Aphrodite represents this utterness of woe and this fulness of heart-sympathy for the calamities of others.

The goddess Demeter even, when sorrow had all but slain immortality within her, was rescued by the gracious promise of hope in Aphrodite's smile; and this may justify us in maintaining once more that the Greek conception of Aphrodite was that of a consoling goddess, the enemy of despair, the harbinger of joys unlooked for, and the moderator of unruly pleasures.

This noble and consoling figure has dominated the destinies of nations since history began. Arising among the unknown tribes of Accad in the far-off east, she was honoured and worshipped at Niniveh and Babylon, at Tyre and Sidon and Carthage. Before the taint of monstrous licentiousness had brought corruption upon her, she found

---

[1] To this extent and in this sense I should incline to dissent from Professor Gildersleeve, who says, "the worship of Aphrodite is no less profound while it is infinitely more graceful than the Oriental." With the latter part of this I agree too thoroughly to be able to subscribe to the former. Demeter's awkward and mysterious strains go together, and both of them make her the Greek equivalent of the tragic Ishtar who laments for Tammuz.

[2] Euripides, in the *Helena*, almost seems to have the Assyrian poem before him in his beautiful song of the sorrows of Demeter-Cybele, who falls fainting and lifeless on the snowdrifts of mountains in Asia,—fainting and lifeless because she finds not Persephone. The earth meanwhile is stricken with barrenness. Until the Graces and Aphrodite sought her there and ministered to her, there was no fruitfulness, no springs would flow, and feasting fled from earth and forsook the gods even.

from the purifying sea a new birth, and came to her rising in Greece from Cyprian Paphos. When the power of self-repression, with which the nobler thought of Greece associated Aphrodite, began to falter and fail, Rome saved the sea-born goddess and her higher worship. Indeed the Roman Mother Venus of Virgilian song was as intensely kind, as irresistibly winning, as that most primally and exclusively Greek goddess the darling daughter of Zeus and Dione, the slender maid[1] who was worshipped and feared by Sappho. Nor does the broader and more mature as well as more oriental conception of Paphian Aphrodite, into which this goddess of Sappho was finally merged, reach quite the heights and depths of the all-nourishing mother Venus to whom Lucretius makes melodious prayer.

Perhaps the poor Cypriote papissa or priest's wife was not wrong in correcting the learned Ludwig Ross. He spoke to her of a sanctuary of Aphrodite. "No," she said, "not Aphroditissa; it is the Holy Chrysopolitissa."[2] To her is sacred a church on Aphrodite's Hill of Old Paphos. The Mother of God surnamed the Golden has taken the place once filled by Homer's golden Aphrodite.

[1] Γλύκεια μᾶτερ, οὔτοι δύναμαι κρέκην τὸν ἴστον
πόθῳ δάμεισα παῖδος, βραδίναν δι' Ἀφροδίταν.

See Euripides, *Helena*, 1098: κόρη Διώνης Κύπρι, μή μ' ἐξεργάσῃ.

[2] τώρα δὲν τὴν λαλοῦσιν Ἀφροδίτισσαν, τώρα τὴν λαλοῦσι Χρυσοπολίτισσαν.

APPENDIX VI

THE TEMPLE AT OLD PAPHOS

THE irregular trapezium[1] which the temple and its contiguous buildings once occupied lies at some distance—a stone's throw, be it said—from the brow of the hill. Before this trapezium area is reached you come upon the most remarkable remains upon the site. I cannot describe these better than in the words of Mr. R. Elsey Smith.[2] "Starting from the south-west corner, and examining the walls in detail as proposed, we find first of all a very large massive wall extending for some eighty-five feet in a nearly northerly direction, with a short return at the south end. It consists of a basement of polygonal blocks mostly of massive proportions brought to a fairly even face, and with a carefully wrought and levelled upper bed, on which rests a series of magnificent rectangular blocks, the largest of which measures seven feet by over fifteen. These blocks are of limestone, and have been laid with their beds vertical, so that they have suffered severely from the effects

---

[1] *Excavations in Cyprus* (1887-1888), reprinted from the *Journal of Hellenic Studies* (1888). See pp. 58 and ff., where Mr. Ernest Gardner conclusively disposes of all plans previously published, and clearly sets forth Mr. Elsey Smith's plan in connection with ancient authorities and coins. For my own detailed account of the site and of Cesnola's so-called plan, see *Nation* (Sept. 6 and 13, 1888).

[2] *Ibid.* See Mr. Elsey Smith's discussion of his own plan in the *Journal of Hellenic Studies* as cited above. The plan is by his kind permission here reproduced.

of weather. The stones both of the basement and upper parts of the wall are pierced with holes for the purpose of hauling them; the larger stones have two holes, but some of the smaller ones are pierced with a single hole only. In the upper stones these holes run from the vertical face at one end in a quadrant form up and down to the upper and lower beds of the stone; in the basement stones, which of course were below the pavement level, these holes generally run from the face backward to the vertical joints."

This remarkable and puzzling remnant is undoubtedly, Mr. Elsey Smith and all others conclude, the oldest feature discoverable at Couclià. Curiously enough it contains the only evidence upon the whole site that there was any doorway in any particular place. The two socket-holes for door-posts have two steps leading down to them. This door was, however, much less than ten feet wide from post to post, and can hardly have been the principal entrance to any court, such as Mr. Elsey Smith thinks was possibly enclosed by this the oldest structure at Old Paphos.[1] The piercings in these huge monoliths are said strongly to resemble what is discoverable upon the site of temples presumably of Phoenician origin on the island of Malta. Among the ruins of Sicilian Selinus, which was, like Old Paphos, a meeting ground for Greeks and Phoenicians in the earliest days, Ludwig Ross saw stones similarly pierced, and he attributed them to Phoenician workmanship. Can it be amiss to recall here the Phoenician method of preparing for the building of walls, as reported in the account of the building of Solomon's temple?

"And the house when it was in building was built of stone made ready before it was brought thither; so that there was neither hammer nor axe nor any tool of iron heard in the house while it was in building."

Piercings of some kind must have been made in the

---

[1] Of course the theory is that all traces of the main door have disappeared. Wherever it was, it certainly was not the small door of which traces remain.

quarry by Hiram's builders and stone squarers, otherwise it would not have been possible to transport huge blocks and put them in their place without leaving some projection upon the blocks, which must then have been removed upon the site itself by chiselling. This would have involved the sound of hammer, of axe, or some tool of iron. The Greek[1] way of getting stones in place was entirely different, since they had no objection to hammering on the site. They shaped the stones very accurately, but finished them only roughly in the quarry. The final smooth finish, together with the chiselling down of square projections left for a hold in transportation, was done when the walls were up. The first builders at Paphos, then, may have been Phoenicians, since they probably used the methods of Hiram's builders, and not those of the Greeks.

A change not only in the manner of building walls but in the way of finishing stones, and in the methods used for their transportation, took place among the workmen at Old Paphos before a stone of what became the temple of Aphrodite was laid. The proof of this is ready at hand in the remains of walls which are close to the supposably Phoenician work just described in detail. Here are marks (A) of an ancient reconstruction of parts of walls, and (B) of an addition made at the same ancient date. All these reconstructed parts—including two rows of columns—indicate a new manner of workmanship. "The stones employed," says Mr. Elsey Smith,[2] "are of smaller and more regular dimensions . . . and they are very evenly laid without mortar; each stone has a broad draught along the upper edge, and down the two sides of its outer face,

---

[1] To understand this only a glance at the unfinished Propylaea of Mnesicles at Athens is needful. The downward (westerly) face of this building was so far finished that the square projections used for transport have been chiselled off, but the smooth chiselling of the outward surfaces has never been completed. The upward (easterly) face is left wholly unfinished, and is still covered with the curious square projections intact. See Appendix XI. i. 8 and 9.

[2] *Journal of Hellenic Studies*, 1888, p. 48, at the bottom.

leaving a rough panel in the centre."¹ This rough dressing of the stone with a draught around the edge—it commonly goes around the whole edge—is a mark of workmanship which may have been Phoenician, and is probably not Greek. The other technical details, however, show a nearer approach to Greek workmanship.

In these early walls of two kinds some discover an earlier temple which became in later and more magnificent days an appendage to the enlarged sanctuary: something which, for want of a better name, has been called the South Wing. The unmistakably unique and possibly Phoenician character of some of the walls here not unnaturally leads one to look for a parallel at the monuments in Phoenicia. Here is Professor Reber's brief description (taken from M. Renan's account of his expedition) of the "Snail's-Tower" at Marathus, the ancient Amrit, not far from the Byblus of which the Paphian Cinyras was the fabled king. This building, with four others, forms the most considerable mass of Phoenician work preserved in Phoenicia. The effect of them from afar is said to be very wonderful. A closer view shows a certain helpless heaviness that makes them less interesting. The "Snail's-Tower" is constructed out of huge square-hewn blocks of limestone. It is a cube

---

[1] This rough dressing of the stone with a draught around the edge is known as Rustica, and has been supposed to be a mark of Phoenician workmanship. But though such chiselling has been found in Phoenicia, it is also plentiful elsewhere and does not prove Phoenician handiwork here. Perhaps it is vain to seek any real knowledge of Phoenician buildings, or to identify anything as certainly Phoenician, outside of Phoenicia itself. Dr. Franz Reber has truly said in his *Kunstgeschichte des Alterthums* (p. 134) that the characteristically Phoenician adornments of buildings, private and public, were of wood. The cedars of Lebanon were so near at hand. It is therefore possible—since Cyprus of old abounded in forests—that the first temple at Paphos was chiefly of wood. The tradition of abundant wood upon the island existed in 1532, when Ziegler wrote—"Silvosa primitus fuit, sed quia metalli aeris ferax esset silva excisa in caminos et opera metalli campos aperuerunt arabiles." Ortelius, 1573, gives Ammianus Marcellinus (book xiv.) and other authorities for forests and shipbuilding in Cyprus. Evagoras and Conon both resorted to these forests for shipbuilding, which must have had great importance from the end of the fifth century B.C. downward.

eleven metres high and nine metres square, and there are traces of a pyramid that once surmounted this cube. Its hewn stones five metres in length—longer, that is to say, than the longest of the pierced monoliths of the south wing at Paphos—are treated in Rustica, like the later walls of the same south wing at Paphos. The "Snail's-Tower" has within it two mortuary chambers, and it was undoubtedly a tomb, as were also the four smaller buildings not far away.

I venture to suggest that in these remarkably puzzling walls of the so-called south wing we may have the remains of one or more tombs built by the Phoenicians. These buildings were partly suggested by the pyramids of Egypt, no doubt; the subterranean mortuary chambers hollowed out in the rock under all the great tombs at Marathus, excepting the "Snail's-Tower," are indeed an attempt to reproduce the conditions of the chamber of the dead in the bowels of the Egyptian pyramid. In the "Snail's-Tower" and—if it be a tomb—also at Paphos we have a departure from this type. The builders at last contented themselves with massively built chambers above ground. What leads me to think of the south wing here at Paphos as having possibly been a tomb is the matter-of-course way in which Clement of Alexandria,[1] quoting from the first book of a work by Ptolemy the son of Agesarchus, talks of the tombs of Cinyras and his descendants as being at Paphos within the precinct of Aphrodite. They are, he as much as says, well-known features of the sanctuary at Old Paphos. We need not, in spite of some traditions to that effect, assume a tomb of Aphrodite, but merely that there was at Paphos one tomb or several for the great king-priests of importance. But if Clement the Roman were taken literally in what he says of a tomb of Aphrodite at Old Paphos,[2] this might very well be paralleled by the statue of Aphrodite surnamed *of*

---

[1] Clemens Alexandrinus (*Protrept.* cap. iii. *ad fin.*)—Πτολεμαῖος δὲ ὁ τοῦ Ἀγησάρχου ἐν τῷ πρώτῳ τῶν περὶ τὸν Φιλοπάτορα ἐν Πάφῳ λέγει ἐν τῷ τῆς Ἀφροδίτης ἱερῷ Κινύραν τε καὶ τοὺς Κινύρου ἀπογόνους κεκηδεῦσθαι.
[2] *Homil.* v. 23.

the tomb (ἐπιτυμβία)[1] and the tomb of Chthonian Dionysus which were features of the great temple at Delphi. At Delphi the tomb of Dionysus was a half-understood relic of an order of worship long superseded. At Paphos the Phoenician-built tomb of Aphrodite would represent an early and perhaps a purely Phoenician phase of worship, and would commemorate the descent of Ishtar—her death —into Urugal.

But now, if these oldest ruins are the remains of tombs, it is certainly time to turn to the temple itself, which is only a few steps north of the northernmost portion of the remains just mentioned. I have called the whole space occupied by the temple ruins, as Mr. Gardner does, an irregular trapezium. Its west and south sides measure 220 feet, its east side 228 feet, and its north side 207 feet. This great quadrilateral enclosure is not rectangular, though the Romans, when they repaired and rebuilt it, did their best to make a rectangle out of it. Its eastern side consisted of a range of chambers and a way out; the whole of its northern side probably, and certainly the whole of its southern side, consisted of a long porch.[2] These porches, had their unmistakable traces not appeared, would have been suggested not only by what is known of cognate temples, but also by the heats of Cyprus. These imperatively demanded a shelter within the precinct for the processions wearied by the long way from New Paphos.[3] These considerations suggest that upon the remaining side —the western one—may also have been a portico. Unfortunately there are absolutely no remains of any kind

---

[1] Plutarch, *Q. Rom.* 23. The other Clement (of Alexandria), speaking of the Argives, describes them as οἱ 'Αφροδίτην τυμβωρύχον θρησκεύουσιν.

[2] I use porch here, as in chap. vi. above, in the sense of *stoa* or *porticus*.

[3] A remarkably interesting proof of the great good sense which guided the learned authors Perrot and Chipiez in their account of Paphos may be found in their statement that such porticoes were required upon the site. It is not often that subsequent excavations on a site bear such clear testimony in favour of those who had to speak without all the facts.

PLAN OF THE TEMPLE AT OLD PAPHOS

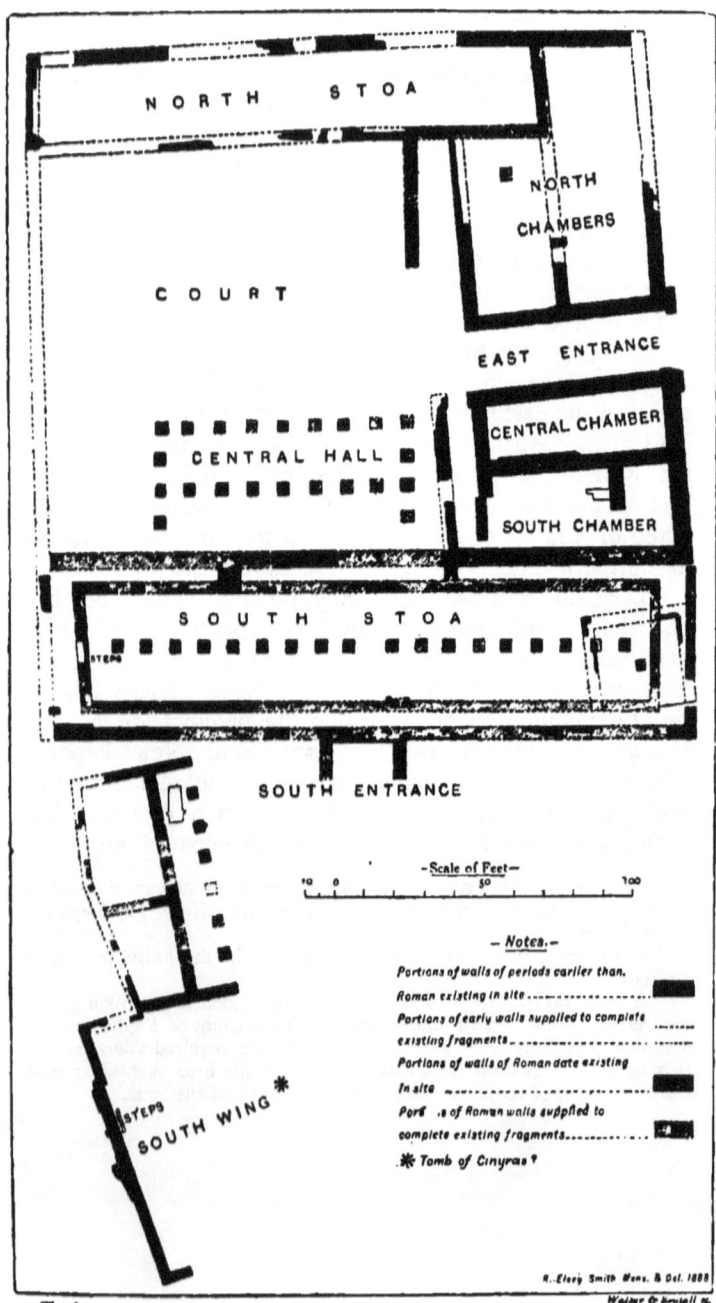

To face page 310

upon the western side, and, therefore, only the natural requirements of worshippers, and the not wholly convincing parallel of Solomon's temple, can be appealed to in favour of a porch or anything else.[1] With this general description of the temple after the excavation, let us compare what was supposed to be known before excavations took place. Professor Reber, with admirable judgment and brevity, says —" Within a circular fence enclosure there was a group of buildings consisting of two lower wings overtopped by a higher central nave. The wings were supported by columns, perhaps they were porticoes. Two columns shaped like those of Egyptian architecture stood disengaged and unburdened. It is likely that these last had no architectural function, but were like Jachin and Boaz." These last, it will be remembered, were either in the front of or in front of the entrance to the Hebrew sanctuary. This whole description is based upon representations of the temple on coins and upon an intaglio.

Excavation on the site has done away with the notion of a circular enclosure. The shape of the coin, Mr. Gardner suggests, left no choice to the artist. The quadrilateral court really has no curved lines on any of its sides. It is hard to determine the exact position of the sanctuary where was the pyramid of white stone worshipped at Paphos as at Byblus. It was in all probability one of the chambers built along the east side of the quadrilateral. Of these chambers three are now traceable, and strange to relate, by the side of the central one of these three is an open way out. This has been called the east entrance. North of this entrance are the north chambers, not supposed by any one to have been the sanctuary. South of it is the central chamber, which was almost certainly the sanctuary in later Roman days, because in the open court opposite its front the Romans built a colonnaded approach

---

[1] Many cross trenches were made in the hope that further excavation to the west might be justified. Nothing, however, was found except, at a few inches below the soil, the bed rock.

on a higher level than the south portico. This we may call the Central Hall. Thus the sanctuary of later Roman days—a chamber older than the Roman Hall in front of it—was approached through a hall of Roman construction. When this hall was built the Romans undertook to make the open court square, and there resulted an irregular passage just in front of the chambers and east entrance which they very probably roofed over.

In spite of the fact that the Romans have made it easy to identify the central chamber as the sanctuary by building a hall in front of it, some extremely minute observations about the manner of construction exhibited by various walls have made certain visitors of the site incline to think that at one time (before serious earthquakes made Roman rebuilding necessary) there was one more chamber on the east side of the court. At that time the Roman sanctuary (central chamber) was not the sanctuary but one of two lower wings flanking the sanctuary, which was part of the present south chamber. Thus we should have for the earlier Greek period of the temple a plan which the coins continued to reproduce in late Roman days, although earthquakes and alterations had sadly interfered, and had even made it necessary to shift the sanctuary. The oldest walls belonging to the temple proper are all of them of an epoch later than any of the walls south of the temple, and constituting the south wing. The central and the south chambers and the north portico were apparently built long before the Romans, and were merely patched by them. This third species of early work on the site—the two earlier exemplified only in the south wing being supposably Phoenician—may be called the Greco-Phoenician walls. A common feature distinguishing them all from Roman work is that there is no mortar used.

The temple then consists of four main parts whose existence is established, and one missing part whose existence is problematical but may for the moment be taken for granted.

1st. The Chambers and Entrance, which are its east side. Traces of a curiously modified Greek work (Greco-Phoenician) coexist with Roman mending in these walls.

2nd. The North Portico, which is the north side. Here the work is Roman with just enough traces of what I have called Greco-Phoenician to make it exceedingly improbable that the original ground-plan was materially departed from.

3rd. The entirely Roman Southern Portico, which is the south side. Here, again, dim traces of an original building are visible, and confirm the notion that the Romans did not seriously innovate. Under the mosaic pavement here were found various fragments of undoubtedly Greek workmanship.

4th. The entirely Roman Hall, by which the later sanctuary—marked Central Hall on the plan—was approached. This ran parallel to the two porticoes, passing through or near the middle of the great would-be quadrangle or court of the temple. Beyond the construction of this hall of approach no serious departure from the original ground-plan was apparently made by the Romans. That their south portico should have been a great enlargement of what had been there before, and should have wiped out nearly all vestiges of it, is natural. The analogy of the Jewish temple requires a far more spacious portico here than on the opposite and northern side of the court. The temple built by Herod had its royal portico on the south. Finally, if there were no other reason for a more spacious portico on the south side of the court at Paphos, the fact that processions from New Paphos must have entered from the south would settle the question as a practical one.

To sum up, the temple ruins at Old Paphos have proved on examination not to be those of a Grecian temple similar to those built in honour of the Paphian goddess in Greece. We have at Old Paphos the very interesting but unfortunately defaced remains of a temple resembling in many ascertainable points that of Solomon. It must be admitted, however, that a comparison between two things so insufficiently known as the plans of these two temples must of necessity be somewhat barren of tangible results.

The remains called the South Wing, which have chiefly excited the curiosity of all travellers, have not, I think, anything to do with the temple-building as such, but are the remains of a Phoenician tomb, like the "Snail's-Tower" at Amrit.

Would that we had more knowledge. If other temples and more tombs built by the Phoenicians or on the Phoenician plan had been examined and understood, it would be perhaps easy to know all manner of things about the remains at Old Paphos. As it is, the biblical accounts of temple-building at Jerusalem, supplemented by Josephus and his description of Herod's temple-building, afford only the palest side-lights—the only lights available for illustrating the temple ruins discovered at Old Paphos.[1] And, as for the walls of the South Wing, it is by no means certain that they can be confidently described as the Tomb of Cinyras; but this account of it is the best to be had, I am sure.

[1] The plan just discussed results from the most thorough and scientific exploration of remains existing upon the traditional site of the Paphian temple. Yet it is quite possible to explain all that is shown upon this plan without being sure that any part of it was the real temple of the Paphian goddess. This uncertainty has been recently expressed by no less an authority than Mr. F. C. Penrose (new series of the *Transactions of the Royal Society of British Architects*, vol. vi. p. 66). Mr. Penrose, after recognising a possible connection between this plan of the Paphian temple and that of Solomon's temple, says: "On this account alone the examination of the Temple of Aphrodite in Cyprus has not been labour wasted. The finds indeed have not been very beautiful architecturally, but still the plan is remarkable, and its use, I think, has yet to be made out." Unlikely as any new discoveries near the site already excavated will seem to any who know the spot, their impossibility has certainly not been ocularly demonstrated. Until such demonstration shall have been given, other archaeologists will be not unlikely to share the uncertainty of Mr. Penrose. This being the case, it is a great satisfaction to know that a project for eventual excavations at Couclià which shall make uncertainty impossible has been discussed. The best guarantee for its efficient management—in case it should ever be carried out—is that those who have been moving in the matter were the originators and prosecutors of the excavations just described.

APPENDIX VII

APHRODITE OF THE GREEKS, HITTITES, AND PHOENICIANS

MANY who are learned in Greek have a pardonable bias in favour of a Greek rather than a Phoenician origin for so important a goddess of the Greeks as Aphrodite. Others who have studied the monuments of Asia Minor, and found there new and interesting materials about the "Hittites," are beginning to suspect that Paphian Aphrodite was originally a goddess of the "Hittites," and to maintain that neither in her origin nor in her main characteristics was she of Greek or of Phoenician derivation. In one doctrine only do these two jarring sects agree—both maintain the non-Phoenician birth and breeding of the goddess worshipped at Paphos and in Greece as of Paphos.

Engel and Heffter, who are anxious to prove the Greek origin of this Greek goddess, have the following case:[1]— The Homeric poems contain many allusions to Aphrodite, the daughter of Zeus and Dione. Now Dione is the feminine form of Zeus, and these names both lead back to a primitive cult as far from Cyprus and the east as anything on Greek soil possibly could be. Dodona and the extreme north-west—not Cyprus and the east—would then be the cradle of Aphrodite-worship. It may be maintained that a knowledge on Homer's part of Paphos and

[1] I am perhaps bound to say that the statement of their case is mine.

Cyprus disappears with the application of critical standards to the text of the *Odyssey* and the relegation to a later date of the Aphrodite-Ares episode in the eighth book, at the end of which the goddess betakes her to Paphos. Every one must, I think, admit that the oldest portions of the *Iliad* and *Odyssey* know nothing of Aphrodite as Cypris or the Paphian goddess. But to return to the vindicators of the purely Hellenic origin of our goddess; Herodotus, they say, and other Greeks[1] who talk confidently of the Cypro-Phoenician beginnings of the Greek goddess, take this view partly from a perceptible bias in favour of the east as the place for all origins, especially religious ones, and partly from a lack of the critical point of view.

This critical treatment of Homer must not, however, be half applied, and if it is conscientiously brought to bear on all the places where Aphrodite is mentioned by Homer, the result is not by any means in favour of her Greek origin. The most undeniably primitive portions of the *Iliad* and the *Odyssey*, the oldest groundwork of Homeric song, contain no word or words to show that the poets of primeval Greece knew at all either whence or from what parentage Aphrodite came. All the passages of Homer where Aphrodite is called the daughter of Zeus and Dione, like all those where she is spoken of as Cypris, or in any way connected with Paphos, are, by a remarkably general consensus of otherwise discordant critics, pronounced to belong to a comparatively late period when the Homeric poems underwent what may be called revision and amplification.[2]

---

[1] For the various authorities see note 1, p. 284, above.

[2] There are eleven passages of the Homeric poems where Aphrodite is mentioned as the daughter of Zeus, or of Dione. They occur in the Third, Fifth, Fourteenth, Twentieth, and Twenty-first books of the *Iliad*, and in the Eighth book of the *Odyssey*. They are to be naturally grouped as follows :—(1) *Il.* iii. 374; (2) *Il.* v. 131, 312, 371, 382, 820; (3) *Il.* xiv. 193, 224; (4) *Il.* xx. 105; (5) *Il.* xxi. 416; and (6) *Od.* viii. 308. A number of these passages cannot possibly count in favour of the greater antiquity of a purely Greek Aphrodite, since they associate her as the daughter of Zeus and Dione, not with Dodona or any place in Greece, but by calling her Cypris, or otherwise, identify her with Paphos and Cyprus. At the

APHRODITE—GREEK, HITTITE, PHOENICIAN 317

As far then as the testimony of the Homeric poems can avail to prove anything about the earliest Greek knowledge of Aphrodite, it shows that her powers and her charms were known long before her origin was thought of. Furthermore it is plain that when the question of her birthplace and parentage did arise, it received a twofold answer. In absolute unconsciousness of the contradiction involved, Homer tells us that Aphrodite, the daughter of Zeus and Dione, was named Cypris, and had, for her favoured place of abiding, Paphos. Homer begins by knowing too little and ends by knowing too much about the Paphian divinity.

same time (*Od.* viii. 288 and xviii. 193) the *Odyssey* indicates that this Paphian goddess was immediately identified with the Phoenician divinity of the island of Cythera (Cerigo) by calling her Cytherea (see Pausanias, III. xxiii. 1).

All the passages—see (2) above—in the Fifth *Iliad* are off-set by others, 330, 422, 458, 760, 883, where this Greek daughter of Zeus and Dione is called Cypris, *i.e.* not Greek but of Cyprus. Indeed this whole episode of the wounding of Aphrodite is quite as certainly of late composition as is the tale of the loves of Ares and Aphrodite in the Eighth *Odyssey*, where Aphrodite, daughter of Zeus and Dione—(6) above—claims Cyprus as her own, and takes refuge in Paphos. See lines 363 ff. Thus (2) and (6) are ruled out as evidence of the greater antiquity of a Greek Aphrodite for the early Greeks, and (1), (3), (4), (5) remain.

As to (1), Bergk (*Litteraturgeschichte*, vol. i. p. 566) declares it to be a late addition. For many opinions to the same effect see Ameis-Hentze's *Iliad* (Anhang, Heft i. pp. 159-176). The Fourteenth *Iliad* (3), so far as it concerns us, as also the Twentieth (4), and the Twenty-first (5), are similarly divorced by the consensus of competent critics from the undoubtedly oldest groundwork of the *Iliad*. These facts are the more worth considering because none of these exclusions was made with any reference to or knowledge of the question here under discussion. See for (3) the Fourteenth *Iliad*, Bernhardy (*Litteraturgeschichte*, pp. 164 and 165 of the first part of the *History of Greek Poetry*). At p. 169 (*ibid.*) Bernhardy begins his careful presentation of the various views of various scholars about the closing books of the *Iliad*, and makes it tolerably plain that (4) and (5) are to be classed with (1), (2), (3), and (6), as belonging to a comparatively modern phase of the Homeric era. In confirmation of this view see Bergk in the work above cited, pp. 609-613 for (3), pp. 633-634 for (4), and p. 636 for (5). If still further confirmation be desired, it may be found in Ameis-Hentze's *Iliad* (*Erläuterungen zu* xiii.-xv. pp. 45-69, and *ibid., Erläuterungen zu* xix.-xxi. pp. 45-63, and p. 95).

If Aphrodite was the daughter of Zeus and Dione, she was a native goddess of the Greeks; and her name was not Cypris, nor was her home at Paphos or elsewhere in Cyprus. Logic does not, however, avail when you are dealing with poetry and religion. Homer and the other poets are so independent of "arguments about it and about" that, in a far later day, Theocritus, when he wrote his seventeenth Idyll [1] in praise of Ptolemy, spoke of "The mistress of Cyprus, daughter revered of Zeus and Dione."

The most reasonable way of explaining this poetical vagueness of Homer points to a confirmation of the usual theory that Aphrodite was essentially of Paphos and the east. The earliest Homeric presentation of her divinity by giving her no birthplace, and by silence as to her parents, treats her as a comparatively unknown power. Later on, when her commanding influence secures attention to her antecedents, a native and aboriginally Greek worship asserts its claims, which ran parallel to hers. This Greek goddess was no daughter of Zeus and Dione, but Dione herself. Dione was apparently for the early Greeks what Freya was to the Germans, and what Venus was to the early Romans. Dione [2] was worshipped by the side of Zeus at Dodona. Euripides—fragment 177, from the lost play of *Antigone*—apostrophises Dionysus as the son of Dione, and thus makes her the same with Thyone-Semele, originally an earth-goddess. All this goes to show what were the most ancient Greek associations, surviving vaguely in all pious minds of Greece, which would sometimes lay hold upon the smiling goddess of the east. These associations have an undeniable solemnity and a real dignity which are often lacking in the more eastern aspect of the goddess, and they doubtless played a part in the ennobling transformation which that goddess underwent at the hands of Hellas; but the fact remains that Dione of the early Greeks was very completely overshadowed and supplanted

---

[1] Line 36, Κύπρον ἔχοισα Διώνας πότνια Κώρα.
[2] See Plew's revision of Preller's *Greek Mythology*, p. 271.

by Cypris, the goddess of Paphos, and through Paphos of Phoenicia and Assyria.

The first victory won by Cypris was in the matter of the name. Where the case is of conflicting divinities, everything is in a name, and the name of Dione was practically driven out by Cypris-Aphrodite. Whatever may be the derivation of Aphrodite, it is not Greek, and Cypris speaks for itself, in spite of the forced attempt of an over-ingenious Homeric commentator to derive it from a Greek word [1] meaning to be pregnant. Then, with this prevalence of the new name partly as the cause and partly as the effect of it, came the increasing renown of the great places of the eastern worship of the goddess. Paphos and Cythera, both of them, played a remarkable *rôle* in the development of early commerce on the Mediterranean. No wonder then if the early Greek poets fancied that the real divinity was Aphrodite-Cypris, and not Dione of Dodona. No wonder if the old Greek divinity merely retained sufficient hold upon the imaginations of Greek-speaking men to live on as mother of the goddess. A conflict between Dodonaean Dione and Aphrodite-Cypris, where the latter was victorious, is the sufficient explanation of the anomalies in Homer's account of Aphrodite.

If this account of the overshadowing of the native Greek figure of Dione-Aphrodite by the Cypris-Aphrodite of Cythera and of Paphos is deemed convincing, and if it be admitted that, so far as her Greek worshippers were concerned, Cypris-Aphrodite was above and before all the Paphian goddess, then the question of her origin at Paphos must be reopened. Some of those who are especially entitled to a respectful hearing upon any question where Cyprus is concerned are inclined to believe that the preponderance in earliest times, at Paphos and in Cyprus, of Phoenician influence has been so seriously overstated as to obscure the really characteristic and original strain of the Paphian goddess, who will, they think, be eventually recog-

[1] κύειν.

nised as the Paphian and Cyprian modification of a divinity of Asia Minor. The dissemination of the cult of this goddess they attribute to a conquering race known hitherto only by name, and chiefly from the annals of Canaan and Egypt. This is Aphrodite of the "Hittites."

In the chapter above on Paphian Aphrodite room has been made in the process of reshaping submitted to by the Phoenician Ashtaroth-Astarte for a noteworthy element from Asia Minor added at Paphos to the goddess's character. This Paphian and non-Phoenician strain may conveniently be called by the name of the "Hittites." It certainly constitutes an important difference between Cypris-Aphrodite and Ashtaroth, but for all that I do not find myself convinced of its all-importance. I am still convinced that Phoenician influence was the "tone-giving" one at the temple of Aphrodite at Old Paphos, as it evidently was at Cythera and at Eryx. In order, therefore, that the last great light which shines upon the Paphian goddess from a rising interest now felt in the new-found "Hittite" theory may not be dimmed by prepossessions of my own, I have asked and obtained the permission of my friend, Mr. D. G. Hogarth, to print portions of a private letter which he was good enough to address to me. Little as I think anything which one of his competent knowledge and especial research may say on this subject requires either explanation or apology, I am perhaps bound to quote his remark that "future research may easily upset" various confirmations of the view which he so acutely defends, and to repeat his observation that the knowledge of the "Hittites" is only at its beginnings. The following, then, is his account of Aphrodite of the "Hittites," communicated to me in connection with my attempt to criticise a note in his *Devia Cypria*,[1] a book which I have always used with advantage.

"Now, as to the general question of my note in *Devia Cypria*, p. 26, the Phoenician origin of Aphrodite, and the part played by Phoenicians in Cyprus, I may as well state

[1] See above, note 1, p. 282.

my own theory for what it is worth. My idea in writing that note was that Aphrodite is the Asiatic goddess, derived from Asia Minor, where she was universally worshipped at an early period—not from Phoenicia, though I know that Ashtaroth is only another avatar of the same divinity. It seems to me a very significant fact that the Cypriote Syllabary is entirely non-Phoenician; it is also so clumsy a vehicle for a Greek language that it must have been *rooted* before Phoenician was brought into contact with the islanders. If not, it is difficult to understand either how it was not supplanted by the more convenient script, or how, on the other hand, it could itself have supplanted the latter. This postulates, therefore, an ancient pre-Phoenician population in Cyprus. Whom did they worship? In early Cypriote inscriptions 'Aphrodite' does not occur, but ἡ Fάνασσα and ἡ Πάφῐja do occur. Is she the original goddess, only called Aphrodite much later?

"If the date of Cypriote texts were better assured, I believe that it could be proved that ἡ Fάνασσα is pre-Phoenician. It is not yet proved, but it is probable, that the Cypriote script comes from the 'Hittites'; it was employed by a people speaking a language in which there were no Semitic elements. Why, then, should the great goddess of that people be Semitic?

"You say there is no positive evidence against Phoenicians being the originators of the goddess and the main influence in the island. Certainly I can adduce nothing more convincing than the above considerations. I find it hard to believe that a people who left so little influence on the speech of an island originated its chief worship, and I point, rather as confirmation than anything else, to the scantiness and local distribution of Phoenician remains in Cyprus. I know that future research may easily upset that confirmation; but at present the fact that only Citium, where there was an independent Phoenician kingdom in late times, and Idalium, which depended on it, have yielded anything of importance, is remarkable. By the way, have you noticed that at the latter there has been found no dedication to or mention of Aphrodite, whereas Athena is common?

"Neither Herodotus nor Homer can furnish very strong evidence for events previous to their time. I take it that 'Hittites' never came in contact with western Greeks, and were always unknown to the literature of the latter; what they did directly or indirectly in Cyprus would naturally be ascribed to Phoenicians. You say yourself, and most truly, that Cinyras is more like Attis than Tamuz.

"This is a crude statement of the idea which led me to write the note to which you refer. There is, I admit, another theory which would account for some of the facts, though it will not explain the absence of Phoenician remains, namely, that the immigration of a people from Asia Minor at an early period drove out Phoenicians who had peopled the island previously. It is not hard to believe that such Asiatic immigrants, being worshippers of the great Nature goddess, would identify her with their predecessor's Ashtaroth, who would accordingly survive in Cyprus while the other gods returned to Sidon and Tyre. Some day I hope to discuss this problem more fully, but do not see how either theory is to be established unless a date can be found for the earliest Cypriote inscriptions. When we found such complete incised 'Hittite' texts this past summer in Cappadocia, I thought that we might be able to show a fairly close relationship between their conventionalised symbols and the Cypriote; but there is no more resemblance than in the case of the well-known symbols in relief. True that the number of incised 'Hittite' inscriptions known at present is very small; still it cannot be said that the prospect of finding a *terminus a quo* for Cypriote by comparing these (probably) late examples of 'Hittite' is particularly bright at present.

"By the way, *à propos* of what you say about a Thracian wave on page 280, Ramsay has shown conclusively now that this wave was that which introduced a father god; Cyprus owns a mother, and her aboriginal must belong to the earlier time."

After all, the above account of the aboriginal mother goddess of Cyprus differs from my own only in the comparative importance attached to the main elements—of Phoenician and of "Hittite" origin — in the Paphian goddess as she conceivably existed at Paphos before the first advent of the Greeks. Chiefly to Mr. Hogarth, but somewhat also to Engel, I owe the conviction that there was an aboriginal pre-Phoenician goddess at Paphos. I would like to persuade him that the belief of Herodotus and others, who had some facts before them which are inaccessible to us, that the Phoenicians did visit and abide at Paphos, was well founded, and cannot possibly be due to a confusion between "Hittites" and Phoenicians. Furthermore, I would urge upon him that these Phoenicians so transformed the Mother Queen of the "Hittites" that the resulting Paphian divinity found at Paphos, and adopted by the early Greeks, was Phoenician rather than "Hittite."

Any other view of the case makes it difficult to understand the legend of the founding from Eryx, *i.e.* by the Sicilian Phoenicians, of a temple of Aphrodite at Psophis, in Arcadia. It is also difficult to explain upon any other theory the early bestowal upon Aphrodite of the name Cytherea derived from a worship established at Cythera by purple-fishing Phoenicians. And yet this epithet seems to be about as old as that of Cypris.

In fact, if Paphian Aphrodite was of the "Hittites," when Greeks first found her at Paphos, then she "suffered a sea-change" on her way to Greece, which left her indistinguishable, so far as Greek worshippers were concerned, from the Greco-Phoenician goddess on Cythera and at Eryx.

APPENDIX VIII

THE OLYMPUS AND THE BOCARUS IN CYPRUS —HETTORE PODOCATHARO AND JOHN MEURSIUS

THE most minute and comparatively unimportant questions require sometimes an unusual expenditure of time, and what seems a vast deal of talk about nothing at all. This general truth will, I fear, receive illustration in what follows. If it were possible without controversy to call Mount Troödos—the highest mountain of Cyprus—Olympus, the "mons mamillae similis" of certain well-known old[1] maps of Cyprus, and one or two unknown or hardly known modern[2] ones; and if I could ignore the trivial fact that a blunder of the elder John Meursius has imported the river-name Bocarus from the Athenian island of Salamis,

[1] See the finest of Cardinal Bessarion's MSS., a copy of the work of Ptolemy, whose original goes back, they say, to the twelfth or thirteenth century. However that may be, Bessarion's copy now in the Marcian Library has a beautiful map of Cyprus,—somewhat misshapen,—where Olympus figures. A. Ortelius published in 1573 a map entitled "Cypri Insulae Nova Descript." Here Troödos does not appear at all (*Trodisi* occurs as the name of a village), although the map is for modern purposes and contains only modern geographical names, *i.e.* names used by the Lusignans and Venetians. Paphos for instance is marked *Baffo, olim Paphos*.

[2] *Chypre: Histoire et Géographie*, par le Marquis de Sassenay: Paris 1878. On the excellent map here published and originally made for the "Revue de Géographie," the Troödos is rightly identified as the ancient Olympus.

where it belongs, into Cyprus where it has no place,—then the tiresome minutiae of this appendix might be dispensed with. But I have already been asked by the kindest and most competent of critics what is my authority for saying that the Troödos, and therefore not Mount Santa Croce, or Della Croce (Stavrovuni), was anciently called Olympus. The question is justified; for the best accredited maps—that of Major (then Captain) Kitchener and those of Kiepert—identify the ancient Olympus in question with Mount Santa Croce (Stavrovuni), and leave us to believe that Strabo had never heard of the only remarkable mountain in Cyprus. To answer this question and to protect my account of the shrine of Aphrodite at Old Paphos from the reproach of containing no mention of the wonderful river Bocarus of one hundred mouths, the following description of blunders within blunders, of confusions ancient and modern, is offered to such as may be minded to read it.

The question whether the ancients applied the name Olympus to Mount Troödos or Mount Santa Croce in Cyprus is eventually settled, I think—first, by Strabo's epithet of μαστοειδές, which is absurd when applied to Stavrovuni and exactly suits Troödos; and secondly, by a good MS. of Strabo.[1] The restoration of a period there found, in place

[1] The ordinarily accepted text (Teubner) of Meineke for this crucial passage, of Strabo, book xiv. p. 683, is as follows,—he has just mentioned Κίτιον (Larnaca): εἶτ' Ἀμαθοῦς πόλις καὶ μεταξὺ πολίχνη Παλαιὰ καλουμένη, καὶ ὄρος μαστοειδὲς "Ὄλυμπος· εἶτα Κουριὰς (ἄκρα) χερρονησώδης. . . . Thus Olympus would be Stavrovuni or Mount Santa Croce, which lies just inland from the place assigned by Strabo to Palaea between Larnaca and Limassol. The punctuation of the same passage which I propose to adopt is that of the Marcian Strabo catalogued in Venice as "Cod. 378 (Arm. lxviii. Th. xc.) in 4 minori membr. fol. 43; Saeculi circiter xi." εἶτ' Ἀμαθοῦς πόλις· καὶ μεταξὺ πολίχνη Παλαιὰ καλουμένη. Καὶ ὄρος μαστοειδὲς "Ὄλυμπος· εἶτα Κουριὰς χερρονησώδης. . . . This dissociates Palaia—which is mentioned, as it were, parenthetically—from Olympus, and puts the latter between Amathus (Limassol) and Curias. This description exactly applies to the Troödos, since Strabo thought of the coast directly after Curias as trending northward, see lower down on the same p. 683: ἀρχὴ δ' οὖν τοῦ δυσμικοῦ παράπλου τὸ Κούριον,—Curium is the town just beyond Curias from Limassol (Amathus),—τοῦ βλέποντος

of the comma substituted for it in the generally accepted text, settles the question. Still the present punctuation of Strabo's text is of very ancient date, since, as we shall see, Eustathius read it as Meineke does. It will be well therefore to go into many details and fully to understand how such a conflict of opinions has gathered around so simple a matter as the identification of this Cypriote Olympus. Above all we must remember that the same name of Olympus is also applied by Strabo to a headland-promontory at the extremest north-eastern point of the island.[1] About the situation of this, the lesser Olympus of Cyprus, there are not two opinions. Now I will pass in review some of the accounts given at various more or less modern times of the greater Olympus. No more commanding authority than that of His Holiness Pope Pius the Second can be appealed to in the fifteenth century. In the chapter on Asia Minor of his *Opera Geographica et Historica*,[2] he translates from Strabo the passage where Olympus is mentioned,—he does not speak of Strabo, but simply adopts the passage as his own. Having mentioned Citium [Larnaca], he writes: " Deinde Amathus civitas, et intermedio spatio oppidum nomine Palae et Olympus mons qui mamillae speciem praebuit et Curias peninsulam, et Curium urbs." Thus the Pope Aeneas Sylvius de' Piccolomini plainly ignored the highest mountain of Cyprus and applied the name Olympus to Mount Santa Croce; or did he simply follow the punctuation of the

πρὸς 'Ρόδον. . . . It is impossible, I think, to suppose with the ingenious d'Anville (*Mémoires de l'Institut*, Ancienne Série, vol. xxxii. p. 259) in his *Recherches Géographiques sur l'île de Chypre*, that Strabo meant both Stavrovuni and Troödos by his Olympus.

[1] Thus the name Olympus rightfully occurs twice on maps of ancient Cyprus. Ortelius in his *ancient* map (1580) brings it in thrice, and so does M. le Comte de Mas Latrie on a map published in 1862.

[2] Pius II. is not speaking from personal observation, as in his *Commentarii*, where he so graphically describes the situation of Monte Oliveto and the Alban Hills. Cyprus, throughout the fifteenth century, was little visited, and indeed even in Venice was regarded as a place of banishment, as was shown by the banishment of two inconvenient nobles to Nicosia in 1492.

Strabo which lay open before him?[1] Pius the Second wrote the above while he was pope (1458-1464).[2] Let us now appeal from him to the German Ziegler (1532). Ziegler simply places Olympus in the southern part of the island: "Orientalia ... Salaminia comprehendunt, Occidentalia Paphia, Meridionalia Amathusia et Olympus mons, Septentrionalia Lapathea." Now this unfortunately is very non-committal, but the difference is very appreciable between a statement that Olympus is between Citium (Larnaca) and Amathus (Limassol), and that it lies in the district of Amathus, with the district of Lapethus to the north. The latter description of the mountain's whereabouts almost inevitably attaches the name Olympus to the Troödos which would to-day be described as in the district of Limassol, since the road leading to its summit begins there. But after all Ziegler is only translating the well-known passage in Ptolemy, as Aeneas Sylvius translated Strabo. Ptolemy, as explained by the traditional map in the best MSS., is decidedly though not decisively in favour of identifying the ancient Mount Olympus with the Troödos. What is really needed is not an accumulation of slightly varying translations of two well-known passages in Strabo and Ptolemy respectively, but if possible some trace of the local survival in Cyprus of the name Olympus. So far as ancient testimony leaves the matter in doubt, this sort of evidence has a decisive value; particularly when the great mountain of all Cyprus is involved. Traditions about smaller things are easily changed and shifted.

If tradition of this kind exists, its traces will be found in the utterances of a cloud of witnesses belonging to the sixteenth century. These men knew Cyprus at the time

---

[1] The same mistake, if mistake there be, was made by Eustathius on *Il.* i. 18 : εἰσὶ δὲ καὶ ἕτεροι "Ολυμποι· ἔν τε γὰρ Πελοποννήσῳ, ὡς καὶ ἐν τοῖς τοῦ περιηγητοῦ ἐγράφη, καὶ ἐν Κύπρῳ δὲ ὄρος μαστοειδὲς μεταξὺ Κιτίου καὶ 'Αμαθοῦντος "Ολυμπος λέγεται· καὶ ἄλλη δέ τις ἀκρώρεια Κύπρου ἐκαλεῖτο οὕτως ἐν ᾗ ναὸς 'Ακραίας 'Αφροδίτης, ἄδυτος γυναιξί.

[2] I quote from the Helmstadt republication by Joh. Melchior Gustermann, 1690.

when that island was more nearly in the centre of
European affairs than ever before or since. Many of them
had an especial hold upon Venice and Cyprus as well.
Like the Athenians of old, the Venetians in the sixteenth
century, having failed to acquire any foothold on the
mainland which was at all commensurate to their maritime
and commercial importance, were forced by circumstances
to make much of their islands, and the popular interest in
these possessions gave rise to a new sort of geographical
literature in the numerous books published about islands
exclusively. That the Venetian public laid stress upon
accuracy in the depiction of any scene where their island
domain was involved is curiously exemplified by the dim
outline of the mediaeval Acropolis of Naxia (the capital of
Venetian Naxos) which adorns the middle distance of
one of the most beautiful of all Venetian pictures—
Tintoretto's "Marriage of Ariadne and Bacchus." Tintoretto was born, it will be remembered, in 1518, and
lived until 1594, and therefore the various "Isolarii"
of the century were the new books of his day. The
earliest of these which I have consulted is that of Benedetto Bordone of Padua. This curious book was
published under a quaint and apparently irrelevant[1]
authorisation from Leo the Tenth (Giovanni de' Medici).
"Da. Rome, apud Sanctum Petrum sub annulo piscatoris.
die V. Junii 1521 Pont. Nostri Anno Nono." But it is
evident that this imprimatur was not enough, and a
petition had to be addressed to the Venetian Signoria as
follows: "Benedetto Bordone miniator compare humilmente
davanti a le Signorie vostre narrando cum sit che molti
anni si habbi faticato di & notte in cōponere uno libro,
nel quale si tratta de tutte l' Isole del mondo si antiche
come etiā moderne &c. . . ." This narration secured a
monopoly of the sale for ten years from the 6th of March
1526. The date of Bordone's *Isolario* was 1508: see

[1] The title of Bordone's book does not appear among those recited in the document, and his book is not apparently authorised by it.

Horatio Brown's *Venetian Printing Press* (1891) p. 103. Bordone thought himself learned in books, and gives much space to a remarkably confusing disquisition on *La Musica*, the "terza sorella" of *Astrologia*. Of this last he says "e nell numero delle Muse, adonque ell' è vera." His real claim to a hearing, however, is that he has travelled himself,[1] or at least that he has talked with others who have travelled, and can be depended upon to give a fresh and unbookish account of Cyprus or any one of his "isole si antiche come etiã moderne." Of the art of drawing an accurate map Bordone was not a master, since he was almost the inventor of woodcutting for maps.[2] For this reason no doubt, speaking in the third person, he tells the Signoria of "le sue tante fatiche . . . volendo quelle far imprimere di molte spese si nel stampare, come anchor nel far tagliar la forma di ciaschuna Isola come essa sta. . . ." However, for the purpose in hand, Bordone's sketch map is all-sufficient. He places "la croce," the equivalent of Mount Santa Croce (Stavrovuni), close to the southern shore of the island with "il chito" (Larnaca-Citium) close at hand. He finds no way of indicating Mount Olympus on this map, but that is readily explained when we read what he says of Olympus in the text of his work. Speaking of Cyprus, he there says: "& ha nel mezzo il monte olimpo." Bordone was so completely of his day and generation that his idea of a map did not contemplate the possibility of anything more complete than are those rude sailors' charts called Portulani of which the Marcian Library and the Museo Correr at Venice are full.[3] Olympus, then, was in the centre of the

[1] This is shown by the letter of dedication: "allo eccellente chirurgico Meser. Baldassaro Bordone, Nepote Suo, accetti queste nostre fatiche . . . cagion potrano esser, che alchuno pellegrino ingegno la strada dinanzi fatta vedendosi" etc., etc., the passage becomes hopelessly muddled, but seems to imply some travelling on Bordone's part.
[2] See Brown, *The Venetian Printing Press*, p. 103.
[3] These never give any features of the interior; frequently the space where such details would come is taken up with pictures for the delectation of the jolly sailor's eye. See Portulan No. 9 (in the Marcian

island, and was not the well-known mountain on the coast where every Venetian sailor knew the monastery and church of the Holy Cross. Bordone emphasises this familiar fact on his map by drawing a picture of the church and the mountain, making the church just a little larger than the mountain. The whole impression left by the excellent Bordone is that of a sailor telling of his travels after they are over in language so artless that it is often absolutely unintelligible. An *Isolario* exists from which Bordone undoubtedly took the general idea of his book. It is that of the sea captain Bartolommeo who names himself "da li Sonetti" in his book of geographical sonnets on the islands of the Aegean Sea, which he dedicated to the doge Giovanni Mocenigo, and published shortly after 1500.[1] That is about eight years before Bordone's book of the same name.

But this form of geographical-historical literature, the peculiar invention of the Venice of the sixteenth century, did not perish with these rude first attempts. Its perfection was achieved just while the Turk was outrageously hurling himself on the island empire of Venice. The first edition of *L'Isole piu famose del mondo*, by Tommaso Procacci da Cosiglione, was published in 1571, and the author prefaces his account of Cyprus with the following allusion to a work on that island which he had seen in MS.: "Nel descriuer la nobilissima e famosissima Isola di Cipro; io farò piu breve che la grandezza & gloria sua merita; non perchè le cose non siano molte in numero; ma perchè essendo stata fatta questa descrittione auanti a me dall' illustre & uirtuosissimo Signore Hettore

Library) by Battista Agnese. There a figure labelled "Philipus Rex Hispaniae Rex Angliae" is throned in mid-Spain, while, somewhat inconsistently, England is adorned with the "Regina Angliae" who sits bolt upright and holds a sword. In Italy "Pontifes Ivlivs Tercius" holds up the cross, while over against him in Bosnia is the terrible "Suleymanssach imperator turcorum." The date of this sailor's chart and picture-book is 1553.

[1] The date of publication is apparently very doubtful, 1477 and 1485 are both given by competent authorities.

Podocatharo,[1] cauallier di quel Regno, & non essendo anchora stata data in luce,[2] hauendola io per cortesia di quell' honorato & cortese signore letta, & ueduta tutta; non è honor mio, ne creanza di nobile spirito far torto a quel magnanimo gentil' huomo a cui son grandemente obligato. Però coloro che al presente legeranno questa descrittion da me fatta, sappianno che io toccherò sommariamente alcuni soli passi piu importanti, & del resto aspettino di douer da quel libro, che il Signor Hettore Podocatharo chiama *Ritratte* del Regno di Cipro, ueder pienamente, e in giudizioso stile, quanto a questo proposito appartenga."

Procacci's first edition came, as above remarked, in 1571; one of the publishers, Simone Galignani by name, dedicated it to Don John of Austria, who was in a few short months to win the glorious victory of Lepanto, for which Venice is still full of his praises. But in spite of this rebuff the unmentionable Turk pressed forward still, and before Procacci's second edition appeared Cyprus had, by process of fire and sword, and by murderous treachery, been torn violently away from the European empire of Venice, just

---

[1] Hettore Podocatharo was a man of some wit. Cicogna speaks of his praises in Ludovico Domenichi's *Facezia*, Venice, 1574. Procacci dedicated to Hettore the first volume of his *Cagione delle Guerre Antiche*, see Cicogna's *Iscr. Venet.* p. 142. The name Podocatharo (Lightfoot) is variously spelled in old documents, but Procacci's orthography is correct, for Cardinal Ludovico Podocatharo has adopted it on the illuminated page which marks one of the treasures of the *Bibliothèque Nationale* as having been originally his. He bequeathed the book to the Pope's Library. How it came to be in Paris is shown by a scrawled inscription on a scrap of paper pasted on the inside of its boards: "Exempl. du Vatican, avec fig. 2, dont la 1ière est coupée par moitié. le 25 Pluv. an 9." It is the 1481 *Dante*, with Landino's notes and two of Botticelli's illustrations. Ludovico Podocatharo was born in Cyprus in 1430. Most of his precious collection of antiquities, etc. was left to Livio Podocatharo. Some few of the Podocathari migrated to Venice in the fifteenth century, says Cicogna. Certainly the name is not unfamiliar on tombs in the churches of Venice.

[2] Procacci also mentions Hettore Podocatharo's "*Ritratte del Regno di Cipro*" in his work *de' Funerali Antichi*, with the comment "non credo che sia stampata questa storia."

at the time when the chance of some measure of justice for her immemorially downtrodden natives was at last arriving. The Hettore Podocatharo, from whose forthcoming book the scrupulous Procacci had feared to borrow too much, fought under Astorre Baglioni in defence of Nicosia. He was one of the eleven captains from whom the eleven "Beluardi" or Bulwarks of the town were named. One of these last was on the point of succumbing, but, as may be read in the life of Astorre Baglioni, published at Verona in 1591 under the name of Brenzone,[1] "accorserò appresso Gio. Antonio da Soelle, & Eftore Podocatsaro, & ualorosamente scacciarono i nemici. Indi il Podocatsaro seguitò il nimico fino fuori del Parapetto, se ben la sua mala sorte volse che una scheggia di pietra spezzata dall' artigliaria lo percuotesse nel capo ove bisognò iacere in letto. Fu feruto anco Ercole Podocatsaro." The above mentioned Podocathari both survived these wounds and the earlier horrors of the sack of Nicosia, where they lost their kinsmen Giulio and Ludovico of the same name; Brenzone can hardly spell it twice in the same way. The grievously wounded Hettore only escaped for a time however. With various fugitives and 300 soldiers he was defending as well as he might the house of his sister the Countess of Tripoli, when the wily Mustafa urged him to accept terms which were instantly violated. Mustafa[2]

---

[1] There are many reasons for thinking that this is a mutilated version of Procacci's life of Baglioni, of which I have found some mention, but which was never published unless this be it. The curious relation in which many passages of the life of Baglioni stand on the one hand to Procacci's book on Islands, and on the other to Estienne de Lusignan's *Chorograffia*, which last especially represents Hettore Podocatharo's MSS., makes it probable that, if Brenzone wrote the book, both Procacci and the *Chorograffia* were freely used. If Procacci wrote it, he may have used the details (gathered from Hettore's MSS.) which delicacy had prevented his using in his book on Islands.

[2] The intense hatred of Turks, common in those days as in these, is exhibited characteristically by Brenzone in his account of the names of those who headed the invasion of Cyprus: "che nome piu stravagante e bestiale di quello che trovano i Turchi? Mustafa, indegno, imaginario, bestiale, diabolico. Pialy, nome da mulatieri. Giurerci che s'uno fosse

ordered his prisoner's head to be cut off, pretending to be in a passion with him.[1]

After his friend Podocatharo's lamentable death, Procacci might well have put all that he could of the missing and unpublished *Ritratte del regno di Cipro* into his second edition, which was published shortly after his edition of the *Isolani* of Bembo, about 1590. But in that preface he does not say more of the book soon to come than that he has included in it many new islands. A comparison of the two editions shows that in fact little or nothing has been altered in the very good account of Cyprus originally composed with Podocatharo's helping MS. It is high time now to give without further explanation Procacci's account of the Cypriote mountains—Santa Croce and Troödos—which have been identified with Olympus by one authority or another. After giving a description of the northern range of mountains, Procacci addresses himself to the southern group, to which both of the heights in question belong, saying: "L' altra parte de' monti trauersa l' Isola, cominciando dall' antica città Solia [Soli], ch' era XVIII miglia lontana da Cormachiti [Strabo's Cape Crommyon], & andando per mezzo dell' isola fino al monte della Croce [Stavrovuni] che risponde a Capo Masoto [Ptolemy's Cape Dades near Larnaca-Citium], & uanno fino a Baffo [Paphos] a marina; d' onde uoltano dall' altra parte, & pure a marina uanno fino a Solia. In mezo a questi e il monte Olimpo, chiamato con uoce Greca *Trohodos*, che è altissimo & pieno d' alberi d' ogni sorte, gira di circonfer-

---

nel mezzo di cinquanta asini, anzi lupi e dicessi Pialy, Occhiaij, o Mustafa fuggirebbono piu che lepri i cani, o le colombe lo spaviero."

[1] Such is Brenzone's account, differing materially from that given in the *Chorograffia* above mentioned and written by " Padre Maestro Angelo, della famiglia de Caletus Vicario generale di terra Santa " who was in Nicosia during the siege and whose qualifications as a "persona iuditiosa, dotta, & sanza passione & veridica" are much vaunted. Angelo says that the Countess of Tripoli declared herself Mustafa's prisoner in his absence and barricaded herself in her house till he should come. Her brother "Hector Podochataro" was summoned for a pretended cure of his wounds and treacherously slain on the road.

entia LIIII miglia, che son XVIII leghe, & ad ogni lega è posto un monastero di monaci di San Basilio, Greci: e, in ciascuno si trovano fontane in abbondanza, & frutti d' ogni qualità, onde la state soleuano i nobili Cipriotti venire a questi luoghi per lor diporta."

The absolute equivalent of this description, though its pure Italian is somewhat defaced, recurs in the life of Astorre Baglioni above quoted, where it runs as follows: ". . . principalmente il monte Olimpo, monte altissimo, monte d' ogni bene monte che dal piedi gira XVIII leghe. Monte che in ogni lega si trova un monastero de' Calseri, Monaci di San Basilio Monasterij copiosi d' ogni gratia, per igrani, frutti & fonti d' acque soauissime. Indi erano chiamati le delitie della nobilta, perchè l' estate andauano a prender aria per sanarsi : sanati conseruarsi."

It would be evident, if we did not know it from the express statement of the scrupulous Procacci, that such a description as either of the above originated with one who was more than casually familiar with the facts whereof he spoke. It is still more evident that, since the great name of Podocatharo is connected with it, a new value immediately attaches to it. The Podocathari form a link between Cyprus under Byzantine rule and the Cyprus ruled and misruled by Venice and the Lusignans. One of the earliest records of the family which I have been able to discover is in a curious book which I have often alluded to above, and which was prepared for publication—in the monastery of Santa Catherina di Formello — in the month of November 1570 at Naples by Frate Stephano Lusignano di Cipro, or rather Estienne de Lusignan, whose name appears on its title-page. He fled the kingdom ruled by his ancestors in the flurry caused by the first arrival of the Turks, and probably reached Naples as early as September—Nicosia capitulated on September the 9th : the invaders appeared at Paphos on the 1st of July. Considering the minute nature of this uncommonly good account of Cyprus, it is incredible that any man, let alone so inefficient [1] a man as Estienne de Lusignan, should have written it in so short a time as that which elapsed between his flight and the aforesaid month of November in the same year, unless it is a compilation from various documents, among the most valuable of which would be Hettore Podocatharo's missing MSS.[2]

[1] The inefficiency of Estienne appears especially in his foolish additions to the simple title of Podocatharo's work, in his helpless but somewhat pathetic apology about the misprints in the Italian version. He left the book a whole year in the printer's hands while he was travelling up and down Italy to gather money for the ransom of his friends in Turkish captivity, "il correttore hebbe molti dinari non hauendo Io la lingua Toschana ne Italiana naturale," then it was brought to Bologna and kept another year, it was "quasi dicono veduto & riueduto, nondimeno contiene molti errori, & qui remediar volesse, necessario sarebbe rinouarlo, & le mie forze sono debolissime," then follow quantities of errata. But the most foolish thing about this Italian edition is its dedication, "Al Christianiss. et glorioso Carlo nono, re di Franza, et al felicissimo, et vittorioso Henrico novo re de Polonia." He did not take the precaution to prove his royal descent, and therefore the book passed unnoticed of his brothers of France and Poland. It is ludicrous to notice how elaborately Estienne proves his Lusignan genealogy in documents prefixed to the French version (Paris, 1580), which is, however, dedicated no longer to two kings, but to the edification of one boy, Guy de Saint Gelais, son of Estienne's kinsman, Loys, of the same name.

[2] In the dedication of his French version Estienne says, "Je vous ay voulu donc faire présent de ceste Chronique, restant du sac de Cypre & sauvée des mains cruelles des Barbares." In the Italian *Chorografia* at p. 75 he says "La predetta Cronica cominciando dal Re Giouanni fino a qui, l' ho cauata dalla cronica Greca di Giorgio Bustrone il quale era compagno del Re Giacomo auanti che fusse Re, & anchora dipoi. Vero è che noi habbiamo aggiunto alcune cose di altri Auttori, & multe altre lasciate per breuità." Careful comparison of the parts of his work which deal with the various classes (Parici, Perpiari, Lefteri, Albanesi, Venetiani bianchi) and describe the government with similar passages on the same subject in Procacci's book shows that the two undoubtedly derive this information from the same source, since neither can possibly have copied the other. A comparison of the brief description given of Cyprus in Florio Bustrone's *Istoria di Cipro* (the Cronica alluded to) on sheets 1-12 of the MSS. shows that both Procacci and Estienne certainly neglected it, and as certainly used better and fuller information. Bustrone does not mention Giovanni Podocatharo's name in his account of the ransom of King Iano (sheet 173). Estienne says that Giovanni Podocatharo sold all he had to free the king, giving a version not unlikely to have been found in Hettore Podocatharo's book. Procacci tells us that he used Hettore Podocatharo's *Ritratte del Regno di Cipro*. The inference is irresistible that Estienne de Lusignan derives his most interesting and important matter (found

However that may be, the title of the book in question is *Chorograffia et breve Historia universale dell' Isola di Cipro principiando al tempo di Noe per insino al* 1572; and in it we find the most ample information (from a prejudiced source, be it said) about the Podocathari, their first exhibition of the devoted and self-sacrificing patriotism which characterises the family being recorded as follows: "Giouanni Podochataro gentilhuomo Ciprioto, vendette tutto il suo mobile & immobile, & ciò che haueua, & con quelli danari riscattò il Re dal Cairo; al quale da indì in poi fù imposto, che, pagasse ogni anno il tributo al Cairo: il qual tributo fù cresciuto al tempo del Re bastardo: dipoi l' anno 1516, il Turco estirpò il Soldano: & quel tributo che si pagava al Sultano, si pagaua al Turco, come dominatore del Sultano: & hora non vuole più il tributo; ma come si dice, ha preso tutta l' Isola, & cosi è finito il tributo."

This King Iano, so loyally ransomed by Giovanni Podocatharo, was the father of Agnesa who married Ludovico, Duke of Savoy; and the title of kings of Cyprus and Jerusalem, still attaching to the house of Savoy, is through her derived from this monarch, of whom after his ransom we hear that he spent the rest of his days in continual starvation because of the constant raids of the Mamelukes. Undiscouraged by all these reverses, Iano's epitaph (given by Bustrone) says of him:

Caesar erat bello, superans grauitate Catonem.

In the time of the "re bastardo," this Iano's grandson, a "Pietro Podochataro" figures very creditably—so far as can be ascertained. Indeed it is satisfactory to see

in Procacci and not in Bustrone) from Podocatharo's MSS., "saved," as he himself says,—though he is talking vaguely, and appears to mean his own book or Bustrone's—"from the sack of Cyprus and snatched from the cruel barbarians' hand." This view of his debt to Podocatharo is confirmed by the unusually familiar knowledge possessed by Estienne's book of the doings and havings of that great family. For Bustrone's *Chronicle*, see MSS., British Museum (additional MSS., Earl of Guilford), No. 8630. Bustrone (Florio), Istoria di Cipro.

that the family recuperated itself financially[1] so that the Podocathari were in a position to buy from the Venetian Signoria (after 1489, the date of Caterina Cornaro's formal abdication) one of the most valuable and the most ancient of all the domains of Cyprus, Chiti or Citium (Larnaca): "Chitheon era città primieramente edificata auanti d' ogni altra, & fu edificata dal primo habitatore dell' Isola, cioè da Cethin pronepote di Noe: Il che testificano li sacri espositori, Girolamo, la Glosa ordinaria, & altri sopra al 23. capitolo di Isaia, & al secōdo di Gieremia. Questa città è posta alla marina, discosta dalla città di Marium cinque leghe, & è verso mezo giorno, & haueua già vn Porto bello, & serrato, come dice Strabone: il quale hora è distrutto affatto; & si vede bene il vestigio. Questa era città Regale anticamente, . . . Hora la predetta città si chiama il casale Chiti: il quale è grande e pieno di giardini, & d' ogni frutto, & questo fù feudo di Chiarione, ouer Gariu Lusugnano: del quale fù priuato dall' ultimo Re bastardo, & dipoi fù venduto dalla Signoria di Venetia alli Podochatari."[2] There is great probability in favour of supposing that the "Re bastardo" rewarded[3] Pietro Podo-

[1] See the *Chorograffia*, p. 30 *verso*, "Ma poi al tempo del Re di Cipro bastardo, furono molti Nobili di Cipro morti, & altri fuggiuano, & altri furono disnobilitati per le priuationi delle loro facultà: perche non voleano adherire àesso bastardo." The confiscated estates were given to "nobili & ignobili" from Italy, and Pietro Podocatharo (who was sent as ambassador to Cairo in the interest of Carlotta, but changed sides on reaching Egypt) was handsomely rewarded, and retrieved the family fortunes. Bustrone (197-199) gives a list of those benefited. Pietro Podocatharo (198) comes in for enormous estates, Giovanni and Philippo, his kinsmen, get handsome presents.

[2] The parallel passage in Procacci is as follows: "nè meno d' essa (Amathus) fu seggio reale la città di Chitheon, prima di tutte l' altre edificata, da Cithin, nipote di Noè, ch' è posta alla Marina verso mezo giorno, c' haueua un bel porto; & hora ridotta in casale, si chiama Chiti, ch' era le delitie di quel regno, posseduto da *Hettore Podocatharo*, Cauallier Cipriotto, *che di queste cose scrisse*: il qual u' aueua giardini bellissimi & ripieni di preciosi frutti." The differences between this and the corresponding passage of the *Chorograffia* go to show that Estienne simply published the original text of Hettore Podocatharo.

[3] Of the four names of places bestowed upon him according to Bustrone's list (p. 198 *recto*), I can only locate two which were not near Chiti.

catharo for his support by giving him certain rights at or near Chiti. However that may be, the family came into regular possession of the property when Venetian rule was established. Procacci gives a most appreciative account of the life which Hettore Podocatharo led there, and of his generous hospitality. Evidently this brave man lived there the life which he loved, and the splendid courage with which he defended his native Cyprus was born of a most deep and loyal attachment attested at the last by the sacrifice of his life. Against the sombre background formed by the savage onslaught of those ruthless Turks in the last half of the year 1570, Hettore Podocatharo at his peaceful home of Chiti stands out as a gracious and genial representative of all the good that might have come to miserable Cyprus if he and such as he had been suffered to guide the counsels of those in power. That Hettore did have great influence at Venice is abundantly proved by the terms in which his fugitive brother Zuanne Podocatharo apostrophises him in a hitherto unpublished appeal which Zuanne delivered on the 17th of May 1573 "auanti il serenissimo prencipe Aluise Mocenigo, doppo la perdita del regno di Cipro." Standing forth with the orphaned children of the heroic Hettore by his side, Zuanne feels for the first time to the full how much he has lost in Hettore, and how completely alone are he and the orphans his nephews. There is a human pathos in the situation, and a Homeric directness in his words, that makes it well to quote them: "Dhe! Pietosissimo Prencipe, uengavi oramai pietà di noi, risguardi hormai Vostra Serenità con la serena fronte questi infelici figliuoli. Questi son quelli che non hanno esperienza alcuna di pecato, si può noi con qualche nostro difetto siamo posti nella miseria, che si trouamo. . . . Questi sono quelli c' hanno perduto tanta espetatione, e tale che poteua farli uiuer per sempre contenti, e felici. Vostra Serenita risguardi quest' innocenza, risguardi quella purità, e considerando in che grado poteuano esser, et in quale si trovino al presente, cerchi con la sua pietade uincer in parte l' impeso della nostra fortuna. . . . Dhe! Clementissimo Principe, aprite hormai le uostre misericordiose bracchia, riceuete noi con quella carità, che si richiede ad un tanto Prencipe, e il debito della pietà Christiana, e la riputatione del uostro benignissimo Impero, e per edificatione, et essempio, delli uostri altri sudditi porgeteci hormai il uostro Clementissimo agiuto, acciò possiamo sostentar questi figli, acciò possiamo recuperar gl' altri, che sono dispersi per le bande degl' infedeli, e quà li potiemo hauere, quà li cauaremo fuori delle mani de' nostri empij nemici, quà li metteremo nel consortio d' altri Christiani, quà li donaremo gl' amplessi materni:[1] ci parà assai esser ristoradi di cotanta nostra perdita. Ma hoi me! me misero! o me infelice! perche non sono io atto a poter con quelle efficace parole, che si conuiene persuader questo cosi pietoso offitio! Doue sei sfortunato fratello, qual crudele et improuisa morte mi t' ha tolto? Perche non sei qui in tanta necessità presente ad aiutarmi? Tu, fratello, hai potuto molte altre volte in questo medesimo luogho per beneficio della nostra Patria con le tue parole intenerir i cuori di questi sapientissimi senatori ad impetrar quanto sapessi dimandare, ed io col tuo medesimo spirito rappresentando questi tuoi orfani figli, e questi altri delli tuoi amici e parenti, non potrò mouer a pietà li piu pietosi Christiani del mondo! Tu, fratello, molte fiate col tuo ornato parlar hai potuto saluar la uitta, le facoltà, et honor de molti, et io in questo nostro esterminio non potrò impetrar dalla benignità istessa il uiuer de tuoi figliuoli, che si muorono della fame! Almeno, fratello, poichè qui presente esser non puoi, poscia che di

---

[1] Several of these captives were ransomed, see the *Relatione di Alessandro Podocatharo de' successi di Famagosta*, Venice, (?) 1656. He gives a moving account of the horrible death of Bragadino, and of various horrors. He tells in detail of the devastation of the Messarea, the Carpass, part of the Viscontado, and of the Baffo district. He says that he was ransomed for 325 cecchini. Cicogna mentions a letter from Pietro Podocatharo of March 3rd, 1577, to Cardinal Comendone, where he says that Livio Podocatharo came to Venice for money to ransom himself, his brother Giovanni, and his son. Probably the Giovanni in question is the Zuanne who is speaking.

far questo officio non t' è concesso, tu insieme con l' altre
anime beate delli nostri Cittadini li quali si hanno tanto
volontariamente, fedelmente, e prontamente offerti alla
morte per la Patria, presentatevi tutti insieme nell' imagination di questi Clementissimi Signori, scoprite loro in questo
ponto le uostre crudelissime ferite, rappresentate il lago del
uostro sangue sparso, mostrate le uostre ardenti ceneri e
con quest' Imagine tutti congionti insieme, come se fosse
uiui, aprite le uostre supplicheuoli braccia alli misericordosi
piedi di questo gran Prencipe, con lui vi dolete, con lui ui
lamentate, con lui piangete, da lui per noi e per uostri
figliuoli impetrate qualche pietade, e qualche agiuto
acciò noi raconsolati alquanto possiamo passar questo
pocco di uiuer che auanza, sotto la santa e benigna
protettione di questa gloriosia Republica, la qual piacerà
alla Maestà di Dio di conservar, et crescer con ogni felice
euento." [1]

With this moving apostrophe made in his name, Hettore
Podocatharo, "quel magnanimo gentil'huomo" disappears
from view. Procacci's description of Troödos-Olympus
given above was no doubt inspired by Hettore's fuller
account, but still it gives little of his "ornato parlar," which
was evidently as well remembered by his contemporaries as
his wit. One of the most valuable parts of the precious
MS. which Procacci saw and praised is, however, preserved
in the description of Mount Olympus-Troödos given in
Estienne de Lusignan's *Chorograffia*. This account of the
great mountain of Cyprus has only to be compared with
Procacci's to appear plainly as the original. "L' altra parte
delli monti comincia da Solia città antica discosta da Cormachiti 6. leghe in circa : & vanno essi monti per mezo
dell' Isola insino al monte della Croce; il qual monte
risponde al capo Masotto, & li monti vengono lì vicino, &
vanno à marina per insino a Baffo; & poi voltano dall'
altra parte, & vanno à marina à marina per insino à Solia.
In mezo de questi monti è il monte Olimpo; il quale in

[1] *Marciana*, Classe VII., Cod. DCXLIX.

greco si adimanda Trohodos;[1] il quale è altissimo; & come si ha salito alcuni monti, come si è al piede di esso; & ancho è dibisogno salire vna lega buona, che sono miglia 3. & quando si è giunto alla cima, si discopre quasi il mare intorno dell' Isola; eccetto che da Carpasso, che non si pò bene conoscer la terrā: però si vede bene il mare. Vedesi anchora li monti di Cilicia, & quando è chiaro nello spuntare del Sole, si vede anchora li monti della Soria [Syria]. Questo monte è pieno di alberi di ogni sorte; & hà una pianura grande in cima. Il piede del monte circonda 18. leghe che fanno miglia 54. & ad ogni lega è posto vn monasterio de' Calloiri [an Italianised form of καλογήροι, the modern Greek for monk or priest] ouer Monaci di San Basilio: quali Monasterii sono pieni d'ogni frutto, & di fontane in abondanza; onde questi, & altri, che si ritrouano nell' Isola, sono li sollazzi delli Cipriotti al tempo della estade. . . . In cima del monte Olimpo è vna Chiesa di San Michele, & lì di fuora è un sasso grande simile a quelli, che si ritrouano nelli torrenti: & intorno intorno à quel monte alto vna lega per insino al piede non si ritroua vn altro simile: & li Greci villani dicono una fauola, che quella pietra è[2] quando che l' arca di Noe riposò di sopra: & questa è grande, perche quattro huomini apena la possono eleuare da terra: & quando che nell' Isola sta assai à piouer; uanno tutti quelli Casali vicini del monte in processione in cima di quell' alto monte, & con certi legni leuano in alto quel sasso, &

---

[1] This seems to mean that the "nobili" always called it "Olympo," while the villani used the name Trohodos. See the map of Ortelius (1573), prepared for these "nobili," where Olympus is the only name given, and Trohodos does not appear. Bustrone identifies the Monte della Croce as the Olympus where was a temple of Aphrodite Acraea. This of course is a blunder, since that temple was in the district of the Carpass. The real Olympus Bustrone calls *Lambadista* or *Chionodes*, appealing to the author of the life of S. Barnaba, who does not bear him out. The modern name he gives as *Triodos*, MS. p. 10, *verso*.

[2] There is confusion here, as often happens, because Estienne did not understand Italian, and has, for that reason, made sad work of his original.

sempre cantando : & cosi finito, dicono, che non passa molto, che pioue, & assai ; laqual cosa io giudico essere superstitione ; però lasso il giudicio a chi ne hà cura."[1]

Here then is a description of Mount Olympus of Cyprus, and an identification of it with the Troödos, which might well be set up against the authority of Strabo, if Strabo, read as he should be, were not wholly in agreement with it. It is not rash to assume that Hettore Podocatharo was educated in one of the great universities of Italy.[2] He was acquainted with the text of Strabo, and yet never dreamed of suspecting him of identifying Olympus with the Monte Della Croce. But, more than that, his long life in Cyprus, where he was born, the long line of Cypriote ancestry from which he sprung, the traditional sympathy with the down-trodden Parici—descendants of the mass of people found in the island by King Richard Cœur de Lion, and sold by him first to the Knights Templars, and then, upon their speedy expulsion, to Guy (Guido or Guyes) of Lusignan—which characterised the Podocathari, and none more than Hettore himself, all this makes of him the representative of any continuous traditions which may have survived in Cyprus. One of the most likely things to have survived from days even before Strabo's time would certainly be the ancient name of the delight of all the nobility of Cyprus, their refuge from the infamous heats of lower parts of the island—Mount Troödos-Olympus. I therefore have no hesitation whatsoever in quoting Hettore Podocatharo in proof against all available authorities, ancient and modern, of the identity in ancient Greek and Roman times of the Troödos and Mount Olympus.

None of the numerous and confusing accounts of the mountains in question, given after the sixteenth century,

[1] *Chorograffia*, pp. 4 *verso*, 5 *recto*.
[2] Cicogna mentions a letter from Hettore to his brother Pietro, who was at college under Paolo Manuzio. This justifies the assumption that Hettore had been to college himself. He could hardly have taken the position among learned Venetians which he plainly occupied unless he had been at a university in Italy.

need now detain us. With the occupation of Cyprus by the Turks all opportunity of understanding anything about it at first hand was at an end. Perhaps it is worth while to note that the much admired geographer, Abraham Ortelius, called by Cambden "eximius veteris geographiae restaurator," did nothing for the understanding of Cyprus beyond repeating what Bordone had said, appropriating Procacci's work without acknowledgment, and giving the testimony of his map of 1573 to show that the name Olympus was current then for Mount Troödos.

Very similar to the unsystematised and ill-digested treatment of Ortelius is that which John Blaeuw [1] gives to Cyprus in 1662. Blaeuw takes Ortelius' map of 1573, in flagrant disagreement with a smaller one elsewhere in the same book, without any acknowledgment; then he accompanies it with Procacci's commentary, so far as the Olympus is concerned. Plainly no one cared or knew about Cyprus in the seventeenth century, although a multitude of maps and descriptions of the island continued to appear. The one exception is a belated Venetian "Isolario" by the enterprising Geographer in Ordinary to the republic, Coronelli. His Isolario appeared in 1696, and is absolutely correct in giving (according to Strabo) a promontory Olympus, which lies close to the north-eastern extremity of the island, and then a Mount Olympus, which is the Troödos half-way between Alesandreta and Piscopia. Coronelli may have had before him the old MS. of Strabo (still at Venice), which I have quoted as punctuating the passage about Olympus correctly, but he certainly did have in mind the traditions about Cyprus and its Olympus, which Venice still preserved from the days of her Ægean supremacy. No one knowing Cyprus well, and going to Strabo and Ptolemy, would differ from Coronelli, I am sure.

[1] It was really the work of his father William, quite as much as his. See its dedication as "Parentis sui suosque labores geographicos." Various editors and compilers were employed.

The only reason that existed between 1675 and 1870 for connecting with Cyprus the name Bocarus as that of a river or of anything else, was a curious series of blunders made in a posthumously published MS. by John Meursius. But then Dr. J. P. Six discovered one more letter than the Duc de Luynes or Dr. Deeke could see on a coin in the British Museum. Dr. Six is the greatest expert in the reading of Cypriote characters, and while he was in doubt all was uncertain; but he has finally decided that that inscription on that coin will not after all bear his first interpretation, and does not therefore contain any name even remotely resembling " Bocarus " or PO-KA-RO-SE.[1] What now remains is to see what are the passages in ancient authorities where the name Bocarus occurs. The lexicographer Hesychius has made the following entry: Βώκαρος· ποταμὸς ἐν Σαλαμῖνι ἐκ τοῦ 'Ακάμαντος ὄρους φερόμενος.[2] This passage gives for the island of Salamis two names not ordinarily seen upon its maps, Acamas, as the name of a mountain, and Bocarus, as the name of a river. This last name does appear on the map of Salamis given by K. O. Müller in Ersch and Gruber's *Allgemeine Encyclopaedie* (see the article "Attica"). In the *Etymologicum Magnum* may be found: ΒΩΚΑΡΟΣ: Τὸ ἔαρ ὑπὸ Τροιζηνίων· παρὰ τὸ τῷ βίῳ χαρὰν φέρειν, βώχαρος, καὶ βώκαρος. Καὶ ποταμὸς δὲ Σαλαμῖνος οὕτω καλούμενος. From this *Hesychius* gains confirmation, and we learn moreover that the name Bocarus meant *spring* in the speech of the men of Troezen, just across the Saronic gulf from the Salaminian river Bocarus. From Stephanus and Eustathius[3] no additional information but further confirmation is to be derived. After these

---

[1] According to a note shown me at the British Museum as containing Dr. Six's amended reading, the letters are not what he first thought them, and the word should begin, not end, with the sigma syllable.

[2] Meursius, as will appear, cites this one passage four times. Once of the river Bocarus on the island of Salamis, thrice as referring to a stream in Cyprus.

[3] See his commentary on the *Iliad*, ii. 637, and on Dionysius Periegetes, 511.

commentators and lexicographers, it is well to search Strabo. In his ninth book, at page 394, you may read: Βώκαρος δ' ἐστὶν ἐν Σαλαμῖνι ποταμός, ὁ νῦν Βωκαλία καλούμενος. Then comes to hand a passage in that dreariest of poems, Lycophron's *Alexandra*, vv. 447-452, where Teucer, Agapenor, Acamas, and two others are spoken of as five early colonists of Cyprus, which is called by two of its most obscure and completely forgotten names, Sphekia and Kerastia. Lycophron, not content with these hard names, alludes to Paphos in Cyprus by the forgotten name of its river Satrachus,[1] to Curium on the coast near Paphos by the epithet ὑλάτης, there given to Apollo (see *Devia Cypria*, 24 and ff.), to Paphian Aphrodite by an obscure name given her at Sparta coupled with the qualification "Zerynthian," alluding to a cave in Thrace where the goddess was worshipped. Finally, having thus done every ingenious thing to prevent our knowing that the heroes went to Cyprus, and settled near the shrine of Aphrodite at Paphos and at Curium, Lycophron plays a final trick upon our wits by describing Salamis (from which Teucer departed for Cyprus) as the "Caves of Cychreus, and the dells of Bocarus." Salaminian Cychreus was, like Cecrops, half man and half serpent, and, by virtue of the lower half of him, a denizen of caves. Now that by a tedious process of excavation their meaning has been laid bare, these lines of Lycophron may be cited in full:

[1] Satrachus is a name which wanders up and down on the various maps of Cyprus. Usually it is bestowed upon a river rising from Troödos-Olympus. Sometimes a city is improvised and called Satrachos. The passage of Lycophron given in the text, together with the following four lines of Nonnus, *Dionysiac.* xiii. 458 ff., ought to make it certain that the *Diarrhizo* at Old Paphos bore the name Satrachos or Sestrachos. For the most learned and conclusive paper on the subject, see the *Philologus* for 1874, vol. xxxiii. Dr. Robert Unger there (pp. 419-430) proves that, wherever the Bocarus may have been, it was not at Paphos, because the Satrachos was there as Nonnus says:

ἐξ ὑδάτων ἐπίβαθρον ἀνερχομένης Ἀφροδίτης
ἦχι θαλασσιγόνου Παφίης νυμφήϊον ὕδωρ
Σάτραχον ἱμερόεις, ὅθι πολλάκις οἶδμα λιποῦσα
Κύπρις ἀνεχαίνωσε λελουμένον υἱέα Μύρρης.

οἱ πέντε δὲ Σφήκειαν εἰς Κεραστίαν
καὶ Σάτραχον βλώξαντες Ὑλάτου τε γῆν,
Μορφὼ παροικήσουσι τὴν Ζηρυνθίαν.
ὁ μὲν πατρὸς μομφαῖσιν ἠλαστρημένος
Κυχρεῖος ἄντρων Βωκάρου τε ναμάτων, . . .

"*But five there are who shall house them near to the Zerynthian Morpho* (Paphian Aphrodite) *and go to the Horned Isle Sphekeian* (Cyprus), *even to Satrachos* (Paphos on the Satrachos[1]), *and the land of Hylates* (Curium, where Apollo Hylates was worshipped). *By his father's blame the first* (Teucer) *driven out from the caves of Cychreus and the dells of the Bocarus* (Salamis). . . ."

These are the only places in ancient literature where the Bocarus is mentioned. And yet many find it difficult to give up the idea that there is some authority to show that the ancients called a river at Old Paphos (the river Satrachos) by the name Bocarus. This is not the case, however, with Bursian, who gives, in his description of Salamis, the following account of its streams (i. p. 363 of his large work): "Zahlreiche . . . Gussbäche, deren ansehnlichster (wahrscheinlich der an der Südwestseite der Insel) den Namen Βώκαρος, später Βωκαλία führte, durchfahren die Abhänge der ziemlich spärlich mit Strandkiefern und Strauchwerk bewachsenen Berge." Ancient authorities should be the only warrant for ancient usage, but still let us further appeal to John Blaeuw and his *Atlas Major* of 1662, already cited above. The description there given of Salamis is as follows: "*Posita est ea contra Eleusin, Atticae urbem, & confinia Megaridis Atticaeque. Longitudo eius est stadiorum 70. Primarium insulae oppidum ei cog-*

---

[1] See John Meursius' own note on this line in his juvenile commentary; see also Tzetzes, who speaks of a town and a river named Satrachus. Jacob Geel and Emperius seem to have written in 1773 saying that Paphos was on the Satrachus, but I have failed to find the letters in question. See also Musgrave's note on Eurip. *Bacchae*, 404: "Audiamus modo Sestrachi apud Nonnum descriptionem . . . Sestrachus enim dicitur, non Bocarus, qui Paphum alluit fluvius."

nomine est; et Bocarus sive Bucolius amnis, nunc Italis Bumna indigetatur." Whoever, among the numerous contributors to "Blaevius'" *Atlas Major*, may have written this description of Salamis, certainly could not yet have heard of the transference to Cyprus of this Salaminian river Bocarus; for it did not take place, so far as the world at large was concerned, until 1675, when John George Graev or Graevius promulgated at Amsterdam the *Cyprus, Rhodes, and Crete* of Meursius. The writer in Blacuw's *Atlas* did, however, have access to other works of Meursius, published during the author's life, which ended at Soroë in 1639. Meursius, in his *Pisistratus*, cites, with no word of dissenting comment, Strabo's account of the Bocarus as a river in Salamis off Attica. This proves at least that the learned Meursius was not always of his later opinion about the Bocarus.

In fact, without unduly disparaging the merit of Meursius as a pioneer in that laborious research which, when accompanied by a sound judgment, is the bone and sinew of scholarship, I may say of his work in general that he accumulates quotations for the sake of having many of them, and often falls into the error of using the same authority on both sides of a difficult question. Meursius lacked common sense; his work has not the luminous and life-giving quality that would have made him a worthy successor to the traditions of Erasmus or have won the unqualified admiration of men of learning who came after him.[1] The most concise qualification of Meursius and his scholarship will be found in Professor Frederick Allen's address on the University of Leyden, given as president of the American Philological Association in 1882. Professor Allen there said that Meursius, the antiquary, had great diligence and some

[1] Of Johann Friedrich Gronovius, for instance, who came to a professorship at Leyden in 1658, upwards of thirty years after Meursius resigned. It is possible that he was a pupil of Meursius; they certainly carried on a correspondence. His opinion of Meursius is perhaps reflected by his son Jacob Gronovius, who succeeded him in the Leyden professorship.

constructive power, and that his monographs laid a good foundation for subsequent work. Every one who is interested in Cyprus is in fact interested in Meursius, and owes to his industry a debt of gratitude. It is therefore a thankless task to talk of the serious errors in Cypriote geography whose origin can be traced to Meursius. But for all that Meursius may fairly be held responsible for the idea current in his day among scholars that ancient geography was independent of the configuration of the earth. He certainly has treated Cyprus as a sort of fairyland, where rivers may run over mountain-tops in order to enable scholars to defend the most random and unpremeditated emendations.

The fact is that John Meursius is one of those who early showed a fatal precocity. At the age of thirteen, says an appreciative biographer (Schramm), he was preternaturally fond of Greek: "Quippe iam Anno aetatis XIII carmen Graecum suo Auctori haud inficiandum elaborabat." This is faint praise, not at all like that bestowed upon the feat by which Meursius in his sixteenth year indicated his preference for the least poetical of Greek writers. He actually wrote at that tender age a commentary on Lycophron! It is for this that D. Heinsius praises him and declares him an Apollo:—

> Talis erat, famam cui pristina tempora debent,
>   Meursius, et debent tempora nostra suam ;
> Qui Siculi vatis,[1] noctemque Lycophronis atri,
>   Dispulit et Phoebus post tria lustra fuit.

Meursius taught Greek at Leyden as professor for fourteen years, and then was glad to get away from his native country and accept the post of Professor of Danish History at Soroe, on the island of Seeland. Thither he went in 1625, escaping from Calvinism and the Synod of Dort, and abandoning for the most part his Greek studies. If there had been any chance of his further intellectual growth, this

[1] This alludes to Meursius' juvenile essays on Theocritus.

change from Leyden to Denmark cut it off. His publications on classical subjects ceased, and his study of Danish history was so perfunctory that he never even learned enough Danish to master the most necessary records. Hence when Lami asked for the MS. left behind on this subject, he was assured that there was nothing extant which would not if published mar the reputation already achieved by Meursius. As a boy he tried to do work which many a man would shirk; in the prime of his manhood at forty-five he was subject to lapses of judgment, and at times he could become hopelessly infantile.[1] He did, however, preserve to the last that command over many books which Graevius praises, saying of Meursius: " Nihil enim hoc viro in evolvendis omnibus omnium aetatum scriptoribus qui ex illetabile illi barbariei nocte salvi in lucem horum temporum emerserunt, fieri potuit diligentius."

It is this wonderful acquaintance of his with swarms of writers whose dulness few ever had the courage to penetrate that gives to Meursius' work on Cyprus its great value. As I am speaking of his shortcomings in that work, let me first quote competent criticisms of defects in his work at large. To begin with his mechanical habit of always translating Greek quotations into Latin, it would seem that he sometimes made these translations while he was half asleep. In some remarks appended to Meursius' *Ceramicus*—see Lami's complete edition—Gronovius[2] objects, as well he

[1] In justice to his later work it should be remembered that he long suffered from and eventually died of a most painful disease.

[2] Lami publishes a curious letter which shows that Abraham Gronovius had not forgotten how thoroughly his father, Jacob—and for that matter his grandfather—had found out the weak points in Meursius' scholarship. Abraham, though not of much learning or consequence, was, if only for the name he bore, deemed of sufficient consequence to receive Lami's circular describing the projected edition of Meursius. In answer he writes, April 1736, to Valentio Gonzaga, complimenting Italian printing, saying: "Non possum non recordari felicitatis qua olim istic usi fuerunt *avus meus, Parens atque Patruus.*" He then feelingly alludes to the odium which Meursius incurred by devoting time to the study of the Christian fathers: "Quamvis hac sedula opera sua, et Christiano digna, ingens odium Meursius apud nescio quos dum inter vivos ageret,

may, to Meursius' translation of Καλλίστη ἡ Θήρα τὸ πρότερον—"*Pulcherrima venatio prius*;" he also finds fault with Meursius for confusing Hermes καταιβάτης with Zeus of the same epithet and a clap of thunder: "Quae sunt arenae sine calce," *too much sand and no mortar*, humorously adds the indulgent Gronovius. There are indeed many of these trackless waste places in Meursius' best work. James Brucker truthfully says that Meursius was much imposed upon "in Themide Attica," where he quotes as the real laws of Athens fictions composed as rhetorical exercises. Also Brucker is right in speaking severely of Meursius' "De denario Pythagorico."[1]

Let us turn now to chapter xxii. of the first of Meursius' two books on Cyprus, as printed by Graevius, reprinted by Lami, and revised in an autograph MS. of the Marcian Library. From this last[2] in Meursius' own handwriting, with his own corrections and additions, I shall make my

in se contraxerit. Ego vero ab ipso iuventutis meae lubrico, *paternis* institutis ita formatus, eos qui scripta vel ad ritus vel ad historiam veteris Ecclesiae spectantia primi luce donaverint . . . Meursium . . . Montefalconem . . . venerari nunquam desinam."

[1] It would seem that some rated Meursius so low that they threw cold water on Lami's idea of publishing his complete works. See the letters in answer to Lami's circular printed at the beginning of the Florence edition (Florence, 1741-63, 12 vols. folio). See also the end of Lami's dedication.

[2] Meursius, while in Denmark, did no classical work apparently except this one on *Cyprus, Rhodes, and Crete*. Of this he made two copies, both of which came by his death into the hands of his son. One of these passed by sale into the library of George Seefeld, out of which it was forcibly taken in 1658 when Charles X. of Sweden made his famous march across the frozen Belt. Most of the looted books, and Meursius' *Cyprus*, etc. among them, were added to the royal library at Stockholm. Thence Graevius borrowed the Meursian MS. in 1675, and by way of recognising the kindness of the loan dedicated the printed book to Charles XI. whose father stole the MS. All this happened thirty-nine years after Meursius died; twelve years later this MS. was burned with the rest of the Stockholm library. John Meursius, junior, being a worldly-minded person, had presented the other autograph MS. of *Cyprus, Rhodes, and Crete* (one which had received annotations and various polishings and reshapings in the last years of his father's life) to the Senate and Doge of Venice with a request that he be recompensed for this and other services by the title of "Cavaliere di San Marco." This title was conferred, and the three volumes—one for each island, Cyprus, Rhodes, and Crete—were duly consigned to entire oblivion

OLYMPUS AND BOCARUS IN CYPRUS 351

quotations. After citing a line from a Homeric Hymn to Aphrodite, where the Cypriote town of Salamis is mentioned, Meursius goes on : " Perluebat autem eam [1] (Salaminem) fluvius Bocarus, ex Acamante monte profluens. Hesychius : Βώκαρος ποταμὸς ἐν Σαλαμῖνι, ἐκ τοῦ Ἀκάμαντος ὄρους φερόμενος, *Bocarus fluvius in Salamine, ex Acamante monte profluens*." The writer of this has apparently never dreamt that Cyprus really exists to check by its shape any suggestions or emendations. Such a thing as a map of Cyprus—he might easily have had that of Abraham Ortelius—he has never looked at. In chapter xxvii. he again quotes Hesychius, whose account of Acamas he

in the library of the Council of Ten. Thus, thirty-three years before Graevius published the unfinished Stockholm MS., the completed one was placed beyond the reach of probable publication. When the library of the Council of Ten was dispersed and for the most part absorbed into the Marcian library (1795), there were no longer three but two parts of the MS.—*Cyprus* and *Rhodes*. The MS. on *Crete* was apparently stolen or lost at some earlier time, and it was finally bought by Cicogna. With his books and MSS. it passed into the Museo Correr, where I have examined it in detail, as also the *Rhodes* MS. in the Marcian library. To the Marcian MS. of *Cyprus* I gave even more time, comparing it with Graevius' Amsterdam edition, after satisfying myself that there is no independent value attaching to Lami's Florence reprint of Graevius. (Lami has corrected a few gross misprints of Graevius, but did not for instance use the table of errata given at the end of Graevius' *Crete*, nor did he rectify cross references, omissions, or wrong numbering of chapters.) As reproductions of the MS. burnt at Stockholm, both of these editions of Amsterdam and of Florence are disgraceful. The Venice MS. shows enough about the Stockholm version to make that much absolutely certain. As for the difference between the Stockholm MS. and the Venetian revised one, I challenge any one to find a single error of judgment which Meursius, on mature second thought, saw fit to correct. He has made himself doubly answerable for all the worst of his blunders by rewriting them in smoother Latin and by a careful index, where he passes them all and assigns to each its place in alphabetical succession. But it must be allowed that he has added many new and some important citations. These give a slight value to the Venice MS., but they need never be published.

[1] Curiously enough, no one has ever taken this blunder of Meursius seriously, as many have taken the blunder about Paphos and the Bocarus. The Pediaeus is too prominent a river to have its name changed with ease by any one. Perhaps if the name Satrachus had been equally well known the Bocarus would never have invaded Cyprus.

thus translates: "Acamanta indefessum, et nomen proprium unius filiorum Antenoris." He quoted just above from Sextus Empiricus to show that Acamas was a son of Theseus, from whom the promontory was named, and now adds from Hesychius: "Etiam mons in Cypro, ita dictus, nominatus vero est ab Acamante, Demophontis quidem fratre sed Thesei filio, ex hoc Bocarus amnis profluebat. Idem Hesychius alio loco. . . ." Then he repeats the quotation and translation given in chapter xxii. The heading of chapter xxx. Meursius has written out as follows: "*Fluuii. Aous. Bocarus. Locus Euripidis correctus. Salaminem, et Paphum, perluebat in plures alveos distributus, etc.*" Then in the body of the chapter,[1] when he has disposed of the Aous,[2] he again attacks the Bocarus: "Bocarus. Hesychius . . ."—here follows the same quotation twice made before—"Scio ab aliis[3] Bocarum in Salamine Atticae commemorari: sed hic fuerit sane Cypri, in qua Acamas, unde ortus. Ac corruptum esse puto eius nomen apud Euripidem in Bacchis—

> Ἵκοίμαν ποτὶ τὰν Κύπρου
> Νᾶσον τᾶς Ἀφροδίτας
> Πάφον θ', ἃν ἑκατόστομοι
> Βωκάρου[4] ποταμοῦ ῥοαί
> Καρπίζουσιν ἄνομβροι.
> *Utinam veniam in Ciprum*
> *Insulam Veneris:*
> *Et Paphum, quam centum habentis ostia*
> *Bocari fluuii fluxus*
> *Foecundant sine imbribus.*

---

[1] This chapter is practically identical in Graevius, Lami, and the Marcian MSS., probably because the latter has by accident no margin for additions.

[2] The Aous, be it said, is the name anciently given to Mount Santa Croce, so constantly miscalled Olympus.

[3] These "*other*" people include himself, in the passage of his *Pisistratus*, and also in his early commentary on Lycophron, line 450.

[4] I take it that Engel is responsible for the adoption of this absurd invention of Meursius, Ross following him.

Hodie editur, Βαρβάρου ποταμοῦ, *Barbari fluuii.* Ubi etiam obseruandus : Paphum quoque perluisse, aut alluisse : et in plures alueos scissum proluxisse."

I suppose that a river which could flow from the Acamas to the sea at Salamis could also empty into the sea through a hundred mouths at Paphos, but it would certainly, in so doing, crowd out the other Paphian river called Barbarus, which Meursius mentions on the strength of this same passage in Euripides at the fourteenth chapter of this same book. The heading of this chapter, in Meursius' own hand, runs as follows : " Paphus antiqua ; quam Agieos condidit ; Typhonis filius ; sive Cinyras ; sive Paphus unde dicta & quando condita: prius Erythra appelata. In 'excelso loco sita agro pingui, quem sine pluuia Barbarus fluuius irrigabat," etc. Then in the body of the chapter comes, after an account of the excellent fertility of the surroundings of Paphos : " Et irrigabat fluuius Barbarus, etiam sine ulla pluuia, Euripides Bacchis—

Πάφον θ' ἂν ἑκατοστόμοι
Βαρβάρου[1] ποταμοῦ ῥοαὶ
Καρπίζουσιν ἄνομβροι.
*Et Paphum quam centum ostia habentis
Barbari fluuii fluxus
Frugiferam reddunt sine imbribus.*"

The indices, carefully prepared by Meursius for this book, and written by his own hand in the Venice MS., show both the Bocarus and the Barbarus,[2] as well as the name of Euripides among the authors "qui hic illustrantur, emendantur aut errare ostenduntur." The object of this

[1] Mannert and others are guilty of taking the capital B of this line as seriously as Meursius does. It was zeal in correcting this mistake that led Engel to leap from the frying-pan into the fire and speak of a " vielarmiges Flüsschen, der von den alten Bokarus, nicht Barbarus . . . genannt war" (*Cyprus,* i. p. 126).

[2] These are far completer than the indices which Graevius published in his edition. Probably these last were done by some hard-pressed scribe of Amsterdam.

long account of much blundering will be reached if a comparison of the above passages will only show that Meursius' *Cyprus* is an unsteady guide, and that until it was written the Bocarus was never connected either by uttered speech or in writing, or on any map, coin, or inscription, with Cyprus where it has no place.

VIII

APOLLO AT DELOS

THE place of our choice when first we set foot on Delos is the altar where Odysseus worshipped in the spring-time of our world.

"At Delos once by Apollo's altar I saw thy like," says Odysseus the castaway to Princess Nausicaa, going on to compare that maiden's peerless beauty and grace to "a palm's tender shoot growing upward."[1] Such a vision, as of a delicate tree uplifting its graceful branches and exquisite stem against the pure and glowing sky of some well-loved Italian picture, is a fitting symbol of the worship of Delian Apollo and his sister Artemis, guardians of purity and truth for Hellas and the ancient world.

Purification and purity, these two words must always be on men's lips when they talk of Delos. The spiritual needs and the moral perfections which these words imply were in the hearts of the votaries who came to worship and observe the rights prescribed. Unspeakable feelings and inexplicable associations clustered for religious Greeks about the story of Leto's wanderings and her final deliverance

[1] *Odyssey*, vi. 162 and ff.

upon the barren Delian rock—the birth of Apollo and Artemis.[1]

All the efforts of poets, philosophers, geographers, and historians have been expended in the most various utterance of the terror and the pity, the awful gladness that assailed the mind when contemplating Delos, and the moment when Apollo "leaped forth to the light of day."[2] Certain pious representations of the birth of the Virgin and of various saints may be appealed to as a Christian analogy. We hear from Theognis[3] how at that hour "The universal shores of Delos all were loaded with ambrosial fragrance, and the immense earth was moved to laughter, while rejoicing visited the depths of gray ocean." "Earth smiled beneath her," says the Homeric bard[4] of Leto, and we hear from Euripides in two of his most pathetic strains[5] how the "first parent of palm-trees and the earliest growth of the laurel" were called into being for the comfort of Leto, the mother. Her bed was near the Inopus, a stream specially hallowed in the minds of latter-day believers by its fabulous connection with the far-off river Nile whose floods found an underground way to rocky Delos.[6] Moreover Leto had close at hand the most sacred lake, which in some versions of the birth-legend quite takes the place of the Inopus, and in almost all is mentioned with a peculiar

---

[1] According to the *Homeric Hymn to Delian Apollo* (16 and ff.) Artemis was born on Ortygia and Apollo on Delos. Baumeister seems justified in rejecting these lines. Ortygia was an older name for Delos. Some have tried to make out that it means Rhenea.
[2] *Homeric Hymn to Delian Apollo*, 119.
[3] Bergk's ed., vv. 7-10.
[4] *Hymn to Delian Apollo*, 118.
[5] *Hecuba*, 459; *Iph. Taur.* 1100.
[6] Strabo, 271, Callimachus's *Hymn to Delos*, 206 ff. See also the sonnets on "Sdiles" in the curious book of Bartolommeo da li Sonnetti. The story of to-day substitutes the Jordan for the Nile.

reverence.[1] From the predestined moment of fate when Apollo and Artemis were born, Delos was changed : " Of gold from that hour were all her foundations, the ripples of her wheel-shaped lake were liquid gold, golden was the sheltering palm-tree, Inopus rolled a flood all gold, and golden was the ground from which the mother lifted up her son new-born."[2] " A flush of golden flowers, as it were a forest flowering on a mountain-peak, covered the chosen island where no flowers had grown till then."[3] To-day a wealth of flowers, gold and red, is almost the only remnant of past glories that time and man's destructive hand have left on Delos.

Few scenes upon which the religious imagination of man has loved to dwell have been made more touching or filled more full of the pathos which consoles than the stay upon Delos of lonely Leto,[4] who sealed with suffering an "argument of never ending love." Euripides discoursing upon this theme might use the further words of Shakspeare saying—

> The pretie and sweet maner of it
> Forst those waters from me, which I would have stopt,
> But I had not so much of man in me
> But all my mother came into my eyes,
> And gave me up to tears.

Truly human are the "tricklings of tears down dropping fast" whereof the exiled maidens speak in the play just after their thoughts have dwelt upon the touching tale of

[1] Herod. ii. 170.   [2] Callimachus' *Hymn to Delos*, 260 ff.
[3] *Homeric Hymn to Delian Apollo*, 135 and 139, Baumeister's text, cf. *ibid*, 53 and ff.
[4] The literary record of Leto's character is less vivid and complete than would be expected from the prominence given to her in various pictorial and sculptured records. Hesiod gives, however, a most beautiful account of her, *Theogony*, 406 and ff. "She was a comforter always, and gentle to mortal men as to the deathless gods,—a comforter from the beginning, the most soothing presence of all on Olympus."

Leto, into which they plaintively weave the sorrows of their loneliness and exile.[1]

> Bird, that adown the rock-ridged main,
> Halcyon, a pitiful refrain
>   Singest, to all thy knowers known,
>   For husband lost thy tuneful moan
> Shrilled forth ! be other lays to thine
> Likened, a wingless songster's—mine,
> For noon-tide throngs in Greece my yearning strain,
> Yearning for Artemis, easer of pain,
>   'Neath Cynthus' heights abiding where
>   Thrive palms with delicate leafage clean,
> And laurels' tender shoots and fair,
>   Sprouts of the olive blest, gray-green,
> That Leto's birth-pangs dear helped bear ;
> There swirls the lake's disc too in eddying coils
>   Whereon the sweet-voiced swan is seen
> Who for the muse's sake melodious toils.

The religious-minded Greek might well attach an importance to the commonest things in such a land of miracles as Delos. For the very island itself had been originally a wanderer over the seas, driven forth from the starry heavens where it shone in the beginning.[2] When the twin gods

---

[1] *Iph. Taur.* 1089-1105.
[2] There is a curious confusion of geography, astronomy, and mythology in accounts given—all of them by late writers such as Apollodorus, Callimachus—of Delos before the birth of Apollo and Artemis. The learned fabulist Hyginus has gathered them together ; and underlying the whole was probably some genuine religious myth at which we dimly guess. It appears that according to one current version Poseidon hid in his watery depths the floating island with Leto upon it while the grim emissary of Hera, Pytho, vainly searched for her. This harmonises with the tradition that originally Delos, like its neighbour Tenos, was a possession of Poseidon (Strabo, 37, *Aeneid*, iii. 74). But now comes an inexplicably barren tale which seems chiefly to exist in order to account for certain names of Delos, and which most effectually hides any traces which may be nvolved in it of genuine popular myth-making. A sister of Leto, Asteria, in order to escape from the love of Zeus, is changed into a quail and finally into Ortygia or quail island. Asteria was at the beginning a

were born the holy Cyclades, motionless till then, danced for very joy around Delos, while the holy island itself—always a wanderer over seas till then—was made to stand still. "For in the foretime it was a wanderer," says Pindar,[1] "at the mercy of every dashing wave and of the whirling winds; but the daughter of Coeus set foot upon it wild with shooting pains the forerunners of her deliverance; then it was that on earth's stablished foundations four upright pillars arose, and upon their capitals columns that were footed in adamant held firmly aloft the rock[2] where she first in her travail had sight of her blessed progeny." Meanwhile the islands centered round about Delos, the chosen Cyclades,[3] went through their dance, and swans from Asia went singing seven times around the holy island, and then the babes were born. In memory of these joyous circlings of the swans before his birth, Apollo afterwards set seven strings upon his lyre.[4] Because, moreover, Leto had respite from travail-pangs on the seventh day of the month, that day was made holy.[5]

star in the sky, and her two names were merged with herself in the floating island. When Apollo and Artemis were finally born, their birth-place Asteria-Ortygia became Delos for insufficient reasons more than sufficiently dwelt upon by Callimachus in his *Hymn to Delos*.

[1] Quoted by Strabo, p. 485.
[2] Virgil, *Aeneid*, iii. 73 ff., gives an alternative account of the early career of Delos which amounts to much the same as Pindar's, only in place of pillars chains fasten the island. Its anchors are Myconos and Gyaros. In common with Myconos the two sacred isles Delos and Rhenea are of granite. Hence the notion that in the record (1) of Delos as an island not originally fixed in its place like others, but left a wanderer (Callimachus' *Hymn to Delos*, 30 ff. and 92 f.), (2) of Delos as being hidden under water till Zeus or Poseidon drew it out (see *Etym. Mag.*, s. v. Δῆλος), we have a mythological account of the comparatively recent and volcanic origin of Delos. If this way of treating the myth could only be deemed reasonable it would have a certain value for geologists which it now entirely lacks.
[3] See Appendix IX. on the Cyclades.
[4] Callim. *Hymn to Delos*, 300 and ff.
[5] Hesiod, *Works and Days*, 770 and f.

In thinking of Delos, the first importance was given by religious Greeks to a feeling that the birth of Apollo and Artemis made the island especially pure, and in order to preserve that quality without stain it was in time enacted by a gradual process of evolution in the idea of what purity required (somewhat accelerated and much discredited by political circumstances) that there should be no birth, no death, and no burial upon the holy isle.[1] Because Leto and her children had communicated to Delos by contact the inherent virtues indwelling in them, it was meet that all occasions of contamination from mortals at the supreme physical moments of birth and death should be removed.[2] Delos itself was in the end so over-jealously guarded from the contaminations of birth and death, that the dying had to be moved across the sheltered narrows to Rhenea before they quite gave up the ghost, and anticipated births were at last so regulated as to take place also upon that adjacent island. These regulations for defence against contamina-

[1] There was, furthermore, a curious provision that no dogs be allowed on Delos (Strabo, 486).
[2] A certain help in gaining the Greek point of view may be derived from the fourth chapter of Mr. Frazer's *Golden Bough*, where many curious customs really far removed from the Greeks are described. In some of these the view of supreme physical moments here suggested may be found. The notion that there is a taint derived from the presence of death has not survived with any religious sanction, though the Old Testament is full of it. Perhaps though a touch of it has lingered to give special point to Mérimée's saying that he came near dying while calling at the house of a person with whom he was not sufficiently intimate to justify his taking that liberty. The taint derived from proximity to a birth, however, was quite as much provided against by the priests of the medieval church as by those of Apollo and Aesculapius. That the same view was entertained under the Jewish dispensation is noted in our own Milton's touching lines,

"Methought I saw my late espoused saint
Brought to me like Alcestis from the grave, . . .
Mine, as whom washt from spot of child-bed taint
Purification in the old law did save."

tion seem to have passed from Delos to the Epidaurian shrine and precinct of the Apolline god Aesculapius. In imperial times certainly there was constructed outside of the Epidaurian precinct a place of refuge called the house of birth and of death.

But before Rhenea could become a sort of second Delos, and take upon itself contaminations for the sake of leaving the Holy Island pure, an ideal consecration was required. In the record of this may be found another and real though not logical proof that in Delos resided a virtue of inherent purity, greater perhaps than that attributed by the faithful to the shrines of most powerful saints. The record in question is of a gift that Polycrates made to Delian Apollo.[1] Polycrates, among his many proverbial strokes of good luck, hit upon the idea of dedicating to Apollo at Delos the island of Rhenea which he had conquered. He decided to offer the island in just the same way that he would have chosen for offering a statue or a piece of furniture to the temple. How then was his island,—a small island it was, to be sure, but still at least four times the size of Delos,—how was Rhenea to be offered up at the shrine of Apollo? The universally prevalent religious conception of Delos as the purest of all spots helped him to the way. He stretched across the not very deep roadstead between Rhenea and Delos cables or chains of iron, and brought about through the 500 yards of water that intervened a contact of the impure with the pure. Thus the greater was contained by the less, thus the island now called Megale Dili, Great Delos, was made for certain purposes a part of its smaller neighbour. It was a very fortunate stroke for Polycrates, since the world was amazed and delighted, and at the same

[1] Thuc. iii. 104.

time was informed that the new master of the island of Samos had made himself the best friend of Apollo at Delos.

The most spiritual bond, however, that ever attached a whole community to the distant shrine of a god was that which bound Athens to Delos, during the absence of the holy ship on its yearly visit to the island. During that month all Athens was consecrate to Apollo, and thus a month was added to the life of Socrates. No death could be inflicted by the state while it was in official congress with the Holy Island, for this would blot, through indirect contact, the perfect purity of Apollo's home.[1]

The early history of Delos is a chapter of lustrations and purifications. Pisistratus of Athens devoted his efforts in the archipelago to a removal of all tombs that were within sight of Apollo's temple.[2] A century later, in 426 B.C., the Athenians, self-governed at last and not ruled by any tyrant, renewed and improved upon the policy of Pisistratus. In this year they began to take possession of Delos for avowedly religious but also for commercial reasons, and instituted the great Delian festival called the Delia. At this time all mortal remains were dug up and removed from Delos.[3] Thus even at Delos it was only gradually that the stringent regulations of ceremonial purity were developed, and generations of increasing stringency were required before the taint of births and deaths was secluded from Delos and

---

[1] A similar sanctity by spiritual contact is constantly implied in the terms in which the Cyclades are spoken of by various authors. In return for this their homage glorified Delos. As Strabo says, 485: ἔνδοξον δ' ἐποίησαν αὐτὴν αἱ περιοικίδες νῆσοι καλούμεναι Κυκλάδες, κατὰ τιμὴν πέμπουσαι δημοσίᾳ θεωρούς τε καὶ θυσίας, καὶ χοροὺς παρθένων, πανηγύρεις τε ἐν αὐτῇ συνάγουσαι μεγάλας.
[2] Thuc. iii. 104.   [3] Ibid.

confined to Rhenea. Moreover the harsh rules set up by Athens for her own purposes were a real violation of the spirit of Apolline religion.¹ The climax was reached four years after this second purification of Delos by Athens. In 422 B.C. the Athenians declared that all the Delians were a source of contamination to the island, and thus, having previously removed the dead, they now drove out the living.²

The conduct of Athens at Delos from 426-422 B.C. did not deceive religious Greeks, who saw in it a determination on her part to suffer no commercial rivalry, and resented the outrage offered by the Athenians elsewhere to a sanctuary of Delian Apollo.³ Apollo himself from his Delphian oracle interfered and secured the restoration of the Delians after a most unhappy period of exile.⁴ An echo of the public interest taken by religious Greece in Delos and the Delians, an interest which would resent their unmerited wrongs, is found in the *Hecuba*, which was brought out between 426 B.C.—the date of the establishment of the Delia, and 422 B.C.—the date of the expulsion by Athens of the Delians from Delos. The captive Trojan maidens thus sing of Delos and the Delians:

"Where the first of palms that grew, and the laurel-tree shot upward holy branches of tender green to give comfort to blessed Leto in her travail-pangs for Zeus. With Delian maids shall I there join in praise of the fillet and bow of heavenly Artemis?"⁵

---

[1] See M. Homolle's article "Delia" in Daremberg and Saglio.
[2] Thuc. v. i.
[3] At Delium in Boeotia (Thuc. iv. 89-100). After the battle in 424, the Boeotians organised a Delian festival at Delium. This was a protest against the policy of Athens at Delos.
[4] Thuc. v. 32.
[5] *Hecuba*, 457 ff.; and cf. *Iph. Taur.* 1089-1105, quoted above.

Great as was the interest of Euripides in the Delians and their traditional observances, he yielded to none in a sense that Delos must be perfectly pure. This abundantly appears in the *Ion*, where Creüsa cries out in the temple at Delphi, making appeal from injustice to the holiness of Delos. She thinks that Delphian Apollo has grievously wronged her, and believes momentarily that he has no purpose of reparation: therefore she cries aloud against him. But even under these circumstances the genuine piety of her heart did not escape the poet. What more true and more touching proof of it can be found indeed than the closing words of Creüsa, whereby the harshness and horror of the tale she has just told of Apollo's wrongdoing are made but another means of proclaiming the beauty of holiness that guards his sacred island?

"Delos abhors thee, she cries; even the laurel-shoot growing close to the palm-tree of delicate leafage, where in the pangs of her holy travail Leto brought thee to birth for Zeus."[1]

This amounts very nearly to a worship of the island itself, and certainly Euripides, by a magnificently religious exaggeration, has here gone farther even than the celebrated apostrophe of Delos by Pindar, who addressed the island as follows:

"Hail! thou that wert stablished by a god, thy upspringing was most longed for of the children of bright-vestured Leto! Moveless miracle of all the breadth of earth, Delos named by mortals, and by the blessed gods called the far-gleaming star of darkling earth."

The natural beauty which flashes from Delos in these lines of Pindar is a glittering loveliness shared with her by

[1] *Ion*, 919 and ff.

all the holy Cyclades; and like the holiness which brought worshippers of yore, it is a garment bestowed by the coming of the sun god. Untouched of sunlight Delos and Rhenea with all the twelve that circle round them, white Paros and fertile Naxos, rugged Myconos and Tenos with rocky Syros —all of them, untouched of sunlight, seem desolate and drear; but let Apollo touch them with the arrows of his day, and they are then like flashing prisms that he has set upon the sea, or blossom-like they glisten white on blue, and the poet of to-day still marvels to see them there—

> Lily on lily that o'erlace the sea.

The sea and the sunlight of his Aegean home entered long since into the heart of the ancient Aegean poet Archilochus and made him, even more than Pindar, capable of worthily setting forth the strong and beautifully awful majesty of Delian Apollo. Archilochus chose rather for his theme, and for his native land, the whole breadth of the Aegean than the pent-up Paros where he came to birth.

"Away with Paros, her figs and fishy life!"[1] he cries, and launches his barque upon the sparkling sea, singing,

> Wood makes the trough to knead my bread withal,
> Wood makes the cask to keep Ismarian wine,
> Wood makes the deck where drinking I recline.[2]

Although the poetry of great Archilochus has disappeared with the exception of a few lines, in some of those few that remain we may read of the presence in his heart of the glorious Delian sun-god Apollo. The very flame of swift power in the death-dealing sun, pouring ceaselessly upon the fervid flanks of Delian Cynthus, or making the white

[1] Bergk, *Frag.* 51. [2] *Ibid.* 3.

sea-walls of Paros glow again with intolerable heat, was felt by Archilochus, when indignant he cries :

> Sirius will flash, I hope, most fiercely out,
> And utterly consume them.[1]

There were moments in the life of this man, the poet of the whole Archipelago, and more especially of that greater Delos formed by all the Cyclades,—moments, I say, there were in this poet's life when the intensity of his scorn swept him away as completely as if he had been caught in the whirl of the tides of his native seas. At such times he would look in wrathful and untolerating expectation towards the Holy Isle of Delos and thence invoke Apollo, the dealer of sudden death :

> Apollo, take the guilty ones away,
> Unmask them, Lord, and slay as thou canst slay.[2]

For a moment the largeness of such noble scorn transfigures Archilochus; the inspiration of deep utterance makes him for one instant like the god whose power he invokes, but it lasts but the space of a moment. Though our poet's anger resembles that of high Apollo, he is otherwise not like him. Archilochus never dreamt even of that chivalrous regard for womankind which belonged to the ideal godhead of Apollo.

Let us now examine first this great quality, which sometimes tempts one to call Apollo a King Arthur of the Greeks.

Does Apollo the giver of swift and painless death slay women as well as men? Here is one test of his chivalry. Homer may be called in for the first witness, he knew

[1] Bergk, *Frag.* 61.   [2] *Ibid.* 27

Apollo first. In describing Syrie, commonly identified with Syros one of the twelve Cyclades, Homer says:

> When it cometh to pass that men grow old in that country, The god of the silver bow, Apollo, and Artemis with him Suddenly comes upon them and slays with shafts that are gentle.[1]

Again Apollo and Artemis come together and avenge upon Niobe and her children the blasphemous outrage uttered against their dear mother Leto. The two, brother and sister, act in concert; Apollo's shafts strike down the sons of Niobe, her daughters are slain by the unerring aim of Artemis.

Sometimes, we hear, these twin gods dealt destruction by command of the other gods. Sometimes Artemis acts alone, as in the case so bitterly complained of by Calypso when,

> Artemis dread, the golden-throned, on the island Ortygia,[2] Suddenly came upon him[3] and slew with her shafts that are gentle.[4]

Apollo's anger against the guilt of his love Coronis, soon to be mother of the blameless Aesculapius, could not make him raise his hands against her,—she died, "slain," says Pindar, "by golden shafts of Artemis shot forth. She went from her chamber down to Hades' house through contrivance of Apollo."[5] Thus it appears that Apollo and Artemis are appointed to bring a sudden death, whether painless and peaceful—as to those who have lived righteously through a long life—or a destruction whirled on the guilty like a flash from the death-dealing anger of heaven.

[1] *Odyssey*, xv. 409 and ff. [2] Delos.
[3] Orion the lover of the Dawn. [4] *Odyssey*, v. 123 and ff.
[5] *Pyth.*, iii. 8 and ff.

In any case Apollo gives no death to womankind, in all such cases his sister Artemis intervenes.

Other Greek divinities are not, like Apollo, incapable of bringing death to women. Furthermore, Apollo's conduct towards his various loves shows often in other ways the true aspect of chivalry. The love of Apollo and Daphne, the story of Marpessa's marriage, both represent Apollo the lover submitting to be scorned and rejected with no thought of revenge, but rather (in Daphne's case at least) with a persistency in loving which foreshadows the more complete ideal of devoted chivalry. As a lover Apollo is not angered by refusal, and entire rejection does not end his suit. Though Daphne eluded him utterly, he takes to be his own the laurel tree, which was peculiarly hers, since it was she. This laurel became one of the symbols of purification and purity in the Apolline ritual. It is even possible that the whole myth of the love of Apollo for Daphne sprang up as a link to join a form of native and immemorial tree-worship to the later and higher service of Apollo. That a myth of this kind, chiefly intended as a connecting-link, should come, by the way, to present pictorially so high-minded a mood of unsensual and unselfish love is most significant. A similar link between the Thracian Dionysus and the native Icarian tree-worship was that of the suicide of Erigone and the mania for self-destruction that came upon all the maidens of Icaria. These two episodes embody the popular appraisal, so to speak, of Dionysus and Apollo. Dionysus was wrapped in a mystery of cruel horror, he drove men to nameless destruction, whereas Apollo was the noble-minded god, shining before men as a beacon of purity, and supporting their moral weakness by his own sublime and undying strength.

Zeus in his loves forms a great contrast to the unsensual Apollo. Zeus transforms himself into this animal or that for more certain and secret pursuit. These animals are an incarnation, as it were, of the carnal impulse in the god. Such a mark of sensuality is not set upon the love-pursuit of Apollo. Moreover Apollo is represented as accepting the *duties* along with the privileges of a lover.[1] The responsibilities of fatherhood, so little and so ineffectually heeded by Zeus, come home in all their fulness to Apollo.

Many stories present these high aspects of Apollo's commerce with men. For one of them, his appreciation of those charms which elude perception by mere sense, Pindar's account of the loves of Apollo and Cyrene is perhaps the most adequate.[2] Wandering in the woods, Apollo comes of a sudden upon Cyrene engaged in a hand to hand struggle with a lion. The maiden is alone, but unafraid. The god calls out straightway to Chiron, that gentlest and wisest of all centaurs: "Leave thy dread cave, come forth and marvel at this great prowess; how with mind undaunted the girl maintains her struggle, showing a spirit that towers above trials, a stedfast soul unstormed by fear. What mortal begat her? Plucked from what tribe doth she dwell in the hidden nooks of the shadow-flinging hills?" Truly Apollo's bearing is chivalrous and the nobility of passion can no farther go.

In the answer made by Chiron to Apollo's questions about Cyrene, the god is spoken of as one for whom it is unlawful to have part in a lie,[3] and this recalls another place where Pindar says that Apollo sets not his hand to falsehood,[4] and also various passages where Plato maintains

---
[1] See the *Ion* of Euripides, *passim*.   [2] *Pyth.* ix.
[3] *Ibid.* 42.   [4] *Pyth.* iii. 9, ψευδέων οὐχ ἅπτεται.

the unerring and unswerving truthfulness of the god.[1] Truthfulness is also among the cardinal virtues of the Knights of the Round Table, and thus again is the chivalry of Apollo made manifest. Apollo was in fact bound not to come near to falsehood by a law, a *Thesmos*. This law was an obligation, self-imposed no doubt, but yet stronger than any other impulse in the god, and therefore stronger than himself. He would not speak untruth because he could not, and he could not because he would not. This is a standard which suffers nothing by comparison with the medieval point of honour.

Further consideration of Apollo as the infallible speaker of truth by his oracles would lead rather to his Delphian than his Delian shrine, for the oracle at Delos never had great influence until Alexandrine times[2] when oracles began already to be neglected. Apollo, we are told, gave oracles at Delos in the summer season, but not during the winter. Then he gave answers at Patara in Lycia. According to still another account Apollo absented himself during the winter months to sojourn among the Hyperboreans in the uttermost parts of the earth. Kindred stories about regular absences of the god from Delphi are told and have been dealt with in the opening chapter of this book. Dismissing these questions without going more deeply into them, we may briefly add that the two great Apolline principles were represented by his two great shrines at Delphi and Delos. Apollo was everywhere the god of purity and truth, but his Delian worshippers had first in their minds his purity, while men flocked to Delphi that before all things else they might hear truth. This is broadly true of Apollo, and it also

---
[1] *Apol.* 21 B, *Rep.* ii. 382 E and 383 B.
[2] Callimachus, *Hymn to Delos*, vv. 1-5 ; Virg. *Aen.* iii. 85-101.

seems true to say that in many local stories, notably in those of Delphi, the god is represented as having attained the purity of his heart and the clearness of his infallible mind by a process of trial, a period of tribulation, which so regenerated him that he was fitted to be the moral protagonist of Olympus.[1] There was a commemoration at Delphi of Apollo's self-purification after he slew the dread serpent Pytho. Apollo was condemned in another story to serve a mortal for nine years in expiation of his slaying the Cyclops. These are Apollo's victories over himself, his acts of submission to that higher and self-imposed *thesmos*, which among other things forbade him—as Pindar's Chiron says—from touching falsehood. Through the moral superiority to other ideal figures in Greek mythology thus achieved, Apollo was enabled to possess for his own both Delphi and Delos, where other gods were in possession when he came. For instance, Delos apparently belonged to Poseidon before it came to Apollo, and the same seems true of Delphi. Actual record of the superiority of strenuous and self-disciplining Apollo is preserved, first by the great Delphian motto on his temple "Know thyself," and secondly, by legends of Apollo's superiority in various strenuous ways to other gods. The contest between him and Heracles for the tripod ended in a compromise where Apollo's superiority is plainly shown. M. Ronchaud[2] has indeed most admirably said that "Apollo, when he has dealings with other divinities, always shows a certain moral

---

[1] See chapter iv. of C. F. Keary's *Outlines of Primitive Belief*. Mr. Keary says, p. 191: "The history of the development of Apollo's character, then, is the gradual exaltation of his nature to suit the growing needs of men. In the *Iliad*, though Zeus is the most mighty of the two, Apollo's is certainly the more majestic figure."

[2] Article "Apollo," in Daremberg and Saglio.

superiority. His standard is higher than theirs. Poseidon was his fellow-labourer in the building of the walls of Troy, but the possession of Delphi and its oracle, originally shared by Poseidon with Earth, passed into Apollo's hands, and Poseidon was dispossessed. Apollo's superiority shows itself also in the Homeric record of his strife with Hermes. He is the rival of Hermes in inventing the lyre, and wins the day over him in a race at Olympia. Ares himself cannot withstand Apollo at boxing, and as for the insolent Phorbas, Apollo punishes him with death. Apollo taught Heracles the use of the bow, and in various points the legends of Heracles run parallel to those of Apollo. But Apollo stands far above Heracles, and looks down from the heights of his divine perfection."

A further insight into the nature of the purifier purified, of Delian Apollo and his services at Delos, will be gained by looking into the various festivals celebrated on the island at various periods. The festival in honour of Apollo's birthday was—like the flower festivals of Dionysus—in the spring. Upon the sixth of the month Thargelion began this Apolline Christmas season, of which a glorified record is preserved in the Homeric Hymn to Delian Apollo. This may be summarised as follows:—

Apollo has many sanctuaries, "thick-growing forests," "high points of far outlook,"[1] "high-standing headlands,"— Delos, though, is his best beloved shrine.

> There Ionians, trailing long robes, are wont to assemble.
> With them they bring the wives they wedded, and children
>   are with them.
> They meanwhile, on combats of boxing, singing, and dances,

---

[1] Such is the temple of Apollo at Bassae.

Always intent, whenever the contest begins, are contented,
Seeming predestined to live thus ageless for ever and deathless.

The joy of the occasion lent to all that partook of it a glamour of immortality; the stranger standing by thinks he is seeing the "Charm of the World," and rejoices exceedingly at sight of "goodly men and women with beauteous girdles," of swift ships and abundance of treasures. Finally, as a climax to his description of the festal joy, the bard exclaims in wondering delight :—

Look! the daughters of Delos, handmaidens of him the fardarter,
Singing begin, first of all with hymns in praise of Apollo,
Of Leto next they sing, and of Artemis shooting her arrows.
Heroes of old they praise, and the glories of men and of women.

The tribes of mankind are enchanted with these songs wherein

All men's manner of speech, the castanet's rhythm and motion,
Well they counterfeit all, so that each would feel sure he had spoken,
Spoken himself, so deftly devised are their songs and so sweetly.

This is the earliest record of the Ionian festival in honour of Delian Apollo, and after reading this, it becomes difficult to believe that Apollo was of purely Dorian origin, as some have maintained.[1]

A later testimony to this earliest festival of Apollo at

[1] As this Homeric Hymn throws a welcome light upon Delos, it is satisfactory to note, before turning away from it, that inscriptions found on the island have thrown light upon the questioned authenticity of its second part. See the interesting article by Gabriel Daurès on " Excavations at

Delos is found in Thucydides (iii. 104) above referred to. From him we learn that it was a yearly celebration, and did not occur every fourth year like the festival called the Delia, founded at Delos by Athens in 426 B.C.

In fact the successful attempt begun in that year by the Athenian democracy to supplant the local traditions of Delos by closely allied Athenian ones, and the remodelling of the ancient Apollonian festival, has given rise to much confusion both in mythology and ritual. It would be useless to attempt now a disentanglement of such confusion. It is enough to bear in mind what M. Homolle has so clearly pointed out, that (1) the earliest festivals described in the Homeric Hymn were quite distinct both from (2) the Athenian Delia which supplanted them, and also from (3) the festival called the Apollonia, which was an attempt to revive something like them, made so late in the day that all the traditions that surrounded the Homeric bard had died away. The Apollonia were celebrated during the century and a half of independence enjoyed by Delos. The last stage of Delian merry-making begins in 166 B.C., a year memorable for the final reappearance at Delos, under Roman auspices, of Athenian power. Abundant testimony from the end of the second century B.C. tells of the second revival of the Delia[1] in those latter days. The celebration was only in part religious and, as had been the case with every festival ever celebrated at Delos, there was also a sort of

Delos," *Nouvelle Revue*, Sept. 1880. M. Homolle found an inscription which proves that the last half of the hymn was called Homeric in the third century B.C., not only popularly but by a competently qualified judge.

[1] Thus, to summarise, the Delia were founded in 426 B.C., suspended in Lysander's day after he took Athens, until 386 B.C. With the second sea-supremacy of Athens they were revived and lasted until 330 B.C., then came the revival in 166 B.C.

fair.[1] But apparently the commercial spirit finally got the upper hand in these latest days; and Delos, at the time when Menophanes, a lieutenant of Mithridates, brought final destruction upon it, was largely in the hands of enterprising Phoenicians, and Jews who knew not Apollo. Delos became more famous as the greatest slave market in the world than as the birth-place of Leto's twin children. Perhaps it was some sense of the incongruity of this which made the praises of Delos so irksome a theme to Virgil.

But even in Virgil's day the eye of faith could see much that was beautiful and inspiring. All the shrines at Delos had been deserted for years before Ovid wrote his description of *candida Delos* crowded with gifts from kings and peopled everywhere with votive statues. But still the splendour of Athenian festivals there celebrated irradiated the memory of what Delos had been. And religious-minded and imaginative men remembered more vividly the glories of the remoter past when the sordid and commercial thing that Delos had become was swept away. Hence, if we try to gain some fragmentary knowledge of the manner of Athenian celebrations at Delos, we shall but do (as far as may be) what those who knew the island in the day of her decay and destruction were prone to do.

The celebration was in mid-spring, before May was one week old, lasting at least two days,—the first was Apollo's birthday, the second was that of Artemis. For this festival [2]

[1] Tenos has reproduced in modern Christian times many of the features of ancient festivals at Delos. Twice a year the Evangelistria draws crowds who come to pray, and many of whom stay to buy and sell. These Tenian festivals were begun towards the end of the first quarter of this century.

[2] I am speaking of the quadrennial festival; there were minor celebrations on the "off years."

extensive preparations were made at Athens. Choruses were trained,[1] deputations were chosen and qualified, victims were bought and put into a good condition for sacrifice, the sacred Delian ship was made in every way seaworthy, and the signs of heaven were consulted for a favourable time of departure.

The Delian deputation or Theory—whose members were called by the special name of Deliastae — must not be confused with the singing choruses of youths and maidens that accompanied them. The whole number of celebrants who constituted the Athenian contribution to the quadrennial festivities at Delos would therefore be very large. When Callias, the son of Hipponicus, was the head of the deputation, its numbers were 118. Nicias went with 103. This whole array, collectively named the Delias, had to sail from the Piraeus, and go out past Sunium into the open sea where began the Cyclades. As Attic Sunium disappeared in the distance, they passed Ceos, Cythnos, Seriphos, and Syros on the right, and on the left Andros and Tenos. When they came in sight of Myconos to the far east, they stopped short of it and ran into the narrow and sheltered channel between Delos and Rhenea—the gift of Polycrates to Apollo. In the beautiful days of late April and early May they would have a glimpse from afar of Naxos [2] and Paros in the southern group of the holy Cyclades.

[1] The choruses from Athens were renowned for beauty and for artistic perfections, Xen. *Mem.* III. iii. 12. The Deliastae — a committee in special charge of the representation of Athens at the Delian festival—were chosen from the Eumolpidae and the Kerykes, families identified with the worship at Eleusis. They had to see that the deputation took its departure as soon as favouring signs appeared in the heavens. The Deliastae were required to have passed a year of probation, say in the Marathonian Delion. For references and further details see M. Homolle's article "Delia" in Daremberg and Saglio.

[2] For views of Naxos, see Appendix XI. i. 84-86.

Without unfavourable winds the journey could be made in four days, although to be sure the ship dedicated to Apollo's service was none of the newest or swiftest. This Delian boat was called the *Theoris*, and was a small old-fangled craft, with thirty oars, a triaconter, kept always in the very best repair. The very faithful tried to believe it was the identical boat upon which Theseus set sail for Crete, vowing to found a festival for Apollo,[1] if victory crowned his expedition. Evidently other boats were needed, for, apart from the five score persons, more or less, who had to find ship room, enough victims for a hecatomb had to be transported to Delos.[2] Often, too, the high-born Athenians who wished their horses to compete in the races at the Delian festival[3] must have required additional transport. For Delos still more than Ithaca is and always was "a place for goats" rather than horses. In Delos there were no wide courses, and no meadow save the one around the sacred lake.[4] When the fleet was ready in the harbour and the ministrant who made sacrifice daily at the altar of Apollo gave word that a favouring flash of lightning indicated the right moment for weighing anchor, a wreath was set upon the prow of the sacred *Theoris* and the pilgrims sailed away with appropriate ceremonies and the singing of songs, which were sung all the way to Delos.[5]

---

[1] Plutarch, *Theseus*, 23, and cf. Pausanias, VIII. xlviii. 3.

[2] The accounts for 377-374, M. Homolle says, cover a purchase of 109 animals for sacrifice.

[3] The Athenians of wealth and position took all this trouble,—at the time the Delia were first founded,—the more readily if the Peloponnesian managers of the Olympic games, being Spartan sympathisers, are supposed to have made participation in the races at Olympia more or less disagreeable for them.

[4] See Appendix XI. i. 71, 72.

[5] M. Homolle quotes the words ᾄδεις ὥσπερ εἰς Δῆλον πλέων, *Paroem-iogr.* (Göttingen), p. 42.

Around the sacred boats sent by the state swarmed many others carrying pilgrims on their own account, and some of them freighted with merchandise. The same thing happens to-day, *mutatis mutandis*, when the faithful sail to Tenos for the festival and fair of the Holy Evangelistria.

Perhaps the most memorably magnificent of all these sacred embassies to Delos was that already mentioned despatched from Athens shortly after the conclusion of the Peace of Nicias. It may be remembered that just before this time the repentant Athenians had rescinded their harsh decree of banishment, and thus the Delians had but recently returned from exile. This sacred embassy was headed by Nicias, an Athenian whose rather mechanical piety coupled with misfortunes bravely borne made his career most touching, and all but nobly tragic. In company of a number of boats bearing the youthful chorus, and of other craft of the heavier kind for freight, the *Theoris* brought up not, as in former years, in Delos proper, but across the way on Rhenea. This landing must have been on the eve of the great Delian festival. All night long rumblings and voices were borne over the waters to the listening Delians. In the morning a gorgeous pontoon bridge connected Rhenea with the Holy Island. Across it came the procession and Nicias, all in festal array, and wearing golden crowns. After the bridge was crossed they passed northward singing all the way to where in later years the roadway was hemmed in by the portico of Philip (the Fifth of Macedonia), and they entered the precinct by a Ceremonial Gate (the southward gate built by the Athenians). After this, they moved northward still, passing to the westward of the great temple of Apollo, and also of the smaller temple of Leto by its side. The processional way here as at Eleusis was lined on either side with various statues and monuments, and these were more numerous as the neighbourhood of the temple was reached. After joining the sacred way that led inward from the larger North Propylaea, Nicias came to the ancient temple of Artemis or, as some think of the Seven Gods.[1] Here were deposited the laurel crowns of gold periodically sent to Apollo of Delos from Athens during Athenian supremacy.

After the procession had gone the rounds prescribed, visiting shrines and temples, crowning the ancient wooden statue of Aphrodite left at Delos by Ariadne,[2] who had it from Daedalus, its fashioner, the second stage of the celebration was reached, the sacrifice.[3] The hundred kine decked for the offering and with their horns gilded were sacrificed on all the altars save one alone—the bloodless altar of Apollo, the father of the Ionian race. There only first-fruits were offered, and no doubt thither the gifts of the mysterious Hyperboreans[4] found their way. Then came perhaps certain ceremonies of dedication and purification,

[1] The uncertainty about this temple, the existence and approximate position of which are known through inscriptions, is due to subsequent building, which in the Middle Ages swept all its foundation marks from the face of the rock. Here stood perhaps the only Christian building of any pretensions that Delos has ever possessed—some sort of a chapel built by the Knights Hospitallers, which had in turn almost completely disappeared when excavations began in earnest under M. Homolle. He found here one of the most remarkable statues of antiquity—representing, let us say, Artemis. Take, if you will, a very tall tombstone and round off its angles and corners till its form is nearly cylindrical. Divide the result into three parts, not equal, but nearly so, one for the legs, one for the body, one for the head. Something should be done, no matter what, about the arms. Then your Delian statue of Artemis, not beautiful, but most ancient, is complete. Brunn has published it in his *Denkmäler*.

[2] Pausan. IX. xl. 3 and 4 ; Callimach. *Hymn to Delos*, 308 ff.

[3] Plutarch, *Nicias*, 3.

[4] Mannhardt has an ingenious theory that they were Thracians or Macedonians.

after which the games began—contests of physical strength and skill, horse racing, and musical competition. Everything which Athens could do was done here in Apollo's honour, with all the more splendour because Athens was solely responsible for the festival. Nicias saw, no doubt, the older temple of Apollo, supplanted later on by the one whose ruins we contemplate to-day. That temple, like its successor, fronted eastward and therefore away from the channel and towards Mount Cynthus. Between its back or western end and the sea stood in the day of Nicias the colossal statue of Apollo dedicated by the Naxians. This figure towered up to a height of twenty-four feet, and the ancient Nicias seems to have been deeply moved by its god-like proportions. That he might vie with the ancient Naxian worshippers of Apollo, he gave money before he left for setting up a colossal palm-tree of bronze by the side of their colossus. This was done, and the two stood there for many a year side by side. So close were they, indeed, that there was a great disaster generations afterwards when a windstorm swept across from Tenos, where Aeolus himself was housed on Mount Cycnias. The too blustering Aeolus visited Apollo's precinct rudely, and caused the brazen palm-tree to crash down against the statue of Apollo and overturn it utterly. Such was the unlucky gift given by one who at the time considered himself no doubt the luckiest of men.

But the pious Nicias did more than this: he gave ground to the temple worth 10,000 drachmae. He provided that the income from this should be spent for celebrating what sounds very much like a mass for his soul. He stipulated for a yearly sacrifice and an accompanying entertainment at which the Delians were to pray for the gods to grant an abundant good fortune to Nicias. The time came only too soon when Nicias—overwhelmed by the incessant agonies of the most painful and incurable of diseases—needed sorely all these prayers and more. A hopeless invalid, he died under the most tragical circumstances, slain by decree of the Syracusan mob, and at Athens his pious name was execrated.

Such, in outline, was the manner of honouring Apollo used by the Athenians during the various periods of assured supremacy when Athenian officers took from the Delians all control over the concerns of Delian worship. Such was the Athenian festival called the Delia and first celebrated in 426 B.C.

For the earliest festival we are constrained to fall back chiefly upon the pleasing picture of the Homeric Hymn to Delian Apollo. A sufficient account of this has been given above. There are also some verses of Theognis[1] more or less plainly referring to it. Aside from this we only know a detail here and there about ancient images, and remarkable practices associated with a fabulous and more or less prehistoric past. There is the story given by Aris-

[1] Φοῖβε ἄναξ, αὐτὸς μὲν ἐπύργωσας πόλιν ἄκρην,
'Αλκαθόῳ Πέλοπος παιδὶ χαριζόμενος.
αὐτὸς δὲ στρατὸν ὑβριστὴν Μήδων ἀπέρυκε
τῆσδε πόλευς, ἵνα σοι λαοὶ ἐν εὐφροσύνῃ
ἦρος ἐπερχομένου κλειτὰς πέμπωσ' ἑκατόμβας,
τερπόμενοι κιθάρης ἠδ' ἐρατῇ θαλίῃ
παιάνων τε χοροῖς ἰαχῇσί τε σὸν περὶ βωμόν.

Bergk, 773-779. The last four lines are thus translated by Frere:

So shall thy people each returning spring
Slay fatted hecatombs; and gladly bring
Fair gifts with chaunted hymns and lively song,
Dances and feasts, and happy shouts among;
Before thy altar, glorifying thee,
In peace and health, and wealth, cheerful and free.

totle¹ of Pythagoras' visit to Delos, wherein we hear that, passing others by, he made sacrifice upon the altar of Apollo Genétor or Patroos, where the shedding of no blood was tolerated. We cannot know what may have been the Delian version of the first appearance at Delos of the ancient wooden image of Aphrodite,² because the Athenian tale has alone survived, making it a gift from Ariadne when she passed that way with Theseus. That the ante-Athenian phase of worship was represented by many curious and clumsy works of most primitive art is abundantly shown by the seven ancient images discovered by excavation near the Delian shrine of Apollo. Of the most remarkable of these mention has been made above.³ Furthermore it appears that the mother goddess Leto was represented in her Delian temple by a wooden idol more grotesquely inadequate, according to later notions of Greek art, than M. Homolle's famous Artemis. That the art-critics of later times had much to say on this score appears from the following anecdote quoted by Athenæus⁴ from Semus,—a Delian, the loss of whose writings has no doubt deprived us of much information about Delos and Delian Apollo.

Parmeniscus, "the man who never laughed," consulted the Boeotian oracle in the dark cave of Trophonius that he might in some way break the spell. The god gave him answer hexametrically:

> Go to mother at home, honour her with exceeding great kindness.

---

[1] Ar. Fragm. 447, quoted by Diog. Laertius and Iamblichus, who gives it twice.
[2] For the curious outline of Aphrodite's history at Delos, see Appendix X.
[3] See above, note 1, p. 379.   [4] xiv. 614 B.

The obedient Parmeniscus sought out his mother, and amazed her by his unusual attentions. The effect of all this was apparently to make them both more hopelessly solemn than ever. Not too many years afterwards, our solemn friend came to Delos, — as Aegean voyagers from west to east always did in those days. While going the pious rounds on the island Parmeniscus worshipped in the Letoon or Temple of Leto, next that of Apollo. Accustomed to the more knowing art in vogue at his native Metapontum, he was not prepared for the wooden idol which represented Apollo's mother in this ancient shrine. Therefore on catching sight of the idol his devotions were interrupted by uncontrollable fits of laughter. Leto, Apollo's mother, was the mother whom he had been commanded to "honour with exceeding great kindness."

Aristotle has quoted in his *Ethics* [1] the curious inscription which met the eyes of worshippers at this temple of Leto,

> Righteousness the noblest is ;
> Health is better than the best ;
> Sweetest though, of all that is,
> Is getting what you love.

These words, if connected with Leto, who was "a comforter from the beginning, the most soothing presence of all on Olympus," must be expressive of her typical attitude. Like an indulgent mother with her children, she chiefly wished that men should have their heart's desire. Attached to the personality of the goddess of self-devoted and uncomplaining love, they gain a new

---

[1] *Eudemian Ethics*, at the beginning of the first book, and also toward the end of the eighth chapter of the first book of the *Nicomachean Ethics*. In the former place it is described as on the Delian Letoon, in the latter simply as τὸ Δηλιακὸν ἐπίγραμμα.

and a higher meaning, and with Leto's life to point their moral, are full of a religious significance. Therefore, it ceases to surprise us to find Aristotle twice quoting the saying, and also we can better understand why this same sentiment without substantial variation occurs among the maxims of Theognis,[1] a poet to whose imagination the Delian myth of Leto strongly appealed.[2] Let the motto of the Delian Letoon be an offset to the Delphian motto, "Know thyself," and temper its too exclusively intellectual bias. Here too is the needed contradiction (always given by the heart to the head) of the other Delphian motto "Nothing too much." The mother goddess Leto was given over to unmeasured love, and the affection which her love inspired in her children Apollo and Artemis was the best proof that you can never go too far in love.

As a touching mark of the spirit of grateful affection and simple trust which could find expression at Apollo's Delian shrine, the inscribed gift picked up there by Professor Ulrichs is very precious. It was a cheap leaden quiver, the gift of shipwrecked sailors who had come near to starvation, upon which was stamped,

> For by these we were rescued from starving.

Such indications as a discovery of this kind gives of the living spirit of religion working in men's hearts and guiding their lives are of far more real importance than the record preserved by Callimachus and others of the building of an altar by Apollo with materials sought on Mount Cynthus by his sister Artemis.[3] It was made, we are told, entirely

[1] Bergk, 255 and f.   [2] See above, note 1, p. 381.
[3] Callimachus, *Hymn to Apollo*, 58-63.

of horns such as the goddess could gather among the granite boulders of that eminence, too irreverently designated by the traveller Tournefort as a *colline désagréable*. Another curiosity which attaches itself also to the very earliest forms of worship used before the dawn of known history is far away from the town of Delos and the precinct of Apollo visited by Nicias. For lack of a better name it may be called the "Cave Temple of Apollo,"[1] though it has been called the "Grotto of the Sun" by Burnouf and the "Cave of the Dragon" by another, and more prosaically still by the unenthusiastic Tournefort "a stone sentry box." This cave-temple is formed by placing aslant against each other, on the top of a natural rift in the solid rock, five huge and rough-hewn granite slabs, two on the north and three on the south. These two rows rest upon and are crowded against uneven ledges, rudely fashioned at their lower edges in the side of the reshaped rift or gully in the Cynthian mountainside. Their upper edges meet together forming the point to the most inartificial seeming gable. This appearance of inartificiality is enhanced by a heap of granite boulders accumulated on the sides of this rude pediment, which seems the chance product of nature's workmanship. This impression is increased by the circumstance that a huge spot at the back of this cave was probably never roofed over. Within this strange place, half natural and half artificial, half cave and half temple, were found by Lebègue,[2] who excavated here for Burnouf early in the seventies, the feet of what he thinks must have been a fine statue of Apollo. A curious stone of unshapely form upon which

[1] For photographs of this and of various Delian scenes, see Appendix XI. i. *The Cyclades*, 71-83.
[2] See for more details his *Recherches sur Délos*, where M. Burnouf's astronomical points are also presented.

these feet rested is talked of by M. Lebègue as undoubtedly a Baetylus or fetish stone, which according to this view must have been worshipped here, as a cone was worshipped in Aphrodite's ancient Paphian precinct. In front of this sentry-box cave-temple is a terrace built up by means of a most carefully constructed wall. This, though of very early workmanship, is of much later date than the cave-temple itself. Upon this terrace there are traces of something like a tomb and of the charred remains of sacrifice. Also a stone footing for a very large tripod appears there, and furthermore, in front of and close to the cave-temple itself is a row of stone bases; perhaps these were for small tripods.

And now, having given as full an account briefly as might be of the Athenian Delia, and of the more ancient observances and objects of worship at Delos, what yet remains to be spoken of is the festival of Apollo as it was celebrated during the day of Delian independence. When Athenian interference ceased, the intellectual leadership of Athens was still felt, and therefore the new Apollonia, which should have been a revival of the most ancient observances, were in fact almost the same thing which the Athenians called the Delia, only no *Theoris* came from Athens. The four crowns of gold sent periodically by Athens while she ruled the festival were sent no more, and no more votive gifts were made to the god by Athenians. Delos was no longer beautified by Athenian architects, such as those whose ruined work is still seen in the scattered fragments of the most important temple of Delos.[1] It was to the munificence of a Macedonian,

---

[1] The temple was built about a century after 422 (when Nicias headed the Athenian Delias), and certainly before 315 B.C. It was of about the

Philip the Fifth, that Apollo owed the chief addition to his splendid buildings made during the era of Delian independence.[1] During these years Delos welcomed as the votaries of its god not Athenians but merchants from Eastern Tyre and Sidon, traders from far-off Panticapaeum on the sea of Azof, and also from the far West. The part in Delian affairs played by the islands round about, the Cyclades, was also greater than in the day when Athens ruled supreme. Indeed, the sanctuary became a centre of Aegean affairs as well as of Aegean religion. It was, as M. Homolle puts it, not a place for worship only, but equally a "Recorder's office for the safe-keeping of important decrees, a sort of treasury department or bank for the whole Archipelago, and also a central museum for the islands of the Aegean."[2]

Meanwhile festivals under the name of Apollonia took place with but few alterations from the Athenian programme at the Delia which they supplanted. There were all sorts

size and dimensions of the Theseum at Athens, it had almost precisely the same width, but was appreciably shorter. For all manner of archaeological details concerning Delos, it is a pleasure to refer to so charming a book as that just published by M. Ch. Diehl under the title of *Excursions archéologiques en Grèce* (Paris, 1890). M. Diehl has written just the entertaining and untechnical sort of book which was required, and has been extremely happy in what he says about Delos.

[1] The porch of Philip, whose massive blocks form one of the most imposing (and to the hasty sightseer impeding) of the present Delian ruin-heaps, was built toward the close of the era of independence, *circa* 180 B.C. It is interesting to the student of architecture, because in it is represented the last and worst extremity of the Doric style. Its columns have lost the strength and the upbearing swing that belong to those of the Parthenon, and are transformed into dull and unprofitable posts. See the instructive account of this whole matter in the *Antiquities of Ionia*, Part IV. 1881, published by the Dilettanti Society.

[2] See in the *Bulletin de la société de géographie de l'est*, 1881 (1er trimestre), M. Homolle's lecture on Delos given at Nancy. To understand what the temple was, he tells us to combine the Musée de Cluny, a garde-meuble, a cour de comtes, the Bank of France, the Crédit Foncier, and the Madeleine.

of foot races, the *stadion*, the *diaulos*, the *dolichos*, the *hoplite race*,—and there was the *pentathlon*. Furthermore *torch races* were indulged in. It may be difficult to be sure how many of these features were new, and how many were simply in continuation of the established Athenian programme. It may not be possible to know whether the far-fetched practice of horse-racing introduced by the Athenians at Delos was maintained by the islanders when freed from Athenian supervision. Of one thing though we may be certain: there was abundant dancing. One has but to visit the Archipelago in carnival time to-day to see a tolerably good reproduction in modern surroundings of what has always characterised Aegean merrymakings. "At Delos," says Lucian, "they could not so much as make sacrifices without dancing and music as well." After that he proceeds to describe the measures trod at Delian merrymakings by especially chosen dancers, and by choirs of picked youths trained for the delectation of those who resorted to Apollo's festival.[1]

The Greeks of the Archipelago have at all times been under the spell of the swaying surges of ocean, which was the background of their home life and home joy. These islanders live now as of old face to face with the strongest moods of the great sea, not as in the far recesses of Venetian lagoons, where the whims of ocean are moderated. Accordingly, while the graceful swerve of the moderated

[1] This spirit of the ancient dances took shape before my eyes in a band of Syriote peasants whom I saw dancing in front of a village church on the last day of the carnival. There they were, old men and young men, maidens and women of maturer years, all merrily dancing and singing, while the kindly priest whom the refrain of their song was chaffing looked on contentedly. I recollect particularly the hilarious conduct of a certain genial and one-eyed villager, Socrates, who danced until he lost both shoes. For a band of Syriote butchers caught and photographed in the act of dancing the Caramanian dance, see Appendix XI. i. 64.

pulses of the sea has shaped the motions of Venetians, and lent a swaying outline to the houses men live in at Venice, in the Archipelago the very quicksilver rhythm and instant sweep of ocean have passed into the limbs and hearts of the Greek islanders.

By the mark of good-humoured merriment and kindly spirit of comradeship we know under its modern disguise the ancient spirit of Apollo's Delian festivals, which may be studied with especial advantage when the faithful gather at Tenos. Three neighbouring islands cast lots as it were for the rich vestment of sanctity, splendour, and power which magnified Delos of yore and exalted Delian Apollo. The period of storm and stress which issued in Greek independence built up at Syra[1] a great commercial port, instituted at Tenos the sanctuary of the Evangelistria,[2] and finally assured to the inhabitants of Myconos the possession of untenanted Delos and Rhenea.

To this same establishment of Greek independence we owe the opportunity for studying the worship of Apollo at Delos unmolested of Turks or other wild beasts. To the indefatigable labours and the wonderful resources of the first established school at Athens we owe the abundant material now open to the student of Delian secular and religious antiquities. The head and front of the latest and most important discoveries there is M. Theophile Homolle. To that distinguished scholar we owe the deepest gratitude for

[1] Ross tells of a scheme for diverting the trade of Syra to Delos which was seriously considered, but finally abandoned early in this century. See for the best account of the growth of Syra, *Loukis Laras*, by D. Bikélas (the English translation is by Mr. Gennadius). For pictures of the modern life of the Cyclades, see Appendix XI. i. 58-70.

[2] Agitation for building the church where the miraculous picture is housed began about 1820, just at the time when the picture itself had been unearthed in accordance with the dream which persistently visited a pious nun of Tenos. See Appendix XI. i. 87.

all the self-denying enthusiasm and undiscouraged perseverance which have led to his brilliant results. The work which shall embody and bring to a climax all M. Homolle's studies is as yet incomplete, but he has already done so much with his accumulated material that scholars declare him, and rightly, to be one of the few foremost archaeologists of our day.

APPENDIX IX

THE CYCLADES AND SPORADES

IT is difficult to understand the relation borne by the various islands of the Aegean to the worship of Apollo at Delos and to each other, without going into the history of the two terms Cyclades and Sporades. Neither of these terms was known in Homer's or Hesiod's day, and of the two the term Cyclades was not only the first to be used later on, but was also far more widely known throughout antiquity. The word Sporades was used apparently, so far as it came into a general usage, by a sort of analogy to the use of the word Cyclades. It covers somewhat vaguely the smaller islands, too insignificant either to be named singly and stand alone or to be classed among the Cyclades. In most cases, also, the islands so named are too far away from Delos to make the term Cyclades possible for them. The Cyclades were certain illustrious[1] islands more or less accurately described as centred around Delos and Rhenea, and were especially favoured by Apollo, who colonised them through his son Ion;[2] the Sporades were small islands to whose population might be more especially applied the Euripidean line (*Rhesus*, 701), νησιώτην σποράδα κέκτηται βίον. They were in no sense a group, but were scattered broadcast,[3] and each one was so small that any life but an

[1] Theocritus, *Id*. XVII. 90 and f.   [2] Euripides, *Ion*, 1571-1600.
[3] *Etym. Magn.* s.v. Σποράδες νῆσοι: ἢ διὰ τὸ σποράδην κεῖσθαι, ἢ ἀπὸ τοῦ σπαρτὸν καὶ σπρατόν.

unsettled and vagrant one was more or less difficult upon it. As the islands answering to this description were chiefly toward the western coast of Asia Minor, there was a tendency from the moment the term Sporades came into use to divide the islands, as they are now definitely divided, into two categories, an eastern one of Sporades, and a western one—which alone could be called a group—of Cyclades. But this was never strictly done in antiquity.

In the Homeric Hymn to Delian Apollo[1] there still survives a certain confusion noticeable in the *Odyssey* between islands and such peninsulas as were in any literal way almost islands; therefore it would be vain to expect from this source any classification of islands. The same imperfect knowledge of islands, as such, characterises Hesiod. Undoubtedly the notion of a group of Cyclades around Delos grew up after the day of the Homeric poems and hymns, and its use was at first primarily determined by religious and mythological considerations which, being in a sense the reverse of geographical, did not require anything so definite as a catalogue of islands to which the name was applied. Herodotus may have been more definite and strictly geographical in his understanding of how the word applied. He says nothing, however, to encourage the idea, for he declares that none of the Cyclades were subject to Darius (v. 30), and means evidently to distinguish them from islands toward Asia Minor, whose Ionian inhabitants voluntarily submitted to Persia (i. 169). He had no general name for these latter, and the only phrase of general import which he uses for all the islands in question is "the islands in the Aegean" (ii. 97), where it may perhaps be claimed that the context suggests chiefly the Cyclades. Thucydides, on the other hand, evidently thought it important to be rather more clear in his own mind about the islands of the Aegean. He speaks (ii. 9) collectively of the Cyclades and the islands later known as the Sporades as "the islands inside of the Peloponnesus

[1] vv. 30-45.

and Crete." That he had a definite list or group of islands which he designated as the Cyclades is made very probable by this same passage, where he uses the phrase, "all the Cyclades except Melos and Thera." For the islands afterwards called the Sporades, Thucydides had no name whatsoever, and may so far forth be classed with the early poets and Herodotus. In the speech of Athena at the close of the *Ion*, we have finally the most important mention of the Cyclades from a religious and mythological point of view. There they are plainly mentioned as chosen islands, in whose colonisation and civilisation Apollo Genetor or Patroos, the patron and father of all Ionians, was immediately concerned.[1] This Apolline consecration of the Cyclades is often made prominent in later writers, such as Callimachus,[2] and there is a trace of it in the general tone of Herodotus, who distinguishes the Cyclades from common islands by saying that they never became subject to Darius.

In the days of the organised Roman empire all this was changed; it became imperative to have clearly defined geographical terms, and therefore the religious mystery of vagueness in the use of the term Cyclades disappeared. A list of Cyclades was made out, and the newer term Sporades was applied to the excluded islands, most of them east of Delos. It must be remembered, however, that none of these were important and well known. Rhodes, Chios, Samos, and islands of that ilk, were not counted either as Cyclades or as Sporades.[3] A learned Spaniard Hyginus, and the accom-

[1] *Ion*, 1583. For the point here made it is not necessary to suppose that Euripides used the word κυκλάδας as a proper name, though I incline to think he does, as do also most editors of the play.

[2] *Hymn to Delos*, 300 and ff.

[3] The only exception to this would be the name of ἐπαρχία νήσων Κυκλάδων, sometimes given to Diocletian's *Insularum provincia*. This was one of seven subdivisions of the province Asia, and included 53 islands, among which were Rhodes, Cos, Samos, Chios, Mytilene, Methymne, Tenedos, Porselene, Andros, Tenos, Naxos, Paros, Siphnos, Melos, Ios, Thera, Amorgos, Astypalaea. See Marquardt, *Römische Staatsverwaltung*, vol. i. p. 348; cf. also note 2, p. 397 below.

plished Greek geographer Strabo, both of them, give some knowledge of the definite and purely geographical meaning which in the days of Augustus and later attached itself to the two terms in question. Under the title of "Insulae maximae,"[1] Hyginus begins a long enumeration, where may be found Sicily, Sardinia, Crete, Cyprus, Rhodes, Euboea, Tenedos, and Corsica. As his very last item he gives a list of the Cyclades:—"Cyclades insulae sunt novem, id est Andros, Myconos, Delos, Tenos, Naxos, Seriphus, Gyarus, Paros, Rhene" (Rhenea). The first point noticeable here is that the only two islands specifically named by Thucydides as Cyclades, Melos and Thera, are not included in Hyginus' list. Another point against the list is that Delos and Rhenea appear in it, and thus themselves figure among their own surroundings. This is enough to discredit Hyginus' list, even if we had not Strabo's.[2]

Strabo has evidently considered the whole question in all its bearings, for he not only gives his own opinion in

[1] *Fab.* 276. Curiously enough Mauritania, Egypt, and Sicyon are classed here among *insulae*. This has something to do with an ambiguity in the Latin word *insula*, which applied to buildings and precincts which were definitely marked off from their surroundings. That there was, however, some real confusion in Hyginus' mind is shown by his phrase for Egypt : "quam Nilus circumlavat."

[2] See Theocritus, *Id.* XVII. 58 and ff., where there is a curious reproduction of the Delian birth legend of Apollo. Ptolemy, whose praises the poem sings, was born on Cos, which comparatively unwieldy island cried aloud for joy, and took Ptolemy new-born into her arms, exclaiming in substance : "Blessings on thee, and mayest thou honour me even as Apollo honoured Delos, and love me as Apollo loved Rhenea." This shows how inseparable were Delos and Rhenea in the poet's mind, and makes evident that it was as absurd to count the one as the other among the Cyclades. Delos and Rhenea were the centre, while the Cyclades were the circumference. In the *Encyclopædia Britannica*, be it said, only ten Cyclades are named, for two of the twelve there given are Delos and Rhenea. Now the only two authorities who name Delos and Rhenea among the islands that surrounded them are Hyginus, whose list is of nine only, and Stephanus Byzantius, who names twenty-three : twenty-one beside the two centre islands. It seems useless to attempt thus to tamper with the authorities at this late day, and by far the best considered list is undoubtedly Strabo's, from which Delos and Rhenea are excluded. See Pauly, *s.v.* "Sporades."

the matter by naming the Cyclades, but also he corrects Artemidorus. He enables us, furthermore, to get a fairly adequate list of the islands which he considered to be Sporades, and he separates from both Cyclades and Sporades various important islands and groups of islands along the coast of Asia Minor.

To begin with, Strabo does not regard the Cyclades solely as a collective name for a group of islands. They are, as contrasted with the Sporades, famous islands singled out from among less noteworthy ones: ἐν δὲ ταύταις (islands near Crete) αἵ τε Κυκλάδες εἰσὶ καὶ αἱ Σποράδες, αἱ μὲν ἄξιαι μνήμης αἱ δ' ἀσημότεραι, p. 474, book x.; again in speaking of islands in the Aegean sea—a much smaller expanse, according to his definition of it, than what we call the Aegean—he says ἐν δὲ τῷ Αἰγαίῳ μᾶλλον αὐτή τε ἡ Δῆλος καὶ αἱ περὶ αὐτὴν Κυκλάδες καὶ αἱ ταύταις προσκείμεναι Σποράδες, ὧν εἰσι καὶ αἱ λεχθεῖσαι περὶ τὴν Κρήτην, p. 485, *ibid.*; and again, a little farther down the same page, Strabo indicates the religious nature of the bond between Delos and the Cyclades, not without a confirmation of his previous implication that the Cyclades are islands of especial note, and therefore set apart from the others. These are his words: ἔνδοξον δ' ἐποίησαν αὐτὴν (Delos) αἱ περιοικίδες νῆσοι, καλούμεναι Κυκλάδες, κατὰ τιμὴν πέμπουσαι δημοσίᾳ θεωρούς τε καὶ θυσίας καὶ χοροὺς παρθένων πανηγύρεις τε ἐν αὐτῇ συνάγουσαι μεγάλας. The substance of this important passage is that Delos largely owed its glory to the honours paid it by the surrounding Cyclades, whose communities as such constantly deputed sacred embassies, provided solemn sacrifices, and sent choirs of maidens to add beauty and solemnity to Delian festal gatherings. Such in general terms were the Cyclades, islands far more noteworthy than the Sporades. A detailed examination of Strabo's account and list first of the Sporades and then of the Cyclades is now necessary. If it be desired to give a list of the Sporades according to Strabo, the matter will be a difficult one. But though he does not mention all, the following are some of them. Thera (p. 484, and cf. p. 485 quoted above), Thucydides to the contrary notwithstanding, is one of Strabo's Aegean Sporades, Amorgos is distinctly classed as such (p. 487 end). Anaphe is classed along with Thera (p. 485, cf. Apollonius Rhod. iv. 1709), Sicinos, Ios, Pholegandros, and Gyaros, as of the Sporades, so that all insignificant islands in the neighbourhood of the Cyclades are added to those of equally small pretensions to the eastward—the Carpathos group, the Calydnae isles, and all manner of small fry in the neighbourhood of Rhodes, Cos, and Samos —these are the Sporades.[1]

And now for the list of the chosen Cyclades given by Strabo (p. 485, book x.) He says somewhat vaguely: "The number given to begin with was twelve,[2] but several have been added to the list." Then he quotes Artemidorus—an Ephesian who wrote eleven books on geography

[1] For fuller information from other authors as well as Strabo, see the article "Sporades" in Pape's *Wörterbuch der Eigennamen*, where a list is given as follows :—Anaphe, Astypalaea, Amorgos-Patage, Autoniate or Hiera, Ascania, Azibinthia, Atragia, Aigilia, Bouporthmos-Machia, Gyaros, Gerus, Donusa, Dionysia, Elaphonesos, Helene and Eulimna, Thera, Therasia, Icaria (Icaros), Ios, Hieracia, Hippouris, Casos, Crapathos (Carpathos), Calydnä and Calydna, Calymna, *Cimolos*, Cos (Coos), Corsia, Cinaethos, Corassiae, Caminia, Cinara, *Cythnos* and Cothon, Leros, Lebinthos, Lea, *Melos*, Nisyros, Nicasia, Patmos, Proconnesos, *Paros*, Platea, Sicinos, *Seriphos*, Scylos, Sapyle, Syrnos, Schinussa, Syme, Telos, *Tenos*, Tenedos, Hypere, Pholegandros, Phacusia, Chalcia, Odia, Oletandros, Olearos. I have italicised those names which are also to be found on Strabo's list of twelve Cyclades. The result is that there are sixty-three islands to which, by some one or another, the name Sporades has been given, and that only six islands (Andros, Myconos, Naxos, Syros, Ceos, and Siphnos) on the usual list of Cyclades have never, so far as we know, been classed as Sporades.

[2] Pape, quoting (*s.v.* Κυκλάς) Steph. Byz., says that according to the ancients there were more than twelve, and then gives the list of Stephanus, as follows :—(1) Aegina; (2) Amorgos; (3) *Andros*; (4) Antissa; (5) Aspis; (6) Astypalaea; (7) Delos; (8) Icaros; (9) Ios; (10) Kos; (11) Casos and Nasion; (12) *Cythnos*; (13) *Melos*; (14) *Myconos*; (15) *Naxos*; (16) Nisyros; (17) *Paros*; (18) Peparethos; (19) *Siphnos*; (20) Telos; (21) *Tenos*; (22) Tragiae; (23) Olearos. It will be seen that except Cimolos, Syros, Seriphos, and Ceos, all of Strabo's twelve are on this list in italics.

early in the first century B.C.—who enumerates fifteen Cyclades as follows :—(1) Ceos; (2) Sithnos; (3) Seriphos; (4) Melos; (5) Siphnos; (6) Cimolos; (7) Prepesinthos; (8) Oliaros; (9) Paros; (10) Naxos; (11) Syros; (12) Myconos; (13) Tenos; (14) Andros;[1] (15) Gyaros. Out of these Strabo takes, without comment, (8) Oliaros and (7) Prepesinthos, and with a reason (15) Gyaros, leaving just twelve, which number, he says, figured as that of the Cyclades at the very first. It is plain that Thucydides had a somewhat different list, since Thera was upon it, an island not thought of by Artemidorus, and classed by Strabo among the Sporades.

The reason which Strabo gives for excluding Gyaros from the chosen islands is evidently the fact that it was bare of all resources. He tells an anecdote to illustrate this, and finally quotes a line from the *Elegant Trifles* of Aratus, where Leto is reproachfully apostrophised for passing her votary by, even as she passed Pholegandros or Gyaros by. Thus we are brought round again to the divine selection of certain islands to be the holy Cyclades.

After the day of Strabo the number twelve was apparently adhered to, for the phrase Dodekanisia—*Twelve-islands*—survived into Byzantine and mediaeval times, and finally seems to have stood for many, if not all, islands in the Aegean.[2] The word Archipelago, which arose in the later days of Italian supremacy, seems never wholly to have lost its reference to the sea. Bursian (quoting Forbiger) is my authority for understanding it as a corruption of *Aegaeon pelagos*.[3]

[1] It is interesting to note that two of the Bahamas bear the name Andros, not, however, taken from the Aegean, but probably from Governor Andros of memory unblessed in the colonial records of the United States of America. A French navigator also tried to fix the name *Grandes Cyclades* upon a group lying south of the Caroline Islands.

[2] It would seem that Diocletian's ἐπαρχία νήσων Κυκλάδων survived under this altered name, which corrected the implication that all its fifty-three islands were of the sacred twelve.

[3] Bursian, iii. p. 351, note 2; Forbiger, *Handbuch der alten Geographie*, ii. p. 19 ff. : Αἰγαῖον πέλαγος, Aegeopelago, Agiopelago, Azopelago,

It remains now to consider what are the modern Cyclades and Sporades. The modern Department of the Cyclades covers practically all islands that group themselves around Delos, Rhenea, and the twelve Cyclades of old. These are those islands lying east of the Peloponnesus and north of Crete which are not misruled by Turkey, but enjoy freedom under the kingdom of Greece. East of these lie the Turkish islands, to which (large and small alike) is given the name of Sporades. Certain Greek islands, north and east of Euboea, are now sometimes called the Northern Sporades, a convenient use of the term which Strabo would not have found it easy to understand.

Archipelago. The form Arcipelago occurs first in a treaty of June 30th, 1268, between Michel Palaeologus and Venice.

APPENDIX X

THE WORSHIP OF APHRODITE AND OF STRANGE GODS AT DELOS

PAUSANIAS (IX. xl. 3), in speaking of ancient wooden idols (ξόανα) traditionally attributed to Daedalus, says: "The Delians also have a rather small wooden image of Aphrodite, the right arm of which by the lapse of years has suffered grievous disfigurement. The lower part of it is square, and there are no feet. I am convinced that Ariadne received this image from Daedalus, and that when she went with Theseus she took it with her from home. Now the Delians say that when Theseus had been parted from her he dedicated the image to Delian Apollo, that he might not, by bringing it home with him, have the remembrance of Ariadne revived and be constantly renewing his griefs [1] on account of the love of her."

The form in which Pausanias gives this legend, which is no doubt its latest one, throws an interesting light upon the following observation [2] of M. Homolle: "Il n'est pour ainsi dire, pas une légende délienne qui n'ait sa contre-partie dans une légende athénienne,[3] destinée à prouver la primauté religieuse d'Athènes et ses droits sur Délos." In the above passage of Pausanias we read an Athenian legend which had

[1] Paus. I. xxii. 5. [2] Note 32 to his article "Delia" above quoted.
[3] This is true even of the birth-legend of Apollo and Artemis, partially transferred by Attic legend to Cape Zoster, in Attica. Pausanias, I. xxxii. 1. Cf. Baiter and Sauppe, *Orat. Att.*, Hyperides, fr. 286, 39, and 286, 65.

evidently driven the original Delian account of the ancient statue of Aphrodite from the minds even of the native Delians. If Theseus played any part in their original story, it was probably not the *beau rôle* of a faithful lover; it is only or chiefly in Athenian legends that Theseus is the plaintiff (ὁ ἀφαιρεθείς).[1]

This story of Theseus then may be classed with the other Attico-Delian legend to the effect that Theseus taught the islanders their characteristic *crane-dance*. They danced this around the altar of horns in a strange building[2] placed in front of Apollo's Delian temple, which has been ingeniously described under the name of the Hall of Bulls. This dance is reported to have been a representation of the way of Theseus through the mazes of the Cretan Labyrinth. If the name crane-dance implies resemblance to the lines of flocking cranes that move across Greek skies, then the comparison to Theseus in the Labyrinth falls of its own weight, and a far nearer parallel is the modern peasant's dance called the Syrtos.[3]

To reconstruct the forgotten Delian legend of the crane-dance would be as impossible as to ascertain what account the ancient Delians gave of their wooden idol of Aphrodite. It is probable that anciently the local cults of Delos and Naxos were most closely united; the antiquity of the colossal statue set up by the Naxians at Delos proves their especial devotion to Apollo, as do also abundant traces of his early worship on Naxos. The reasons for identifying Ariadne with Aphrodite, as one phase of that

[1] Cf. Pausanias, X. xxix. 4.
[2] It appears to have been upwards of 220 feet long and only 40 feet wide. See M. Homolle's account in the *Bulletin de Correspondance Hellénique*.
[3] This dance is consecrated in the minds of Greek patriots by the fact that it is associated with the heroic defence of the Khan of Gravia. There, as the enemy approached, and it became evident that a picked company must stand out against them, the gallant Odysseus led off the Syrtos whereby he gathered his chosen band of 180 into the Khan of Gravia, that modern Greek Thermopylae whose Leonidas survived with nearly all his men.

elusive godhead, are abundant, and therefore it seems likely that the most ancient worship of Aphrodite at Delos was the same in origin with that of Ariadne upon Naxos. There appear in fact to have been two aspects of this Aphrodite-Ariadne, (1) the one whom Dionysus espoused, a triumphant and immortal goddess, (2) she who was forsaken of Theseus and doomed to a lonely death. As the springtime bride of Dionysus, Ariadne was the gladsome spirit of love and vegetation. As the forsaken spouse of Theseus, she was that same spirit doomed to a wintry eclipse. Both of these phases recur in Cypriote as in Assyrian legends. In Cyprus Aphrodite was entombed as Ariadne-Aphrodite. The legend of Theseus' abandonment of Ariadne in the form less creditable to him was also current in Cyprus.

The other links between Delos and Aphrodite, not the Paphian goddess in particular, but the goddess at large, and more especially her eastern prototypes and parallels, belong to the latter days of Delian independence and to that final period when, after 166 B.C., Delos was restored to control nominally Athenian but really Roman. This was a time when distinctions between the gods of one people and those of another were falling away, and when each god of Greece and Rome tended to become every other one. By this time Apollo certainly may well have begun to feel that he had little pre-eminence at Delos, and could hardly recognise in the great emporium for buying and selling *slaves* the island of his birth.

Not far from the most ancient cave temple on the flanks of Mount Cynthus was set apart what may be called the precinct of the foreign gods, and there an inscription has been found *to Eros Harpocrates Apollo.*[1]

Here is combination and to spare. In the Eleusinian rites divinities such as Rhea Cybele and Demeter were merged into one, but only in the fulness of time, when their worships and their stories, after running parallel, had

---

[1] See upon this whole subject two admirable articles by M. Hauvette Besnault in the *Bulletin de Correspondance Hellénique* for 1882.

gradually been united. This gradual fusion was impossible in the case of Apollo and Harpocrates or Horus, two names for one Egyptian god whose resemblance to Apollo was purely superficial. Through this Egyptian interloper Apollo on his own native soil becomes one with the god Eros, and thus enters into union with Aphrodite the mother of all loves. But perhaps this point should not be insisted upon, and we should rather say that the precinct of the foreign gods on Mount Cynthus of Delos became foreign soil, where Apollo was neither really himself nor even first among the strange gods who there broke down the reserve of his nature and made themselves identical with him. Such an exterritorial character in this precinct seems implied by an inscribed enumeration of divinities where Apollo is neither first nor last among a whole procession of Egyptian gods and goddesses—Harpocrates, Serapis, Apollo, Isis, and Anubis. This precinct was certainly not in existence until the days of the breaking up of pagan divinities, and its Egyptian gods were unknown in the early days of the purer, nobler, and more exclusively Grecian rite of Delian Apollo. And yet its nearest neighbouring shrines are the oldest on the whole island. The precinct itself is on the western slope of Mount Cynthus, next to the most ancient holy way. This holy way led from the summit—where was the old-time temple of Zeus Cynthius and Athena Cynthia—to that mysteriously primeval place of Delian worship called the cave-temple of Apollo. Near by and a little below on the downward journey to the plain and city of Delos lay this precinct of the foreign gods. In it were two diminutive temples or shrines, one of Serapis and one of Isis. Just below and northward runs the bed of a ravine bordered by what is believed to have been the Cabirion, a temple for the worship of the more or less unclean and unmentionable Cabiri.[1] These gods came originally from Phoenicia, and

[1] The German School at Athens made important discoveries in excavating the Cabirion close to Thebes in Boeotia. This was in the winter 1888-89.

were associated with the mysteries of Samothrace, a northward island where were cultivated the less noble and more questionable aspects of a nature worship in substance not unlike that of Eleusis.

The presence here of Phoenician Cabiri may prepare us for another Phoenician divinity with whom we have been lately occupied: I mean the so-called Syrian goddess. The ready confusions and hastily made conglomerations of latter-day pagan worship are nowhere more conspicuous than in the latest, the cosmopolitan era of Delos. No worship more fully illustrates it than this of Syrian Aphrodite. We must not, though we rightly call her Aphrodite, connect her too closely with the Paphian goddess. On the other hand she was in the latter days not purely Phoenician, but was associated in worship with Egyptian Isis; and her cult, with that of the other strange gods in this precinct, was supervised and administered by Greek officials.

This had a curious result, *i.e.* the establishment by Phoenicians under native management of a second worship of the Syrian goddess Atargatis. The reason for this striking duplication of sanctuaries and observances in honour of one and the same goddess is that newly arrived Syrians, merchants fresh from Beyrut, from Antioch and from Sidon, found at Delos, in the Syrian goddess worshipped in Greek fashion on the north-western spur of Mount Cynthus, nothing which they recognised as their own.

Three several times, then, and under three guises, did Aphrodite visit Delos. Once as Ariadne forsaken of the hero Theseus, once as a sort of Isis in the company of the Cabiri and the chief gods of Egypt, and once as the Atargatis worshipped by the Phoenician and Syrian colony established for commerce in later days.

APPENDIX XI

PHOTOGRAPHS REFERRED TO FOR ILLUSTRATIONS

N.B.—*By the kindness of Mr. Leaf I am able to place certain numbers on his list, as well as many upon that for which I am now chiefly responsible, at the disposal of those who might wish to procure illustrations. The lists in question are issued by the Society for the Promotion of Hellenic Studies. Those of my readers who belong to that society can procure all these and many other Greek pictures at cost price. Those who are not members of the Hellenic Society will find below the prices at which they can procure various illustrations as enumerated.*—L. D.

I.— LIST OF PHOTOGRAPHS TAKEN IN GREECE AND CYPRUS, JANUARY TO JUNE 1888, BY MR. MALCOLM MACMILLAN AND MR. LOUIS DYER.

Notice.—These photographs measure 8×6 inches and may be procured at a cost, including postage, of 12s. per dozen from Messrs. Walker & Boutall, 16 Clifford's Inn, Fleet Street, London, E.C. Single prints may be obtained at 1s. each.

(a) ATHENS

The Acropolis

No.
1. The Theatre of Dionysus.
2. A Cyclopean wall (near the Asclepieum).
3. A Cyclopean pit (near the same).
7. The Bastion of Odysseus, the defender of Gravia (since destroyed).
8. The Propylaea (from Cimon's Wall).
9. ,,   ,,   (from the top of the Parthenon).
14. The Parthenon, N.W. corner through a Byzantine arch of the Erechtheum, showing in the middle distance foundations attributed to the age of Pisistratus.
18. The same (foundations seen from the roof of the Acropolis Museum).

Acropolis Museum

21. An ephebus (of the Apolline type).

Lower Town

23. The Temple of Zeus (Olympieum)—connected by its final dedication with the deification of the Roman emperors—and the Bed of Illissus.

The Carapanos Museum

25. Aphrodite and Eros (terra cotta).

Central Museum

30. A satyr found near Lamia.
32. A sleeping maenad found S. of the Acropolis.

(b) ATTICA

Suburbs of Athens

No
34. Colonos, the Cephissus (crossed lower down by the Eleusinian procession).
35.   „   Hill of Demeter Euchloos.

The Piraeus

40. The babe Plutus found in the water near Eetionea (Central Museum).

Eleusis

42. General view including the "Secos."
43. Lower gateway, medallion.
44. Appius Pulcher's gateway, débris.

Icaria (Sto Dionyso)

46. Rapendosa valley and cave.
47.   „   cave.
48. View from the brow of Rapendosa cliff, forming the Sto Dionyso valley towards Marathon and Styra in Euboea.
49. View from the same toward the Pentelic range.

The American Find at Icaria

50. The ruined church untouched.
51. The ruined church pulled down.
52. Replica of "Marathonian Soldier," a head (archaic) and a Bas-relief (stele).
53. The replica and a muleteer.
54. A crown of Icarian ivy devoted to Dionysus.
55. A bas-relief from the Icarian Pythion.

Sunium

No.
56. The temple of Athena, near view.
57. The same, far view, being "Cap Colonnas."

(c) THE CYCLADES

Syra

58. Old Syra—The Roman Catholic Upper Town.
59. The same (distant view).
60. A glimpse down a street of Old Syra.
61. Hermupolis—Shipping, a Chiote Bombarda.
62.   „   „   a Perama.
63.   „   „ .   a Trechanderi from Siphnos, a Goelette and a Trechanderi from Santorin (Thera).
64. " La Caramanienne "—performed by Syriote butchers.
65. The Psariana.
66. The Potamos: a street in Hermupolis.
67. Episcopio, view from the church terrace (inland).
68. The same, towards Rhenea.

The Syriote Museum

69. Stele from Paros, a poor man's gravestone.
70. Inscription from Ios.

Delos

71. The Lake of Leto.
72. Mount Cynthus, from the lake.
73.   „   from Apollo's temple.
74. Mount Cynthus, Cave temple from a Roman house.
75.   „   Cave temple (foundations).
76.   „   „

No.
77. Temple (on the slope of Mount Cynthus). Draped female statue of Isis.
78. Portrait-statue of Caius Ofellius by Dionysius and Timarchides of Athens.
79. Ruins of Apollo's temple.
80. Acroterion from same (Central Museum).
81.   ,,   ,,
82. The Naxian Colossus.
83. Rhenea from Mt. Cynthus and the lesser of the Rheumatiari Reefs.

NAXOS

84. The Gateway of Dionysus.
85. Mt. Coronis.
86. The Valley of Paratrecho, and Mt. Zia or Ozia.

TENOS

87. Mt. Burgo and the Sanctuary of the Evangelistria.

(d)—CYPRUS

LIMASSOL

88. St. Nicholas monastery, a ruin near Cape Gatto.
89. The castle of the Knights Templars at Colossi.

BAFFO

90. The ruins at Old Paphos (Couclià), after the British excavations.
91. Inscription from Old Paphos (elaeochristion).
92. The Eros of Paphos, from temple of Aphrodite. *Ibid.*
93. Same, profile view.
94. A terra cotta head from Old Paphos.
95. The Coucliote Diggers at Old Paphos.
96. The Bleeding Column, New Paphos.

LAPETHIA—CERYNIA

No.
97. A tomb and a monastery at Lapethus.
98. A Byzantine fort in Cerynia.
99. The cloister at Bello Pais.
100. The castle " Dieu d'Amour."

SALAMIS

101. The rampart and moat of Famagosta.
102. St. George and the cathedral-mosque of Famagosta.
103. Famagosta cathedral, from the rampart.
104. The same, nearer view.
105. The same, chantry door.
106. The same, minaret.
107. Gateway of the Lusignan palace at Famagosta.

THE VISCONTA

108. St. Sophia, the cathedral-mosque of Nicosia.

(e)—WESTERN GREECE

AEGINA

109. The temple of Athena, from below.
110. The same from nearer N.E.
111.   ,,   ,,   S.E.

ARGOLIS

112. Tiryns citadel from the west.
113. The same, gallery toward Nauplia.
114. Argos museum, a Medusa.
115. Mycenae, the Lions' gate.
116. A Cyclopean bridge near Epidaurus
117. Theatre seats at Epidaurus.
118.   ,,   (orchestra)   ,,
119.   ,,   (stage)   ,,

ARCADIA

No.
120. The battlefield of Tegea.
121. Heads from a Tegean temple (of Athena Alea), C.M.
122. Bassae-Phigalia, temple from N.E.
123. The same, interior.

LACONIA

124. Sellasia valley (Skiritis).
125. The valley of the Eurotas from Vryliàs (Skiritis).
126. Spartan museum, the Omphalos relief.
127. An Amazon, etc. *Ibid.*
129. The Langgada, Pass (Taygetus) and distant Parnon.
130. The summit of Langgada Pass, Mt. Rindomo (Biscuit-mountain).
131. The same in another direction, southerly Mt. Pigadià.

OLYMPIA

133. Ruins of the Heraeum from the gymnasium.
134. The Hermes (bearing the babe Dionysus) from the Heraeum, now in the Syngro Museum.
135. Temple of Zeus, from Pelopion, E.$\frac{1}{2}$
136. ,,   ,,   ,,   W.$\frac{1}{2}$
137. The same, Metope, Nemean labour of Heracles, Syngro Museum.
138. The same, Metope, Athena, nearer and front view.
139. ,,   ,,   Augean labour, Syngro Museum.
140. ,,   ,,   the fetching of Cerberus, Syngro Museum.
141. ,,   Western pediment, Syngro Museum.
142. ,,   Eastern   ,,   ,,   ,,
143. ,,   Apollo from western pediment, Syngro Museum.
144. The Kladeos, from the eastern pediment.
145. The same, débris on the south side.
146. A well near the same.
147. N.W. entrance of the Stadium.
148. A pugilist of note, bronze in the Syngro Museum.

CEPHALLENIA

No.
149. A view toward Ithaca from the road near Same.

ITHACA

150. View from Mount Aëtos northward.
151. View on Mount Aëtos (cyclopean wall of "Odysseus' castle ").
152. The Grotto of the Nymphs (so called).

II.—CATALOGUE OF PHOTOGRAPHS OF GREECE BY MR. WALTER LEAF.

These Photographs measure about 7 × 5 inches, and may be procured at a cost of 1s. each in silver, or 1s. 6d. in platinum, from Mr. CASSTINE, Photographic Studio, Swanley, Kent. Platinum is recommended only for those marked with an asterisk. The profits on the sale will go to the Homes for Working Boys, Swanley.

ATHENS

2. *The British School: Lycabettus in background.
4. *The Acropolis from monument of Philopappus.
5. *The same : larger scale.
7. *Acropolis from Areopagus.

ELEUSIS

33. *Sekos from S.W. angle.
34. *View towards S.E.
35, 36, 37. Sekos from N.W. angle. (These three form a panoramic view.)
38. *Precinct of Pluto from S.
39. *Precinct of Pluto from N.
40. *Substructures of Sekos.

SUNIUM

No.
42. *From S.E.
44. *From E.
46. *From W.

43. *From N.E.
45. *From N.
47. *Interior, looking W.

OROPOS

51. Theatre at Amphiareion.
52. *The same, showing Proscenium.
53. *The same, from N.W.
56. *The same, showing Seat of Priest.

CORINTH

65. Temple from N.E.   66. Temple from E.

DELPHI

73. *General View.
74. *Substructure of Peribolos and Athenian Stoa.
76. *Castalian Spring.
77. *Relief in Museum.

MONASTERY OF ST. LUKE, STIRIS.

80. Church, West Front.
81. Church, South Side.
82, 83. East End (these two form a single view).
86. General View from S.E.: Parnassus in background.

HELICON (HIERON OF THE MUSES)

87. General View: Hill of Ascra to right.
88, 89. Proscenium of Theatre.

III.—List of Enlargements from Mr. Walter
Leaf's Photographs.

‍‍* These are selected from the list of eighty-nine small photographs which are already accessible to members of the Society for the Promotion of Hellenic Studies. *They are also to be had by the public at large through the Autotype Company, at No. 74 New Oxford Street, London, W.C.*

No.	Subjects	Dimensions
1.	Athens from the Monument of Philopappus	$17\frac{1}{2} \times 11\frac{3}{4}$ in.
2.	Temple of Sunium, from N.E.	$17\frac{1}{2} \times 11\frac{1}{2}$,,
3.	Temple of Sunium, East end	$17\frac{1}{2} \times 12$,,
4.	Temple of Corinth	$17\frac{1}{2} \times 11$,,
5.	Delphi: General View	$17\frac{1}{2} \times 11$,,
6.	Delphi: Peribolos Wall and Stoa of the Athenians	$17\frac{1}{2} \times 11$,,
7.	Eleusis: Remains of the Hall of the Mysteries	$17\frac{1}{2} \times 11\frac{1}{2}$,,
8.	Eleusis: Precinct of Pluto	$17\frac{1}{4} \times 11\frac{1}{2}$,,
9.	View of St. Luke, Stiris: Parnassus in the background	$17\frac{1}{2} \times 11\frac{1}{4}$,,

INDICES

I.—INDEX OF AUTHORS AND SOURCES

ACTS, chap. xiii., *290*
Adams, Henry, *History of United States*, *267*
Aelian, story of the cure of a horse by Serapis from, *254*
Aeneas Sylvius de' Piccolomini, *326*
Aeschylus, *Edoni*, fr. 55, *158*; *Eumen.* 22 ff., *25*; *Prom.* 806, *177*
Agnese, Battista, Portulano of, described, *329* f.
Allen, Professor F. D., on the University of Leyden, *347*
Ameis-Hentze's *Iliad*, *317*
Andocides, *de Mysteriis*, 110-112, *175*
Anthology, ix. 75, *108*
Anthropological Institute, Journal of, *169* f.
d'Anville, *Recherches Géographiques sur l'île de Chypre*, *326*
Apollinaris Sidonius, witness for Apollonius, *265* f.
Apollodorus, *Bibliotheca*, I. iii. 5, *49*; I. v. 2, *64*; I. v. 4, *63*; III. x. 1, *119*; III. xiii. 6, *63*; III. xiv. 7, *105*, *107*
Apollonius Rhodius, iv. 1709, *396*
Apollonius of Tyana, letters attributed to, xxxiii., *223*
Apuleius, *261* f.
Arabantinos, work on Epirus, *89*

Aratus, *Elegant Trifles* by, *397*; *Phaen.* 91, 138, *111*
Archaeological Society, the Greek, at Eleusis, *186*
Archaeology (American), Journal of, 2, *104*
Archéologique, Revue, 227, 229
Archilochus, *Frag.* 3, *Frag.* 51, *365*
Architects, Royal Society of British, Proceedings of, 252, *314*; plan reproduced from, *398*
Aristides, prayer of, to inspired dreams, *236*, *242*
Aristophanes, *Birds*, 28, schol. on, 874, *85*, 96. *Frogs*, jibes at Dionysus, *78*; 312, 154 ff., 316-459, *212*; 372-459, *185*; schol. on 158, *181*. Schol. on *Knights*, 697, *107*. *Peace*, 374, *181*. *Plutus*, 727, *177*. *Thesmophoriazousae*, 68. *Wasps*, 9, *85*
Aristotle, *Const. Ath.* on Epimenides, *123* f.; 3, *130*; 13, *129*; 15, *126*, *137*; 16, *126*. *Eth. Eud.* i.; init. *Eth. Nicom.* i. 8 fin., *383*. Fr. 447, *382*. *Politics*, v. 9, *129*; v. 12, *126*. *Rhetoric*, iii. 16, cites *Antigone*, 911 f., *166*. περὶ θαυμασίων ἀκουσμάτων, cxxii. 133, *93*.
Artemidorus, on the Cyclades, *395* f.

INDEX

Athenaeus, *Deipnos.* ii. 40 A. *111*; iii. 78, *82*; 416 B, *51*; 533 C, *125*; 609, *126*; xiv. 614 B, *382*
Attar, Leonida, unpublished map of Cyprus by, *287*

BACCHYLIDES, fr. 64, *62*
Bachut, E., *Histoire de la Médecine*, etc., *110*
Backofen's *Mutterrecht*, *168*
Baglione, life of Astorre, *332*
Bähr, on Orpheus, in Pauly, *127*
Barry, F. W., "Report on Census of Cyprus, 1884," *272*
Bartolommeo "da li Sonetti," rhymed account of Venetian islands by, *330*; on Cythera, *286*; sonnets on "Sdiles," *356*
Bayle's *Dictionary*, translated in 1735, *266*
Bede, *Commentary on the Acts*, *290*
Benndorf, *195*
Bentley, *115*, *262*
Bergeat, Herr Alfred, researches of, on Cypriote geology, *275* f.
Bergk, *Griechische Litteraturgeschichte*, *112*, *317*
Bernhardy, G., *Griechische Litteraturgeschichte*, *115*, *116*, *123*, *127*, *136*, *317*. On Philostratus, *260*
Bibliothèque Nationale, *Dante* (1481) from the Vatican in the, *331*
Bie, Oscar, *Die Musen in der Antiken Kunst*, *104*
Bikelas, D., on Greek doctors, *267* ff.; *Loukis Laras* by, *389*
Birdwood, Sir George, K.C.I.E., *85*; on Dionysus, *164* f.
Birmingham Speculative Club, essay read before the, *226*
Blaeuw, *Atlas Major* of John and William, *343*, *346* f.
Boccaccio, *Teseide*, VII. stanza 43, *286*
Boissier, Gaston, "La religion Romaine," *15*
Bordone, Benedetto, *Isolario* of, *328* f.

Braun, Emil, Dr., *Kunstvorstellungen des geflügelten Dionysus*, *179*
Brenzone, life of Astorre Baglioni by, *332*
Britannica, Encyclopaedia, article "Cyclades," criticised, *394*
British Museum, additional MSS., Earl of Guilford, No. 8630. *336*
Brown, Horatio F., *The Venetian Printing Press*, *329*
Brucker, James, on Meursius, *350*
Brunn, *Denkmäler der Antiken Kunst*, by Dr., *195*, *249*, *270*, *379*
Buck, Carl, on the American find at Icaria, *104*
Bursian, *346*, *397*
Bustrone's *Istoria di Cipro* MSS., *335* f.
Byzantius, Stephanus, *394*

CALLIMACHUS, *Hymn to Apollo*, 58-63, *384*. *Hymn to Delos*, 1-5, *370*; 30 ff. and 92 f., *359*; 82 ff., *78*; 206 ff., *356*; 260 ff., *357*; 300 ff., *359*, *393*; 308 ff., *379*
Carr, Lucien, Women among the Huron-Iroquois, *171*
Casaubon, Meric, on Apollonius, *266*
Cassel, Verein deutscher Philologen und Schulmaenner at, *104*
Cervantes, "Journey to Parnassus," *24*
Chaucer, "Knight's Tale," 1363, *286*
Christus Patiens, *4*, *139*
Cicero, *Ad Atticum*, vi. 1, *188*; v. 15, vi. 1, *258*. *Phil.* II. xliii. 110, XIII. xix. 41, *37*
Cicogna, *331*
Claudian, on Cyprus, *274*
Clement, of Alexandria, *Protrept.* iii. ad fin., *309*; p. 30, *177*
Clement the Roman, *Homil.* v. 23, *309*

416   INDEX

Colvin, Mr. Sidney, on the Homeric Hymn to Demeter, *54* f., *57* f., *150*
Comparetti, on date of Orphic fragments, *181*
Corlieu, "Étude médicale sur la retraite des 10,000," *225*
Cornhill, vol. xxxiii. June, 1876, *54*
Coronelli, *Isolario* of, *343*; *Morea* of, *288*
Correr Museo, unpublished map in, *287*
Cudworth, *265* f.

DANTE, *Par.* xix. 22, *74*; xxi. 71, *42*
Daremberg, Charles, *État de la Médecine entre Homère et Hippocrate*, *226*; on Hippocrates, περὶ εὐσχημοσύνης, *238*; *Histoire des Sciences Médicales*, *223*; "Études d'archéologie médicale sur Homère," *227*; list of Alexandrine doctors, *219*
Daremberg et Saglio, *Dictionnaire des Antiquités*, 66, *185* f., *363*, *371*, *376* f., *399*
Daurès, Gabriel, on "Delos," *373* f.
Dawkins, Mr. Clinton, *164*
Diehl, Ch., *Excursions archéologiques en Grèce*, *387*
Dilettanti, Society of, *Unedited Antiquities of Attica, 186*; *Antiquities of Ionia, 387*
Dindorf, rejects *Bacch.* 286-297, *167*
Dio Cassius, 37 f., *261*
Diogenes Laertius, *125*, *382*; a quotation from Aristotle by, *382*
Domenichi, Ludovico, *Facezia*, *331*
Dörpfeld, Dr. William, *1*, *186*, *194*, *197*, 202
Dryden, *Palamon and Arcite*, 286
Duemmler, account of an early Semitic occupation of Cyprus, *280*
Duncker, *272*
Dyer, L., *179*

Ἑβδομάς, Athenian periodical, *89*

Eckermann, Conversations with Göthe, *162*, *166*
Edinburgh, Philosophical Institute of, *3*
Egger, A. E., *15*
Emperius places the Satrachus at Paphos, *346*
Engel, "Cyprus," *315* f., *323*, *352* f.
Epiphanios in Cyprus, *278* f.
Ἐπιθεώρισις, Ἀνατολική, Athenian periodical, *89*
Erasmus, *237*, *260*
Ersch and Grüber, *Allgemeine Encyclopaedie*, "Attica," *344*
Etymologicum Magnum, *107*, *344*, *359*, *391*
Eunapius, *188*
Euripides, *Alcestis*, 360, *177*. *Bacchanals*, *136-162*; lines 274-276, *185*; 303 ff., *99*; 385, 406 ff., *287*; 404 ff., *348*, *352* f.; 877-881, 897-901, *184*; 1344, *4*. *Electra*, *71*. Frag. 177, *318*; 394, *30*; 752, *25*. *Hecuba*, 457 ff., *363*; 459, *356*; 1267, *96*. *Helena*, 1098, *304*. *Heraclidae*, 66. *Ion*, 23, 35; 713, 5; 919 ff., *364*; 1571-1600, *391*; 1583, *393*. *Iph. in Tauris*, *34* f.; 264-274, *146*; 1089-1105, *358*, *363*; 1193, *210*; 1244, 25; 1401 f., *150*. *Rhesus*, 36, 99; 701, *391*. *Phoen.* 205 ff. and 226 ff., 25; 687, *48*
Eusebius of Caesarea, *263*, 290
Eustathius, on Dion. Per., *344*. On *Il.* i. 18, *327*; ii. 637, *165*, *344*; vi. 132, *132*
Evenus, of Ascalon, *Anthol.* ix. 75, *108*

FABRICIUS, note on Dio, 44, 6, 37 f.
Felix, Quintus Minucius, the *Octavius* of, *8*
Fitzgerald's *Rubaiyat*, *91*
Foerster, R., *Raub der Kora*, 70
Folk-Lore, J. G. Frazer on May festival, *89*

Forbiger, quoted by Bursian, *397* f.
Fortnightly, Mr. Pater's articles in the, *27*
Foster, B. W., M.D., Essay read before Birmingham Speculative Club, *226*
Foucart, M., work at Delphi, *33*
Fourcade, unpublished report of, on Cypriote agriculture, *281*
Frazer, J. G., the *Golden Bough*, *27*, *50*, *159*; on May festivals, *89*
Friedlaender, *Darstellungen aus der Sittengeschichte Rom's*, etc., *8*
Furtwaengler, on Alcamenes' *Aphrodite*, *270*; in Roscher's *Lexicon*, *271*

GAILLARD'S *Medical Journal*, *241*
Galen, *234* f.
Gardner, Mr. Ernest, *Excavations in Cyprus*, *305*
Gardner, Professor, on sculptures of Dionysus and Icarius, *105*
Gaudry, M. Albert, *Recherches scientifiques dans l'Orient*, *275-277*, *280*
Geel places Satrachus at Paphos, *346*
Gellius, xv. 10, *110*
Gennadius, *389*
Geographical Societies, publications of, Berlin, *275*; de *l'Est*, *387*; Munich, *275*; France, *275*
Géographie, Revue de, *324*
Geological map of Cyprus, *275*
Géologique, Société, *275*
Gildersleeve, Professor B. L., *Essays and Studies*, *258* f., *297*, *303*
Girard, Paul, *L'Asclépieion*, etc., *2*
Gladstone, the Right Hon. W. E., on Eumaeus, *47*
Gloucester, Warburton, bishop of, *180*
Goethe, on *Aberglaube*, 7; wished *Antigone* 904 ff. proved spurious, *166*. The *Bacchanals*, translation from, *162*; Conversations with Eckermann, *162*, *166*; on the sublime in Euripides, *162*

Grecques, Association des Études (Monuments), 70
Gregory, St., of Nazianzum, *4*
Grohs, Hugo, on Dio Cassius, *38*
Gronovius, A., *349* f.; J. F., *347*
Guardia, *La Médecine à travers les Siècles*, *226*

HARRISON, Miss Jane, and Mrs. Verrall, *Mythology and Monuments of Athens*, 27, *106*, *110*, *119*, *124*, *176*, *195*
Hauvette, M., on strange gods at Delos, *401*
Heffter, *315* f.
Hellenic Studies, Journal of, 2, *33*, *111* f., *181*, *305*
Hellénique, Bulletin de Correspondance, 2, *400* f.
Hermesianax, of Cyprus, *25*
Herodotus, i. 14, *92*; 28, *85*; 30, *122*; 35, *92*; 59, *129*; 105, *273*; 131, *298*; 169, *392*; 199, 298. ii. 48 f., *164*; 52, 77; 81, *164*; 97, *392*; 146, *165*; 170, 357; 171, *51*. iii. 90, *85*; 97, *63*; 119, *166*. iv. 79, 77; 94, 86. v. 4 f., *84*; 30, *392*; 67, *115*; 74, *198*. vi. 64, 75, *198*. vii. 6, *127*; 75, *85*. viii. 32, 25; 65, 209 f.; 138, *92*
Herophilus, *237* f.
Hesiod, *Theogony*, 347, 355, *98*; 406 ff., *357*; 455, *98*; 502, *112*; 769, *98*; 912, *50*; 913, *98*; 969 ff., 62, 97. *Works and Days*, 298, *51*; 463-466, *53*; 466, *52*; 502, *132*; 504 ff., *112*; 700 f., *359*
Hesychius, *82*, *120*, *132*, *344*
Heuzey, M., on Demeter Graia, 70
Hieronymus, note on Eusebius, *290*
Hippocrates, 220, *223*, 225, *234*, *238*; περὶ εὐσχημοσύνης, *238*
Hogarth, Mr. D. G., on Aphrodite of the Hittites, *320-322*; *Devia Cypria*, *282*, *290*, *345*
Holwerda, *272*

2 E

Homer, *Iliad*, ii. 695, *47*. iii. 374, *316*; 413 ff., *273*. v. 125, *47*; 131, 312, 371, 382, *316*; 500, *47*; 820, *316*. vi. 135, 77. xiii. 322, *46*, *52*. xiv. 193, 224, *316*; 325, *91*; 326, *48*. xvi. 514 ff., *29*. xx. 105, *316*. xxi. 76, *46*; 416, *316*. xxiii. 220, *91*. *Odyssey*, i. 93 f., 285, *61*. ii. 125, *48*; 214, 359, *61*. iv. 83, *284*; 702, *61*. v. 123 ff., *367*; 125 ff., *62*. vi. 162 ff., *355*. viii. 288, *317*; 308, *316*; 363, *287*. ix. 196-213, *91*. xi. *91*; 217, *48*. xiii. 250, *61*. xv. 409, *367*. xviii. 193, *317*. xix. 171 ff., *61*
Homeric Hymns, i. *372*; 16 ff., *356*; 30-45, *392*; 53 ff., *357*; 118 f., *356*; 135, 139, *357*. iv. 59, *287*; 247 ff., *271*, *273*. v. *54-68*; 4, *46*; 272, *215*. vii. 28, *284*. xvi. *245*. xxxiv. *163* f.
Homolle, M. Théophile, *2*, *33*, *389* f., 400; work at Delphi, *33*; lecture on Delos, *387*; article "Delia" in Daremberg and Saglio, *363*, *376* f., *399*
Horace, *Od*. iv. 5, 39, *38*; iv. 14, 25, *95*
Hutchinson, W., on *Northumberland*, *49*
Hyginus, *Fab*., 59, *65*; 130, *135*; 147, *64*; 191, *92*; 225, *119*; 276, *394*
Hyperides, fr. 286 (39, 65), *399*

IAMBLICHUS, a quotation from Aristotle by, *382*
Imola, Benvenuto da, Commentary on Dante, *25*
Im Thurm, testimony on couvade, *170*
Inscriptions, *43*; *C.I.G.* 3525, *14*; *C.I.L.* iii. 1, 685, *87*; found at Delos, *274*, *373*; found at Epidaurus, M. Kabbadias and the, *237*; J. P. Six on Cypriote coin bearing an, *344*

Institut, Mémoires de l', *326*
Isaiah, *281*

JACOB, on *Ant*. 904 ff., *166*
Jebb, Professor, *3*, *11*, *133*, *166* f.
Jerusalem, letter to the bishop of, *278*
Jowett, Dr., *127*
Judaeus, Philo, *Legatio ad Caium*, *14*
Justin Martyr, judgment on Apollonius attributed to, *266*

KABBADIAS, M., *2*, *237*
Kalogeropoulos, P. D., *88* f.
Kampouroglous, *89*
Keary, C. F., *6*, *9*, *16*, *52*, *371*
Kenyon, Mr. F. G., *126*, *132*, *137*
Kern, Dr., *194* f.
Kiel, Schriften der Universität zu, *104*
Kitchener, Major, map of Cyprus, *325*
Kock, Dr. Theodor, *215*
Krause, *44*

LAMI, edition of Meursius by, *349* f.
Landor, *150*
Lang, R. Hamilton, *280*, *288*
Largus, Scribonius, *237*
La Roche, edition of *Odyssey*, *61* !
Lebègue, *Recherches sur Délos*, *385*
Lehrs, *Populäre Aufsätze*, *10*, *20* f.
Lenormant, M. F., *66*, *70*, *185*, *217*
Leunclavius, *37*
Lloyd, Bishop, letter to Bentley, *262*
Lobeck's *Aglaophamus*, *127*
Lucan, *24* f.
Lucian, *107*, *259*, *261-263*, *270*, *388*
Lucretius, *300*, *304*
Lumbroso, G., *13*
Lusignan, Estienne de, *275*, *285* f., *334* ff., *342*
Lyall, Sir Alfred, *12*
Lycophron's *Alexandra*, 447 - 452, *345* f.
Lyon, Professor D. G., *301*

INDEX

Macmillan's Magazine, 27, 101
Macrobius, 30, 93, 96
Malgaigne, 225
Mannert, 353
Mannhardt, William, 27, 53, 97, 182, 208, 379
Marcellinus, Ammianus, 308
Marcian Library, unpublished MSS. of Meursius, 274; unpublished MS. of a speech by Zuanne Podocatharo, 340; Portulano No. 9, 329 f.; Bessarion's MSS. of Strabo, 325
Marianus, Scotus, 290
Marquardt, 38, 44, 393
Martial, 276
Mas Latrie, Comte de, 278, 326
Maximus Tyrius, 293
Médecine, Gazette de, 225
Medicine, Academy of (N.Y.), 241; Gaillard's *Journal of*, 241
Menander, 151
Merriam, Dr. A. C., 13-15, 32, 107 f., 111, 115-117, 133, 237, 241
Meursius, John, 346-354; *Ceramicus*, 349; (MSS.) *Cyprus*, 274 f., 290, 350-352; (Graev's edition) *Cyprus*, 347; "De denario Pythagorico," 350; on Lycophron, 346; *Pisistratus*, 347; "Themis Attica," 350; on Theocritus, 348
Middleton, Professor J. H., 33
Milton, 79, 360; *Comus*, 146, 148, 150
Minucius Felix, 20
Moellendorf, Wilamovitz, 238
Mommsen, 13, 83
More, Henry, the Platonist, 19, 264
Müller, E., 258
Müller, K. O., map of Salamis by, 344
Munro, J. Arthur R., 280
Musgrave, 346

Nation, The, of New York, 2, 23, 305
Nazianzum, Gregory of, 107
Newton, Sir Charles, 1, 69 f., 195

Nipperdey, on Tacitus, 43
Nonnus, 92, 109, 139; *Dionysiaca*, i. 5, 142; x. init. 99; xiii. 458 ff., 345; xiv. 120 ff., 99; xix. 261 ff., 95; xxvii. 283-307, 107; xlv. 99, 142; xlvi. passim 107-110
Northumberland, A view of, etc., 49 f.
Nouvelle Revue, 374

OBERHUMMER, Dr., 275 f., 278
Olympiodorus, 87
Omar, the Persian, 91
Origen, 258, 264, 278
Orphic Hymns on Dionysus, 22, 162
Orphic fragments, 181
Ortelius, Abraham, maps of Cyprus, 324, 326, 343, 135
Osann, on the Lesser Mysteries, 104, 124
Ovid, 64 f., 375, *Fasti*, iii. 717, 142; v. 145, 38. *Her.* ii. 65

PAMPHOS, 122, 175
Pandora, Athenian periodical, 89
Pape, *Dict. of Proper Names*, 132, 396
Pater, Mr., 26 f., 70, 101, 136, 169, 235 f., 242
Pathe, C. von Wulfften, on Philostratus, 259
Patzig, H., 27
Pauly's *Real-Encyclopaedie der Alterthumswissenschaft*, 44, 118, 127
Pausanias, 32, 218, 247, 285; I. ii. 5, 104; ii. 7, 135; iv. 5, 92; xiv. 1-4, 176; ibid. 3 f., 124; xxii. 1, 5, 399; xxxi. 4, 31, 82; xxxii. 1, 399; xxxviii. 3, 64, 122, 175; ibid. 7, 64. II. ii. 5, 6, 189; ibid. 14, 65; xxiv. 6, 99; xxxv. 4, 176. III. xix. 6, 179; xxiii. 1, 317. IV. iii. 10, 65. V. x. 8, 9. VIII. v. 2, 286; xxiv. 1, 6, 286; xxv. 4, 176; xlviii. 3, 377; liii. 3, 286. IX. xii. 3,

140; xx. 1, *119*; xl. 3, *399*; ibid. 3, 4, *379*. X. iv. 3, *132*; xxix. 4, *400*; xxxii. 6, *25*
Peabody Museum, Report of Trustees of, *171*
Penrose, Mr. F. C., *252*, *314*
Perrot and Chipiez, *310*
Perry, Mr. T. S., *172*
Petelia, Orphic inscriptions found at, *181*
Pfander on Euripides, *157*
Pherecydes, *64*
Philios, Dr., *1*, *196* f.
Philo, Judaeus, *14*
Philological Association, Transactions of the American, *15*, *347*
Philologus, the, *56*, *345*
Philostratus, *258-261*, *263*; *Epist.* 39, *107*
Phurnutus (Cornutus), quoted by Meursius, *274*
Piccolomini, Aeneas Sylvius de', *326* f.
Pindar, *71*, *130*. *Olympian Odes*, 1, *102*; 11, *71*; 12, *102*. *Pythian Odes*, 3, *8* ff., *369*; 9, *369*
Pius II. (de' Piccolomini), *326* f.
Plato, *19*. *Apol.* 21 B, *370*. *Epinomis*, 487 E, *297*. *Laws*, viii. init., *177*. *Rep.* ii. 364 B, *181*; 382 E-383 B, *370*
Plautus, *Mercator*, init., *272*
Pliny, *41* f., *253*. *Nat. Hist.* II. vi. 12, vii. 18, 19, *42*; VII. viii. 45, *42*; 59, *107*; 195, *294*
Plutarch, *Alexander*, 97; *Antony*, 24, 79; *Aristides*, 27, *210*; *Demetrius*, 26, *209*; *Flamininus*, 16, *40*; *Nicias*, 3, *379*; *Pericles*, 13, *191*; *Solon*, 12, *123*; 29, *116*, *126*; *Theseus*, 23, *377*
Plutarch, Pseudo-, *De Anima*, *110*; tract on Isis and Osiris, *22*; *De Fluviis*, *25*; *De primo frigido*, *113*; on Hesiod, *132*; *Quaest. Rom.*, *310*; *Sympos.*, *103*, *106*, *258*
Podocatharo, the family, *330-343*; Alessandro P., *339*; Hettore P.,

Ritratte del Regno di Cipro, *330-335*, *340-342*; Zuanne P., his appeal to Alvise Mocenigo (Marcian MSS.), *338-340*
Polemon, *218*
Porphyry, *72*
Potli, *88*
Praktika, *1*
Preller's *Greek Mythology*, *48*, *98*, *177*; Plew's revision, *318*; Robert's revision, *272*, *298*; Ritter and, *Hist. Phil.*, *177*
Procacci, Tommaso, *L'Isole piu famose del mondo*, *330-333*, *337* f.; *de' Funerali Antichi*, *331*; *Cagione delle Guerre Antiche*, *331*
Propertius, *14*
Ptolemy, Bessarion's MS. of, *324*
Pullan, R. P., *1*

QUINTILIAN, *42*

RAGOZIN, Mme. Zenaïde, *302*
Ralli and Potli, *Church History*, *88*
Rapp, *Beziehungen des Dionysoskultes zu Thracien*, *83*
Reber, Professor, *History of Art*, *308*
Ribbeck, Otto, *Anfaenge des Dionysoskults in Attica*, *104*, *125*, *129*, *132*
Ritter and Preller, *177*
Robert, Carl, interpretation of vase-pictures by, *94*
Ronchaud, M., *371*
Roscher, Dr. W. H., *402*; *Ausführliches Lexicon der Griechischen und Roemischen Mythologie*, *120*, *159*, *270*, *292*
Ross, Dr. L., *290*, *352*, *389*
Royal Institute, lecture before, *39*
Ruhnken, *54*

SALIGNACIUS, BARTHOLOMAEUS, *Itinerarii*, *290*
Sandys, Dr., *142*, *146*, *148*
Sappho, *274*, *304*
Sassenay, le Marquis de, *324*
Scherer, Chr., *176* f., *194*

Schliemann, Dr. H., *106*, *286*
Schöne on Euripides, *157*
Schramm's *Life of Meursius*, *348*
Schwalbe, *166*
Seeley, Professor, on Roman Imperialism, *39*
Semus of Delos, *382*
Seneca, *290*
Servius, confusions about Parnassus, *24*, *85*, *107*
Sibylline Oracles, *290*
Sidonius Apollinaris, *265*
Six, Dr. J. P., *344*
Smith, Mr. Cecil, *181*
Smith, Mr. R. Elsey, *252*, *305-308*
Sophocles, *133*. *Antigone*, 904-915, discussion of interpolation of, *166* f.; 1115-1152, *133* f.; 1119, the reading *Icaria* justified, *133*; 1126, 1144 f., *25*; 1200, *177*. *Philoctetes*, 177, 237. *Triptolemus*, *71*
Stephanus, Byzantinus, *105*, *181*, *274*, *344*
Strabo, *183* f., *325*, *327*, *341*, *395-397*; 37, *358*; 271, *356*; 371, *103*; 375, *237*; 383, *218*; 394, *345*; 395, *189*; 412, *118*; 417 f., *25*; 463-474, *94*; 467, *184*; 468, *132*, *159*; 474, *395*; 479, *123* f.; 484, *396*; 480, *360*; 485, *359*, *362*, *395* f.; 564, *85*; 633, *122*; 683, the traditional punctuation changed according to Bessarion's MSS., *325*
Suetonius, *14*, *37* f.
Sybaris, Orphic fragments found at, *181*
Syncellus, *119*

TACITUS, *Ann.* i. 72, iv. 42, xii. 4, xiii. 11, *43*; iv. 20, *42*; iv. 55, *44*. *Hist.* iv. 81, *42*

Themistius, *116*
Theocritus, *318*, *394*
Theognis, *356*, *381*, *384*
Theopompus, *126*
Thiersch, *130*
Thraemer, *179*
Thucydides, *131*, *361-363*
Tomaschek, *86*
Tournefort's description of Cyprus, *385*
Tylor, Dr., *169* f., *289-297*
Tyrius, Maximus, *293*
Tyrrell, Professor, *157*, *162*, *166* f.

UNGER, Dr. Robert, *345*
Uspergensis, Abbas, *290*

VERCOUTRE, Dr., *229*
Verrall, Mrs., *27*, *124*
Vienna, Reports of Academy, *86*
Virgil, *Aeneid*, iii. 15, *85*; 73, *359*; 74, *358*; 85-101, *370*. *Georgics*, i. 21-31, *124*
Vitruvius, *191*
Voigt, F. A., *97*, *120*, *159*, *176* f.

WARBURTON, *The Divine Legation of Moses*, *180*
Wecklein, rejects *Bacch.* 286-297, *167*
Wegener, Dr., on the Hymn to Demeter, *56*
Wilmans, Dr., on Dio Cassius, *38*

XENOPHON, his record of military medicine, *225*. *Anab.* I. ii. 13, 92. *Mem.* III. iii. 12, *376*; IV. ii. 8 ff., *225*

ZENODOTUS, on *Odyssey* text, *61*
Ziegler, on Cyprus, *308*, *327*
Zonaras, *37*

II.—General Index

ABONOTICHUS, serpent impostures of Alexander of, *254*
Abraham, statue of, in Lararium of Severus, *265*
Academy, Cicero proposes a gate for the, *188*
Acamantis, Philonides named Cyprus, *274*
Acamas, a mountain of Cyprus and of Salamis, *187, 344, 352* f.
Acanthus-leaf, on the capitals of the Epidaurian Tholos, *252*
Accad, Aphrodite came from unknown, *303*
Accounts, inscriptions concerning, found at Eleusis and Delos, *195, 207, 387*
Achilles, the Apolline ideal and, *9*; fire-baptism of, *64*; Chiron's pupil, *232*
Acropolis (Athenian), chamber on, devoted to remains of Aesculapian temple, *249*
Acropolis (Eleusinian), *187, 199, 203* f.
Acta publica, consulted by Dio Cassius, *38*
Actor, inspiration of, by Dionysus, *117*
Adonis, *291* f.
Aeëtes, *231*
Aegae, Apollonius and Maximus at the temple of Aesculapius at, *255, 257* f.
Aegean, Archilochus the poet of the, *365*; festivals of the, *389*; Venetians and Greeks in the, *328, 389*; Delian centre of the, *387*; Archipelago, a name of the, *397*
Aegina, *187, 223*
Aegipan, *98-100*
Aegyptos, river, Nysa close to, *163* f.
Aelian, ridiculous credulity of, *259*

Aeneas, virtues of, *39*; Chiron's pupil, *232*
Aeolus, housed on Tenos, *380*
Aeschylus, the record of the couvade and, *169-171*; Dionysus the tutelary god of, *81*
Aesculapius, *15, 220, 222, 231* f., *235* f., *239* f., *242, 245, 255*; medicine and, *15, 220, 226, 234*, f., *237* f. ; myth of, *15, 220* f., *230* f., *232* f., *234* f., *244-246*, *254, 256*; other gods and, *15, 240, 242* f.; Amphiaraus and, *232*; Aphrodite and, *270* f.; Apollo and, *15, 219* f., *231, 239-242*; Apollonius of Tyana and, *220, 255, 257*; attendant divinities and, *240*; Demeter and, *194, 219* f., *270* f.; Dionysus and, *194, 220* f., *247*; Persephone and, *219* f.; Serapis and, *254*; Zeus and, *15, 21, 219* f., *239*; worship of, *229* f., *236, 238* f., *243, 247, 249, 254, 361*; at Aegae, *255-258*; at Athens, *2, 5, 242, 248* f.; at Cos, *194* f., *221, 225*; at Epidaurus, *2, 5, 219* f., *220, 243-245, 248-254*; among the Lapithae and Phlegyae, *194* f., *221, 233* f.; at and near Rome, *221, 234* f., *243, 254*; in Thessaly, *194* f., *221, 233* f.
Agamemnon, *285, 293*
Aganippe, *24*
Agapenor, *285* f.
Agave, *137, 147, 150, 160-162*
Agelastos petra, the, at Eleusis, *61, 207*
Aglaurus, mother of Ceryx, *122*
ἀγνή, used of Persephone, *48*
Agriculture, in Cyprus, *281*; knowledge of, came from Demeter through Triptolemus, *71*; im-

plements of, Cinyras invented, *294*
Agrionia, *103*
Aidoneus, *49* f., *55, 57, 178, 194*
Αἰγαῖον πέλαγος, corrupted into Archipelago, *397* f.
Aiorai, *106*
Aithousa, mother of Eleuther, daughter of Alcyone and Poseidon, etc., *119*
Ajax, *46, 78*
Alaric, *188, 265*
Alban hills, *326*
Albanians, May festivals of, *89*; wasting of Eleusis by the, *188* f., *196*
Alcaeus, *102*
Alcamenes, statue of Aphrodite by, *270, 273*
Alcibiades, *215*
Alcmaeon, dissection of animals by, *223*
Alcmaeonidae, arraignment of, *124*
Aletis, song in memory of Erigone, *106, 115*
Alexander, Bacchanals of the house of, *138*; Dionysus and, *79*; the empire of, *44* f.; the Emathian conqueror, *79*
Alexander, of Abonotichus, *254, 263*
Alexandria, Caesareum at, *13* f.
Alexandrine doctors, Daremberg's list of, *219*; sailors, worship of Caesar ἐπιβατήριος by, *14*
Ali Pasha, of Janina, *268*
Alliance, the Eleusinian, of divinities, *77, 176, 211, 216*
Alpheius, *163*
Amadis de Gaule, anatomy of, compared to Homer's, *228*
Amathus, a Phoenician foundation, *281, 291* f.
Amathusia, Xenagoras called Cyprus, *274*
Amazons, *38, 249*
American excavation at Icaria, *104, 114*
Amphiaraus, a Boeotian Aesculapius and a pupil of Chiron, shrine at Oropus of, *232*
Amphictyon, in Dionysus-legend, *119*
Amphipolis, Phyllis on the shore near, *65*
Amphipolitans, deified Brasidas, *40* f.
Anacreon, sang under inspiration of wine, *102*
Anatomy, Homer's clear notions of, *227-230*; origin of, *234, 237*; heroic interest in, *227*; influence of Homer in, *229*
Anaxagoras, loftier teachings of, in the *Bacchanals*, *138*
Andania, competition with Celeae and Eleusis of, *65*
Androclus, son of Codrus, *122*
Andros, on the way to Delos, *376*; among the Bahamas, *397*
Anemones, on the Tholos of Polycletus, *251*
Animism, *27*
Anthesteria, at Athens, *130* f.
Anthesterion, month of the Lesser Mysteries, *208*
Anthropology, scientific method in, *169* f.
Anthroporraistes, ἀνθρωποῤῥαίστης, or man wrecker, Dionysus' surname, *100*
Antigone, the, interpolation in, *166* f.
Antonines, the age of the, an age of valetudinarians, *235*
Antony, Mark, as Caesar's flamen, *38*; masquerade of, as Dionysus, *79*
Anubis and Apollo at Delos, *402*
Apamea, *14*
Aphrodite, *2, 5*; nature of, *273*; powers of, *271*; came from everywhere, *272*; a nature goddess, *271, 273*; a jealous power, *273*; a restraining power, *300*; bore a sword, *46, 270, 273*; a consoling power, *271, 298, 303*; a goddess of the dead, *292, 309* f.; sur-

named Sosandra, *271, 298, 303*; ancient influence of, *271, 303* f.; modern views about the origin of, *315*; had a strain neither Greek nor Phoenician, *282, 324*; came from Accad, *303*; worship of, in the East, *273* f., *293, 297* f.; Greek influences never quite prevailed with, *271-273, 297, 317*
Aphrodite, of the Greeks, *270-273, 284, 297* f., *303* f., *315* f., *319*; of the Hittites, *315, 320* f.; of the Phoenicians, *273* f., *282, 284-286, 297* f., *303, 315, 318, 320, 323*
—— of the poets.—Euripides on, *298-300*; Homer on, *298* f., *304, 317* f.; Pindar on, *299* f.
Aphrodite's associates.—Adonis and, *291*; Aesculapius and, *270* f.; Apollo and, *271, 379, 382, 399-403*; Ariadne and, *400* f.; Cybele and, *21, 303*; Demeter and, *21, 69, 303*; Dionysus and, *148, 273, 310*
—— sanctuaries (Greek). — At Athens, *270* f.; at Cythera, *285* f., *323*; at Delos, *379, 382, 399, 403*; towards Eleusis, *218, 271, 296* f., *304, 314*; at Psophis and Tegea, *285* f., *323*
—— sanctuaries (Cypriote).— *153, 274, 285, 287, 296, 317, 321* f.; at Old Paphos, *272, 279, 292*
—— Zerynthian sanctuary, *345* f.
Apolline perfection, Apollonius of Tyana and, *220*
Apollo, *5, 8, 9, 14* f., *17* f., *24, 28-30, 33* f., *169-171, 219, 242, 264, 366-369, 371* f.
Apollo's associates. — Aesculapius, *220, 240-242*; Aphrodite, *271, 300*; Ares, *372*; Artemis, *355, 367*; Athena, *218*; Augustus, *14*; Bacchus, *25*; Coronis, *245*; Daphne, *368*; Demeter, *159, 218*; Diana, *150*; Dionysus, *21, 30* f., *34, 36, 81, 102, 104, 159, 162, 368*; Eleuther, *119* f.; Harpocrates, *401* f.; Hecate, *159*; Heracles, *371* f.; Hermes, *372*; Horus, *401* f.; Marpessa, *368*; the Muses, *102, 104, 159*; Nero, *114*; Poseidon, *372*; Proserpina, *159*; Pythagoras, *219*; Zagreus, *128*; Zeus, *26, 369*

Apollo's sanctuaries.—At Bassae, *372*; at Curium, *345* f.; on Mt. Cynortion, *246*; at Daphne, *218*; at Delos, *2, 5, 35, 201, 360-363, 370, 372, 375, 378-380, 382, 384-389, 394, 401* f.; at Delphi, *17, 26, 29, 33-36, 370, 372*; at Icaria, *102, 104*; at Marathon, *104*; on Parnassus, *104*

—— story, *110, 128, 219, 231, 239, 294, 356-359, 369, 372, 379, 382, 391, 393, 399*

Apollonia, celebrated during Delian independence, *374, 386-389*

Apollonius means one under Apollo's guidance, *219*; seven Alexandrine doctors named, *219*

Apollonius of Tyana, reasons for the discredit of, *258* f., *261* f.; important facts concerning, *220, 255, 257, 261, 263-266*; relation to Christians and Christianity of, *258, 260* f., *263* f.

Appius, Claudius Pulcher, gate of, at Eleusis, *188, 190*

Arabian strain of Dionysus, *168*

Araby the blest worships Dionysos, *140*

Arcadia, temples of Aphrodite in *285* f.

Arcadian forms in Cypriote, *280*; legends of Demeter Erinys and her daughter Persephone Δέσποινα, 48

Arcadians, the, when and whence they entered Cyprus, *280*

Archaeological Society, Greek, *1* f.

Archaeology, 7

Archedemus, his Athenian grinders, *214*

INDEX 425

Archelaus, wild religion at the court of, *137*
Archilochus, the poet of the Aegean, *365*; and Apollo, *366*; and Paros, *365*
Archipelago, a corruption of Αἰγαῖον πέλαγος, *397* f.
Archipelago, Athens in close communion with the islands of, *81*; the carnival of, and the Delia and Apollonia, *388* f.; tales of Dionysus in, *111*; Thracians in earliest days controlled the, *80*; seat of Thracian power in, was Naxos, *80*
Archon, marriage of Dionysus with the wife of king, *130* f.
Arcturus-Icarius, *110*
Ares, Apollo boxed with, *372*
Aresthanos found Aesculapius on Mt. Titthion, *244* f.
Argive account of Eubouleus-Dionysus, *176*
Argolis, Polycletus of, his two Epidaurian masterpieces, *246*
Ariadne, *130*, *379*, *401*; Aphrodite and, *400* f.; Daedalus and, *399*; Demeter and, *62*; Dionysus and, *130*; Persephone and, *62*; Theseus and, at Delos, *382*
Arician Grove, picturesque but comparatively unimportant rites of, *27*
Aristaeus, the giver of honey, reared Dionysus, *143*
Aristophanes, *68*, *212-216*; Apollo and, *28*; Dionysus and, *81*; Eleusinia and, *212-216*
Aristotle on Dithyrambs and Tragedy, *116*; corroborates the Parian Marble, *132*
Art, Delian and Metapontine, *383*
Artemis, *245*, *355* f., *367*, *399*; at Delos, *356*, *379*, *385*; at Eleusis, *189* f.; at Epidaurus, *250*
Arts, Pygmalion and Cinyras originated the useful, *294*
Ascalon, Evenus of, *108*
Asclepieion at Athens, *2*

Ascoliasmos, at Dionysiac festivals, origin of, *108*
Ashdod, Dagon at, and Eastern Aphrodite, *297* f.
Ashtaroth and Cypris - Aphrodite differentiated, *320* f.
Asia, Central, *12*
Asia Minor, *1*, *2*; attempt to derive Aphrodite from, *271* f., *320*, *322*; Athenians in, *122*, *132*; contributions from, to the myth of Cinyras, *293*, *295*; Cnidian sanctuary in, *70*; north Cyprus, an extract from, *277*; Maenads followed Dionysus from, *141*; Lenaeon, a month name of, *132*; land of Phrygian flute and Lydian airs, *294*; Sporades lie near, *392*; Taurus range and north range of Cyprus, *275*; Thrace of, *84*
Ἀσιάρχαι, ten in Asia, *44*
Ἀσίας, ἀρχιερεὺς τῆς, *45*
Aspelia, Xenagoras called Cyprus, *274*
Assumption, the, and the bringing of Semele to Olympus, *177*
Assurbanipal, Sardanapalus, poem on Ishtar found in library of, *300*
Assyria, Aphrodite ultimately from, *272*; Cinyras, king of, *291*
Assyrian and Greek strains in Aphrodite, *298*; idea of Ishtar, *273*, *303*; stranger, Phoenician wine trade and Dionysus the, *165*; rosettes an inheritance from, *251*
Astarte - Aschera, and Aphrodite, *277*
Asteria and Ortygia, barren legend of, *358*
Astronomy, of Icarian story, *110* f.; in a Delian legend, *358*
Astynomus, called Cyprus Crypton and Colinia, *274*
Atargatis, worship of, added to that of the Syrian goddess at Delos, *403*
Athena, appeared to Alaric and saved Athens, *265*

426 INDEX

Athena, frequent mention of, at Citium, *322*; Cynthia, Delian temple of, *402*; and Demeter, shared Apollo's temple at Daphne, *218*

Athene Sotera, Pisistratus and, *126*; and the heart of Zagreus, *181*

Athenian shrine of Rome and Augustus on the Acropolis, *40*; temple of Aesculapius next the Acropolis (inscription), *241*; and Argive account of Eubouleus-Dionysus, *176*; Confederacy, *12*; religion, became the same with Attic, *122* f.

Athenian worship, at Delos (*a*) architecture, *386*, (*b*) festivals, *374-381*, (*c*) legends, *382*, *399* f.; at Eleusis, *122*, *124*, *207-218*

Athenian worship of Dionysus, *123*, *134*; derivation of, *81*, *130*, *137*, *162*; festivals of, *128-132*, *134*

Athenian theatre of Dionysus, *114*, *119*

Athenians in Asia Minor, *122*, *132*; Venetians and, *131*, *328*

Athens typically free, *11*; the Archipelago and, *81*; Cecrops at, *64*; commercial jealousy of, *363*; Democedes at, *224*; Eleusinion at, *124*, *207*; Eleusis and, *122*, *208*; Eleutherae and, *118* f.; Epimenides at, *124*; Icarian influences at, *114*, *117*, *129*, *132*; religious innovations at, *129* f.; worship of Aphrodite at, *270*; worship of Apollo (Delian) at, *362* f., *376* f., *386* f.; worship of Apollo (Delphian) at, *34*; worship of Aesculapius at, *219*, *222*, *241*, *248* f., *256*; worship of Demeter and the Eleusinian divinities at, *77*, *118*, *122*, *124*, *207-211*, *215-217*; worship of Dionysus at, *36*, *77*, *80* f., *89* f., *117-119*, *121* f., *125*, *129-131*, *133-135*

Athens and Venice, religions contrasted, *131*

Atlas, father of Aithousa's mother Alcyone, *119*

Atthis, Adonis closely connected with, *291*, *322*

Attic Demeter legend, *60*; Dionysus legend and worship, *34*, *104* f., *113*, *143*; confederation, *60*; religion, *122* f., *129* f., *218*; sense of measure, *34*, *104* f., *113*; tragedy, *117*

Attica, the *Bacchanals* called the Passion Play of, *137*; song of Bacchanals and winter festivals of, *156*; country demes of, and Dionysus, *34*; Demeter and Dionysus came to, *105*; Euripides wrote for Greece as well as for, *143*; exclusiveness of local religions in, *122* f.; Icaria the Pieria of, *111*; belief in Pisistratus of countrymen of, *126*; political and religious fusion of, *122*; early influence of Thracians on, *111*; beautiful Triptolemus myth of, *71*

Atticus, lukewarm about building in Academy, *188*, *190*

Aufidus, bull-shaped, *95*

Augustales, in Italy, Sicily, Gaul, Spain, etc., *43*

Augustalia, local celebrations analogous to, *43* f.

Augustan poets, imperial religion and the, *38*

Augusti, oaths In acta divi, *43*

Augustin, St., commends self-control of Apollonius, *264*

Augustus, deification of genius of, *38*; worshipped as 'Αλεξίκακος, Zeus, Apollo, Poseidon, *14*; Egyptian style of, *14*; Julius Caesar and, *37*; masquerading scheme of, *37* f.; Rome and worship of, *40*; wished to govern not to reign, *37*; worship of, Rome and, *45*; worshipped by "circumlocution," *40*; and temples for imperial worship, *38*; temple at Jerusalem and, *8*

INDEX

Aurelian, vision by, of Apollonius, *265*
Autonoe, on Cithaeron, *150*
Autopsy of the Greater Mysteries, *209*
Axius, Dionysus crosses the, *157*

BABYLON, Aphrodite-Mylitta at, *303*
Bacchanal, Apollo a prophet, *30*
Bacchanalian revels, Euripides' understanding of, *150* f.; victory, *184* f.
Bacchanals of everyday life, *112, 138*; full of Dionysus, *136*; comparison of, with Pans, *99* f.; in the *Thiasos*, *100*; Thebes the mother of, *133*; Thracian originals of, *97*
Bacchanals, The, of Euripides, prefigures future and sums up the past, *138*; music of, *144*; called the Passion Play of Attica, *137*; many aspects of, *136* f., *153*; relation of, to Dionysus, (*a*) its scene is full of Dionysus, *139* f., (*b*) it presents in full the Bacchic cult, *157*, (*c*) a gospel of Dionysus, *136*, (*d*) fullest presentation of Dionysus, *121*, (*e*) contains proto-Thracian Dionysus and teachings of philosophy, *138*; all characters in, are prophets of Dionysus, *156* f.; stand for Dionysus, *139*; Dionysus not the sole representative of the god in, *139, 155*; analysis of the action of, *140-143, 145-160, 162*; details of, (*a*) written in Macedonia, *137*, (*b*) lines of, preserved in *Christus Patiens, 139*; (*c*) Milton's emendation of, *146*, (*d*) interpolation in, *166* f.; (*e*) Cadmus in, *140, 145-147* f., (*f*) Tiresias in, *145*
Baccheios, Dionysus, at Corinth, *159*
Bacchic power, wine represented as the sterner as well as the more charming side of, *91*
—— cult, presented in full by the Bacchanals, *157*

Bacchic worship, stage of, investigated by Americans, *104*; reverence for Cybele in, *141*; the wanton ferule in, *142*; ivy and oak for, *142*
—— dance, its graceful undulations and fitful variations, *103, 146*
—— images at Corinth of Pentheus' tree, *150*
—— instruments, mention of, *143*
—— madness, the method of, *145*
Bacchus, Homeric notion of, *77*; dance of, *142*; lover of laurel, *30*; torches of, *247*; religious consolation of, *135*
Bactrian forts, Dionysus worshipped at, *140*
Bactylus, on Mt. Cynthus, *386*
Baffo olim Paphos, 324
Balkan Peninsula, *85, 89*
Bank, the Delian shrine a, *387*
Baptism, analogy of, to Lesser Mysteries, *209*
βάρβαρος, Meursius makes a river of adjective, *353* f.
Barnabas, St., in Cyprus, *290*
βασιλεύς, the ἄρχων, with four ἐπιμελεταί, administered cult of Athens and Eleusis, *208*
Basilissa, marriage of Dionysus with, *130* f.
Basque country, persistence of *couvade* in the, *170*
Bas-relief of Dionysus and Icarius, *106*
Bassae, temple of Apollo at, *204, 206, 372*
Bassarids of Dionysus, *79, 97*. See Maenads.
Bavarian killing of *Pfingstl*, *159*
Beans, Cyamites the giver of, and the Mystae, *217*; excluded from Demeter's sanctuary at Eleusis, *217*; horror of, felt by Pythagoreans, *218*
Bentley, abandoned edition of Apollonius, *262*
Bermius, rose gardens on flanks of, *92*

Birth, forbidden on Delos, *360*; principle of second, justifies Orestes, *169* f.
Birth-legend of Aesculapius, *15*, *233*, *245*; of Aphrodite, *271*, *284*, *296*, *317* f., *356-359*, *399*; of Dionysus, *128*, *149*, *165*, *168-173*
Birthday-festival of Apollo and Dionysus' flower feast, *372*
Bishop, functions of, analogous to those of 'Ασιάρχης, *44*
Βιθυνιάρχης, *44*
Blizzard, the most ancient record of a, *113*
Bocalia, an alternative name for Bocarus, *345* f.
Bocarus, a Salaminian river-name wrongly connected with Cyprus, *324* f., *344-347*, *352-354*
Body, mind cured through, *235*
Boedromion, month of the Greater Mysteries, *208*
Boeotia, Amphiaraus the Aesculapius of, *232*; Eleutherae on Attic borders of, *118*; Lenaeon in, *112*, *132*; early Thracians in various parts of, *80*
Boeotian festival of Agrionia, connection of Dionysus and Muses in, *103*
Boeotians organised a Delian festival, *363*
Bondholders, the Turkish, and modern Cyprus, *278*
Boötes-Icarius as vindemiator, *111*; Icarius and his wain become, *110*
Bordone, identifies Troödos and Olympus, *329*
Botticelli and spirit of mystery at Eleusis, *182*; illustrations of Dante by, *331*
Brasidas, deified by Amphipolitans, *40* f.
Brenzone, account of sack of Nicosia by, *332* f.; reproduces Procacci on Troödos-Olympus, *334*
Bricks, devised by Cinyras, *294*;

transport of, from Athens to Eleusis, *207*
Bridge, jibes at, in procession of Mystae, *214*, *217*
Brightness, elements of Dionysus coupled with swift, *102*
British Museum, Demotic stelae in, *14*
Bromius, wine gift of, *109*; mystic maids sealed for service of, *87*
Brotherhood of Dionysus and Apollo, *31*
Brumalia, Roman and Thracian festival of, *86-88*, *112*. See Rosalia
Bucolion, scene of marriage of Dionysus, *131*
Bull, represents water, *95*; Dionysus shaped as a, *95*
Bulls, the Delian Hall of, *400*
Bumna, a modern name for the Bocarus, *347*
Bustrone, calls Troödos *Lambadista* or *Chionodes*, *341*
Butes, leader of the early Thracian migration to the Aegean, *80*
Byblus, Aphrodite worshipped at, as a cone, *293*; Cinyras, a founder priest and king at, *293*
Byzantium, Cyprus under rule of, *278* f.

CABIRION, the Delian, and the Theban, *402*
Cadmus, the *Bacchanals* of Euripides and, *140*, *145-147*; the Dionysus-legend and, *161* f., *164*
Caesar, Julius, *14*, *37*
Caesarea-by-the sea, *14*
Caesareum at Alexandria, the, *13-15*
Calamis, statue of Aphrodite Sosandra by, *299*
Calendar, juggle with, at Athens for initiation of Demetrius, *209*
Callias at the Delia, *376*
Callichorus, the well where Demeter sorrowed, *207*
Canicula-Maera, *110*
Capitoline Museum, bust of Virgil in, *195*

INDEX 429

Cappadocian, Apollonius the, sneered at by Dio Cassius, *261*
Caracalla, coins of, *44*; son of Julia Domna, *264*; partiality for Apollonius of Tyana, *261*, *265*
Caramania, anciently invaded by Thracians, *280*; mountains of, *276*
Caratheodori, two cousins, both fathers of, were doctors, *268*
Carinondas and Apollonius, magicians, *262*
Carnival-time in the Archipelago and the Delia and Apollonia, *388* f.
Carthage, Aphrodite-Ashtaroth at, *303*
Castalia, streams of, *23*, *35*, *133*
Caste, *11*
Castor, a pupil of Chiron, *232*
Cavafy, Dr., at St. George's Hospital, *269*
Cavaliere di San Marco, gift of Meursius' MS. *Cyprus* gained his son the title of, *350*
Cave at Icaria, *109*
Cave-like arches at Eleusis, *191*
Cave-temple of Apollo on Delos, *385* f.
Caves, frequency of, in Cyprus, *289*
Cecrops, Cychreus as, *345*; Eleusis as, *64*; Pandion, the fifth since, *105*
Celeae, Eleusinian Demeter-legend and, *64* f., *105*
Celeus and Eleusin, *61*, *64* f.; a hero at Celeae, *65*; an interlocutor at Eleusis, *65*; Demeter's visit to, *63*, *68*, *105*; discrowned by Ovid, *71*; Icarius contrasted with, *107*; the sons of, *62* f.; the daughters of, *65*, *122*, *175*
Centaurs, *138*, *231*, *249*
Central Museum at Athens, Epidaurian victories in, *249*
Ceos, on the way from Athens to Delos, *376*
Cephissus, jibes at bridge over, *214*, *217*

Cerastis, Xenagoras, called Cyprus, *274*
Ceres, the Roman, *50*
Cerynia, the only centre of life in North Cyprus, *277*
Ceryx, son of Hermes, successor to Eumolpus, *122*
Cestus of Aphrodite, borrowed by Hera, *299*
Chalcidice, Greeks of, deified Flamininus, *40*
Chastity and Cypris, *149-153*
Children, growth of, linked to growth in the field, *53*; surviving European customs about, *53*
Chinese, use of play-actors' masks by, *172*
Chios, not of Cyclades or Sporades, *393*
Chiotes, *101*
Chiron, the character of, *231*; Aesculapius, reared by, *246*; loves of Apollo and, *369*; pupils of, *232*
Chiti (Citium), Podocatharo estate of, *337* f.; Procacci's account of, *337*
Chittim, Cyprus named, *274*; Tarshish and, in Isaiah, *281*
Chivalry, of Apollo in love, *368* f.; Homeric, scorned Dionysus, *78*
Cholargia, Xenocles of, at Eleusis, *191*
Choruses, tragic, at Sicyon, *115*
Christ, deification of emperors led to the imitation of, *265*; statue of, in the Lararium of Severus, *265*
Christian art, spirit of ancient mysteries in, *182*
Christian birth-legends, compared with the Delian story, *356*
—— building at Delos, *379*
—— opponents took trouble to understand Apollonius, *263*
—— ritual, *4*
Christian, mimic fight between Turk and, *90*
Christianity, *3*, *5*, *6*, *15* f., *19*; Paganism and, *44* f., *258*, *260*,

266; in Thrace, *84*, *88*; the Dionysus-worship of the Bacchanals and, *138*
Christians, Apollonius respected by, *261*; ransomed from Turks, *339*
Christopoulos, a lyric poet, studied medicine at Buda, *268*
Chrysopator, epithet of Dionysus, *92*
Chrysopolitissa, the holy, and Aphrodite Paphia, *304*
Church, the hall at Eleusis a, *189*
Church universal, *11*, *15*
Churches, ruins of, in Cyprus, *283*
Cicero, his mocking allusion to Caesar's divine honours, *37*; proposes a building like the gate of Appius, *188-190*
Cilicia, mountains of, *276*
Cimon, Hall of, at Eleusis, *199*, *204*
Cinnamon tree, the, and Nysa, *164* f.
Cinyradae, the, at Paphos, *291*
Cinyras, legend of, *291-295*; the Paphian south wing is perhaps the tomb of, *309*, *314*
Circe had knowledge of miraculous drugs, *231*
Cithaeron, Mount, *118*; Dionysus-legend and, *141*, *147*, *150*, *153* f., *158*; false connection with Cythera of, *286*; never connected with Aphrodite, *286*
Citium, the Roman form for Chittim, *281*; Athena, not Aphrodite, mentioned at, *322*; Phoenician remains at, *282*, *321*; Podocathari estate at, *337*
Citizenship, political, invented by Greece, *12*
Clairvoyance of Apollonius in Dio and Philostratus, *261*
Clan and commonwealth, *11*
Classicists, romanticists compared with, *150*
Clemency of Augustus, worship of, *40*
Cleomenes, devastation of Eleusinian sanctuary by, *198*, *216*
Clisthenes, effect of Sicyonian choruses on, *115*

Clodones, the, are Thracian originals of Bacchants, *97*
Clytemnestra, murder of, and the *couvade*, *169*, *170*; struggle of, for Iphigenia and the *couvade*, *171*
Cnidus, *1*, *5*, *59* f., *70*, *194*, *195*
Cnossus, Epimenides from district of, *124*
Coan practice of medicine, work on, attributed to Hippocrates, *225*; school and early medicine, *234*
Cock, debt of Socrates and Crito to Aesculapius, *239*
Codrus, father of Androclus, *122*
Coins, head of Apollonius on, *265*
Colettis, the Prime Minister, was a doctor, *268*
Colontas, Demeter and, *176*
Colos, Garin du, at Colossi, *288*
Colossi, name and history of, *287* f.
Colossus of Naxians at Delos, *380*; of Rhodes and the Cypriote Colossi, *287* f.
Columbus of a new world, Thespis the, *116*
Comedies, at Athenian festivals, *134*
Comedy, Icaria the cradle of, *111*, *115*, *117*; Susarion invited to Icaria with the first, *114* f.; tragedy and, began together, *117*
Commanderia and Madeira wines, *288*
Commanders, Knights, the, at Colossi, *287*
Commandery at Colossi, *288*
Commandment, Demeter's, *72*
Commercial spirit of Delia after second revival, *375*
Commonwealth and clan, *11*
Concord, of Dionysus and Apollo, *104*
Cone, worship of Aphrodite as a, at Byblus and Paphos, *293*, *386*
Confirmation, analogy of, to the Greater Mysteries, *209*
Conon and Evagoras used forests of Cyprus, *308*
Contradictions, in the pose and look of Demeter and Persephone, *73*;

INDEX

inherent in Dionysus, *78* f., *113*, *136*
Coray, a doctor at Montpellier, *268*
Corfu, May festival at, *89*
Corinth, Aphrodite at, *271* ; Bacchic images of Pentheus' wood at, *159*
Corinthian capital, the earliest known, *252*
Corn, contrasted with wine and the vine, *107* ; lady, the, of, *50* ; mother of, or Kornmutter, *470*
Coroebus, a builder of the temple at Eleusis, *191*
Coronelli calls the Troödos Olympus, *343*
Coronis, daughter of Thessalian Phlegyas, *233*, *244* f., *367*
Corybantes, at birth of Zeus-Dionysus, *99*, *142* f.
Corycian, cave, *133* ; Dionysus on the heights, *157*
Cos, inscriptions at, *237* ; coming of Aesculapius to, *221* ; date of Aesculapian foundation of, *243* ; Ptolemy and, likened to Apollo and Delos, *394*
—— temple of Aesculapius at, the school of Hippocrates, *225*
Cothonea, given for Metanira, *65*
Couclià, modern name of Old Paphos, *289* ; description of the village of, *296* ; Tschiflik at, *290* ; further excavations at, desirable, *314*
Courage, Homeric conception of, *78*
Couvade, Apollo in the *Eumenides* and, *169* f. ; the, and Clytemnestra's death, *169* f. ; Dionysus' second birth and, *168-170* ; the, and Dionysus' love for Semele, *169* ; Greek transformation of problem of, to beauty, *171* ; survival of, to-day in Spain and France, *170* ; struggle for Iphigenia and the, *171* ; Zamacola on the, *170*
Couvocles, old French for Couclià, modern name of Old Paphos, *296*
Cowardice, the, of Dionysus, personified by Satyrs, *99* ; grotesqueness as of, attached to Dionysus, *78*
Crane dance, legend of, at Athens and Delos, *400*
Creed, *6* f., *16*, *18*, *153*
Cretan birth of Epimenides, effect of, *127* ; legends, Dionysus in, *81*, *139*, *142*
Crete, Aphrodite in, *271* ; Ariadne came from, *62* ; Curetes from, *97* ; Demeter-worship in, *61* f. ; Iasion in, *62* ; Rhea and Cybele in, *143* ; Zeus of, a Dionysus, *142*
Crissaean plain, *23*
Crito, debt of a cock to Aesculapius, *239*
Croce, Mount St., wrongly identified with Olympus of Cyprus, *325* ; is probably the ancient Aous, *352*
Cronos, Aphrodite on the Olympian hill of, *271* ; Demeter's father, *50*
Cross of the penitent thief, discovery of, in Cyprus, *275* ; tempests stilled by a nail of the true, *275*
Croton, Aesculapius probably not worshipped at, *225* f. ; Alcmaeon the Pythagorean of, *223* ; Democedes came from, *223* ; renown of its school of medicine, *223* ; the centre of Pythagoreanism, *223*
Cruelty, in Thracian Dionysus-worship, *100*
Cruz, Santa, Cal., and Cape Curias, *288*
Crypton, Astynomus, called Cyprus, *274*
Cuneiform, version from the, *301*
Curetes, are the Satyrs of Crete, *94*, *97*, *142* f.
Curias, cape, and Santa Cruz, Cal., *288* ; Strabo's account of coast west of cape, *325*
Curium, Apollo ὑλάτης at, *345* f.
Customs, justice done by Euripides to, *157* ; variety of local, connected with Eleusinian procession, *218*

Cyamites, the Mystae and, *217*
Cybele, Bacchic worship of, *141*; Corybantes of, *97*; Demeter and Rhea combined with, *401* f. ; one of eight Eleusinian gods, *178*; Rhea acts in Crete as, *143*
Cychreus (Salaminian), Cecrops Eleusis and, *64*, *345* f.
Cyclades, influence on Athens of, *81*; Delos and the, *359*, *362*, *364* f., *387*; history of the name, *391-398*; the Holy Islands called, *376*
Cyclopean sanctuary at Eleusis, *200* f.
Cyclops, Apollo's expiation for slaying the, *371*
Cycnias, a mountain of Tenos, *380*
Cyllene, seen from Eleusis, *187*
Cylon avenged, *124*
Cylon's failure the people's victory, *122*
Cynortion, mountain sacred to Apollo, *246*
Cynthian Cabirion at Delos, *402*; cave-temple of Apollo, *385* f. ; precinct of foreign gods became foreign soil to Apollo, *402*
Cynthus, *365*; temple to Zeus Cynthius and Athena Cynthia on Mount, *402*; altar of horns brought by Artemis from, *384* f.
Cyprians knew that Aphrodite was from the East, *273*
Cypriote agriculture, Lang and Fourcade on, *281*; characters, who used them? *280*, *321*; peasantry, Lang's sympathy for, *280* f.
Cypris-Aphrodite and Ashtaroth differentiated, *320*; not of Greek birth, *318*
Cypris and chastity, *150* f., *153*; Homer mentions Aphrodite as, *284*, *316*; Pontia, Phaedra's name for Aphrodite, *297*
Cyprogeneia, Aphrodite's epithet, *296*
Cyprus, *2*; Aphrodite's isle is, *153*, *274*, *287*; in ancient times, *272*, *274*, *278*, *280*, *284*, *292*, *294*, *321* f. ; description of, *275-277*, *288* f., *308*, *328*; general history of, *276-280*; in medieval times, *275*, *278*, *326-328*, *331-335*, *342*; in modern times, *272*, *274*, *278* f., *288*
Cyrene and Apollo, *300*, *369*
Cythera, Aphrodite on, *271*, *286* f., *296*, *317*; confused with Cithaeron and Cythrea, *286*; Phoenicians on, *286*, *323*
Cythnos on the way to Delos, *376*
Cythrea of Cyprus, confusion of, with Cythera, *286*

DAEDALUS, Delian image of Aphrodite by, *379*, *399*
Daeira, surname of Persephone at Eleusis, *48*
Dagon at Ashdod and Eastern Aphrodite, *297* f.
Daimon, the mystical, of early Eleusis, and Dionysus - Zagreus - Iacchos, *174*
Daisy, the Greek, on capitals of the Tholos, *252*
Dalin (Idalium), earthquake at, *290*
Damaschino, Dr., professor in the Faculty of Paris, *269*
Damasias, Mr. Kenyon's note on, *132*
Damigeron and Apollonius, sorcerers, *262*
Damis the Ninivite, travellers' tales of, *257-259*; notes of, given to Philostratus by Julia, *260*
Dance, Apollo and the, *29*; the Archipelago and the, *388*; Apollo and Dionysus, two gods of the, *104*; Dionysus and the, *96*, *103*, *133*, *142*, *146* f., *213*; of Dionysus on Parnassus, *133*, *149*; of Silenus, *95*; represented Eleusinian and Icarian legends, *107*
Dante, Apollo invoked, *24* f. ; Botticelli's illustrations of, *331*; idea of Parnassus in, *111*; Orphic

ideas in, *25*; remembers Lucan, *24*
Daphnae on the Sacred Way, *218*
Daphne and Erigone, myths of, *368*
Dardanus and Apollonius as magicians, *262*
Darius cured by Democedes, *224*
Daulis, *80*, *111*
Dead, Dionysus translated from the world of the, *102*; streams poured by Odysseus for the, *91*
Death, Aesculapius the awakener from, *239*, *245*; Apollo the dealer of, *366*; of Dionysus, *112*; represented by Dionysus, *28*; taint of, mentioned in the Old Testament, *360*; Thracian idea of, *84*
Decelea, fortification of, by Spartans, *215*
Deification of emperors led to imitation of Christ, *265*
Delian festivals of Apollo, *104*, *363*, *372-381*, *386-389*
Delians, exile and restoration of, *363*, *378*
Deliastae, *376*
Delion, the Marathonian, *104*, *376*
Delium, festival organised at, and battle of, *363*
Delos, *2*, *9*; description and general history of, *361*, *363*, *372-377*, *379*, *383*, *387*, *389*, *394*, *401*; monuments at, *355*, *371*, *378-380*, *384*, *386* f., *400*; mythology of, *35*, *350*, *356-359*, *371*, *379*, *382-384*, *394*, *399* f., *403*; ritual and worship in general at, *255*, *355*, *360-364*, *370*, *376*, *378-382*, *387*
Delphi, description of, *22-24*; known details of monuments and worship at, *21* f., *31-33*, *310*; history and mythology of, *22*, *31-35*, *119*, *371*; oracle at, *26*, *34-36*, *81*, *122*, *363*, *370* f.; revellers blocked by snow above, *113*; worship and ritual at, *22*, *29-33*, *35*, *364*, *370*, *384*
Demaratus inquires about the Eleusinia, *209* f.

Demeter, *1*, *4*, *5*, *8*, *17*; association and combination of, with other gods, *21*, *69*, *73* f., *77*, *107*, *159*, *174*, *176*, *178* f., *182-185*, *208*, *218-220*, *273*, *303*, *401* f.; character and meaning of the divinity of, *19* f., *47*, *51* f., *67-69*, *71-74*, *133*, *180*, *182*, *185*, *215*, *303*; leading points in the myth of, *50*, *55*, *57*, *59*, *61-63*, *66-68*, *71* f., *105*, *111*, *119*, *175* f., *185*, *206* f., *215*, *217*, *303*; development of the worship and myth of, *46*, *48* f., *51* f., *54*, *56*, *60* f., *75*, *77*, *104*, *111*, *122* f., *125* f., *163*, *175* f., *194*, *221*, *233*; monuments of the worship of, *70*, *72* f., *189-196*, *124*, *271*; processional song in honour of, *213*; Dionysus of the Lesser Mysteries with, *125*
Demetrius the Phalerean at Eleusis, *191*
Demetrius Poliorcetes, violated the degrees of Eleusinian initiation, *209*
Democedes, *223* f., *226*, *234*
Democracy, triumph of Dionysus with, *122*
Democratic reform of the greater Dionysia, *134*
Demophoon, legends of, *62-66*, *94*, *175*, *229*
Demotic stelae from Memphis, *14*
Dendrites, Dionysus as, *106*, *159*, *176*
Dendrophoria, Thraco - Phrygian annual custom, *159*
" Denis, vive notre bon père," old French song, *179*
Denmark, Meursius in, *348* f.
Deo, the Eleusinian, *133*
Diana and Apollo, *150*
Diaulos, at the Delia and Apollonia, *388*
διάξωμα of Eleusinian temple, meaning of, *191*, *203*
Dicaeus, describes Eleusinia, *209* f.
Dido-Anna and Aphrodite, *272*
Dili, Megale, the modern name of Delos, *361*

Dio Cassius, trustworthiness of his account of honours voted to Julius Caesar, *37* f. ; inconsistently endorses clairvoyance of Apollonius, *261* f.
Diocles, summoned by departing Demeter, *63*
Diocletian's *Insularum provincia* included 53 islands called Cyclades, *393* ; Cyclades came to be called Dodecanisia, *397*
Diogenia, daughter of Celeus (Pamphos), *65*
Dione and Aphrodite, *272*, *284*, *315* f., *318* f.
Dionysia, the City, are the Greater, *135* ; foundation of the Greater, *132*, *134* f. ; the Anthesteria contrasted with the Greater, *131* ; Thucydides calls the Anthesteria the older, *131* ; the Lesser are the Rural, *131* ; the Rural took shape in Icaria, *113*
Dionysiac customs, persistence in Thrace of, *88*
Dionysiaca, the, of Nonnus, *139*
Dionysodotos, Apollo, *31*
Dionysus, *1*, *4*, *5*, *9*, *15*, *17* f. ; the god of song and dance and tragedy, *29*, *31*, *75*, *79*, *86*, *97*, *102-104*, *115*, *117*, *133*, *136*, *143* ; the god of the nether-world, *29*, *31*, *34*, *79*, *91*, *96* f., *112*, *127*, *132*, *153-157*, *168-173*, *176-178*, *181*, *185*, *310*; the god of the real world, —(*a*) in general, *90*, *92*, *102* f., *130*, *140*, *144*, *217*,—(*b*) of trees and vegetation, *82* f., *106*, *159*,—(*c*) of various elements, parts, and events in nature, *24*, *92-96*, *100*, *102*, *107*, *133*, *139* f., *143*, *145*, *149*, *152*, *156*, *158*, *178* f., *212* ; attendants and others variously possessed by, (*a*) inspiration and possession by (generally considered), *94*, *97* f., *133*, *136*, *139*, *141*, *144*, *155*, *158* f.,—(*b*) Bacchanals possessed by, *112*, *156* f.,—(*c*) Bassarids possessed by, *79*,— (*d*) Corybantes and Curetes at the birth of, *142*,—(*e*) Graces led by, *104*, *135*,—(*f*) Maenads possessed by, *112*, *141*, *184* f.,—(*g*) Midas as, *79*, *93*,—(*h*) the Muses and, *31*, *96*, *103* f., *135*,—(*i*) nymphs, naiads, and waterfolk of, *94*,—(*j*) Pans of, *99*,—(*k*) seasons of, *96*, —(*l*) Satyrs and, *79*, *99*,—(*m*) the Thyades of, *133* ; the Saviour God (of Eleutherae), *22*, *34*, *79*, *118-120*, *133*, *145*, *159*, *161* f. ; festivals of, and ritual in general, (*a*) characteristics of festivals of, *4*, *85*, *89* f., *106*, *112* f., *132*, *134*, *140*, *372*,—(*b*) Thracian festivals of, *86-90*,—(*c*) Athenian festivals of, *113*, *128-132*,—(*d*) Boeotian festivals of, *103*,—(*e*) Icarian country festivals of, *108*, *112-114*,— (*f*) Eleusinian rites of, *214*,—(*g*) observances in honour of, *36*, *140*, *155* ; Thracian origin of, *22*, *77*, *79*, *82*, *84*, *86-90*, *92*, *94*, *96*, *99* f., *103*, *106*, *113*, *126*, *138*, *162*, *164*, *177*, *189*, *194* ; Orphic features in the myth of, *112*, *125-128*, *156* f., *168-173*, *177*, *181*; other gods and, (*a*) Adonis as, *291*,—(*b*) Aesculapius and, *220* f., *247*,—(*c*) Aphrodite and, *273*,— (*d*) Apollo and, *21* f., *29*, *31*, *102*, *104*, *159*, *162*, *185*, *372*,—(*e*) Ariadne and, *130*, *328*,—(*f*) Eleusinian Demeter and, *77*, *107*, *125*, *174-176*, *178* f., *182-185*, *208*, *210*, *212*,—(*g*) Hades of Eleusis and, *176-178*,—(*h*) Persephone and, *144*, *178*,—(*i*) Plutus and, *98*,—(*j*) Zeus and, *22*, *142* ; leading points in the myth of, (*a*) general, *34*, *77*, *101* f., *143*, *158*, *318*,—(*b*)birth-legends of, *81*, *111*, *114*, *142*, *148*, *163-165*, *318*, —(*c*) Attic legend of (i.) early Icarian legends of, *80*, *105*, *111*, (ii.) Semachidae legends of, *105*, (iii.) Eleutheraean legends of, *118* f., (iv.) later Attic story of,

INDEX 435

105, 111, 117, 119, 128, 132,— (d) Eastern myth of, *92, 140* f., *154, 157, 163-165, 168,*—(e) Euboean legend of, *143,*—(f) Theban legend of, *140* f., *148, 177*; development of the myth of, *81* f., (a) from points outside Greece, *34, 79, 81* f., *85, 140* f., *163-165, 168* f., *233,*—(b) from places outside of Athens, *34, 104, 111, 118* f., *121, 123, 139, 175,*— (c) progress to and in Athens, *34, 101, 121-123, 125* f., *130-132, 154, 175,*—(d) to its latter-day shape, *21* f., *36, 79, 106, 143, 186*; characteristics of, (A) violence, extremes, and contradictions in, (i.) contradictions in general, *30, 78, 83, 85, 93, 101, 113, 115, 136, 144, 149, 156,* (ii.) the pitiless and outrageous god, *22, 79, 99-101, 110, 128, 157, 159* f., (iii.) the cowardly and crazed god, *77* f., *99, 179*; (B) higher religious and moral aspects of, (i.) the elusive mystery and truth of his being, *22, 29, 80, 95, 101-104, 133* f., *136, 148, 179* f., *183-185, 368,* (ii.) Christian aspects of, *34, 79, 111, 134, 138, 145, 153-157,* (iii.) Athenian perfections of, *80* f., *102, 105, 113, 117, 162, 178,* (iv.) power of faith in, *29, 76* f., *91, 108, 130* f., *133* f., *140* f., *152-154, 156* f.

Diophantus of Sphettus, his prayer to Aesculapius, *241*

Dirce, Cadmus sowed dragon's teeth near, *147*; Achelous' daughter, invoked for Dionysus, *156*

Dissection practised by Pythagorean Alcmaeon at Croton, *223*

Dithyrambic contests, tripod awarded for prize in, *36*

Dithyrambus, contradictions of Dionysus mirrored in, *115*; influence of, on Thespis and tragedy, *115* f.

Divine man, ideal of, evolved among Greek gods, *20*

Divinity of Aesculapius, Demeter, and Dionysus, hardly recognised by Homer, *233*

Divus, implications of the use of, *43*

Doctors (Greek), Homeric status of, *222, 226, 230*; deference for Apollo and Aesculapius of ancient, *220, 230, 234, 238*; career of Democedes as a public, *223* f. ; modern status of, *222, 267-269*

Dodecanisia, a name for many Aegean islands, *397*

Dodona, *10*; Aphrodite's origin at, *315* f. ; Dione was the Aphrodite of, *318*

Dog-star, Maera became the, *111*

Doge, marriage of, with the Sea, *131*

Dogs, the nocturnal touch of, brought healing, *235* f. ; forbidden at Delos, *360*; frieze of, on Artemis' temple at Epidaurus, *250*

Dolichos, the, at the Delia and Apollonia, *388*

Domitian, Apollonius saw from Ephesus the murder of, *261*

Doric style, bad example of, in Hadrian's gate at Eleusis, *190, 192*; last extremity of, at Delos, *387*; of the Tholos at Epidaurus, *250*

Dotian plain, Demeter came south from, to Attica and Cnidus, *195*

Draconus, promontory of Nicaria, where Dionysus was born, *163*

Drama, contrast of Greek with Chinese and Japanese, *172*

Dreams, circumstances attending, and results gained by, in Aesculapian temples, *235* f. ; prayed to, as the children of Apollo, *242*; porches in Aesculapian sanctuaries for awaiting, *248*

Drugs, Homeric knowledge of, *228* f. ; miraculous power of certain, in Homer, *231*; knowledge possessed by Medea and Circe from Aeëtes of miraculous, *231*;

Chiron in relation to knowledge of, *232*; Aesculapius and his sons associated with miraculous, *231*; Herophilus called the hands of the gods, *237*; the sun-god is the source of miraculous knowledge of, *231*, *237*

Drunkards, Dionysus and brawls of leering, *79*

Dryads, the, and Dionysus, *96*

Dyalos, Dionysus surnamed, *94*

EAGLES, golden, at the Delphian navel-stone, *31*

Earth, Agave and Maenads are angry powers of, *160*; clung to the Telesterion at Eleusis, *206*; Delphi the centre of, *32*; kingdom of, in the heavens, *13*; oracles of, supplanted at Delphi, *35*; Pentheus' father's mother, *156*, *158*, *160*; and Poseidon at Delphi, *372*; stricken for woes of Demeter-Cybele and Ishtar, *302* f.

Earthquake, Dionysus directs the, *100*, *144*, *158*; Maenads as the many - handed, *145*, *159* f.; earthquakes in Cyprus, at Dalin (Idalium) and Old Paphos, *290*

East, gods from the, *17*; Aphrodite from the, *273*; Dionysus entangled with, in Euboea, Nicaria, and Naxos, *163*; second birth of Dionysus connected with, *164*

Eastern pedigree of Aphrodite and Cinyras, *291*; uncleanliness of Aphrodite, *297*; affinities of Adonis can be overstated, *291*

Echion the Earth-sprung, Pentheus' father, *147*, *156*, *158*

Egypt, one of Hyginus' insulae, *394*; the gods of, *17*—unknown to early Delos, *402*—invasion of Delos by, *401* f.—influence on Aesculapius worship through Serapis of, *254*

Egyptians, their knowledge of herbs in Homer, *231*

Egyptian poet of Dionysiaca, *92*; doctors and Democedes, *224*; strain of Dionysus, *168*; use of rosettes, *251*

εἰραφιώτης, Dionysus called, *166*

Elagabalus, coins of, *41*; his reign a Nightmare of Religious Reformation, *260*

Elements, Dionysus becomes the incarnation of the, *90*; wine, fire, water, gold, and unusual brightness are the Dionysiac, *91*, *92*, *102*; fusion through song and the dance of the Dionysiac, *103*

Eleusinion at Athens, the, *124*, *207* f.

Eleusis, *165*; landscape and position of, *55*, *57*, *187* f., *218*; Athens and, *60*, *122*, *208*, *376*; account of monuments of, *1*, *5*, *44*, *60* f., *186*, *188-193*, *197-207*, *218*, *379*; chief points in the legend of, *55*, *57*, *59-61*, *63-65*, *111*, *119*, *195*; legend of, compared with others, *55*, *59*, *243*; compared (i.) with Icarian legends, *104*, *107*, *133*; (ii.) with Peleponnesian legends, *65*, *105*; the mysteries of, *4* f., *68*, *76*, *122*, *180-182*, *209* f., *215* f., *376*, *403*; the Holy Alliance of, *77*, *176-178*, *211*, *401* f.; Aesculapius at, *219*; Aphrodite near, *271*, *273*; Dionysus at, *97*, *121*, *125*, *174-177*, *202*; Eubouleus at, *176*; Hades at, *174*, *176*; Persephone Daeira at, *48*

Eleutherae, Dionysus of, *34*, *104*, *111*, *118-120*, *145*, *162*; image of Dionysus at Athens from the temple at, *119*

Elis, Aphrodite in, *271*

Elysium, *75* f., *87* f.

Emanations from Dionysus, Muses, Hours, etc., as, *96*

Emathia, the cradle of Philip's power, *79*; north of Olympus, where was Mount Bermius and the gardens of Midas, *79*; harboured myth of Dionysus, *79*

Emathia and Pieria, *87*
Emathian conqueror, the great, *79*
Emesa, Julia Domna, daughter of priest at, *260*
Emperius, places Satrachos at Paphos, *346*
Emperors of Rome, allegiance to Venus-Aphrodite of, *300*; sanctity of Apollonius compared with divinity of, *265*; deification of, rooted in previous habits of mind, *40*; not work of clever men, *37, 40*
Engel argues that Aphrodite was Greek, *272, 315* f.; is responsible for adoption of Paphian Bocarus, *352*
English occupation of Cyprus, *277, 279*
Epacria,—Plothea, Semachidae, and Icaria,—confederation of mountaineers, *105, 119*
Epacria, Icarian legend of the visit of Dionysus to, *105, 111*
ἐπαινή, as an epithet of Persephone in *Iliad* and *Odyssey*, *48*
Ephesus, place for yearly assembly of 'Ασιάρχαι, *44*; founded by Androcles, *122*; privileges of βασιλεῖς at, *122*; Domitian's death witnessed from, by Apollonius, *261*
ἐπιβατήρια and ἐπιβατήριος, *13* f.
Epicureanism, a refuge, *41*; first master of Apollonius believed in, *257*; Apollonius rejected, *255*; Lucian biassed against Apollonius by, *263*
Epicurios, Apollo, father of Aesculapius, *219*
Epidaurus, *2, 5, 243*; journey to Hieron of, *246*; description of Hieron at, *247*; precinct of Aesculapius near, *248-254*; Tholos of Polycletus at, *250-254*; theatre of Polycletus at, *246* f.; inscriptions describing miracles at, *237, 254*; statue of Aphrodite found at, *270, 273*; legendary

claims of, *243* f.; legend of, *219, 221, 233, 244* f.; importance in history of surgery and medicine of, *222, 237*
Epimenides prepared Athens for Solon's laws, *123, 131, 175*; from Phaestus near Cnossus, *124*; the Eleusinion and Lesser Mysteries and, *124, 129*; statue at Athens of, *124, 208*; Dionysus and, *127, 175*
Epione, Gentleheart, wife of Aesculapius, *243, 249*
Epirus, theatrical features in May festivals of, *89*
Episcopia of the Venetian Cornari, *289*
ἐπιτυμβία, epithet of Aphrodite, *310*
Epoptical Mysteries, the, time of, *208* f.
Eprius Marcellus, the career of, *43*
Erechtheus killed in war with Eleusis, *122*
Erichthonius, succeeded Amphictyon, *119*
Erigone, legends and ritual concerning, *105, 107, 109* f., *114* f., *135, 368*
Erinys, epithet of Demeter, *176*
Eros, painting of, in the Tholos, *253*; Harpocrates, Apollo and, *401*
Eryx, foundation of Aphrodite-temple from, *286, 323*
Euboean legends of Dionysus, *143, 163*
Eubouleus at Eleusis, *174, 176, 194*
Eucharis, a purely Greek epithet of Aphrodite, *298*
Euhemerus, his views applied to traditions of Mt. Meroe, *166*
Eumaeus, character of, *47*
Eumenides, The, protest against matriarchy in, *171*
Eumolpidae, the Deliastae chosen from the, *174, 176, 376*
Eumolpus from Thrace, *174*; father of Immarados, *122*; station of the Mystae at the tomb of, *218*;

cultivation of the vine and trees by, *107* ; a son of Celeus, *63*
Eunapius, testimony in favour of Apollonius, *264*
Euripides, general account of, as a thinker and poet, *18* f., *29*, *71*, *136*, *138*, *143*, *149*, *157*, *159*, *161* f., *166* f., *169-171*, *178* ; Aphrodite as represented by, *298-300*, *303* ; Apolline legends in, *35*, *358*, *364* ; Dionysus-worship and legends of, *81*, *136*, *142* f., *150* f., *181* ; the Tiresias of, *145* f. ; debt of Milton and Goethe to, *146*, *148*, *150*, *162*
Eusebius, tribute to Apollonius, *263* f.
Euthydemus, Socrates thinks his books are on medicine, *224*
Evagoras and Conon, used forests of Cyprus, *308*
Evangel of Apollonius, Philostratus called to write the, *259*
Evangelistria, Tenian feast of the Holy, *378*, *389*
Evariges, letter of Sidonius Apollinaris to, *265* f.
Evian god, the, Evoe to, *144*
Evoe, *97*, *144*
Evolution, natural, of politics and religion, *16*, *19-21*, *53*
Examples of Odysseus and Pandarus an incentive to know medicine, *228*
ἐξοχώτατε, "your excellence," was the style of Greek doctors, *268*

FAITH, required by Aesculapius, *255*
Falsehood, divinities free from, *18*; Apollo could not touch, *369* f.
Famagosta-Salamis, history of ruins at, *283*
Family, change in, the Dionysus' birth-legend and, *163*
Family-life, Demeter who sanctified the bonds of, *72*
Farmer's god, Dionysus the, *105*, *217*

Fast-day, Icarian observances like, *112*
Fates, Aphrodite the eldest of the, *272* ; measure led by the glorious, in yearly Eleusinia, *215*
Father-god of Thracians in Cyprus, *322*
Fatherhood, the duties of Apollo and Zeus, *369*
Fathers of the Christian Church, *3*
Fawn skins, symbolise for Dionysus the starry sky, *140*, *142*
Ferule, the, in Bacchic worship, *142*
Festivals, Aegean and Apolline, *372-381*, *386-388* ; Dionysiac, *106*, *112-114*, *128-130*, *134*
Fetichism and primitive religion, far below Greek religion, *27*
Fetich-stone or Baetylus, on Mt. Cynthos, *386*
Feuilletonist, Philostratus a Parisian, *260*
Fig-man, Phytalus the, at Lakkiadae, *217*
Fig-tree, in bas-relief of Dionysus at the house of Icarius, *106*
Filius dei, Aesculapius as, *240* f.
Finances the, of modern Cyprus, *278*
Fir-tree, the, of Pentheus at Corinth, Thraco-Phrygian dendrophoria, *159*
Fire, association of Dionysus with, *16*, *62*, *64*, *78*, *92* f., *103*, *133*, *145*, *149*, *156*, *158* f., *179* f., *212*, *245*
Flames, personified by Agave and Maenads, *137*
Flamininus, deification of, *40*
Flash of the elements of Dionysus, *92*
Flattery, attributed to Greeks, *14*
Fleet, the clay fleet of Cinyras, *293*
Flesh, Dionysus an eater of raw, *96*
Flowers, festival of, at Athens, *130* f. ; flowers of Greece inspired Polycletus, *251*, *253*
Forests abounded in Cyprus, *308* ; forests, Scandinavian, *6*

Fortification, Eleusis a, in early days, *190, 198*
Frari church in Venice, picture in, of Cornari of Episcopia, *289*
Freedmen, part assigned to, in imperial services, *39*
Frenzy, inspired by Dionysus, *100*
Frogs, immense success of, due to religious causes, *216*

GAIA, *56, 64*
Galignani, Simone, a Venetian publisher, *331*
Gamelion and Lenaeon, *132*
Gardens, statue of Aphrodite in the, at Athens, *271*
Garin, Nicholas du Colos, at Colossi, *288*
Gebeleizis, a name for the primitive Dionysus, *86*
Genetor, the Cyclades are chosen islands of Apollo, *393*; Delian altar of Apollo, *379, 382*
Genii, of later Emperors, *38*
Genius of Roman people, time-honoured worship of, *40*
Genoese, the, in Cyprus, *278*
Geographical use of term Cyclades under Rome, *393*
Geography, astronomy and mythology and, confused in a Delian legend, *358*; Meursius' idea of ancient, *348*
Geologists, on Cyprus, *275* f.
Gephyrismoi, gibes at Cephissus-bridge, *218*
Germans, the Great God of, *6*
Gibes, used by Iambe to divert Demeter, *68*
Glaucus, prayer of, *29*
Goat, vine-destroying, slain by Icarius, *108*
Gold, significance of, in Dionysus legends, *92, 97, 102, 140, 178*
Golgoi, perplexing connection with Paphos, *285*
Gorgon's head, sent forth by dread Persephone, *48*

Gospels, Godhead of, *19*; the life of Apollonius and the, *258*
Goths, overran Thrace and Illyria, *87*; letter to the King of the, *265* f.
Götterineinanderleben, of the Olympians, *20*
Gout, appeal of Diophantus for cure of, to Aesculapius, *241* f.
Gozzoli, Benozzo, Pausias and, *253*
Graces, the, Dionysus and, *96, 104, 135, 303*
Γραῖα, Demeter surnamed, *70*
Grasshoppers, invasion of Cyprus by, *280* f.
Gravia, Odysseus danced the Syrtos at, *400*
Grecia (Magna), no proof of early worship of Aesculapius in, *225*; Dionysus in, *186*
Greek religion, *21, 26, 29, 75* f., *179, 210*
Gyaros, not of the Cyclades, *392*; an anchor of Delos, *361*

HADEPHAGIA, Demeter, *51*
Hades, the Eleusinian legend of, *58* f., *69, 73, 75, 98*; the Eleusinian worship of, *77, 176-178, 194, 218*
Hadrian's gate at Eleusis, a bad imitation, *190, 192*
Hagnon deposed, and Brasidas put in his place at Amphipolis, *41*
Hair worn for Dionysus, *155*
Halicarnassus, *1*
Hall of Cimon, the, at Eleusis, *199*
Harpocrates, Horus, and Apollo on Delos, *402*
Harvest Queen, the, *50*
—— home, Demeter and, *69*
—— usages, Dionysus and, *217*
Health (Hygieia), Panacea, Telesphorus (Convalescence), attend on Aesculapius, *240*
Heaven, kingdom on earth of, *13*
Hecate sitting in her cave, *56, 159, 181*
Helena, St., legend of, in Cyprus, *275*

Helicon, placed on Parnassus by Cervantes, *24*; Thracian worship of the Muses on, *103*
Hellas, Eleusinian divinities at the great crisis of, *211*
Hellenic genius in religion met Semitic in Cyprus, *273*; ideal, Apollo, Dionysus, and the, *162*
Hellenism, effect on Aphrodite of, *273*
Henry the Eighth, preface of Erasmus addressed to, *260*
Hephaestus fought for Greeks, *46*
Hera set Titans on Zagreus, *128*, *149*, *167*, *181*; sent Pytho against Leto on Delos, *358*; borrowed Aphrodite's cestus, *299*
Heracles, *87*, *371* f.
Heraclitus and Dionysus, *177*, *179* f., *184*
Hermes, *59*, *114*, *122*, *372*
Hermione, Demeter-legend of, *176*
Hero physician, Athenian shrine of the, *239* f.
Herod, *14*
Heroes, the Homeric, fought hard that we might think clearly, *229*; misprised Demeter's gifts, *46*
Herophilus on the miraculous nature of drugs, *237*
Hierocles set Apollonius up against Christ, *264*
Hieron of Aesculapius, the, *244*, *246*
Hierophant in the Eleusinia, *209*, *212*, *217*
Hieroskipou is Strabo's ἱεροκηπία, *290*
Hill, holy, of Dionysus, *94*
Hipparchus and Onomacritus, *127*
Hippocrene on Parnassus, *24*
History of the worship of Aphrodite, *303* f.
Hittite strain discoverable in Aphrodite, *282*, *320-323*
Hittites, the, in Cyprus, *280*, *321-323*
Home, Demeter the goddess of, *69*
Honey in legends of Dionysus, *108*, *143*

Hope, Demeter still had, *71*
Horned Isle (Kerastia), poetic name of Cyprus, *274*
Horns, Delian altar of, *384* f.
Horse, cure at Delos of a, *254*
Horse-racing at Delos, *377*, *380*
Horus, Apollo and Harpocrates, *402*
Hospitallers, Knights, at Colossi, *288*; on Delos, *379*
Hospitals, the temples of Aesculapius were not, *229* f.
Hostanes and Apollonius, *262*
Hours, the, and Dionysus, *96*
Humanity of Aesculapius, *239*
Humility of Aesculapius, *242*
Huns overran Thrace and Illyria, *87*
Hunter, Dionysus a, *96*, *101*, *128*, *160*, *185*
Huntress, Artemis the, at Epidaurus, *250*
Huntsman, Dionysus the wild, *96*, *101*, *128*, *160*, *185*
Hygieia, *220*, *240*
Hyperboreans at Delos, *379*

IACCHAGOGOS, another name for the Hierophant, *217*
Iacchos, *127* f., *174* f., *178* f., *210*, *212-214*
Iambe, *68*
Iano, King of Cyprus, his ransom, *336*
Iasion, father of Plutus, *97*
Icaria, (1) the Attic deme of, *5*, *32*, *36*, *80*, *101*, *104-115*, *117-119*, *121*, *129*, *133*, *368*; (2) (Icaros or Nicaria) the Island, *111*, *163* (see Italia)
Icarian legends and customs, *104-115*, *117-119*, *123*, *131* f., *164*, *208*
Icarius, *81*, *105*, *107-111*, *114* f., *135*
Icaros (Icarus, Icaria, or Nicaria), *111*, *163*
Ictinus at Bassae, *204*; at Eleusis (Hall of Initiation), *191*, *199* f., *202-206*

INDEX 441

Idalian fields, death of Adonis on, *291*
Idalium, dependent on Chittim of the Phoenicians, at, *282, 291, 321*
Illyrian tribes and Thracians, *86* f.
Inimarados of Eleusis, killed in war with Athens, *122*
Immigration, early Greek, into Cyprus, *280*
Immortality, ideas in the Mysteries about, *176, 181, 211*
Imperialism, Roman, *13-15, 37-39, 43* f.
Incubation in temples of Aesculapius, *236*
India, political state of, *12*
Indian Dionysus, a deification of Alexander's conquests, *29*
Indo-Caucasus, wine first cultivated on, *165*
Initiation and the initiated at Eleusis, *176, 181, 189, 208* f., *218* f.
Ino, a reveller of Cithaeron, *147, 150*
Inopus, Leto's travail on the banks of the, *356*
Inquisition, the Spanish, *8*
Inscriptions, early Cypriote, Aphrodite does not occur on, *321* f.
Inspiration of Dionysus, *29, 96* f., *102, 117, 133, 220*
Instruments used by doctors in days of Democedes, *223*
Insula, Hyginus' idea of, includes Mauritania and Egypt, *394*
Insularum provincia of Diocletian called ἐπαρχία νήσων Κυκλάδων, *393*
Intensity of Dionysus lacking in Aesculapius, *220*
Intolerance, Mohammedan, in Thrace, *85*
Ion colonised Cyclades as Apollo's son, *391*
Ionian festival at Delos, *372-374*;
—— Islands, May festivals of, *89*; British rule of, *277*
—— race, Apollo the father of, *379, 382, 393*

Iophon, *Antigone*, 904 ff., interpolated by, *166*
Iphigenia, love of, for Orestes, *150*; struggle for, and the *couvade*, *171*
Iris, her fruitless message to Demeter, *57*
Ishtar, Aphrodite and, *273, 300*; and Demeter, *303*; descent to Urugal of, *301*; lament for Tammuz of, *300* f.
Isis and Apollo at Delos, *402*
Islands and peninsulas, confusion of, in Homer, *392*
Ismenus, the softly gliding, *133*
Isolarii, Venetian books bearing title of, *328-331*
Israel, *5, 18, 274*
Italia, read Icaria for, in *Ant.* 1119, *133*
Ithaca, no wheat land, *47, 377*
Ivy-god, Apollo, *30* f.
Ivy and parsley, Mystae crowned with, *217*; branches for Bacchic worship, *142*

JACK-IN-THE-GREEN, Dionysus attached to himself the attributes of a, *83*
Japanese and Chinese drama, masks in, *172*
Jason, a pupil of Chiron, *232*
Jealousy of Aphrodite's Assyrian nature, *298*; prayer to Aphrodite for deliverance from, *300*
Jerusalem, Augustus' offerings at, *8*; buildings at Paphos and buildings at, *306*
Jews, religion of, *19*; Moeragenes maintains Dionysis is the god of the, *106*; Delos and the, *375*
Jordan, modern Delian legend of the, *356*
Journalism, Apollonius the victim of, *261*
Joy, mixture of, with sorrow, in Demeter, *73*
Julii, oaths In acta divi, *43*
Julius, Jupiter, *37*

JuliaDomna, Philostratus, Romancer-in-ordinary to, *258-260*
Jupiter, philosophical supreme god, *15, 20, 26*; Julius, *37*

Καππαδοκάρχης, *44*
Καθαροί, on Sybarite inscription, *176*
Kerastia, a name of Cyprus, *345* f.
Kerykes, the Deliastae chosen from, *376*
Kittim, the Phoenician Larnaca-Citium, *281*
Kolossi, Garin de, at Colossi, *288*
Kore in Orphic story, *181*
Κυκλάδων, ἐπαρχία νήσων, Diocletian's *Insularum provincia*, called the, *393*

LABYRINTH below the Epidaurian Tholos, *253* f.; Theseus in the Cretan, *400*
Lakkiadae, station of the Mystae at, *217*
Lapethus, importance of, in North Cyprus, *277*
Lapithae, Aesculapius the tribal god of, *221, 233*; on the Epidaurian temple of Aesculapius, *249*
Lararium of Severus, Christ, Abraham, Orpheus, Apollonius, and emperors in the, *265*
Lares Compitales and genius Augusti, *38*
Larnaca, early foundation at, by Phoenicians, *281*; fortified by Knights Templars, *288*
Lasus of Hermione detected Onomacritus, *127*
Laughless stone at Eleusis, *60* f.
Laurel tree, Lord Bacchus, lover of the, *30* f.; Leto and the, *356, 363*; connection of Apollo through Daphne with, *368*
Layard, Sir Henry, de Mas Latrie's dedication to, *278*
Lazarus found a cross in Cyprus, *275*
Lemnos, destruction of, predicted, *127*

Lenae, biennial procession of, *132*
Lenaea, the, and mid-winter festival of Icaria, *132*; first tragedy at Athenian, *132*
Lenaean Dionysus earlier than Dionysus Eleuthereus, *118, 132*
Lenaeon in Boeotia and Icaria, *112* f., *132*; Gamelion and, *132*; Brumalia in the season of, *112*
Lenides, or Lenae, *132*
Lepanto, the battle of, *331*
Lepidus and the favour of Tiberius, *42*
Lesbos, *14*
Leto, traditions and character of, *355-358, 363, 379, 383* f.
Lightning, Apollo sent the, for signal to Theoris, *377*
Ligyon, Achilles, so named for not taking mother's milk, *64*
Liknites, Iacchos surnamed, *128*
Limassol, land at, for old Paphos, *275, 287*
Limestone in Cyprus is friable, *288* f.
Lions, frieze of, on Aesculapius' Temple at Epidaurus, *248*; on cornice of the Epidaurian Tholos, *251*
Little-in-the-fields, Mr. Browning's name for the rural Dionysia, *131*
Lotus blossom, miraculous effect of, *231*
Lusignan, Hugues I. of, gave Colossi to Hospitallers, *288*
Lusignans, feudalism of, in Cyprus, *278*
Lusios, Dionysus called, *159, 162*
Lustrations of Delos, *362* f.
Lycian Patara, oracles of Apollo at, *370*
Lycians in Cyprus, *279* f.
Lycorea, peak of Parnassus, *25*
Lycurgus and Dionysus, story of, *77*; a Thracian, *77*; his hatchet, *77*
Lydian airs, and the musical escapade of Cinyras, *294*
Lydias, Dionysus and the, *157*

Lyre, Apollo's, lent to Dionysus, *31* ; Apollo and Hermes invented the, *372* ; seven strings of Apollo's, *359*
Lysander, deification of, *41*

MACEDONIA, *79, 86* f., *137, 221, 379, 386* f.
Machaon, son of Aesculapius, *222, 230*
Macris, Mysa, daughter of Aristaeus, nurse of Dionysus, *143*
Madeira, restocked with vines from Cyprus, *288*
Madness, Dionysus - worship and, *110, 120, 141, 145, 147, 161* f.
Maenads, in legends and worship of Dionysus, *31, 79, 100, 112, 128, 137, 139, 141, 145, 150, 158-160, 181, 184* f.
Maera, in the Old Attic Icarian legend, *109-111, 114*
Magdalene, St. Mary, in Cyprus, *275*
Magicians, Apollonius among the, *262*
Magnes of Icaria, *117*
Maidenswell at Eleusis, *60* f.
Malta, ruins on, and Paphian ruins, *306*
Mandra, a sheepfold in Cyprus, often a cave, *289*
Manwrecker, Dionysus, surnamed, *100*
Maps of Cyprus, modern, *274*
Maps, neglect by Meursius of available, *351*
Marathon, mountains near, early Thracians settled on, *11* f., *80, 105* ; journey from, to Icaria overcomes Dionysus, *106* ; the wilderness of, *114* ; the Deliastae at, *376* ; Delion at, *376* ; daisies grow on the field of, *252*
Marathonian tetrapolis, the worship of Apollo from, *104*
Marathus of Phoenicia, the Snail's Tower at, and the south wing at Paphos, *308, 314*

Marco (San), title of Cavaliere di, *350*
Mardonius, devastated the Hall of Pisistratus, *198*
Maron, wine given by, *91*
Marpessa and Apollo, *368*
Marriage of Dionysus and Ariadne, *130* ; of Dionysus and Basilissa, *130* f. ; of Dionysus and Persephone, *178* ; of the doge and the sea, *131.*
Masks, Japanese and Chinese, use of, in plays, *172* ; use of, in tragedy, a barbaric survival, *172*
μαστοειδές, Strabo's epithet of, proves his Olympus was Troodos, *325*
Mater dolorosa, Demeter as, *71*
Matriarchy, protest of Apollo against, *171*
Mauritania, one of Hyginus' insulae, *394*
Mavrocordato, Alex., was a doctor of Padua, *268*
Maximus of Aegae wrote of, and shared, ascetic life of Apollonius, *257* f.
May-day festival, ancient, at Icaria, *112* ; at modern Corfu, *89*
Mayor of Thebes, a doctor, *267*
Measure, Attic sense of, in Dionysus-worship, *105, 113*
Medea had knowledge of miraculous drugs, *231* ; Aphrodite as represented in the, *300*
Media worships Dionysus, *140*
Mediaeval church, laws of purification in, *360* ; churches, ruins of, in Cyprus, *283*
Mediation, final requirement of, by Aesculapius, *254, 256*
Medicine (Greek) early (i.) beginnings of, *223-225*—(ii.) practical bearings of Homeric, *228* f.—(iii.) positive and mythical aspects of, *232-234* ; later perfection of, (i.) sacred, *222, 226, 230, 232, 237* f.—(ii.) secular, *223-225, 229* f., *234* f., *238* f. ; modern Greek, study of, *222, 268*

Meeting-house at Eleusis, and in Thrace, for Dionysus-worship, *189*
Megara, and Icaria, relations of, to early comedy, *115*
Meilichius, Dionysus surnamed, *101*
Melanaigis, Dionysus, seen by daughters of Eleuther, *120*; Dionysus, madness sent by, *120, 133*
Meleager, a pupil of Chiron, *232*
Mell supper, *5*
Melpomene, an emanation from Dionysus Melpomenos of Eleutherae, *104*
Melpomenos, surname of Dionysus, the god of song and dance, *104*
Memphis, *14*
Meroe, thigh mountain, and second birth of Dionysus, *165*
μηροτραφής, Dionysus called, *166*
Mesorea, or mid-mountain of Cyprus, *275-277*; devastation of, *339*
Messianic vision of Euripides in *The Bacchanals, 138*
Metagenes of Xypeta, builder of Eleusinian temple, *191, 204*
Metanira, legends of, *62, 65, 68, 107*
Metapontum, story of Parmeniscus of, *383*
Methe, painted by Pausias in the Tholos, *253*
Meursius, John, his life and work, *324, 344, 353, 347-351*
Midas, Dionysus, and the legends of, *79, 87, 92* f., *294*
Milton's debt to Euripides, *148, 150*
Mimallones, the Thracian originals of Bacchanals, *97*
Mining invented by Cinyras, *294*
Miracles inscribed at Epidaurus, *254*; wrought by Aesculapius, *234, 237* f., *245* ; of Apollonius, sanctioned by Aesculapius, *257*
—— wine a perpetual source of, *91*
—— of Dionysus, *143, 149, 153*

Miraculous drugs in Homer, moly, nepenthe, lotus-blossom, *231*
Mnesicles, Propylaea of, imitated at Eleusis, *190*
Mocenigo, Isolario of Benedetto dedicated to, *330*
Moeragenes, maintained that Dionysus was the god of the Jews, *186*; a bandit of the Taurus, *258*; the Athenian? told of Apollonius' life, *258*
Moesa, and her two daughters, of Julia Domna's clique, *259*
Molière, farce made of Democedes' story, *224*
Moly, Herophilus on drugs compared with Homer's account of, *237, 238*
Monastery of St. Nicholas, on Cape Curias, *288*
Monks, the destroyers of Eleusis were, *188*
Monotheism, of Greek religion, *10*
Morality, the Bacchanals, *137*
Mortality of Aesculapius, his mortal schooling, *231, 232*
Moscow MSS. of hymns to Demeter and Dionysus, *163*
Moses and Apollonius as magicians, *262*
Mother Rye, Demeter as, *51*
Motion, of the elements of Dionysus, *92*
Mountaineer-festivals, two Icarian, *112* f.
Mourning for Dionysus, especially in Icaria, *96* f., *112* f.
Musaeus, Onomacritus falsified, *127*
Musagetes, surname of Apollo, the god of song and dance, *104*
Muses, the worship of, with Apollo and Dionysus, *25, 31, 78, 96, 102-104, 135, 159*
Music, relation of instruments of, to Dionysus, *143* f.
—— at the Delia, *380*
Musical contest of Apollo and Cinyras, *294*
Mustafa, at the sack of Nicosia, *332*

INDEX 445

Mycenae vases, rosettes on, *251*
Myconos and Delos, *359, 365, 376, 389*
Mylitta and Aphrodite - Urania, *298*
Myron, arraignment of Alcmaeonidae by, *124*
Mystae, yearly procession from Athens to Eleusis of, *212-218*
Mysteries, the Eleusinian or Greater, *122, 125, 141, 175* f., *180-189, 207-210, 218* f. ; the Lesser at the Athenian Eleusinion, *124* f., *127* ; the Samothracian, *403*
Mystery, ancient and modern meaning of, *178*
Mystes and Epoptes, degrees of, *208* f.
Mythology, *3, 4, 7;* era of conscious analysis in, *78;* (Greek) contrasted with philosophy and theology, *52* ; the critic of, must not offend the poet, *28*
Myths (Greek), their relation to fetichism, *27* ; lives of Christian saints and late pagan, *265* ; the beautiful, of early Attica, *71, 104- 112*

NAIADS, give not wine but water, *108*; torch-led dance of, *88* (see Fire and Maenads)
Narcissus, the, in myth of Persephone, *56*
Nature - worship in Greece, *73, 136* f. ; personifications of, *78, 97* ; theory of, at the bottom of Eleusinian and Dionysiac worship, *140, 178-180, 182-185* ; Aesculapius and, *220* ; Aphrodite and, *271, 273*
Nauplia, road from, to the Hieron of Aesculapius, *244*
Nausicaa, compared to the Delian palm-tree, *355*
Naxia, Tintoretto painted Acropolis of, in his Bacchus and Ariadne, *328*
Naxos, Delian Apollo and, *365, 376,*

389, 400 ; Dionysus, legends of, *81, 111, 130, 163*
νεωκορία, competition for, *44*
Neocorion at Eleusis, the, *197*
νεωκόρος, finally removed from meaning temple-sweeper, *44*
Nepenthe, Helen's, stands for curing mind through body, *234* f.
Nero, the foe of mankind, *42* ; manner of his birth, *42* ; probably gave the Icarian sculptures to the Athenian stage, *114*; as Apollo in the flesh, *114*
Nestor, high esteem of doctors felt by, *222* ; a pupil of Chiron, *232* ; wounding and fall of horse of, *254*
Netherworld-god, Aesculapius like Dionysus a, *220*
New York, Varoschia, Famagosta, Salamis, and, *283*
Nicaria (Icaros or Icaria), an Aegean island where Dionysus was born, *163* ; Draconus, a promontory on, *163*
Nicholas, St., a monastery on Cape Curias, *288*
Nicias at Delos, *378-381* ; endowment of prayers by, *380*
Nicosia, cathedral of, built by Knights Templars, *288*; Venetians banished to, *326* ; siege and sack of, *332-334*
Nile, connected with the Delian Inopus, *356* ; the Cypriote Pediacus and the, *276*
Nineveh, Aphrodite-Ishtar at, *303* ; poem on Ishtar found at, *301* ; Adonis of Amathus and the Tammuz-Adonis of, *292*
Ninivite, Damis the, told credulous tales of Apollonius' travels, *257* f.
Niobids, Apollo and Artemis pursue, *367*
North Cyprus, an elegant extract from Asia Minor, *277*
North range of Cyprus, age of, *275* f.

Northern origin of Aesculapius and gods at Eleusis, *220* f.
Northumberland, Demeter's counterpart in, *49* f.
Notables, connection with imperial worship of provincial meetings of, *43* f.
Notre Dame de Bon Secours, Aphrodite Sosandra as, *298*
Novices, the Eleusinian, *182, 208*
Nymphs and naiads, *78, 94*
Nysa, curious legends of, *78, 134, 143, 163-166, 168*

OAK, branches for Bacchic worship, *142*
Oath, doctors', by Apollo, Aesculapius, etc., *220*
Oaths, "In acta divi Augusti" and "divi Julii," *43*
Oceanus, Persephone seized near, *58*
Oceanus, Eleusis son of, *64*
Octavius, an, of the Emperor's Gens, *14*
Odysseus, the domain of, no wheatland, *47*; streams poured for the dead by, *91, 94*; anatomical knowledge of, *228*; Chiron's instruction of, *232*; the shipwrecked, *275*
Odysseus of Gravia, a modern Leonidas, *400*
Oil contrasted with wine, *108*
Oliveto, Pius II. describes Monte, *326*
Olympia, *9* f. ; *271, 372*
Olympian Zeus, capitals of Athenian temple of, *252*; mildness of, in Aesculapius, *220*
Olympus of the gods, *15, 20, 26, 28, 57, 177, 240, 371*; of Thrace and Macedonia, *29, 87, 153*; of Cyprus, an investigation of its whereabouts, *324-343*
Omadios, Dionysus surnamed, *101*
Omestes, Dionysus surnamed, *101*
Omnipotence, not chiefly reprehended by Greeks in Christian ideal, *20*; Greek gods had local, *10*
Onomacritus, *125-127, 174* f., *181*
ὀπαῖον of Eleusinian temple, *191*
Opposites, Demeter a curious mingling of, *73*
Oracles, *34-36, 96, 238, 255*
Oreads, Dionysus and the, *96*
Orestes, Iphigenia's love for, *150*; justified by the principle of Dionysus' second birth, *169* f.
Orgies of Dionysus, *34, 154*; of Demeter, *63*
Orientation of temples, facts about the, *192*
Origen, read four books of Moeragenes on Apollonius, *258, 264*
Oropus, discoveries about Amphiaraus at, *232*
Orpheotelestae, the, *181*
Orpheus, Thracian tradition of, *9, 103, 157, 182*; in the Lararium of Severus, *265*
Orphic doctrines and myths, *25, 87, 125, 127, 178, 181*
Ortygia and Asteria, barren legend of, *356, 358*
Ostrogoths at Eleusis, *188*
Otherness, equivalent to reality in Thracian conception of Dionysus and his world, *90*
Otherworlds of *Iliad* and *Odyssey*, *49*
Ovid, his lowly setting of the stay of Demeter with Celeus, *71*

PACTOLUS, Dionysus bade Midas wash in floods of, *92, 178*
Paean Apollo, the sun-god, father of Aesculapius, *231, 241* f.
Pagans, it is best to make tolerable sense of the affairs of, *19*; criticism of the solitary Christian god by, *20*; testimony for Apollonius of, *264* f.
Paganism, *3, 7*; last days of, *21, 45, 258, 261, 266*
Palaia, a town between Larnaca and

Limassol not next to Olympus, *325*
Palm tree and laurel of Leto at Delos, *356, 363, 380*
Palm tree in bas-relief of Dionysus at the house of Icarius, *106*
Pammerope, daughter of Celeus, *65*
Pan, distinguished from Satyr, *99*; personifies cruelty of Dionysus, *99*
Panacea named in doctors' oath, *220*; attends on Aesculapius, *240*
Panas, Dr., of the Paris faculty, *269*
Pandarus, ignorance of anatomy punished in, *228*
Pandemos, Aphrodite, shrine of, near Asclepieium at Athens, *270*; Mylitta represented by, *298*
Pandion, dealings with Thracians of king, *111*; the fifth king since Cecrops is, *105*; Demeter came to Eleusis under king, *119*; Attic Dionysus-legends and king, *119*
Panic terrors inspired of Dionysus and his Pans, *99*
Pans, or Aegipans, *98-100*
Papticapneum, men of, at Delos, *387*
Πάφιja, ἡ, later Aphrodite, represented by, *321*
Paphian Aphrodite, distinguished from the Syrian Goddess on Delos, *403*; cone of, and Delian Baetylus, *386*; Aphrodite at Tegea and, *285*
Paphos (new), *285*
—— (old), *2, 5*; history of the temple and worship of Aphrodite at, *272, 279, 281* f., *284* f., *289-291, 293, 295-297, 304-308, 312* f., *324, 345* f.
Parian Marble, Susarion and the, *117*; Aristotle's *Constitution of Athens* and the, *132*; fixes the date of the first tragedy at Athens, *132*
Parisian feuilletonist, Philostratus a, *260*
Parmeniscus at Delos, story of, *382*

Parnassus, description of, *23-25, 33, 36, 133*; Dionysus and winter festivals on the, *112* f., *132* f., *149, 156* f.; Apollo and Dionysus on the, *104*; Daulis on the, *111*
Paros, Archilochus and, *365*; Delos and, *365, 376*
Parsley and ivy, Mystae crowned with, *217*
Paspati, Dr., a well-known author, *269*
Passion, the, *4*; in the Dionysus-legend, *153-157, 181*
Passion-Play of Attica, *The Bacchanals* called, *137*
Patara, winter oracles of Apollo at, *370*
Patriarchy, in the primitive family, *170*
Patrician worship of Eleusis, Icarian Dionysus added to the, *208*
Patroos, Apollo, altar at Delos of, *379, 382*; the Cyclades are chosen isles of Apollo, *393*
Paul, St., Simon Magus, Apollonius and, *258, 260*
Pausias, paintings of, in the Tholos, *252* f.
Pauson, compared unfavourably with Polygnotus, *252*
Peasant, the Greek, of to-day and his taste in wine, *106*; the Cypriote, *335, 341*; admiration for doctors of the Greek, *222*
Pediaeus, the, a Cypriote river Nile, *275, 351*
Pegasus, of Eleutherae, *34, 120*; on Parnassus, *24*
Pelasgians, Thracians identified with, *220*
Peleus, the fire-baptism of Achilles and, *64*; a pupil of Chiron, *232*
Peloponnesian War, Greek religion stood intact until time of, *136*; state of Greece after the, *11*
Peninsulas and islands, confusion of, in Homer's day, *392*

Pentelicus, home of Dionysus near, *104* f.
Pentheus, Dionysus flies to Icarius from, *107*; the frenzy of Zagreus-Dionysus and, *139*; in *The Bacchanals* of Euripides, *145-160*
Pericles, and the temple at Eleusis, *187*
Persephone, earliest and forbidding conception of, *47-49*, *128*; later myth of (post-Homeric), *50*, *54* f., *57-59*, *69*, *75* f.; general religious and moral aspects of the divinity of, *48*, *69*, *73-75*, *213*; significance at Eleusis of, *73* f., *77*, *144*, *176*, *178*, *218*; Iacchos and, *174*; Kore, a name of (Orphic), *181*; Adonis plays the part of, *291*; tie between Aesculapius and, *219* f.; Erigone confused with, *107*; Zagreus the son of, *128*; monuments and rites concerning, *59* f., *70*, *194-196*, *213*
Persia, Democedes led captive to, *224*
Persian order, the, *12*, *17*
Persians, destruction of the Eleusinian Hall by the, *198*; interference with Eleusinian procession from Athens by the, *211*
Personification, implications in primitive mind of, *78*
Pfingstl, killing of the, compared to Pentheus' death, *159*
Phaedra calls Aphrodite Cypris Pontia, *297*
Phaedrus, stage built by, at Athens, *114*
Phaedryades, rocks at Delphi, *23*
Phaestus, near Cnossus, Epimenides of, *124*
Pharsalia, watchword of, *300*; Dante remembered Lucan's, *24*
Phidias, Plutarch would leave supervision of Eleusis-buildings to, *191*
Philip, Dionysus and the house of, *79*, *138*
Philip, portico at Delos of, *379*

Philippi, inscription found near, *87*; Dionysus' hill near, *92*
Philo, porch of, at Eleusis, *190* f.
Philonides named Cyprus Acamantis, *274*
Philosophers, Apollonius among the illustrious, *263* f.
Philosophy, mythology and theology contrasted with, *52*
Philostratus, Apollonius not the play-acting personage of, *261* f., *264*
Phlegyae and Lapithae, Aesculapius tribal god of, *221*, *233*
Phlegyas, visit of, to Epidaurus, *243*
Phoebus, *35* f.; leader in the dance, *29*
Phoenicians, name of Dionysus from, *85*; Dionysus as a child of the thigh came with the, *163-165*, *168*; Moesa, Julia Domna, and Ulpian were by descent, *259*; Aphrodite a goddess of the, *277*, *286*, *323*; Atargatis on Delos worshipped by the, *403*; Cabiri brought by the, *402*; Delos and the, *374*; Cyprus and the, *279*, *281-284*, *319*, *321*; Old Paphos of Cyprus and the, *281*, *284* f., *306*, *308*; Hittites confused with the, *322* f.; Selinus and the, *306*
Phrygians, cousins of Thracians, *85*, *90*, *103*; Dionysus and the, *77*, *90*, *95*, *103*, *140*, *164*, *178*; Adonis and the, *291*; Cinyras and the, *294*; Cybele and the, *97*, *143*; Rhea of Crete and Cybele of the, *143*
Phye, Thracian girl named, *126*
Phyllis betrayed by Demophoon, *65*
Phytalus entertained Demeter at Lakkiadae, *217*
Pieria, a centre of Dionysus-worship, *87*, *137*, *153*; spirits of waters the nurses of Dionysus in, *94*; Icaria an Attic, *111*
Pieris, a centre of Dionysus-worship, *87*, *92*, *94*
Pindar remoulds story of Tantalus, *18*; transcends idea of a resistless

and unrelenting God, *19* ; a leader in nobility of religious thought, *29* ; solemn aspect of Aphrodite's charm seen by, *299* f. ; his account of Cinyras as Apollo's and Aphrodite's friend, *292, 294, 299* f. ; account of Parnassus and deluge by, *25* ; birth legend of Aesculapius keeps him in Thessaly, *245* f. ; his pious preludes, *102* ; praises of Delos by, *364*
Pine-tree dedicated to Dionysus, *106* ; Pentheus, perched in a, *150, 158* f.
Pirates carried off Dionysus, *168*
Pirithous or Apollo, in the Olympian pediment, *9*
Piscopia of the Venetian Cornari, *289*
Pisistratidae, *127*
Pisistratus, Solon's censure and acting of, *116, 126* ; Dionysus-legend and worship developed by, *125-132, 137, 175* ; second exile of, *126, 137* ; lustration of Delos by, *362* ; tillers of the soil befriended by, *126* ; Eleusinian Hall of, *198* f., *204*
Pissouri, brighter landscape near, *289*
Pius II. translates Strabo on Cyprus, *326*
Planets, Dionysus and the, *133*
Plataea, *11*
Plato, arguments about Gods of, *18* f. ; on the "Streamers," *179* ; Aphrodite Urania of, *298* ; protest against the poets of, *26* ; leader in nobility of religious thought, *29*
Pleiades, Alcyone of, *119*
Plothea of Epacria, *105, 119*
Pluto, Dionysus brought the epithet to Hades at Eleusis, *174, 177* f. ; precinct of, in Eleusinian sanctuary, *193-195* ; of eight Eleusinian divinities, *178*
Pluto, daughter of Oceanus and Tethys, *98*

Pluto, or Plutus, *97*
Plutus, nature of his divinity like Dionysus', *97* f.
Plutus, Demeter's son, *97*
Podalirius, son of Aesculapius, infallible in Homer, *230*
Podocathari, fortunes of the family of, *331* f., *336-340*
Podocatharo, Giouanni, his loyalty to king Iano, *336* ; Hettore, *330-333, 338-342*
—— Cardinal Ludovico, collections of, *331*
—— Pietro, under the "re bastardo," reward of, *336* f.
Poetic inspiration, *102*
Poet, Plato's prohibition to the, *18* ; Apollo as conceived by the, *25, 33* ; inconsistency demanded in any treatment of Dionysus by the, *136* ; critics of Greek mythology must not offend the, *28* ; Dante the poet's, *33* ; Eleusis and the, *182* ; religion and the, *38, 136*
Poetry, Greek mythology and the abstract spirit of, *28* ; Greek religion is the poetry of, *33* ; Icaria influenced the history of, *111* ; Apollo and Dionysus, the two gods of dancing, song, and, *104*
Politics, ancient and modern, *10, 15*
Pollux, a pupil of Chiron, *232*
Polycletus, the elder and the younger, *246* f. ; the Tholos of, at Epidaurus, *250-254* ; theatre built by, at Epidaurus, *246*
Polycrates, called Democedes, from Athens, *224* ; gave Rhenea to Apollo, *361* f., *376*
Polygnotus, Pauson, compared unfavourably with, *252*
Polyphemus, clever wounding of, *228*
Polytheism, *3, 10, 20*
Polyxenus, a son of Celeus, *63*
Pomegranate-seed, in myth of Persephone, *58*
Πουτάρχης, *44*

2 G

Pontia, Cypris, Phaedra's name for Aphrodite, *297*
Porch, used for stoa or porticus, *236, 248, 310*
Porches, for the sick in Aesculapian sanctuaries, *247* f. ; need of, at Paphos, *310*
Portulani, in the Marcian library, and the Museo Correr, *329*
Poseidon, Delos and Delphi belonged to, *32, 37* f., *358*
—— father of Aithousa, the mother of Eleuther, *119*
—— and Apollo walled Troy, *372*
—— father of Persephone, *48*
Possession, by Dionysus, *9, 110, 133*; the whole play of *The Bacchanals* a case of, *136*
Prayer to Dionysus, *133*
Prayers, endowment of, at Delos, *380* ; to Aesculapius, Apollo named first in, *220*
Preceptorery, older name for commandery, *288*
Prehistoric man in Greek art, *173*; tribe changes, and second birth of Dionysus, *163* (see Primitive)
Prescriptions of Aesculapius given in dreams, *235*
Priests, of Aesculapius, *230, 234* f., *241* ; cleverness of Delphian, *30* ; Delphian, sanctioned brotherhood of Apollo and Dionysus, *31* ; of old Paphos descend from Cinyras, *291*
Primitive belief, in personification, *78*; custom, survives in tragic masks, *172*; Dionysus, confusion about, *90*; family, *169-171*; man, *12*; medicine, Chiron and, *232*; worship, *106, 137, 195, 293*
Probation, Dionysus before he came to Athens underwent a triple, *81*
Procession to Eleusis, many local customs connected with, *218*; of the Mystae from Aristophanes' *Frogs, 212-216*

Processional ways at Athens, Delos, and Eleusis, *193, 379*
Proclus, an Athenian friend of Aesculapius, *256*
Prophecy, coupled with wine, *93*
Prophet, divine, Dionysus a, *78*
Prophets of Dionysus, the Bacchanals are, *156* f.
Propitiation of Dionysus, *134*
—— of Eleusinian gods, desire for, at Athens in 405 B.C., *215* f.
Propylæa, Athenian, *307* ; Eleusinian, *186*
Proserpina, rape of, localised in Sicily, *62* (see Persephone)
Provindemiator, star in the Icarian legend, *111*
Prudentilla, the heiress, wife of Apuleius, *262*
Prussia, East and West, *6*
Psophis, Phoenician foundations at, *285* f., *323*
Ptolemy, Cos and, likened to Apollo and Delos, *394*; Theocritus praises, *318*
—— (the geographer), place of Cypriote Olympus according to, *327*
Public doctors and ancient hospitals, *229*
Punch and Judy show, Greek counterpart of, *90*
Purification, days of, at Athens before the Eleusinia, *209* f. ; at Delos, *355*; Milton's lines upon, *360*
Purifying powers of Dionysus, *133*
Purity, requirement of, by Aesculapius, *235, 255*; ideal of Apollo and Delos, *355, 360-363, 370*
Pygmalion and Cinyras, kinship of, *294*; sculpture invented by, *294*
Pyrasus of Demeter, *47, 221*
Pythagoras and the Pythagoreans, *72, 218* f., *223, 257, 382*
Pythian monster slain, *35* ; Apollo's expiation for slaying the, *371*; sent by Hera against Leto, *358*
Pythoness, description of the, *36*

QUAKER-MEETING, and first tragic actor of Thespis, *117*
Quintilian, Tacitus, and Pliny, reverence for the imperial idea felt by, *41* f.
Quiver, votive gift at Delos of a leaden, *384*

RANSOM of Christians from Turkish captivity, *335* f., *339*
Rapendosa, the valley of, at Icaria, *105, 109, 114*
Rarian plain, the, *55* f., *66, 187, 207*
Reality of Thracian Dionysus-world, *90*
Reason, inapplicable to the gods, *146*; difficulties of, in Dionysus-legend, *148*
Religion, primitive, relation to Greek myths of, *27*; Cyprus a meeting-ground of many a, *277*
—— (Greek) relentlessness of early phases of, *35*; is the poetry of poetry, *33*; was unshaken until the Peloponnesian war, *136*; Athenian innovations in, *129* f.; harmony of Greek medicine and, *226, 230*
Resurrection, and the offering of a cock to Aesculapius, *239*
Retzinato, Dionysus overcome by, *106*
Revels, the night-long, of Dionysus, *140*
Rhea, Demeter's mother, *50, 57*; of the eight Eleusinian divinities, *178, 401*; a Cretan Cybele, *143*
Rhenea, Delos and, *360-362, 376, 394*
Rhodes, Telchines of, *97*; Colossus of, *287* f.; neither of Cyclades nor of Sporades, *393*
Ribaldry of Eleusinia, connected with Iacchos-worship, *214*
Right living, Pythagorean rules of, *72*; Demeter's rules of, *71* f.
Roman Brumalia and Rosalia, *86-88* (see Rosalia)

Roman Church, *15, 21*
—— hall at Eleusis, *201, 203*
—— Aesculapia, distinction between Greek and, *221, 254*
Romanticists compared with classicists, *150*
Rome, *3, 5, 7* f., *10, 13*; and Augustus, worship of, *40, 45*; temples to the emperor discouraged at, *38*; Cyprus under, *278*
Rosalia, Roman and Thracian festival of, *86-88*; centres of, in Macedonia and Thrace, *87*; survival of, *87-90*; and Brumalia compared with Icarian festivals, *112*
Rose-gardens of Midas in Thrace, *92*
Rosettes, history of, as ornaments, *251*
Rotunda (Tholos) of Polycletus at Epidaurus, *246* f., *250-254*
Rustica work at Old Paphos, *308*

SABAE, of Thrace and Phrygia, *96*
Sabazius, a name for the primitive Dionysus, *86*; and the Sabae, *96*; Thracian and Phrygian idea of, *77, 103*
Sacred lake, the, in the Delian legend of Leto, *356*
Sacred and secular medicine, distinction between, *232, 237*
Sahara, mountains of Cyprus and of the, *276*
Sailors, votive inscription to Apollo of, *384*
Saints, lives of Christian, and late Pagan myths, *21, 265*
Saisara, daughter of Celeus (Pamphos), *65*
Salamis, *12*; Mount Acamas on, *187, 344*; Blaeuw's description of, *346* f.; Cychreus and, *64, 345* f.; Bocarus, a river on, *324, 344*; of Cyprus, *283, 344-346, 351-353*
Samos, not of Cyclades or Sporades, *393*; Democedes called by Polycrates to, *224*; sack of, by Pers-

ians, *224*; Prince Carathéodori of, *268*
Samosata, Lucian of, a Voltaire, *262*
Sanctuaries, Greek, *2* f., *5*, *7*; Christian, *2*, *4* f.; Aphrodite at all Greek, *271*
Sappho, invocation of, to Aphrodite, *295*
Sardanapalus (Assurbanipal), poem on Ishtar found in palace of, *300*
Sarmatians, the, overran Thrace and Illyria, *87*
Sathalia, tempestuous gulf of, *275*
Satrachus and Bocarus, *345* f.
Satrae, the indomitable, *84*
Satyr-friend of mystic maids, *88* (see Maenads)
Satyr-play, the Icarian, *132*
Satyrs, half beasts and half men, *78*
—— and Sileni, companions of Dionysus, *94*, *99*, *106*, *128*
Saviour-god, Dionysus the, *134*
Savoy, Democedes' career paralleled at the court of, *224*
Science has its place in nature of Chiron, *232*
—— compatible with superstition in worship of Aesculapius, *234*
—— and religion, harmony of, in Greek medicine, *226*, *238*
—— debt to Homeric fighting of, *229*
Sculpture, skill of Pygmalion in, *294*
Scythian superstition, Hippocrates on a gross, *238*
Sea, the sound of, in forests, *6*; part in Greek worship played by, *210*; power of, to purify, *210*; Dionysus leaps into, *77*
Seasons attend Dionysus, *78*, *96*
Secular and sacred medicine, distinction between, *232*, *237*
Seefeld, library of, looted by Charles X. of Sweden, *350*
σηκός, ὁ μυστικός, *189*
Selinus, pierced stones at, and piercings at Old Paphos, *306*
Semachidae, Dionysus-legend of, *105*, *119*

Semachus, legend of Dionysus coming to visit, *105*, *119*
Semele, Theban place of death of, *140*; Dionysus and, *140-142*, *163*, *177*, *181*; Pentheus and, *148*, *154*; Dione and, *318*
Semitic, Aphrodite's decisive traits are, *272* f., *280*
Senate decrees honours to Julius Caesar, *37*, *40*
Serapis, *3*; priests of Aesculapius and, *254*; Delian Apollo and, *402*
Seriphos on the way to Delos, *376*
Serpent impostures of Alexander of Abonotichus, *254*; Zeus in form of, *181*
Serpents, part played by, in miracles of Aesculapius, *235*, *253* f.
Sestrachus or Satrachus, a river at Old Paphos, *346*
Severus, Alexander, Julia Domna's great-nephew, *265*
Sheep-folds are often in Cypriote caves, *289*
Sicilian life, Aphrodite at centres of, *271*.
Sicily, Greeks in, worshipped Demeter, *51*; myth of Proserpina localised in, *62*
Sicyon, connection of, with tragedy overstated, *115*
Sidon, Cadmus of, and Pentheus, *147*; Aphrodite Ashtaroth at, *303*; Cadmus of, brings eastern tinge into Theban Dionysus story, *164*; sent gifts to Delian Apollo, *387*; early intercourse of, with Cyprus, *281*
Sight, use of terms of, to describe the Mysteries, *209*
Silence, at Eleusis, *180-182*; Pausanias warned to keep, about Eleusinia, *218*
Sileni, innumerable, and Satyrs the mates of Dionysus, *94*, *97*
Silenus, old, the type of things that flow, *78*, *93-95*, *98*
Silvius, Aeneas, *326* f.

INDEX
453

Simon Magus, Apollonius and Paul from the same quarter, *260*
Sisyphus, shadowy punishment of, *76*
Slave-market, Delos a, *375, 401*
Snow, revellers above Delphi blocked by, *113*
Socrates, loftier teachings of, in *The Bacchanals*, *138*; meaning of his dying words, *239*; might not die while Athens was consecrate to Delian Apollo, *362*
Solomon's temple and the Paphian ruin, *306, 313* f.
Solon and Epimenides, *122* f., *175*
—— and the tragedy of Thespis, *116, 123, 126*
Son of God, Aesculapius described as the, *240*
Song and dance in Dionysus-worship, *102-104*
Sophism, the, of Sophocles, *166* f.; the, of Tiresias in *The Bacchanals*, *149*
Sophocles, the Tiresias of, *145, 148* f.
—— Dionysus the tutelary god of, *81*
—— sophism of, *166* f.; Icarian notion of Dionysus simpler than his, *111*
Sorcery, Apuleius in his own defence on the charge of, *262*
Soroë, Meursius at, *348* f.
Sosandra Aphrodite at Athens, *271, 298, 300*
Sotera, Athene, and Pisistratus, *126*
Soudan, Nysa in the Troglodytic country beyond the, *165*
Soumali-country, is the country of the cinnamon, *165*
Sparta, interference at Eleusis under Cleomenes, *216*
Spenser, anatomy of, compared with Homer's, *228*
Sphekia, a name of Cyprus, *345* f.
Sphettus, prayer of Diophantus of Sphettus, *241*

Spintharus, of Corinth, built Delphian temple, *31*
Sporades, the, *391-398*
Spring, celebration of, return of Dionysus in, *112* f.; gibes in celebration of, *213*
Stadion at the Apollonia and Delia, *388*
Stage, Athenian, built by Nero and by Phaedrus, *114*
Stars, fawn-skins symbolise the heaven flecked with, *140*
Statius, linked Icaria and Eleusis, *107*; tells of Erigone's wanderings, *114*
Stavrovuni, Mount, Santa Croce, or Della Croce, *325*
Stockholm, MSS. of Meursius used by Graevius, *351*
Stoicism, a refuge, *41*
Stoics, practically believed in many gods, *20*
Strabo, antiquity of Meineke's mispunctuation of, xiv. p. 683, *325-327*
Strymon, of Orphic fame, and Pieris, *87*; Pisistratus in exile near the, *137*
Styx, mother of Persephone, *49*
Sublime, in Euripides, Göthe on the, *162*
Suicide, epidemic-mania for, of Icarian maidens, *110*; epidemics of, in modern times, *110*
Sultan, Colossi, appropriated by the, *288*
Sun-god, the source of knowledge of miraculous drugs is the, *231*
Sunium, on way to Delos from Athens, *376*
Surgeon, Democedes qualified at Croton as a, *225*
Surgery, Homeric skill in, came down to professional doctors, *224*; necessity of warfare the mother of invention of, *226*; at Epidaurus, *237*; knowledge of, upon which Hippocrates drew, *225*; sprang from positive practi-

cal tendency in early medicine, *233, 237*
Surgical operations inspired by Aesculapius, *226, 237*
Susarion, comedy, his great invention, *114* f., *117*
Suttee, Thracian, custom analogous to, *84*
Swans, song of, at Apollo's birth, *359*
Sybaris, inscription from a tomb at, *176*
Syra has one part of ancient Delian glory, *389*
—— Aphrodite drifted to Paphos from, *296*
Syrian traits in Aphrodite, *297*
—— goddess, worship on Delos, of the, *403*
Syriote peasant dances in carnival, *388*
Syros and Delos, *365, 376*
Syrtos, the modern peasant-dance called the, *400*

TABLE mountains, of Cyprus and the Sahara, *276*
Taboos, account of, in the *Golden Bough*, *360*
Tacitus, reverence of, for the imperial idea, *41* f.
Tammuz-Adonis, plays part of Dionysus and Persephone, *291*; lament for, *300* f.; temple at Amathus of, *292*
Tantalus, Pindar remoulds the story of, *18*; punishment of, *76*
Tar in Cypriote wine, *288*
Tarsus, Apollonius removed from Aegae to, *257*
Taurus mountains of Asia Minor, northern range of Cyprus parallel to, *258, 275*
Taxes, the, levied to-day in Cyprus, *277*
Tegea, temple of Paphian goddess at, *285* f.
Telamon, a pupil of Chiron, *232*
Telchines, *97*

Telesphorus (Convalescence) attends on Aesculapius, *240*
Telesterion, Hall of Initiation at Eleusis, *189*
Tellus the Athenian, death and burial of, at Eleusis, *122*
Tempests, stilled by a nail of the True Cross, *275*
Templars, Knights, in Cyprus, *288, 341*
Tenedos, *101*
Teniote festivals and modern shrine, *375, 389*
Tenos, Aeolus housed on, *380*; of Poseidon, *358*; Delos and, *365, 376*
Tetrapolis, Marathonian, worship of Apollo from, *104*
Theatres, Aesculapian shrines built near, *247*
Theban Maenads, ministers of earthquake, *145*
—— legend of Dionysus and Eastern stories, *164*
Thebes to be decked as a Maenad, *142*; the mother of Bacchanals, *133*; Dionysus-driven women of, in *The Bacchanals, 139*; Dionysus' connection with, *76, 139, 141, 144*
Thelpusa, Demeter legend of, *176*
Themistocles, *11*
Theocracy of Roman Empire, *8, 26*
Theologians, Homer and Hesiod the first of Greece, *26*
Theology, mythology and philosophy contrasted with, *20, 52*
Theoris, the Delian boat of Athens, *376* f.
Theory sent by Deliastae from Athens, *376*
Thera and the Cyclades, *397*
Theseum and temple of Delian Apollo, *387*
Theseus, Demophoon the son of, *65*; the altar of Zeus and, *217*; Chiron's pupil, *232*; *Theoris* and, *377*; Ariadne at Delos and, *382*; Athenian and Delian legends of, *400*

Thesmoi of Demeter, *51*
Thesmophoria, the, *51*, *68*
Thesmos, the self-imposed, of Apollo, *370* f.
Thespis, *115-117*, *126*, *132*, *137*, *139*
Thessaly, myth of Persephone wandering from, *59*; Demeter from, *194*, *221*; Aesculapian legends of, *221*, *234*, *245* f.
Thetis, her attempted fire-baptism of Achilles, *64*; protected the fleeing Dionysus, *77*
Thiasos, *100*; blessings of belonging to, *141*
Thief, discovery of the cross of the penitent, *275*
Thigh-mountain, second birth of Dionysus and, *165*
Tholos, the, of Polycletus at Epidaurus, *250-254*
Thornton, Dr., competed for building the Capitol, *267*
Thrace, Dionysus from, *77*, *86*, *90*, *103*, *119*, *121*, *174*, *189*, *218*; Dionysus in, *85* f., *88*, *90*, *92-94*, *96*, *174*; Phrygia included in the larger, *84*, *90*; chronic disturbances of, *85*; Valerius found three silver statues and strange rites in, *87*; Eumolpus from, *174*, *218*; Pisistratus exiled to, *126*, *137*; Zerynthian Aphrodite in, *345* f.
Thracian elements in the legend and worship of Dionysus, *80*, *82-85*, *94*, *96* f., *100-104*, *106*, *135*, *138*, *162*, *177*; Brumalia and Rosalia, *86-88*; oracle on Mt. Zilmissus, *93*; places of assembly, *94*; history in early days, *80*, *111* f., *221*
Thracians, history of the, *80*, *84*, *86*, *103*, *111*, *220* f., *280*, *322*; character of the, *84-90*; religion of the, *80* f., *83-87*, *90*, *95*, *103*, *106*, *322*; the Delian Hyperboreans were, *379*
Thraco-Eleusinian, Eumolpus the, *122*

Thraco-Phrygian features in all Dionysus-legends from the East, *169*
Thrasymedes, statue of Aesculapius by, *249*
Thriasian plain, *55* f., *187*
Thucydides, unknown sense of the term Cyclades in, *392*, *394*; semi-Thracian parentage of, *84*
Thyades, with Dionysus on Delphian pediment, *31*, *133*; Thyone-Semele and Dione, *318*
Thyone-Semele and Dione, *318*
Tiber, temple of Aesculapius on the island in, *244*
Tiberius, *42* f.
Tintoretto painted Naxia-acropolis, *328*
Tiresias, *145-148*, *166* f.
Titans, Zagreus and the, *128*, *131*, *181*
Tithorea, peak of Parnassus, *25*
Titian, a masterpiece of, *289*
Titthion, Aesculapius exposed on mount, *243*, *245* f.
Tityi, *94*
Tmolus, Dionysus born on, *154*
Tolerance, Apollo's sense of, *8*, *29*, *33*
Tragedy, Icarian legends and, *111*, *115-117*; rise of Athenian, *132*, *134-136*, *159*, *172*; Dionysus and, *78*
Tree-worship, *78*, *82* f., *106* f., *110*, *143*, *159*, *164*
Triaconter, the *Theoris* a, *377*
Tricca, Inscriptions at, *237*
Trinity, mystery of, compared with Eleusinian mystery, *178*
Triopian promontory, Cnidian sanctuary on, *70*
Tripod, *371*; a symbol of unison of Apollo and Dionysus, *35* f.
Tripoli, the country of, in the sack of Nicosia, *332*
Triptolemus, a son of Celeus, *63*; a son of Icarius, *107*; Icarius and, *107*; an Eleusinian demigod, *65* f.; suppression of, in Eleusinian legend, *64-66*, *175*, *194*; Rarian

plain and, *66, 71, 201* ; Demeter's representative, *67, 124, 206* ; one of the gods at Eleusis, *178* f.
Troezen, meaning of *Bocarus* in dialect of, *344*
Troglodytic country, Nysa in the, *165*
Trohodos, used by the villani for Olympus, *341*
Troödos, *276, 324* ; tradition identifying Olympus with, *327-343*
—— Strabo's epithet for Olympus exactly suits, *325*
Trophonius, Parmeniscus and the oracle of, *382*
Trullo, council of, order against the Rosalia at the, *89*
Truthfulness of Apollo conspicuous at Delphi, *370*
Trygaeus, had to be initiated before he died, *181*
τυμβορύχος, epithet of Aphrodite, *310*
Turk, mimic fight of, with a Christian, *90*
Turkish bondholders and modern Cyprus, *278*
Turks besiege and sack Nicosia, *332-334*; Brenzone's hatred of, *332* ; ransoms of Christians from, *335* f., *339* ; their laws and taxes in Cyprus, *277* ; population of, in modern Cyprus, *272* ; special causes for prominence of Greek doctors under the, *267*
Tyana, saved from destruction by Apollonius, *265*
Tyre, Aphrodite-Ashtaroth at, *303*
Tyre and Sidon, early intercourse of, with Cyprus, *281* ; sent gifts to Delos, *381*

ὑλάτης, epithet of Apollo at Curium, *345* f.
Ulpian, of Phoenician descent and of Julia Domna's clique, *259*
Ulrichs, Professor, votive inscription found at Delos by, *384*
Unction (extreme), initiation into the Mysteries compared to, *181*

Unity, of Demeter and Persephone is unity of growth at large, *74* ; of god-doctrine of Xenophanes and of the Mysteries, *180*
Urania, transformation in meaning of epithet, *297* f.
Urugal, Ishtar's descent to, *301*

VALERIUS, in Thrace, *87*
Varoschia, Salamis-Famagosta and, *283*
Vegetation, Dionysus god of abundant, *78*
Venetian rule in Cyprus, *278, 289*
Venetians and marriage of doge with the sea, *131*
Venice and Greeks, religions of, *131, 135, 328, 389*
Venus, *87, 300, 304*
Vespasian, reported miracle of, *41* f. ; the greatest latter-day guide, *42*
Viaticum, *181*
Victory, statues of, on Epidaurian temple, *249*
Vilaras of Janina, a poet and a doctor, *268*
Vindemiator, Boötes-Icarius as, *111*
Vine, the he-goat and the, *108* ; cultivation of the, and Dionysus, *107*
Vintage, autumn Dionysus festivals of the, *129* f.
Virgil, Messianic vision of, *138* ; supposed bust of, *195* ; the mother Venus of his song, *304*
Virgin Mary, the, *4, 71*
Virgo, bright star ε near wrist of, is *provindemiator*, *111* ; Erigone and the, *110*
Volcanic origin of Delos, *359*

WARFARE in Homer, debt of modern science to, *228* f.
Water, given with barley to Demeter, *68* ; wine tempered with, at Eleutherae, *34, 120* ; in Heraclitus' doctrine and Dionysus-worship, *179* f. ; in legend and worship of Dionysus and his

creatures, *78, 94* f., *102* f., *108, 137, 156, 159*
Wine, regarded as an element, *91* f., *103*; first culture of, *165*; Phoenician trade in, and Dionysus, *165*; brought by Dionysus to Icaria, *78, 107-109, 152* f.; power over the dead of, *91*; prophetic power of, *93*; represents the power of Dionysus, *91*; Eleutherae and the use of, *34, 120*; power over poets of, *102*; the story of Midas and the, *93*; Cypriote, *288*; Pramnian given by Maron, *91*
Winged Dionysus, the, *179*
Winter, death of Dionysus, grief of Demeter in, *185*; Icarian observances in, *112* f.; other Dionysiac festivals in, *132, 156*
Winter-oracles of Apollo at Patara, *370*
Wodin, *6*
Wood, Pentheus, like a king of the, *159*

XANTHIAS and Dionysus, witness the march of the Mystae, *212*
Xenagoras, named Cyprus Cerastis, Aspelia, and Amathusia, *274*
Xenocles of Cholargia, builder of Eleusinian ὀπαῖον, *191*
Xenophanes, Demeter stands for the idea of divinity of, *179* f.
Xenophon nearly contemporary with Hippocrates, *225*; military medicine and, *225*; Philostratus imitated passages from, *259*
Xerxes, Onomacritus and Pisistratidae at the court of, *127*
ξόανα, attributed to Daedalus, *399*
Xypeta, Metagenes of, at Eleusis, *191*

ZAGREUS, the myth of, *39, 127* f.; at the Anthesteria, *131*; the mystical δαίμων of Eleusis and, *174*; the doctrine of immortality and, *181*; the pitiless huntsman, *185*
Zamacola, on the *couvade*, *170*
Zamolxis, a name for the primitive Dionysus, *86*
Zerynthian, epithet of Aphrodite from Thrace, *345* f.
Zeus, character of, *12-14, 26, 28, 219* f., *236, 264, 271, 369*; monuments connected with the worship of, *9* f., *14-17, 217, 252, 402*; Aphrodite-legend and, *271* f., *284, 315* f.; Asteria and, *358*; Aesculapius and, *219, 239*; Demeter-legend and, *48, 50, 56* f.; Delphi and the eagles of, *31*; Dionysus legend and, *22, 142* f., *163*; Zagreus-Dionysus and, *128, 181*
Zilmissus, oracle on Mount, *93*
Zoroaster and Apollonius as magicians, *262*
Zoster, birth-legend of Apollo and Artemis transferred to, *399*

THE END

Printed by R. & R. CLARK, *Edinburgh*

www.ingramcontent.com/pod-product-compliance
Lightning Source LLC
Chambersburg PA
CBHW022101300426
44117CB00007B/536